Healthy Aging
Challenges and Solutions

Edited by

Ken Dychtwald, PhD
President and CEO
Age Wave, LLC
Emeryville, California

AN ASPEN PUBLICATION®
Aspen Publishers, Inc.
Gaithersburg, Maryland
1999

Austin College Library

This publication is designed to provide accurate and authoritative information in regard to the Subject Matter covered. It is sold with the understanding that the publisher is not engaged in rendering legal, accounting, or other professional service. If legal advice or other expert assistance is required, the service of a competent professional person should be sought. (From a Declaration of Principles jointly adopted by a Committee of the American Bar Association and a Committee of Publishers and Associations.)

Library of Congress Cataloging-in-Publication Data

Healthy Aging: challenges and solutions / edited by Ken Dychtwald
p. cm.
Includes index.
ISBN 0-8342-1363-X
1. Aged—Health and hygiene. 2. Aged—Medical care. 3. Aging.
I. Dychtwald, Ken, 1950–
RA777.6.H45 1999
362.1'9897—dc21
98-39726
CIP

Copyright © 1999 by Aspen Publishers, Inc.
All rights reserved.

Aspen Publishers, Inc., grants permission for photocopying for limited personal or internal use. This consent does not extend to other kinds of copying, such as copying for general distribution, for advertising or promotional purposes, for creating new collective works, or for resale. For information, address Aspen Publishers, Inc., Permissions Department, 200 Orchard Ridge Drive, Suite 200, Gaithersburg, Maryland 20878.

Orders: (800) 638-8437
Customer Service: (800) 234-1660

About Aspen Publishers • For more than 35 years, Aspen has been a leading professional publisher in a variety of disciplines. Aspen's vast information resources are available in both print and electronic formats. We are committed to providing the highest quality information available in the most appropriate format for our customers. Visit Aspen's Internet site for more information resources, directories, articles, and a searchable version of Aspen's full catalog, including the most recent publications: **http://www.aspenpublishers.com**
Aspen Publishers, Inc. • The hallmark of quality in publishing
Member of the worldwide Wolters Kluwer group.

Editorial Services: Ruth Bloom
Library of Congress Catalog Card Number: 98-39726
ISBN: 0-8342-1363-X

Printed in the United States of America

1 2 3 4 5

Dedicated to Alan Dychtwald

Thank you for a lifetime of solid friendship, support, and love

Contents

CONTRIBUTORS

Chad Boult, M.D.
Associate Professor
University of Minnesota Medical
  School
Department of Family Practice
  and Community Health
Minneapolis, Minnesota

Robert N. Butler, M.D.
CEO
International Longevity Center
New York, New York

Rick Carlson
President and CEO
Health Magic
Denver, Colorado

Bruce Clark, M.D.
Senior Vice President
Age Wave Health Services, Inc.
Emeryville, California

Gene D. Cohen, M.D., Ph.D.
Director
Washington D.C. Center on
  Aging
Washington, D.C.

Ken Dychtwald, Ph.D.
President and CEO
Age Wave, LLC
Emeryville, California

Ronald W. Eastman
President
Geron Corporation
Menlo Park, California

William J. Evans, Ph.D.
Professor of Pediatrics and
  Physiology
Director
Nutrition, Metabolism, and
  Exercise
Department of Geriatrics
UAMS
Little Rock, Arkansas

John W. Farquhar, M.D.
Director
Stanford Center for Research and
  Disease Prevention
Stanford University
Palo Alto, California

Howard Fillit, M.D.
Executive Director
The Institute for the Study of
    Aging
New York, New York
Clinical Professor of Geriatrics
    and Medicare
The Mount Sinai Medical Center
New York, New York

June A. Flora, Ph.D.
Senior Research Associate
Stanford Center for Research in
    Disease Prevention
Stanford, California

James F. Fries, M.D.
Professor of Medicine
Stanford University School of
    Medicine
Stanford, California

Patrick G. Hays
Fellow, American College of
    Healthcare Executives
President and CEO
Blue Cross and Blue Shield
    Association
Chicago, Illinois

Jerrold Hill
Director, Collaborative Research
U.S. Quality Algorithms, Inc.
Subsidiary of Aetna U.S.
    Healthcare
Blue Bell, Pennsylvania

Robert L. Kahn, Ph.D.
Professor Emeritus of Psychology
Institute for Social Research
University of Michigan
Ann Arbor, Michigan

Zaven S. Khachaturian, Ph.D.
Khachaturian, Radebaugh &
    Associates, Inc.
Potomac, Maryland

Paul Kleyman
Editor
American Society on Aging
San Francisco, California

Molly K. Mettler
Senior Vice President
Healthwise, Incorporated
Boise, Idaho

I-Min Lee, M.D.
Department of Epidemiology
Harvard School of Public Health
Boston, Massachusetts

**Patricia E. McDonald, R.N.,
Ph.D.**
Assistant Professor of Nursing
Frances Payne Bolton School of
    Nursing
Cleveland, Ohio

Myron Miller, M.D.
Medical Director, Levindale
    Hebrew Geriatric Center and
    Hospital
Director, Division of Geriatric
    Medicine, Sinai Hospital of
    Baltimore
Professor, Department of
    Medicine, Johns Hopkins
    University School of Medicine
Baltimore, Maryland

Stephen A. Moses
President
Center for Long-Term Care
 Financing
Seattle, Washington

James. T. Pacala, M.D., M.S.
Associate Professor
University of Minnesota Medical
 School
Department of Family Practice
 and Community Health
Minneapolis, Minnesota

Ralph S. Paffenbarger, Jr.,
 M.D., Ph.D.
Professor of Epidemiology
 Emeritus (Active)
Stanford University School of
 Medicine
Division of Epidemiology
Department of Health Research
 and Policy
Stanford, California

Kenneth R. Pelletier, M.D.
Director
Stanford Corporate Health
 Program
Clinical Associate Professor of
 Medicine
Stanford University School of
 Medicine
Palo Alto, California

Daniel Perry
Executive Director
Alliance for Aging Research
Washington, D.C.

Gloria P. Picariello, M.S.N.,
 R.N., C.S.
Corporate Manager Geriatric
 Programs
NYLCare Health Plans, Inc.
New York, New York

Robert Pritikin, Ph.D.
Director
Pritikin Longevity Centers
Santa Monica, California

Michelle Putnam
Doctoral Candidate
UCLA School of Public Policy,
 Social Research
Los Angeles, California

Uwe Reinhardt, Ph.D.
James Madison Professor of
 Political Economy
Princeton University
Princeton, New Jersey

John W. Rowe, M.D.
Professor of Geriatrics and Adult
 Development
Mount Sinai Medical Center
New York, New York

Caroline Schooler, Ph.D.
Director of Research &
 Development
FCB Healthworks
New York, New York

Fernando Torres-Gil, Ph.D.
Associate Dean and Director
Center for Policy
UCLA School of Public Policy
Research on Aging
Los Angeles, California

Donald M. Vickery, Ph.D.
Chairman
Health Decisions International,
    LLC
Golden, Colorado

**Samuel W. Warburton, Jr.,
M.D.**
Senior Vice President Medical
    Affairs
Chief Medical Officer
NYLCare Health Plans, Inc.
New York, New York

May L. Wykle, Ph.D.
Florence Cellar Professor and
    Associate Dean for Community
    Affairs
Director
University Center on Aging and
    Health
Cleveland, Ohio

ACKNOWLEDGMENTS

I would like to extend my deepest appreciation to several people without whose support I could not have brought this book to life: My mom and dad, Pearl and Seymour Dychtwald, whose love and encouragement have consistently added fuel to my fire; my wife, Maddy Kent-Dychtwald, whose brilliance, energy, wisdom, and spirit empower me in every imaginable way; my spectacular children, Casey and Zak Dychtwald, who haven't yet figured out what I do for a living, yet seem to love and enjoy me anyhow; the entire Age Wave team—not quite as precious as the Little Rascals or formidable as the crew of the Starship Enterprise, but much more intelligent, capable, complicated, and energized; Dr. Robert Butler, who has inspired me to tilt at the windmills of healthcare; Charlie Lynch, who has served as an exceptional mentor in the ways of the world, and, in particular, Marcia Freedman, Greta Mart, Julie Penfold, and Rod MacKenzie whose exceptional editorial talents and people management skills helped me to bring the very best out of our wonderful contributors.

Ken Dychtwald
September, 1998

CHAPTER 1

Introduction: Healthy Aging or Tithonius' Revenge?

Ken Dychtwald

In the ancient Greek fable, the beautiful goddess Eos, Goddess of the Dawn, falls in love with the mortal warrior Tithonius. She is so taken by her love and distraught over his mortality that she goes to Zeus's chamber to request a special favor. She tells Zeus she wants to love Tithonius until the end of time and begs him to grant her lover immortal life. "Are you sure that's what you want for him?" Zeus challenges. "Yes," Eos says. "Your wish shall be granted," said Zeus.

As Eos was leaving Zeus's chamber, she realized that while focusing on Tithonius's immortality, she forgot to ask also for his eternal youth. She looked on with horror as, with each passing year, Tithonius got older and older and older. His skin withered and became cancerous. His organs rotted, and his brain became demented. With the passing of decades, his poor aging body became increasingly frail and feeble, but he could not die. Ultimately, Tithonius' body shrunk to a small bag of pained, foul and broken bones—and he continued to live forever.

Tithonius's story is a fitting allegory for what may be occurring within our health care system. We have emphasized the prolongation of life and the denial of death, but we have done little to promote healthy aging. Although in this century we have added 28 years to the average life expectancy at birth, the later years can be a time of illness and disability for far too many older adults. Unless we rethink and reorient our health care priorities, we may be heading toward an era of epidemic levels of chronic disease. Until recently, most people died relatively young of acute, infectious illnesses, accidents, trauma, or in childbirth. Few lived long enough to struggle with hypertension or hypercholesterolemia. Most did not live long enough to experience the frailty that results from osteoporosis, and we

1

seldom struggled with late-life cancers. We did not have large numbers of people with Alzheimer's disease. Until a few decades ago, we did not even know what it was.

Today, more and more people are living long enough to experience these chronic diseases of old age, but our current health care system was not designed to care for them. Few professionals are skilled in the diseases of aging, and our financing mechanisms were not designed to provide long-term chronic care for people with degenerative conditions. Even Medicare is based on an acute-care model most appropriate for younger people. As though Tithonius were seeking revenge, there is a train wreck in our future. We must act *now* to prevent it.

THE DIMENSIONS OF THE CHALLENGE

In 1776, a child born in America could expect to live to age 35, on the average. At the founding of the Republic, the median age of the American population was 16. A century later, life expectancy was only 40, and the median age was 21. As a nation, we were not concerned about such financial transfers between generations as Social Security and Medicare, as there was no mass population of elders.

During the past century, however, extraordinary breakthroughs in health care have been eliminating many of the diseases that once caused us to die young. Smallpox and cholera are almost nonexistent in the United States. The death rate from tuberculosis, the leading cause of premature death a century ago, has been reduced by more than 99%. Measles and streptococcal infections have been transformed from killers to childhood annoyances. Pneumonia and influenza are no longer fatal in and of themselves; their deadlines have been confined to people already enfeebled by trauma or great age. Whooping cough and syphilis, once major epidemic diseases, now kill fewer than 1 in 200,000 people. Typhoid and diphtheria no longer kill Americans (World Almanac Books, 1998). As a result of these incredible advances, we are creating—for the first time in history—a mass population of long-lived men and women. But what kind of old age are we creating? Healthy or ill?

Today, there are tens of millions of men and women over the age of 65 who have high life expectancies but are experiencing a variety of chronic degenerative diseases that our health care system is barely prepared to handle. As thoughtfully explained in *Will You Still Treat Me When I'm*

Sixty-Five, a publication of the Alliance for Aging Research (1996), the cost of being unprepared to handle chronic illness is already very clear. Heart disease alone accounts for more adult deaths than all other causes combined and costs our nation $138 billion in direct and indirect costs annually. Cancer, in all its forms, afflicts 8 million older Americans and drains $107 billion annually, accounting for 10% of the total cost of health care spending in the United States (American Cancer Society, 1997). Though not all types of cancer follow the exponential growth patterns exhibited by other diseases of aging, some types, such as breast and prostate cancer, are much more common in elderly patients, and the risk of most forms of cancer increases dramatically with age.

Strokes among older people are the third leading cause of death, and those who survive are usually left disabled. Strokes alone result in health care costs of almost $30 billion annually. Osteoporosis is also becoming a major health problem of old age, already affecting 20 million women and 5 million men, and leading to more than 250,000 hip fractures each year. The direct and indirect costs of osteoporosis are already more than $12 billion annually and are rising (Alliance for Aging Research, 1996).

GROWTH IN THE OLDEST OLD

Some of the greatest challenges that the aging of our society places on health care come from the fact that the fastest growing segment of the elderly population is women and men aged 85 and older. This population will triple in size from 3.3 million today to more than 10 million—including 1 million centenarians—by the year 2030 (Hobbs & Damon, 1996). It is in these later years of life that the intensity and complexity of health problems compound. Although some segments of today's 85+ population are fit and independent, 62.5% are so disabled that they are no longer able to manage the basic activities of daily living without a good deal of help (Health Insurance Association of America, 1997).

One of the most difficult problems that we will increasingly confront in the years ahead pertains to the rising incidence of diseases of the aging brain most prevalent among the oldest old. Already, an estimated 4 million older Americans suffer from Alzheimer's disease. In many nursing homes and retirement communities, Alzheimer's is often referred to as *elderly AIDS*. Although there are four times the number of people with Alzheimer's as with human immunodeficiency virus (4 million and 1 million), the comparison is appropriate. Although noninfectious, Alzheimer's is a degenerative disorder that steadily robs its victims of memory and judgment, leaves patients unable to carry out the most basic functions on their own, and ultimately destroys the brain. Because it can take 8–10 years for this horrible disease to progress, it often exhausts loving family members along the way.

Alzheimer's disease seldom occurs before middle age, but after age 60, the likelihood doubles about every 5 years. Currently, less than 2% of people aged 60 suffer from Alzheimer's, 3–4% have it by age 65, 6–8% by 70, approximately 15% of those age 75 have it, 25–30% are patients by age 80, and an alarming 47% of people over 85 have this horrible disease. For 1998, the combined direct and indirect annual costs of Alzheimer's disease are estimated to be $100 billion. Unless a cure or treatment is found in our lifetime, it is estimated that 14 million "boomers" and "generation Xers" will be stricken with "elderly AIDS" by the middle of the next century (Khachaturian & Radebaugh, 1996). Alzheimer's disease is very democratic—it strikes without regard for how wealthy, powerful or well-connected one is. As Zaven Khachaturian explains (see Chapter 6), if we care about our future and the future of our children, it is imperative that we commit the talent, energy and financial resources needed to understanding, managing and eventually eliminating Alzheimer's.

Unless we intervene soon, Alzheimer's and the other diseases of aging, with all their pain, suffering and associated costs, will be our inheritance.

ROBUST EXPENDITURES, MEDIOCRE OUTCOMES

The fact that we have added nearly 30 years to the average life expectancy over the past century can be misleading. In reality, the major health-related breakthroughs to date have had an impact on the quality of life and health status primarily of the young. Just a century ago, the average adult spent only 1% of his or her life in a morbid or ill state; today's average adult will be sick more than 10% of her or his life (National Center for Health Statistics, 1997).

Reinhardt points out (see Chapter 15), even though we have the most expensive health care system in the world, the United States lags behind many other nations with regard to longevity. There are 23 countries that can boast a higher life expectancy than ours, including Japan, Switzerland, Greece, Israel, Spain, Sweden, Costa Rica, Italy, the Netherlands, Canada,

Austria, Belgium, France, Norway, the United Kingdom, Cuba, Denmark, Germany, Ireland, Luxembourg, New Zealand, Kuwait and Singapore (World Health Organization, 1998). In spite of the fact that our health care system's measurable results in the areas of longevity and morbidity are mediocre at best, it is not because of inadequate financial support.

Each year, our nation devotes more and more of its resources to health care. In 1960, health care expenditures were 5.2% of the gross national product (GNP); by 1990 health care expenditures had risen to 12.2% of the GNP, or $696.6 billion. In 1996, at 13.6% of the GNP, health care spending in the United States passed the trillion-dollar mark for the first time. If current trends continue, the Health Care Financing Administration (HCFA) projects that health care could consume an incredible 31.5% of the GNP by the year 2020. Of course, if expenditures were to actually reach this level, they would crush our economy (Health Care Financing Administration, 1996).

Not surprisingly, a disproportionate share of these resources is spent on the elderly population. On the eve of the New Deal, all levels of government spent roughly $1 a year on health care for the average older American. By 1965, when Medicare was launched, the figure had risen to roughly $100 per year. In 1995, the latest available figures, funding levels had multiplied 70 times, to roughly $7,000 per older adult. The 33.6 million Americans over 65 that make up 13% of our population now account for 44% of all hospital-bed days and 24.1% of all physician office visits (National Center for Health Statistics, 1995). Medicare covers only about 45% of an older person's health care costs and does not reimburse for many of the real-life medical expenditures of the very constituency it is designed to serve. Medicare will cover the cost of a broken hip or dramatic surgical procedure such as a quadruple bypass. However, Medicare does not reimburse for services to help elders prevent heart disease through proper nutrition and other changes in lifestyle. In addition to public funding, older people themselves pay premiums, co-payments, deductibles, and such noncovered items as prescription drugs, which cost on average $2,750 a year. As Torres-Gil and Putnam, and Moses point out (see Chapters 18 and 19), although more than 60% of all elders will need long-term care at some point in their lives and the average nursing home stay of 2.5 years costs more than $100,000, Medicare pays for only 25% of long-term care services (General Accounting Office, 1996).

It is becoming apparent that we have built a health care system that is very good at maintaining the health of young people and responding to the kinds of accidents and traumas that used to cause many people to die prematurely. The result has been the creation of a growing population of older men and women with the kinds of functional disabilities and chronic degenerative diseases that the health care system is much less capable of preventing or curing.

As politicians debate the merits of Medicare funding adjustments, it would appear that we are captive passengers on a runaway train barreling down the track toward an expensive and unhealthy old age for far too many people. Additional funding alone will not solve the problems of our health care system, but realigning its orientation toward healthy aging will.

A FOUR-PART SOLUTION

Because the problems are not just economic but also systemic, the solutions must come from the reconfiguration of several key elements of our modern approach to health and health care. If we are to solve the problems that lie at the core of our health care system before it collides with the age wave, we must pursue all of the following:

- Commit sufficient attention and resources to the scientific research required to delay or eliminate some of the diseases of aging;
- Provide the academic training and continuing education needed to ensure that health care professionals are fully competent at skillfully, compassionately and cost-effectively meeting the needs of an aging population;
- Orient the philosophy, economic incentives and service design of our health care system toward the goal of producing healthy aging;
- Encourage all aging Americans to actively take greater responsibility for practicing healthy behaviors, thereby reducing demand while increasing well-being.

SCIENTIFIC BREAKTHROUGHS THAT DELAY OR ELIMINATE THE DISEASES OF AGING

There is an emerging consensus in the medical community that the goal of research efforts should be discoveries that would delay or prevent the onset of symptoms of aging-related diseases and conditions, rather than attempts to treat them after-the-fact. If this were possible, it would prevent tens of millions of cases of dysfunction, shorten the length of time that they take their toll on individuals and their families and ultimately save trillions of dollars.

Delaying or preventing the diseases of aging is a relatively new idea but one with great potential. Beginning in middle age, the risks for most disorders—from arthritis to cancer to heart disease—roughly double every 5–7 years. What if we could compress the various diseases of old age into the shortest possible time frame at the very end of life? In his recent book, *We Live Too Short and Die Too Long*, Walter Bortz effectively argues that we must learn how to prolong life and take less time to die. As Rowe and Kahn, and Fries propose (see Chapters 3 and 4), if we could postpone or prevent the onset of any of the painful and costly conditions and diseases of old age, the effect would be that we could have millions of older men and women who would look, feel and act years—and possibly decades— younger than their chronological age, and the economic and social savings would be enormous.

With vigorous research efforts in both the public and private sectors we could raise the possibility of conquering many of the diseases of aging. However, we are currently devoting a very small fraction of total health-related expenditures to this goal. The National Institute on Aging (NIA), which leads the federal aging research effort, reports that federally funded research activities are already making important strides in identifying numerous genetic and environmental factors associated with the aging process. In addition, as Eastman explains (see Chapter 7), within the private sector, increasing amounts of attention and creativity are being applied in the fields of biotechnology and pharmacology to better under-stand the relationship between aging, health and disease. Scientists in many laboratories are now able to isolate not only the genes believed responsible for the onset of aging-related diseases, but also those that confer health and longevity. They are working diligently to find the best ways of preventing frailty and disability and to rehabilitate elders who experience these conditions.

However, as many contributors to this book argue, the dollars being spent are insubstantial in the face of the challenge before us. Because men and women over 65 already consume a third of all health care spending— approximately $342 billion—why does the National Institutes of Health (NIH) spend only 7% of its $11.3 billion medical research budget for aging-related research? This 7% includes the entire budget of the NIA, as well as all aging-specific research conducted by the 23 institutes and research centers that comprise NIH. This amounts to a paltry research investment of two tenths of 1% of the total expenditures pertaining to people over age 65. While it is understood that much of the general research conducted by NIH impacts older adults, there is a growing censensus that the complex health problems of the elderly often require special attention and age-appropriate solutions (National Institute on Aging, 1998).

Compounding the problem of the lack of resources being devoted to research on the diseases of aging is the question of whether medical research is aiming at the right targets. For example, last year 41,800 men died of prostate cancer and 44,190 women died of breast cancer (American Cancer Society, 1997). Yet, the NIH spent $333 million for breast cancer research and only $74 million for prostate cancer research (National Institutes of Health, 1998). With a lower mortality rate (25,695 deaths in 1996), acquired immunedeficiency syndrome (AIDS) research received $1.3 billion of federal funding. My point is *not* that we should be spending less on breast cancer and AIDS research. Rather, we should be spending *much more* on other, less championed but no less destructive diseases.

NEEDED: AGING-READY HEALTH CARE PROFESSIONALS

The Alliance for Aging Research (1996) points out that "50 years ago, the United States first met the postwar baby boom without enough pediatricians, hospitals or kindergartens." Today, with fewer than 15 years before the first baby boomers become eligible for Social Security and Medicare, we are heading toward a future with a dangerous shortage of trained geriatricians and not enough eldercare services to meet the needs of the coming age wave. Our health care system is currently oriented toward the needs and concerns of young people—ear infections, broken bones, colds, flu, pregnancy and childbirth. However, in the decades ahead the battlefield will be made up of an entirely new assortment of illnesses, and we are woefully short of the geriatric samurai needed to win the day.

The term *geriatrics* was coined at the turn of the century by Ignatz L. Nascher (1914), an Austrian-born physician who practiced medicine in New York City. In its broadest sense, by Nascher's definition, geriatrics concerns itself with the "preventive, therapeutic and research aspects of aging-related diseases and conditions." Geriatrics has evolved during this century to encompass the complex needs of older patients. Today, there is a strong emphasis in geriatrics on maintaining functional independence, even in the presence of chronic, age-related diseases. According to the Alliance for Aging Research (1996), "if access to geriatrics-oriented physicians and health care personnel were more widely available, more older people would benefit from improved health status, enhanced personal independence and a substantially lower rate of institutionalization." As Butler, Wykle and McDonald, and Fillit and Miller propose (see Chapters 8, 9 and 10), the result would conceivably be a much healthier population of older Americans, dramatically lower medical, social service and long-term care costs and, as a result, provide a more vital, financially secure twenty-first century.

With the coming age wave, we should be preparing armies of "aging-ready" health care professionals. We are not. From a pool of more than 500,000 physicians, we currently have fewer than 8,000 physicians who have been trained and certified as geriatricians—less than 2% (compared to 30,000 fully trained pediatricians). Though many health professionals assert that we may not need tens of thousands of geriatric specialists, most agree that it would be very helpful if the average health care professional were armed with basic skills in diagnosing, treating and managing the care of elderly patients. It is a sobering fact that most primary-care physicians have received little or no continuing education in geriatrics. In fact, 47% of residents in family practice, 52% in psychiatry, 74% in internal medicine, 83% in physical medicine and 97% in neurology *have never even taken a rotation in geriatrics* (Institute of Medicine, 1993*)*.

To compound this shortage of aging-ready health professionals, very few medical schools in the United States currently include geriatrics in their course work or in their residency training programs. Every medical school in the United Kingdom has a department of geriatrics, and half of the medical schools in Japan have geriatrics departments, but there are only two departments of geriatrics in the United States: Mount Sinai Medical Center in New York and the University of Arkansas. In fact, 113 of America's 126 medical schools do not even require a single course or a clinical rotation in geriatrics, and fewer than 4% of medical students take an elective course in geriatrics (Alliance for Aging Research , 1996). Bruce Clark also argues that far too many of our health care professionals are lacking in the interpersonal communications and basic "customer service" skills so critical to a successful physician–patient interchange (see Chapter 14). Considering the fact that the average graduating medical student will likely spend at least 30 minutes of every working hour for the rest of his or her life with 50+ adults, allowing them to graduate with so few relevant clinical and patient management skills is a cause of great concern, yet this is not being substantially addressed by educators or policy makers.

This theme was examined in May 1998 at a special forum convened by the Senate Special Committee on Aging. At that forum, several alarming statistics were discussed, including: "Of almost 100,000 medical residency and fellowship programs that Medicare helped to support nationwide, only 324 were in geriatric medicine or geriatric psychiatry." In addition, forum attendees were surprised to learn that while "Medicare paid nearly $7 billion in graduate medical education costs in fiscal year 1998, only a fraction of those dollars were directed toward the clinical education of physicians who focus on the health care needs of older adults." Experts at the forum believed that 24,000 geriatricians are currently needed—three times the number we currently have (AOL News, 1998).

Physicians are not the only health care professionals lacking in geriatric education. The same is true in nursing, allied health and pharmacology. In essence, we have created a health care system in which the majority of patients are aged 50–100, but we have neglected to train our health professionals appropriately to work effectively with older adults.

By enabling our health care professionals to be more competent at dealing with the kinds of chronic and often complex medical problems that older people have, we could be taking much better care of our elderly patients while conceivably saving tens of billions of dollars each year. In chapters that follow, Boult, Fillit, Butler, and Wykle all suggest innovative approaches to making health care more "aging-ready."

ORIENTING HEALTH CARE INSTITUTIONS AND REIMBURSEMENT TOWARD HEALTHY AGING

Centuries ago in ancient China, doctors were paid when people were well. It was believed that the healer's job was to do everything in his or her power to prevent the citizenry from becoming ill. If people injured themselves or became ill, the doctor's responsibility was to pay for the costs of care out of his own pocket. Under this arrangement, the goal was a healthy population, and the system was financially aligned to promote it.

In contrast, throughout the contemporary history of the United States, the financial infrastructure of our health care system has been oriented toward disease, not health. Increased illness meant more tests, procedures and hospital-bed days needed, and more money was exchanged. There were few restrictions on the amount of health care doctors and their patients could cause to be purchased, regardless of the actual outcomes.

In recent years, the fee-for-service insurance paradigm has been replaced by a new model that actually has a few things in common with the ancient Chinese approach. The first health maintenance organizations (HMOs) were created in the 1930s with two noble goals: first, to better manage the costs of health care through careful control and distribution of resources and, second, to provide doctors and medical institutions with incentives to keep their patients healthy. The first prepaid health plans, Kaiser Permanente in California and the Health Insurance Plan of Greater New York, emerged as nonprofit alternatives to traditional, fee-for-service medicine. To date, HMOs have done reasonably well at achieving their first goal, cost containment, but they have done poorly at realizing the second, the promotion of health.

The capitated group-practice approach to health insurance moved into the mainstream in the 1970s when the Nixon administration focused on it as a means of providing a reasonable alternative to the status quo without giving in to growing public interest in national health insurance. The administration advanced legislation that would give the federal government's seal of approval to groups that met standards set by law. Under capitated arrangements, group practices attempted to carefully coordinate all treatment and, wherever possible, refrain from using expensive hospital services. In addition, some of these plans have experimented with providing preventive services that traditional insurance does not cover. With HMOs, a new infrastructure was emerging that would allow government, employers and members to better track and manage the relationships between health, health care and the financial resources required to provide it.

Largely spurred by employer concerns, managed care has been at the heart of the health care revolution in the United States during the 1990s. Whereas a decade ago, fewer than 10% of the American public belonged to an HMO or other managed care organization (MCO), today more than 80% of the American public now belong to some form of managed care program. Reflecting the power of managed care, although the fee-for-service rates had been escalating during the 1980s and early 1990s in excess of 15% a year, in 1995 the average premiums for HMOs and preferred provider organizations actually declined by 3.8% and 2.1%, respectively. According to the Tax Equity and Fiscal Responsibility Act Risk Evaluation, Medicare HMO lengths of stay are 17% shorter, and total costs are 10.7% lower than fee-for-service lengths of stay (American Association of Health Plans, 1995).

Even Medicare has begun experimenting with managed care, paying an MCO a monthly capitated rate per enrolled beneficiary. Many HMOs ran into initial problems with capitated Medicare payments due to their unpreparedness for the special problems of older patients. As a result, the number of Medicare HMOs had fallen from 161 in 1987 to only 86 in 1992. (General Accounting Office, 1996). However, during the middle 1990s, pioneering HMOs such as PacifiCare, FHP, Fallon, Kaiser Permanente and BlueCross BlueShield began to better understand how to meet the complex needs of elderly men and women cost-effectively, and the Medicare market saw a steady influx of plans as enrollment burgeoned. There are now 6 million elders (approximately 20%) who apparently like advantages such as coverage for prescription drugs and zero paperwork offered by capitated Medicare plans, compared with only 1 million at the beginning of this decade. One challenge for these organizations is whether or not they will be able to continue to manage the care and costs of mature patients effectively as more older and ill individuals join their ranks.

When MCOs began pursuing Medicare beneficiaries, there was a great deal of concern that these plans might exploit their older members for profit and that they would not be able to provide the same quality of care as traditional fee-for-service plans. To date, these concerns have not proven to be correct. The American Association of Health Plans conducted a study in 1995, using HCFA data, that concluded that even though Medicare beneficiaries can switch plans every month, only 4% return to fee-for-service Medicare after receiving care from an HMO.

Notwithstanding the ongoing concern that managed care runs the risk of cutting quality while cutting costs, many people would now agree that managed care offers a more cost-effective approach to health care, one of its two initial goals. However, if it is to survive the challenge of an aging America, managed care must commit to doing a far better job of realizing its other initial goal, that of keeping people healthy for as much of their long lives as possible. In chapters that follow, Hays, Fillit, and Miller present important strategies and tactics for how this can be accomplished.

HEAL THYSELF: MOST AGING AMERICANS TAKE LITTLE RESPONSIBILITY FOR CARING FOR THEIR BODIES

As concerned as I am about the fact that our health care system is not yet up to the task of caring for our aging population, I am equally concerned by the fact that so many of our aging citizens do not take better care of themselves.

Research such as that discussed by Evans (Chapter 23), Lee and Paffenbarger (Chapter 5), Pelletier (Chapter 22), and Rowe and Kahn (Chapter 3) has consistently shown that we can dramatically influence our health status as we age. We all age 1 minute every 60 seconds but, depending on how we care for our bodies, as the years unfold we become dysfunctional or go the distance with vigor to spare. Of course, this process is determined by our species-specific genetics. If we were carp fish, we would be programmed to live 250 years, and if we were hummingbirds we would live only 3 years. The aging process is also influenced by our family-specific genetics. However, to a large extent, according to the Centers for Disease Control (1996), more than 50% of our potential for lifelong health is determined by our personal behaviors.

The difference that 10 years makes to the body of an individual with good self-care and one without can be compared to the difference that 10 years makes in the life of two cars, one cared for properly and the other neglected. The car that has been well cared for has been parked in a garage every night, its tires have been properly inflated, the wheels have been correctly aligned, it has had regular check-ups and adjustments, and it has been driven on safe roads within the speed limit. After 10 years, it still looks great and drives well. In contrast, the neglected car has been parked out on the street at night under a sappy oak tree, it was rarely brought in for tune-ups and it was run on cheap gas and oil that has caused the engine to knock and rattle. In addition, this car has also been involved in an accident or two. After 10 years it looks terrible and drives worse.

Similarly, recent research has shown overwhelmingly that regular exercise, proper nutrition, stress management, injury prevention, proper use of medication, smoking cessation and the appropriate use of health care services can produce reductions in heart disease, hypertension, non–insulin-dependent diabetes mellitus, colon cancer and osteoporotic fractures—many of the most common diseases of aging. In addition, it is known that healthy behaviors cause increases in bone mass and mineral content, lean muscle mass, metabolic rate, balance, coordination, strength, elimination efficiency, heart/stroke volume and a perceived sense of well-being.

Considering the proven benefits of ongoing preventive self-care, very few older women and men commit the energy or the time to practice the most minimum wellness-oriented behaviors. Two thirds of today's elders do not exercise regularly and approximately 40% are overweight. One half of them do not wear seat belts. Seventy-five percent do not regularly comply with their medication regimens. More than half do not regularly eat healthy and nutritious meals (even among those who can easily afford to), and 4 million elderly men and women (approximately one in eight) are still chronic smokers (National Center for Health Statistics, 1997).

If we can control some portion of our potential for healthy aging, we have a responsibility to do so, not only for our own and our families' sakes, but to help avoid the "unhealthy aging" crisis that our nation could be facing in the decades ahead. Mettler, Vickery, and Farquhar and colleagues (see Chapters 21, 25 and 26) provide insights as to how to promote a higher level of self-care among older adults.

Fortunately, the baby boomers, now entering their fifties, have begun to respond to the public education campaigns of the past decade by changing their habits. Boomer women and men are more likely to belong to health clubs (17% compared to only 8% of nonboomers), and they are more likely to participate in exercise classes and to engage in a variety of sports. Twenty-six percent of boomers say that they jog regularly, 29% enjoy bicycling, and 23% report that they do calisthenics. The proportion of baby boomers who regularly swim, dance, bicycle, jog, ski or participate in team sports is twice as large as the rest of the population (Wellner, 1998).

Similarly, with the boomers migrating into maturity, the food and beverage industry has experienced a major transformation toward healthier products, as evidenced by the fact that between 1975 and 1995 the per capita consumption of beef fell from 94 to 67.2 pounds. In contrast, per capita consumption of leaner poultry rose dramatically, from 28 pounds in 1960 to 70.4 pounds in 1995. Also, compared to 20 years ago, Americans are consuming 21% more vegetables and 27% more fruit (United States Department of Agriculture, 1997 and 1998).

THE CHALLENGE AHEAD

During 99% of all the years that humans have walked this planet, the life expectancy was under 18 years. Most people did not age; they died. Even though there were some who lived to 60, 70 or even 90 years, they were very few and far between. During this century, as a result of dramatic advances in sanitation, public health, food science, pharmacology, surgery, medicine and, lately, wellness-oriented lifestyle management, a change of tsunami proportions has begun. With the average life expectancy having vaulted to 76 and rising, most of us will live very long lives. As a result, we are witnessing the dawn of the twenty-first century "gerontocracy." America was unprepared for the baby boom, the teen boom, the yuppie boom and the middlescent boom. Similarly, we are grossly unprepared for the coming age boom.

Among all of the challenges we will confront as we transform our society to accommodate this coming age wave, perhaps the most critical lies in the realm of health care. Whether we are sick, frail and dependent or vital, active and productive as we grow old will depend on our ability to dramatically alter the orientation, strategies and capabilities of our current health care system. The size of the job that must be done to avoid Tithonius' revenge and to produce new generations of long-lived, healthy elders is daunting. However, if we are to be successful, the time to get started with these changes is *now*. In the chapters that follow, many of America's leading gerontologists, physicians, nurses, allied health professionals, researchers, health economists and public policy analysts offer their views and experience on each of these themes. I am hopeful that, collectively, their insights and suggestions can light a path toward healthy aging.

REFERENCES

Alliance for Aging Research. (1996). *Will you still treat me when I'm 65?* Washington, DC.

American Association of Health Plans. *1995 patterns in HMO enrollment.* Washington, DC. Available at: http://www.aahp.org/menus/index.cfm (1995).

American Cancer Society. (1997). *Cancer facts and figures.* Washington, DC.

Business Wire. (May 20, 1998). *US Senate Special Committee on Aging sponsors forum on the national shortage of health professionals trained in geriatrics.*

General Accounting Office. *Medicare HMOs: Rapid enrollment growth concentrated in selected states.* HEHS Report 96-63. Washington, DC. Available at: http://www.gao.gov/reports.htm (18 January 1996).

Health Care Financing Administration. (1996). *HCFA statistics.* HCFA Pub. No. 03394. Washington, DC.

Health Insurance Association of America. (1997). *Guide to long-term care insurance.* Washington, DC.

Hobbs, F.B., & Damon, B.L. (1996). *65+ in the United States*. Washington, DC: Bureau of the Census Report No. P23-190.

Institute of Medicine Committee on Strengthening Training in Geriatrics for Physicians. (1993). Washington, DC: National Academy Press, 14.

Khachaturian, Z., & Radebaugh, T. (Eds.). (1996). *Alzheimer's disease: Cause(s), diagnosis, treatment, and care*. Boca Raton, FL: CRC Press.

Nascher, I.L. (1914). *The diseases of old age and their treatment, including physiological old age, home and institutional care, and medico-legal relations*. Philadelphia: Blakiston.

National Center for Chronic Disease Prevention and Health Promotion [CDC]. *Surgeon General's report on physical activity and health*. Washington, DC. Available at: http://www.cdc.gov/nccdphp/sgr/sgr.htm (1996).

National Center for Health Statistics. (1995). *Health, United States, 1996–97*. Washington DC.

National Center for Health Statistics. *The third national health and nutrition examination survey, 1988–94*. (NHANES III), Advance Data No. 255. Washington, DC: U.S. Department of Health and Human Services. Available at: http://www.cdc.gov/nchswww/faq/hanesii1.htm (1997).

National Institutes of Health. *Distribution*. Available at: http://www.nih.gov (1998).

United States Department of Agriculture. *Vegetable yearbook. Annual data, 1970–97*. Stock # ERS-89011B. Washington, DC. Available at: http://151.121.66.126/Prodsrvs/dp-sag.htm (1997).

United States Department of Agriculture. *Fruit and nut yearbook. Annual data, 1970–97*. Stock # ERS-89022. Washington, DC. Available at: http://151.121.66.126/Prodsrvs/dp-sag.htm (1998).

Wellner, A. (1998, March). Getting old and staying fit. *American Demographics*.

World Almanac Books. (1998). *World almanac*. Mahwah, NJ: KIII Communications Company, 615.

World Health Organization. (1998). *The world health report 1998: Life in the 21st century—a vision for all*. Geneva, Switzerland.

PART ONE

The Science of Healthy Aging

CHAPTER 2

Revolution in Longevity

Robert N. Butler

In the late 1700s the average life expectancy at birth was 35 years. At the turn of the twentieth century, it was 47 years on average, and only 3% of the population made it past age 65. The twentieth-century revolution in longevity has led to an added 25 or more years of life. In the United States today, average life expectancy at birth has jumped to 75, and a full 80% of all deaths occur after age 65. In addition, people over 85 now constitute the fastest-growing segment of our population. Unfortunately, health maintenance and health promotion among the elderly population have not kept pace. Although it is true that we have postponed death, we have not yet been able to delay the age of onset of a variety of distressing disorders associated with growing older. Dementia, arthritis, diminished hearing and visual acuity, incontinence and hip fracture all continue to occur at the same ages as in the past. The chronic, nonfatal disorders of longevity destroy the quality of life and sap society's resources.

Does this mean that longer life necessarily brings with it more years of chronic disability? The latest evidence seems to support the concept that it does not and that we can indeed defer disease and dysfunction. Such postponement can become the most effective means of prevention, and prevention is essential if we are to reduce the staggering social and economic costs of disease.

---

*Data from the Alliance for Aging Research, which used Health Care Financing Administration data to calculate the savings from delaying the onset of disability in terms of hospital and doctor costs ($1.8 billion per month); nursing home costs ($3.2 billion per month); and home care costs ($.3 billion per month); total savings = $5.3 billion per month.

Source: R. Butler, The Revolution in Longevity, in *Delaying the Onset of Late-Life Dysfunction*, R. Butler and Brody, eds., pp. 1–9, © 1995, Springer Publishing Company, Inc., New York 10012, used by permission.

Were it possible to postpone physical dependence among persons 65 and above in the aggregate, it is estimated that $5 billion or more per month in public and private spending could be saved.* This does not represent a one-time saving only, but would establish a new lower basis for further expenditures in the future, assuming other variables remain constant. Such deferral is complex, and we need to understand better all the actual and biomedical implications, because it is not likely that all variables will remain the same. As a result of deferral, for example, either increased robustness or frailty could occur, new useful medical findings could be introduced in the meantime, cures for diseases might be found, and so on.

There are basically two ways of increasing longevity. One is through health promotion and disease prevention. The other is through basic research—involving all the rich new possibilities of molecular and cellular biology—and application of the results. Increasingly, these two methods will be combined. For example, if we are able to identify a gene for a specific disease such as colon cancer, an individual with such a marker could have the opportunity to alter his or her behavior accordingly, eating less fat and having more frequent checkups.

However, we need not—indeed, we *should* not—wait for the future findings of biology to apply what we already know. This becomes evident when we consider the status of health behavior in the United States today. Exercise, particularly aerobic activity and resistance training, has been shown through outstanding clinical investigations to reduce physical frailty, yet 71% of people do not exercise. Pneumonia and its complications are among the top 10 causes of death, yet 86% of people over age 65 do not receive the pneumococcal vaccine. On average, 10,000 people die of the flu in a given year, and in the course of a major epidemic as many as 70,000 succumb. Yet 50% of persons 65 and over do not get an autumn flu shot. Lung cancer attributable to tobacco use has surpassed breast cancer among women, yet nearly 22.6% of women still smoke. In fact, by all accounts, tobacco and alcohol are directly responsible for the top two causes of premature death—heart disease and cancer. Even so, there are 18 million Americans with alcohol problems, 10 million of whom are considered to have hard-core alcoholic disorders. In addition, the vast majority of Americans continue to eat high-fat diets, even though such foods have been shown to dramatically increase the risks of heart disease and cancer.

Health promotion and disease prevention are a dual responsibility that must be shared by the individual and society. The individual needs to adopt a lower-risk lifestyle, and society must educate the public, support bio-

medical research and elect government officials who will introduce legislation to maintain and improve public health. An example of this synergy
is the issue of smoking and the necessary avoidance of active and passive
smoke. There is no question that we need to continue various efforts to help
current American smokers quit the habit. However, since 1964, when the
Surgeon General's report on smoking was issued, there has been progress,
including a steady decrease in the number of Americans who smoke and
more protection of nonsmokers through legislation requiring smoke-free
environments. It is possible that the present debate over the addictiveness
of nicotine could lead to even greater restrictions on tobacco. This is an
example of what can happen when individuals and society collaborate to
prevent disease.

It is never too late to introduce new health habits. Indeed, the economic
consequences of not doing so and, consequently, of not preventing or
postponing dysfunction, are staggering. Inaction is fatal and costly. We
continue to pay for the care of people with disease rather than paying to
prevent disease. The economic cost of disease to our society is enormous
in terms of both direct costs (resources spent on hospitals, physicians, labs,
pharmacies and other goods and services that go along with medical care)
and indirect costs (not only loss of productivity by the patient but also by
the members of that individual's family and other unpaid caregivers).

Where, then, would our health dollars best be spent? To begin with,
public dissemination of information is absolutely essential if people are to
make informed choices. Federal and state efforts in that direction have
improved in recent years. Dr. Julius Richmond, who became Surgeon
General in 1976, led the way in advancing health promotion and disease
prevention. Human behavior can change, and such change can be maintained. Indeed, informed choices can lead to lifestyle changes which, in
turn, lead to major beneficial transformations in health and social well-
being.

We know, too, that economic determinants change behavior. Tobacco
and alcohol taxes actually reduce consumption, especially among the
young. In Canada, for example, hefty taxes on cigarettes have had a
quantitative impact on tobacco use. How useful it would be if there were an
even greater investment in social and behavioral research to help us
understand better other incentives and disincentives to lifestyle change. It
is especially important to disentangle the roles of genes and socialization
involved in addictive behavior. Clinical studies can help us understand
many physiologic and pathophysiologic issues and can lead us to solutions

that will delay or prevent disability. Most of all, we must invest in basic biology, especially the "new biology"—recombinant DNA, hybridoma and transgenic technologies—which is the wave of the future in both prevention and treatment.

Megascience projects such as the Human Genome Project, which may lead to numerous contributions to human health, should be cooperative, multinational efforts. Animal models remain critical to scientific success as well. Animal resources, especially aging animals, are both essential and expensive.

Among the basic biologic questions are these: What is a symptomatic or phenotypic threshold of a disease? How many cells do we need to lose in the macula before visual impairment occurs, or in the substantia nigra before Parkinson's disease develops? What do we do about infectious disease and the fact that microbes have become so skilled at survival, as Lederberg (1992) described so well in the volume *Emerging Infections*. And what about certain cancers that may have been predetermined genetically years before but may reveal themselves only after certain changes in the environment or in relation to the passage of time? How might we forestall cancer? How do we maintain the immune system? Study of the mechanism of metastases should be a fruitful field. The expression of genetic disease, the ecology of disease in general, is another area of vast importance.

The ultimate goal of this trend of thought, of course, is a disease-free old age in which people remain healthy and functional until the end. It is the classic dream of gerontologists, illustrated so eloquently by the nineteenth-century poem, "The Deacon's Masterpiece or The Wonderful One-Hoss Shay," written by the great doctor and poet, Oliver Wendell Holmes (1955). In effect, we could postpone all disease until a predetermined length of life is over so that we could "go to pieces," as Holmes put it, "All at once, and nothing first,—/Just as bubbles do when they burst." The goal is to counter the famous Gompertzian formulation, which states that the force of mortality proceeds exponentially with age (especially after age 30), doubling every 7 years, and to change the pace of overall aging or the aging processes of specific organs or bodily systems and ultimately to reset the biologic clock. Delaying dysfunction means reducing both the length and the amount of dependence. If we carry this bold concept through to its ultimate conclusion, all disease and disability would be postponed literally beyond death, the very point at which the biologic clock has run out!

What are other mechanisms of delay? The redundancy of systems in the body and the body's surprising plasticity or ability to repair itself are parts of the biologic basis for the mechanism of delay. Caloric restriction, first studied in depth by Clive McCay, causes delay of dysfunction and even of death. Control of free radical damage is relevant, and gene regulation is key. Delaying immunosenescence may prove to be a powerful weapon against disability, as may growth factors. In general, gene therapy approaches seem the most dramatic.

How much should we invest in such biomedical research or, indeed, in all of science? Should it be at the rate of gross national product (GNP) or greater than the GNP rate? Should we invest a percentage of health care expenditures in medical research? Yes, a sizable percentage! Today, on average, less than 20% of approved grants are funded by the National Institutes of Health. Congress and the executive branch of government should double the base of support to 40%. Certainly, there is a great cost to doing nothing. In the case of Alzheimer's disease, for example, it has been projected that by the year 2040, as the number of older people increases, the number of Alzheimer's patients will grow to three to five times the current count, which means that we could be facing a $300 billion to $500 billion national expenditure for Alzheimer's disease alone.

Aging research is worth doing, especially in the context of a longer life expectancy, because we want to keep cutting disability rates while lengthening life. Thus far, indications are that we are on the right track. American physician James Fries (1980) predicted the "compression of morbidity," which, he asserted optimistically, would occur following successful health promotion, disease prevention and research. Recent reports by Manton, Corder and Stallard (1993) suggest that disability rates have indeed declined, both *manifest* disability rates, as a consequence of medical responses, aid devices and housing improvements, and *inherent* disability rates.

The human desire is *not* to take longer to die but to live longer in good health through deferral of nonfatal as well as fatal conditions. This is an important strategy for biomedical science policy to support. From that perspective, biomedical research is the ultimate method of prevention, the ultimate service to humankind and the ultimate cost-containment strategy.

However, can we really plan research, or can we only provide the resources and sketch general priorities? On the one hand, scientists want money to do their work and freedom to explore as they wish. On the other hand, the public—which provides the tax dollars—has a vested interest in the way in which these funds are expended. Taxpayers ultimately finance science and technology, and they want results.

How can we match these simple desires: To have scientific freedom as well as reasonable and productive planning? Perhaps the common ground is the provision of basic resources and the assurance that funds channeled into megascience projects will not subtract funds from investigator-initiated research. We should sponsor major initiatives to tackle specific problems but avoid micromanagement. Science as a profession is no longer a cottage industry. Furthermore, it is troubling that in these austere times, review groups have become very conservative and do not support risky research proposals. There should always be a set-aside for high-risk scientific studies.

It is this author's belief that our nation must strengthen its support of basic science and preserve individual investigator-initiated research. It has been demonstrated over and over again that undifferentiated, untargeted science is the basis of extraordinary discoveries that meet human needs. Thus, we are always engaged in an effort to, on the one hand, balance the public's expectations—reflected in what can be called the *health politics of anguish* and advocacy within our democratic form of government—and, on the other hand, the need to preserve scientific freedom and the possibility of serendipity.

Increasing attention has been paid in the twentieth century to the role of genes and the environment, broadly defined to include lifestyle and the quality of our air and water. Not until the past 20 years, though, has significant attention been focused on the role of the aging of the organism. Yet aging brings about increased vulnerability to disease and disability, and it is necessary to understand all antecedents of dysfunction. The twenty-first century is likely to bring an even greater expansion of research interest in all three interconnected antecedents to disease—genetics, the environment, and aging—for the purpose of postponement as well as cure. The challenge is to delay dysfunction at a rate that outpaces the increase in life expectancy.

REFERENCES

Fries, J.F. (1980). Aging, natural death, and the compression of morbidity. *N Engl J Med, 303*, 130–135.

Holmes, O.W. (1955). The deacon's masterpiece or the wonderful one-hoss shay. In Oscar Williams (Ed.), *American verse from colonial days to the present.* New York: Pocket Books.

Lederberg, J. (1992). *Emerging infections: Microbial threats to health in the U.S.* Washington, DC: National Academy Press.

Manton, K.G., Corder, L.S., & Stallard, E. (1993). Estimates of change in chronic disability and institutional incidence and prevalence rates in the U.S. elderly population from 1982, 1984, and 1989 National Long-Term Care Survey. *Gerontol Soc Sci, 48*(4), S153–S166.

CHAPTER 3

Successful Aging

John W. Rowe and Robert L. Kahn

We define successful aging as including three main components: low probability of disease and disease-related disability, high cognitive and physical functional capacity and active engagement with life. All three terms are relative, and the relationship among them (as seen in Figure 3–1) is to some extent hierarchical. As the figure indicates, successful aging is more than absence of disease, important though that is, and more than the maintenance of functional capacities, important as it is. Both are important components of successful aging, but it is their combination with active engagement with life that represents the concept of successful aging most fully.

Each of the three components of successful aging includes subparts. Low probability of disease refers not only to absence or presence of disease itself, but also to absence, presence or severity of risk factors for disease. High functional level includes both physical and cognitive components. Physical and cognitive capacities are potentials for activity; they tell us what a person can do, not what he or she does do. Successful aging goes beyond potential; it involves activity. While active engagement with life takes many forms, we are most concerned with two—interpersonal relations and productive activity. Interpersonal relations involve contacts and transactions with others, exchange of information, emotional support and direct assistance. An activity is productive if it creates societal value, whether or not it is reimbursed. Thus, a person who cares for a disabled

Source: This chapter adapted with permission from J.W. Rowe and R.L. Kahn, Successful Aging, *The Gerontologist*, Vol. 37, No. 4, pp. 433–440, 1997, Copyright © The Gerontological Society of America.

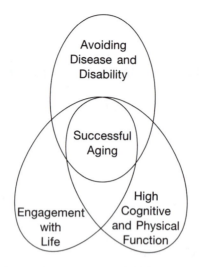

Figure 3–1 A Model of Successful Aging. *Source*: Reprinted with permission from J.W. Rowe and R.L. Kahn, Successful Aging, *The Gerontologist*, Vol. 37, No. 4, 1997, Copyright © 1997 The Gerontological Society of America.

family member or works as a volunteer in a local church or hospital is being productive, although unpaid (Herzog & Morgan, 1992).

STAYING HEALTHY: REDUCING RISK FACTORS FOR DISEASE AND DISABILITY IN LATE LIFE

The concept of usual aging as a large subset of those elderly previously considered to be "normal" is depicted in Figure 3–2 (Rowe, 1990). The curve farthest to the right, labeled *Death*, displays the 1980 age-specific mortality experience of the United States. The area to the left of the curve labeled *Disability*, estimates that portion of the population without disability, and the envelope between the Death and Disability curves denotes the disabled population. The area to the left of the curve labeled *Disease,* represents the nondiseased, nondisabled population. The final curve, labeled *Risk*, estimates the portion of the nondiseased population at significant risk for developing disease. The increasing dominance of this population with advancing age reflects emergence of the "usual aging syndrome"

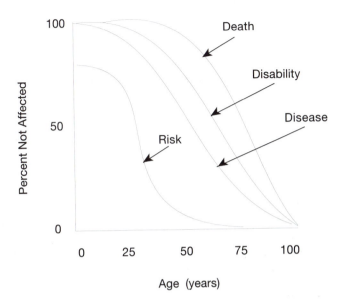

Figure 3–2 Relation of Risk of Disease to Presence of Disease, Disability and Death In an Aging Population. *Source*: Reprinted with permission from J.W. Rowe and R.L. Kahn, Successful Aging, *The Gerontologist*, Vol. 37, No. 4, 1997, Copyright © 1997 The Gerontological Society of America.

associated with risk of chronic disease. The area at the extreme left and bottom of the figure includes the nondiseased population at lowest risk, i.e., those who are aging "successfully" with respect to risk of emergence of disease. While the death, disability and disease curves traditionally originate at 100%, that is, with none of the population affected at birth, the risk curve arbitrarily originates at 80% not affected, to reflect the fact that many individuals begin at risk, either because of genetic factors or the psychosocial environment in which they are born.

HERITABILITY, LIFESTYLE AND AGE-RELATED RISK

The previously held view that increased risk of diseases and disability with advancing age results from inevitable, intrinsic aging processes, for the most part genetically determined, is inconsistent with a rapidly developing body of information that many usual aging characteristics are due to lifestyle and other factors that may be age-related (i.e., they increase with age) but are not age-dependent (not caused by aging itself).

A major source of such information is the Swedish Adoption/Twin Study of Aging (SATSA), a subset of the Swedish National Twin Registry that includes over 300 pairs of aging Swedish twins, mean age 66 years old, half of whom were reared together and half of whom were reared apart. About one third are monozygotic, while two thirds are dizygotic. Comparison of usual aging characteristics in twins of differing zygosity and rearing status enables estimation of the relative contributions of heritable and environmental influences.

SATSA-based studies have determined the heritability coefficients (the proportion of total variance attributable to genetic factors) for major risk factors for cardiovascular and cerebrovascular disease in older persons. These are 0.66–0.70 for body mass index, 0.28–0.78 for individual lipids (total cholesterol, low- and high-density lipoprotein cholesterol, apolipoproteins A-1 and -B and triglycerides), 0.44 for systolic and 0.34 for diastolic blood pressure (Heller, deFaire, Pedersen, Dahlén & McClearn, 1993; Hong, deFaire, Heller, McClearn & Pedersen, 1994; Stunkard, Harris, Pedersen & McClearn, 1990). Heritability trends across decades of advanced age revealed a reduction in the heritability coefficients for apolipoprotein B and triglycerides and for systolic blood pressure (0.62 for people under 65 years old and 0.12 for those over 65).

Consistent with these age-related reductions in heritability are mortality data from a 26-year follow-up of the entire Swedish Twin Registry, 21,004 twins born between 1886 and 1925 (Marenberg, Risch, Berkman, Floderus & deFaire, 1994). Among male identical twins, the risk of death from coronary heart disease was eightfold greater for those whose twin died before age 55 than for those whose twin did not die before age 55, and among male nonidentical twins, the corresponding risk was nearly four times greater. When one female identical twin died before the age of 65, the risk of death for the other twin was 15 times greater than if one's twin did not die before the age of 65 and 2.6 times greater in the case of female nonidentical twins. Overall, the magnitude of the risk associated with one's twin dying of coronary heart disease decreased as the age at which the twin died increased, independent of gender and zygosity.

Beyond twin studies, other evidence indicates the importance of lifestyle factors in the emergence of risk in old age. For instance, advancing age is associated with progressive impairment in carbohydrate tolerance, insufficient to meet diagnostic criteria for diabetes mellitus but characterized by increases in basal and postglucose challenge levels of blood sugar and insulin. The hyperglycemia of aging carries increased risk for coronary heart disease (Donahue, Abbott, Reed & Yano, 1987) and stroke (Abbott, 1987), with progressive increases in the usual aging range associated with increasing risk. Similarly, the hyperinsulinemia associated with aging is an independent risk factor for coronary heart disease (Foster, 1989; Pyorala, 1979). Several studies have now demonstrated that the dominant determinants of this risk are age-related but potentially avoidable factors, such as the amount and distribution of body fat (Elahi, Muller, Tzankoff, Andres & Tobin, 1982; Kohrt, Staten, Kirwan, Wojta & Holloszy, 1990), reduced physical activity and dietary factors (Zavaroni et al., 1986).

Substantial and growing evidence supports the contention that established risk factors for the emergence of diseases in older populations, such as cardiovascular and cerebrovascular disease, can be substantially modified (Hazzard & Bierman, 1990; Sticht & Hazzard, 1995). In a study demonstrating the modifiability of "usual aging," Katzel and colleagues (Katzel, Bleecker, Colman, Rogus & Sorkin, 1995) conducted a randomized, controlled, prospective trial comparing the effects of a 9-month diet-induced weight loss (approximately 10% of body weight) to the effects of a constant-weight aerobic exercise program and a control program on a well-characterized group of middle-aged and older men at risk for cardiovascular disease. The study participants were nondiabetic and were obese (body mass index 30 kg/in), with increased waist-hip ratios and modest increases in blood pressure, blood glucose, insulin and an atherogenic lipid profile. Compared to controls, the reduced-energy intake diet resulted in statistically significant reductions in weight, waist-hip ratio, fasting and postprandial glucose and insulin levels, blood pressure and plasma levels of triglycerides, low-density lipoprotein/cholesterol and increases in high-density lipoprotein/cholesterol. While the older weight loss subjects (over 60 years old) lost less weight than the middle-aged subjects and had more modest improvements in carbohydrate tolerance, they participated fully in the reductions in other risk factors. In general, the weight-loss intervention had greater effects than the constant-weight aerobic exercise intervention.

Taken together, these reports reveal three consistent findings. First, intrinsic factors alone, while highly significant, do not dominate the determination of risk in advancing age. Extrinsic environmental factors, including elements of lifestyle, play a very important role in determining risk for disease. Second, with advancing age the relative contribution of genetic factors decreases and the force of nongenetic factors increases. Third, usual aging characteristics are modifiable. These findings underline the importance of environmental and behavioral factors in determining the risk of disease late in life.

INTRA-INDIVIDUAL VARIABILITY: A NEWLY IDENTIFIED RISK FACTOR IN OLDER PERSONS

The traditional repertoire of risk factors identified in studies of young and middle-aged populations may not include some additional risk factors unique to, or more easily identified in, elderly populations. In this regard, the MacArthur Foundation's Studies of Successful Aging point to a previously unrecognized risk factor—altered within-individual variability in physiologic functions—which may be important in determining the usual aging syndrome.

Most gerontologic research, and indeed research in all age groups, is not geared to the measurement of short-term variations and changes. Study designs generally focus on the absolute level of a variable, perhaps comparing levels at two or more time points that may be separated by months or years. Nesselroade and colleagues (Kim, Nesselroade & Featherman, 1996) reasoned that short-term variability in a number of physiologic or perhaps psychologic characteristics might reflect a loss of underlying physiologic reserve and represent a risk factor for emergence of disease or disability. To study the impact of short-term variability, they examined between-person differences in similarly aged residents of a retirement community. They assessed various aspects of biomedical, cognitive and physical functioning every week for 25 weeks in a group of 31 individuals and a matched group of 30 assessed only at the outset and the end of the 25-week period, and they followed the subjects for several years to ascertain the relationship between within-person variability and its risk.

Within-person variability of a joint index of physical performance and physiologic measures (gait, balance and blood pressure) was an excellent predictor of mortality 5 years later. Variability of the composite measure was a better predictor of mortality than mean level, which did not represent a statistically significant risk factor (Nesselroade, Featherman, Agen & Rowe, 1996). A similar pattern of findings held for the psychologic attributes of perceived control and efficacy, for which average level was not a significant predictor of mortality but intra-individual variability scores predicted 30% of the variance in mortality (Eizenman, Nesselroade, Featherman, & Rowe, 1997).

It should be emphasized that some functions are highly variable under normal conditions and others much less so. The significant aspect of intra-individual variability as a potential measure of decreased capacity and increased risk must be a change from the normal variability, regardless of whether the change is an increase or decrease. For example, a decline in beat-to-beat variability in heart rate has been shown to be a predictor of mortality in patients who have previously suffered a myocardial infarction. While in the physiologic measurement used in this study, an increase in variability was associated with increased risk; in other highly regulated systems, a decrease in variability may be detrimental and represent decreased reserve and increased risk.

MAXIMIZING COGNITIVE AND PHYSICAL FUNCTION IN LATE LIFE

A second essential component of successful aging is maximization of functional status. One common concern of older people relates to cognitive function, especially learning and short-term memory. Another functional area of major interest is physical performance. Modest reductions in the capacity to easily perform common physical functions may prevent full participation in productive and recreational activities of daily life.

The MacArthur Foundation Research Network on Successful Aging conducted a longitudinal study of older persons to identify those physical, psychologic, social and biomedical characteristics predictive of the maintenance of high function in late life. The 1,189 subjects in this three-site longitudinal study were 70–79 years old at initial evaluation and were functionally in the upper one third of the general aging population. Smaller age- and sex-matched samples (80 subjects in the medium-functioning group and 82 subjects in the low-functioning group) were selected to represent the middle and lowest tertiles. Initial data included detailed assessments of physical and cognitive performance, health status and social and psychologic characteristics (the MacArthur battery), as well as the collection of blood and urine samples. After a 2.0–2.5 year interval, 1,115 subjects were re-evaluated, providing a 91% follow-up rate for the study.

Austin College Library

PREDICTORS OF COGNITIVE FUNCTION

Cognitive ability was assessed with neuropsychologic tests of language, nonverbal memory, verbal memory, conceptualization and visual spatial ability. In the initially high-functioning group, four variables—education, strenuous activity in and around the home, peak pulmonary flow rate and self-efficacy—were found to be direct predictors of change or mainte-nance of cognitive function, together explaining 40% of the variance in cognitive test performance. Education was the strongest predictor, with greater years of schooling increasing the likelihood of maintaining high cognitive function (Albert et al., 1995). This finding is consistent with several cross-sectional studies, which identify education as a major protec-tive factor against reductions in cognitive function. Since all the subjects had high cognitive function at first evaluation, it is unlikely that the observed effect merely reflected ability to perform well on cognitive tests or was the result of individuals with greater innate intelligence having received more education. Instead, the results suggest either or both of two explanatory mechanisms: a direct beneficial effect of education early in life on brain circuitry and function, and the possibility that education is a proxy for lifelong intellectual activities (reading, crossword puzzles, and so on), which might serve to maintain cognitive function late in life.

Pulmonary peak expiratory flow rate was the second strongest predictor of maintenance of cognitive function. In previous studies, this function was a predictor of total and cardiovascular mortality, and a correlate of cognitive and physical function in elderly populations (Cook et al., 1989).

A surprising finding of this study was that the amount of strenuous physical activity at and around the home was an important predictor of maintaining cognitive function. In a follow-up study to evaluate a possible mechanism of this effect, Neeper, Gomez-Pinilla, Choi and Cotman (1995) measured the effect of exercise on central nervous system levels of brain-derived neurotrophic factor (BDNF) in adult rats. These investigators found that increasing exercise was associated with very substantial "dose-related" increases in BDNF in the hippocampus and neocortex, brain areas known to be highly responsive to environmental stimuli. These data provide a potential mechanism whereby exercise might enhance central nervous system function, particularly memory function.

A personality measure, perceived self-efficacy, was also predictive of maintaining cognitive function in old age. The concept of self-efficacy developed by Bandura is defined as "people's beliefs in their capabilities to organize and execute the courses of action required to deal with prospective situations (Bandura, 1995)." In students and young adults, self-efficacy influences persistence in solving cognitive problems (Brown & Inouye, 1978), heart rate during performance of cognitive tasks (Bandura, Cioffi, Taylor & Brouillard, 1988), mathematical performance (Collins, 1982) and mastery of computer software procedures (Gist, Schwoerer & Rosen, 1989). Lachman and colleagues have proposed a role for self-efficacy beliefs in maintenance of cognitive function among older people (Lachman & Leff, 1989; Lachman, Weaver, Bandura, Elliott, & Lewkowicz, 1992).

In addition to these findings of predictors of maintenance of cognitive function, evidence is accumulating to indicate that it can be enhanced in old age. For example, older people who showed a clear age-related pattern of decline in fluid intelligence (inductive reasoning and spatial orientation) showed substantial improvement after five training sessions that stressed ways of approaching such problems and provided practice in solving them (Schaie & Willis, 1986). Moreover, repeated measurement indicated that the improvements were maintained. Studies from the Max Planck Institute in Berlin confirm the finding that cognitive losses among healthy older people are reversible by means of training, although they also show a substantial age-related training effect in favor of younger subjects (Kliegl, Smith, & Baltes, 1989). There is a double message in these findings: First, and most important, the capacity for positive change, sometimes called *plasticity*, persists in old age; appropriate interventions can often bring older people back to (or above) some earlier level of function. Second, the same interventions may be still more effective with younger subjects, which suggests an age-related reduction in reserve functional capacity. These demonstrations of plasticity in old age are encouraging in their own right and tell us that positive change is possible.

PREDICTORS OF PHYSICAL FUNCTION

In the MacArthur Studies, maintenance of high physical performance, including hand, trunk and lower extremity movements and integrated movements of balance and gait, was predicted by both sociodemographic and health-status characteristics. Being older and having an income of less than $10,000 a year increased the likelihood of a decline in physical performance, as did higher body mass index (greater fat), high blood pressure and lower initial cognitive performance. Behavioral predictors of maintenance of physical function included moderate or strenuous leisure activity and emotional support from family and friends. Moderate levels of exercise activity (for example, walking leisurely) appeared in these studies to convey similar advantages to more strenuous exercise (for example, brisk walking).

CONTINUING ENGAGEMENT WITH LIFE

The third component of successful aging, engagement with life, has two major elements: maintenance of interpersonal relations and of productive activities.

Social Relations

At least since Durkheim's classic study of suicide (Durkheim, 1951), isolation and lack of connectedness to others have been recognized as predictors of morbidity and mortality. Five prospective studies of substantial populations have now demonstrated causality throughout the life course in such associations: Being part of a social network is a significant determinant of longevity, especially for men (House, Landis, & Umberson 1988).

Research on the health protective aspect of network membership has emphasized two kinds of supportive transactions: socioemotional (expressions of affection, respect and the like) and instrumental (direct assistance, such as giving physical help, doing chores, providing transportation, or giving money (Cassel, 1976; Cobb, 1976; House, Kahn, McLeod, & Williams, 1985; Kahn & Antonucci, 1981; Kahn & Byosiere, 1992).

The three-community MacArthur Study tested both instrumental and emotional support as predictors of neuroendocrine function and physical performance. Neuroendocrine measures were also studied as possible mediators of the effects of support. Over a 3-year period, marital status (being married), presumably a source of emotional support, protected against reduction in productive activity (Glass, Seeman, Herzog, Kahn, & Berkman, 1995). Men with higher emotional support had significantly lower urine excretion of norepinephrine, epinephrine and cortisol, and for both men and women, emotional support was a positive predictor of physical performance. Instrumental support, on the other hand, had few significant neuroendocrine relations for men, none for women, and was associated with lower physical performance, probably as an effect rather than a cause (Seeman, Berkman, Blazer, & Rowe, 1994; Seeman, Berkman, Charpentier, Blazer, Albert, & Tinetti, 1995).

These varying effects of social support are consistent with research relating the effect of support to the specific situation in which it is offered. For example, instrumental support rather than emotional support influenced the promptness with which older people who experienced cancer-suspicious symptoms actually saw a physician (Antonucci, Kahn, & Akiyama, 1989). Opposite results came from a nursing home experiment, however: Socioemotional support (verbal encouragement) had positive performance effects, whereas instrumental support (direct assistance) had negative effects on performance (Avorn & Langer, 1982).

Several conclusions seem warranted regarding the properties of social relations and their effects:

- Isolation (lack of social ties) is a risk factor for health.
- Social support, both emotional and instrumental, can have positive health-relevant effects.
- No single type of support is uniformly effective; effectiveness depends on the appropriateness of the supportive acts to the requirements of the situation and the person.

PRODUCTIVE ACTIVITIES

Older people are not considered "old" by their families and friends, nor do they think of themselves as "old" so long as they remain active and productive in some meaningful sense (Kaufman, 1986). In legislative policy, Congressional discussion as to whether the nation can "afford" its older people is as much a debate about their productivity as their requirements for service, especially medical care.

Part of the confusion stems from lack of clarity about what constitutes a productive activity. Our national statistics define gross domestic product in terms of activities that are paid for and exclude all unpaid activities, however valuable. Several current studies (Americans Changing Lives [ACL], MacArthur, Health and Retirement Study) utilize a broader definition that includes all activities, paid or unpaid, that create goods or services of economic value (Kahn, 1986), and these studies have generated age-related patterns very different from those for paid employment alone (Herzog, Antonucci, Jackson, Kahn, & Morgan, 1987; Herzog, Kahn, Morgan, Jackson, & Antonucci, 1989).

The nationwide ACL study found that, contrary to the stereotype of unproductive old age, most older people make productive contributions of some kind, more as informal help-giving and unpaid volunteer work than paid employment. When all forms of productive activity are combined, the amount of work done by older men and women is substantial. Among those aged 60 or more, 39% reported at least 1,500 hours of productive activity during the preceding year; 41% reported 500–1,499 hours, and 18% reported 1–499 hours. The relationship between age and productive activity depends on the activity. While hours of paid work drop sharply after age 55, hours of volunteer work in organizations peak in the middle years (ages 35–55), and informal help to friends and relatives peaks still later (ages 55–64) and remains significant to age 75 and beyond.

Both the ACL and MacArthur studies address the question of what factors enable sustained productivity in old age. Both include longitudinal as well as cross-sectional data, and in some respects the studies are complementary—national representativeness over the full adult age range in the ACL survey, biomedical and performance measures, as well as self-report in the MacArthur research. Three factors emerge as predictors of productive activity: functional capacity, education and self-efficacy.

FUNCTIONAL CAPACITY

Men and women high in cognitive and physical function are three times as likely to be doing some paid work and more than twice as likely to be doing volunteer work. Moreover, for all forms of productive work except child care, functional status also predicts the amount of such work. Indicators of functional decrement, such as limitations with vision and number of bed days during the 3 months preceding the data collection, predict lesser productive activity.

EDUCATION

Educational level is a well-established predictor of sustained productive behavior, paid and unpaid (Chambre, 1987; Cutler & Hendricks, 1990;

Harris & Associates, 1981; Herzog, Franks, Markus, & Holmberg, 1996; Herzog & Morgan, 1993; Lawton, 1983; Morgan, 1986). The possible mechanisms of this effect include the role of education as a major determinant of occupation and income, both of which are major influences on the life course, the selective process in education that probably includes genetic elements and certainly includes parental socioeconomic status, and the tendency of education to inculcate values and establish habits that express themselves in later life as higher functional status and engagement in productive behavior.

SELF-EFFICACY

Self-efficacy and the related concepts of mastery and control are consistent predictors of sustained activity in old age. The ACL study, in addition to identifying a positive relationship between self-efficacy and productive activity, found that two other variables, labeled *vulnerability* and *fatalism*, essentially inversions of self-efficacy, were negatively related to productivity. Consistent with these findings, in the MacArthur sample only one factor—mastery—emerged as relevant for both increases and decreases in productivity; increases in mastery led to increased productivity; decreases in mastery had the opposite effect.

RESPONSE TO STRESS

If we had continuous rather than occasional measurement of successful aging, we would expect to find that even older people who are aging successfully have not met the criteria at every moment in the past. They have moved "in and out of success," as healthy people can be said to move in and out of illness, even under the most fortunate circumstances, aging brings with it some repetitive experience of chronic or recurrent stresses, the "daily hassles" of life (Lazarus & Folkman, 1984) and their cumulative effects. Most older people have also experienced more acute episodes, the "stressful life events" that have been much studied (Dohrenwend & Dohrenwend, 1974; Holmes & Rahe, 1967). For example, older men and women may have been seriously ill, temporarily disabled by accident or injury, disoriented after a stroke or depressed by the death of a spouse. Apart from such crises of illness and bereavement, but similarly stressful, are the experiences of forced retirement, sudden reduction in income, mugging, and burglary.

We propose the concept of *resilience* to describe the rapidity and completeness with which people recover from such episodes and return to meeting the criteria of success. Determination of resilience in dealing with a specific stressful event would require assessment of relevant functions before the stressing challenge is encountered and subsequent monitoring to observe the initial decremental effect, the time required to regain stability of function, and the level of function regained. While no research has yet robustly evaluated resilience, a number of studies are relevant to it. The work by Nesselroade and his colleagues, described earlier, demonstrated the importance of short-term variability in physical function and blood pressure as a predictor of mortality among elderly subjects. We may interpret low variability in blood pressure as an indicator of resilience, but the interpretation must be tentative; we do not know the challenges or stressors to which these subjects were responding.

CONCLUSION

Recent and projected substantial increases in the relative and absolute number of older persons in our society pose a significant challenge for biology, social and behavioral science, and medicine. Gerontology is broadening its perspective from a prior preoccupation with disease and disability to a more robust view that includes successful aging. As conceptual and empiric research in this area accelerates, successful aging is seen as multidimensional, encompassing three distinct domains: avoidance of disease and disability, maintenance of high physical and cognitive function, and sustained engagement in social and productive activities. For each of these domains, an interdisciplinary database is coalescing that relates to both reducing the risk of adverse events and enhancing resilience in their presence. Many of the predictors of risk and of both functional and activity levels appear to be potentially modifiable, either by individuals or by changes in their immediate environments. The stage is thus set for intervention studies to identify effective strategies that enhance the proportion of our older population that ages successfully.

REFERENCES

Abbott, R.D. (1987). Diabetes and the risk of stroke. The Honolulu Heart Program. *JAMA, 257,* 949–952.

Albert, M.S., Savage, C.R., Jones, K., Berkman, L., Seeman, T., Blazer, D., & Rowe, J.W. (1995). Predictors of cognitive change in older persons: MacArthur Studies of Successful Aging. *Psychol Aging, 10*, 578–589.

Antonucci, T.C., Kahn, R.L., & Akiyama, H. (1989). Psychosocial factors and the response to cancer symptoms. In R. Yancik & J.W. Yates (Eds.), *Cancer in the elderly: Approaches to early detection and treatment* (pp. 40–52). New York: Springer Publishing Co.

Avorn, J., & Langer, E.J. (1982). Induced disability in nursing home patients: A controlled trial. *J Am Geriatr Soc, 30*, 397–400.

Bandura, A. (1995). *Self-efficacy in changing societies*. New York: Cambridge University Press.

Bandura, A., Cioffi, D., Taylor, C.B., & Brouillard, M.E. (1988). Perceived self-efficacy in coping with cognitive stressors and opioid activities. *J Pers Soc Psychol, 55*, 479–488.

Brown, I. Jr., & Inouye, D.K. (1978). Learned helplessness through modeling. *J Pers Soc Psychol, 36*, 900–908.

Cassel, I. (1976). The contribution of the social environment to host resistance: The fourth Wade Hampton Frost Lecture. *Am J Epidemiol, 104*, 107–123.

Chambre, S.M. (1987). *Good deeds in old age: Volunteering by the new leisure class*. Lexington, MA: Lexington Books.

Cobb, S. (1976). Social support as a moderator of life stress. *Psychosom Med, 3*, 300–314.

Collins, J.L. (1982, March). Self-efficacy and ability in achievement behavior. Paper presented at the American Educational Research Association, New York.

Cook, N.R., Evans, D.A., Scherr, P.A., Speizer, F.E., Vedal, S., Branch, L.G., Huntley, J.C., Hennekens, C.H., & Taylor, J.O. (1989). Peak expiratory flow rate and 5- to 6-year mortality in an elderly population. *Am J Epidemiol, 130*, 66–78.

Cutler, S.J., & Hendricks, J. (1990). Leisure and time use across the life course. In R.H. Binstock & L.K. George (Eds.), *Handbook of aging and the social sciences* (3rd ed., pp.169–185). San Diego: Academic Press.

Dohrenwend, B.S., & Dohrenwend, B.P. (1974). *Stressful life events: Their nature and effects*. New York: John Wiley & Sons.

Donahue, R.P., Abbott, R.D., Reed, D.M., & Yano, K. (1987). Post-challenge glucose concentration and coronary heart disease in men of Japanese ancestry: Honolulu Heart Program. *Diabetes, 36*, 689–692.

Durkheim, E. (1951). *Suicide*. Glencoe, IL: Free Press. (Original work published in 1897).

Eizenman, D.R., Nesselroade, J.R., Featherman, D.L, & Rowe, J.W. (1997). Intra-individual variability in perceived control in an older sample: The MacArthur Successful Aging Studies. *Psychol Aging, 12*(3): 489–502.

Elahi, D., Muller, D.C., Tzankoff, S.P., Andres, R., & Tobin, J.D. (1982). Effect of age and obesity on fasting levels of glucose, insulin, glucagon and growth hormone in man. *Gerontol, 37*, 485–491.

Foster, D.W. (1989). Insulin resistance-A secret killer [Editorial]. *N Engl J Med, 320*, 733–734.

Gist, M.E., Schwoerer, C., & Rosen, B. (1989). Effects of alternative training methods on self-efficacy and performance in computer software training. *Appl Psychol, 74*, 884–891.

Glass, T.A., Seeman, T.E., Herzog, A.R., Kahn, R.L., & Berkman, L.F. (1995). Change in productive activity in late adulthood: MacArthur Studies of Successful Aging. *Gerontol Soc Sci, 50B,* S65–S76.

Harris, L., & Associates. (1981). *Aging in the eighties: Americans in transition.* Washington, DC: National Council on the Aging.

Hazzard, W.R., & Bierman, E.L. (1990). Preventative gerontology: Strategies for attenuation of the chronic disease of aging. In W. Hazzard, R. Andres, E. Bierman, & J. Blass (Eds.), *Principles of geriatric medicine and gerontology* (2nd ed., pp. 167–171). New York: McGraw-Hill.

Heller, D., deFaire, U., Pedersen, N., Dahlén, G., & McClearn, G. (1993). Genetic and environmental influences on serum lipid levels in twins. *N Engl J Med, 328,* 1150–1156.

Herzog, A.R., Antonucci, T.C., Jackson, J.S., Kahn, R.L., & Morgan, J.N. (1987, February). *Productive activities and health over the life course.* Paper presented at the annual meeting of the American Association for the Advancement of Science, Chicago, IL.

Herzog, A.R., Franks, M.M., Markus, H.R., & Holmberg, D. (1996). Productive activities and agency in old age. In M. Baltes & L. Montada (Eds.), *Produktives Leben im Alter* [Productive living in old age]. Frankfurt/New York: Campus Verlag.

Herzog, A.R., Kahn, R.L, Morgan, J.N., Jackson, J.S., & Antonucci, T.C. (1989). Age differences in productive activities. *Gerontol Soc Sci, 44,* S129–S138.

Herzog, A.R., & Morgan, J.N. (1992). Age and gender differences in the value of productive activities: Four different approaches. *Res Aging, 14,* 169–198.

Herzog, A.R., & Morgan, J.N. (1993). Formal volunteer work among older Americans. In S. Bass, F. Caro, & Y.P. Chen (Eds.), *Achieving a productive aging society.* Westport, CT: Greenwood Publishing Group.

Holmes, T.H., & Rahe, R.H. (1967). The social readjustment rating scale. *J Psychosom Res, 11,* 213–218.

Hong, Y., deFaire, U., Heller, D., McClearn, G., & Pedersen, N. (1994). Genetic and environmental influences on blood pressure in elderly twins. *Hypertension, 24,* 663–670.

House, J.S., Kahn, R.L, with McLeod, J., & Williams, D. (1985). Measures and concepts of social support. In S. Cohen & S.L. Syme (Eds.), *Social support and health* (pp. 83–108). Orlando, FL: Academic Press.

House, J.S., Landis, K.R., & Umberson, D. (1988). Social relationships and health. *Science, 241,* 540–545.

Kahn, R.L. (1986, November). Productive activities and well-being. Paper presented at the meeting of the Gerontological Society of America, Chicago, IL.

Kahn, R.L., & Antonucci, T.C. (1981). Convoys of social support: A lifecourse approach. In S.B. Kiesler, J.N. Morgan, & V.K. Oppenheimer (Eds.), *Aging: Social change* (pp. 383–405). New York: Academic Press.

Kahn, R.L., & Byosiere, P. (1992). Stress in organizations. In M.D. Dunnette & L.M. Hough (Eds.), *Handbook of industrial and organizational psychology, Vol. 3* (2nd ed., pp. 571–650). Palo Alto, CA: Consulting Psychologists Press.

Katzel, L.I., Bleecker, E.R., Colman, E.G., Rogus, E.M., & Sorkin, J.D. (1995). Effects of weight loss vs. aerobic exercise training on risk factors for coronary disease in healthy, obese, middle-aged and older men: A randomized controlled trial. *JAMA, 274*,1915–1921.

Kaufman, S.R. (1986). *The ageless self: Sources of meaning in late life.* Madison, WI: University of Wisconsin Press.

Kim, M., Nesselroade, J., & Featherman, D. (1996). The state component in self-reported world views and religious beliefs of older adults: The MacArthur Successful Aging Studies. *Psychol Aging, 11,* 396–407.

Kliegl, R., Smith, J., & Baltes, P.B. (1989). Testing-the-limits and the study of adult age differences in cognitive plasticity of a mnemonic skill. *Dev Psychol, 25,* 247–256.

Kohrt, W.M., Staten, M.A., Kirwan, J.P., Wojta, D.M., & Holloszy, J.O. (1990). Insulin resistance of aging is related to body composition. *Gerontologist, 30* (Special Issue), 38A.

Lachman, M.E., & Leff, R. (1989). Perceived control and intellectual functioning in the elderly. *Psychol Aging, 2,* 266–271.

Lachman, M.E., Weaver, S.L, Bandura, M.M., Elliott, E., & Lewkowicz, C.J. (1992). Improving memory and control beliefs through cognitive restructuring and self-generated strategies. *Gerontol Psychol Sci, 47,* 293–299.

Lawton, M.P. (1983). Time, space, and activity. In G.D. Rowles & R.J. Ohta (Eds.), *Aging and milieu: Environmental perspectives on growing old* (pp. 41–61). New York: Academic Press.

Lazarus, R.S., & Folkman, S. (1984). *Stress, appraisal, and coping.* New York: Springer Publishing Co.

Marenberg, M., Risch, N., Berkman, L., Floderus, B., & deFaire, U. (1994). Genetic susceptibility to death from coronary heart disease in a study of twins. *N Engl J Med, 330,* 1041–1046.

Morgan, J.N. (1986). Unpaid productive activity over the life course. In Institute of Medicine/National Research Council (Eds.), *America's aging: Productive roles in an older society.* Washington, DC: National Academy Press.

Neeper, S.A., Gomez-Pinilla, F., Choi, J., & Cotman, C. (1995). Exercise and brain neurotrophins. *Nature, 373,* 109.

Nesselroade, J.R., Featherman, D.L., Agen, S.H., & Rowe, J.W. (1996). *Short-term variability in physical performance and physiological attributes in older adults*: MacArthur Successful Aging Studies (submitted).

Pyorala, K. (1979). Relationship of glucose tolerance and plasma insulin to the incidence of coronary heart disease: Results from two population studies in Finland. *Diabetes Care, 2,* 131–141.

Rowe, J.W. (1990). Toward successful aging: Limitation of the morbidity associated with "normal" aging. In *Principles of geriatric medicine and gerontology* (2nd ed., pp.138–141). New York: McGraw Hill.

Schaie, K.W., & Willis, S.L. (1986). Can adult intellectual decline be reversed? *Dev Psychol, 22,* 223–232.

Seeman, T.F., Berkman, L.F., Blazer, D., & Rowe, J.W. (1994). Social ties and support and neuroendocrine function: The MacArthur Studies of Successful Aging. *Ann Behav Med, 16,* 95–106.

Seeman, T.E., Berkman, L.F., Charpentier, P.A., Blazer, D.G., Albert, M.S., & Tinetti, M.F. (1995). Behavioral and psychosocial predictors of physical performance: MacArthur Studies of Successful Aging. *Gerontol Med Sci, 50A,* M177–M183.

Sticht, J.P., & Hazzard, W.R. (1995). Weight control and exercise: Cardinal features of successful preventative gerontology [Editorial]. *JAMA, 274,* 1964–1965.

Stunkard, A., Harris, J., Pedersen, N., & McClearn, G. (1990). The body-mass index of twins who have been reared apart. *N Engl J Med, 322,* 1483–1487.

Zavaroni, I., Dall'Aglio, E., Bruschi, F., Bonora, E., Alpi, O., Pezzarossa, A., & Butturini, U. (1986). Effect of age and environmental factors on glucose tolerance and insulin secretion in a worker population. *J Am Geriatr Soc, 34,* 271–275.

CHAPTER 4

The Case for Healthy Aging and the Compression of Morbidity

James F. Fries

Live long, live healthy, die fast. Use it or lose it. We don't wear out, we rust out. Each of these now-familiar aphorisms expresses an aspect of the paradigm for the compression of morbidity (or ill health), which envisions the potential for reduction of overall human morbidity and associated health care costs (Fries, 1980). The term *morbidity* broadly includes all illness and infirmity; in formal study, the term *disability* is used, which is the major component of morbidity and which is more easily understood.

At present, the years during which one is ill are heavily concentrated in old age. Compressing the amount of time we spend in ill health would mean delaying the age of onset of a disability or chronic condition and decreasing the amount of time between the average age of onset of disability and the average age of death, which may increase more slowly.

Figure 4–1 introduces the concept of compression of morbidity. On the top line, imagine a typical person's lifetime in the United States today, with the shaded area representing morbidity. Life begins at age zero and ends on average at age 75. The onset of some degree of morbidity or disability occurs, on average, at age 55. Almost all of the morbidity in a typical life occurs between the first arrow representing the age of onset of morbidity and the second arrow representing the age at death. Morbidity in later life is made up of a combination of such chronic diseases as heart disease, lung disease, arthritis, stroke and diabetes, aggravated by the physical and mental frailties of old age.

The second and third lines in Figure 4–1 represent possible scenarios for the year 2050. In the second line, scientific advances have extended life, but the amount of morbidity has actually increased, as the arrow representing onset of morbidity has not moved. This has been termed the *increasing*

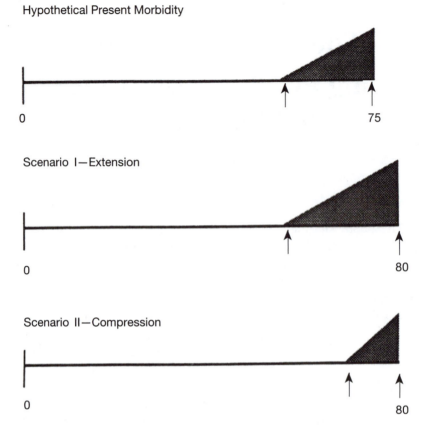

Hypothetical Present Morbidity

0   75

Scenario I—Extension

0   80

Scenario II—Compression

0   80

Figure 4–1 Compression or Extension of Morbidity. *Source:* Reprinted with permission from J.F. Fries, Compression of Morbidity: Near or Far?, *Milbank Quarterly*, Vol. 67, pp. 208–232, © 1990, Milbank Memorial Fund.

misery scenario. In the third line, delay in the onset of morbidity through postponement or prevention of chronic disease has moved the morbidity onset arrow to age 68 or so. Although increased longevity also occurs with postponement of chronic disease, total morbidity decreases.

The same phenomenon is illustrated in Figure 4–2, which represents the lives of twin brothers. The first brother—who smokes heavily and is obese and sedentary—begins to be short of breath about age 40 and subsequently has a premature heart attack, a stroke and eventually dies of lung cancer. The second brother, with fewer health risks, has much less morbidity and

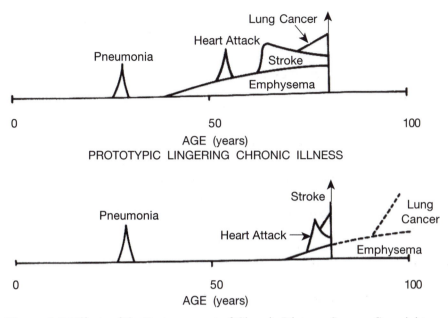

Figure 4–2 Effects of the Postponement of Chronic Disease. *Source:* Copyright © 1981, James F. Fries.

has postponed several illnesses, some of them so much so that they do not occur at all during the life span.

For this scenario to be achieved, largely through prevention of disease and disability, the factors that predict future ill health, improve these risk factors, and document the improvements in health that result must be identified. Increases in physical activity, decreases in cigarette smoking and reduction in body weight are perhaps the most obvious of the variables that might reduce overall lifetime morbidity.

The ideal for the healthy life under the compression-of-morbidity hypothesis, then, is a life that is vigorous and vital until shortly before its natural close. Through the early and middle years of this century, most observers believed that there was movement away from this ideal, with a steady increase in the proportion of a typical life spent being ill or infirm. This increase in infirmity occurred because such common fatal infectious illnesses as pneumonia, tuberculosis and smallpox gave way to chronic diseases (such as heart or lung disease), which involve longer periods of morbidity (Crimmins, 1990; Gruenberg, 1997; Verbrugge, 1984). People began to take longer to die. The first suggestion that this increase in human infirmity might be changing came with the decline in heart disease, the major chronic illness and the major cause of death in the United States, beginning more than 20 years ago.

If acute infectious illnesses are no longer the leading cause of death and major areas of chronic disease are rapidly declining, then what will make us sick and cause us to die? To explain this paradox, it is necessary to conceptualize a new understanding of natural death due to "old age" and of disability due to frailty, which need not be caused by a disease. With the decline in chronic illness and an accompanying increase in life expectancy that occurred in the 1970s, the national illness burden has become increasingly dominated by the frailty of aging. The slowing of many bodily processes with age decreases "organ reserve" and the body's resistance to outside threats.

The shaded areas of Figure 4–1 may also be taken to represent medical costs, which generally parallel morbidity and disability (Crimmins, 1990). Clearly, a scenario of ever-lengthening periods of disability would be financially catastrophic for the nation. Thus, the paradigm of compression of morbidity presents a health policy strategy for addressing our major health care burdens. Recognizing that most illness is currently chronic rather than acute and that the overwhelming portion of the national illness burden falls upon the elderly population, the compression-of-morbidity strategy seeks to compress this period of ill health between an increasing age at onset of disability or illness and a stable or slowly advancing average age at death.

THE RECENT HISTORY OF COMPRESSION OF MORBIDITY

The concept of compression of morbidity was introduced in 1980 by the author, and, in recent years the concept has moved from questionable hypothesis to an accepted paradigm in health education, health promotion and primary prevention programs. However, during the 1980s, the concept of compression of morbidity was controversial. The early controversy appears to have had two roots. First, some in the scientific and demographic communities were uncomfortable with the thought that, in the complete absence of disease or accident, people would not live forever. The concepts of decreasing physical reserve with age and the phenomenon of the frail elder did not sit easily with those who believed that the ultimate goal of gerontologic research was immortality. Of course, the paradigm of the compression of morbidity does not depend on the existence of a fixed upper limit to life, but on the relative movements of the two arrows shown in Figure 4–1, representing the onset of disability and the age of death. If both the onset of morbidity and the age of death increase but draw closer together, then morbidity is compressed.

Second, there was a concern among some scientists that the goal of compression of morbidity would cause greater emphasis on primary prevention of disease and disability and a corresponding shift from cure toward prevention, which might threaten the funding enjoyed by the scientific gerontologic establishment. However, funding for prevention need not come at the expense of medical research. Indeed, because disability and chronic illness are the major drivers of our trillion-dollar-a-year health care industry, compression of morbidity would result in huge dollar savings to society, allowing increases in funding for other areas.

Finally, early critics began to recognize that they had painted themselves into a corner. Prominent gerontologists, including some contributors to this volume, who had initially taken the position that better health habits would lead to increasing misery and a greater frequency of such illnesses as Alzheimer's disease, became associated with programs called *productive aging* or *successful aging* and the like, in which individuals are encouraged to exercise, eat well and maintain satisfactory body weight. To be consistent with the "increasing misery" argument, such programs would have to be called *unsuccessful aging* and deplored, because they would just be increasing the frequency of Alzheimer's disease.

Twenty-five years ago, war was declared on cancer. Nevertheless, cancer mortality has shown a slight increase over the past quarter of a century. Belatedly, the National Cancer Institute now stresses that 70% of cancer mortality and morbidity results from known causes and is preventable. Had we instead made war on the *causes* of cancer, we might today be able to claim at least a partial victory. Other chronic diseases have equally well-defined risk factors, whether they are fatal or nonfatal. If we can make war on the causes of chronic illness, we may as a society begin to realize the compression of morbidity that is theoretically possible.

TRENDS IN LONGEVITY

Survival curves at 20-year intervals in this century are shown in Figure 4–3. In 1900, life expectancy averaged 47 years, and by 1980 it had risen

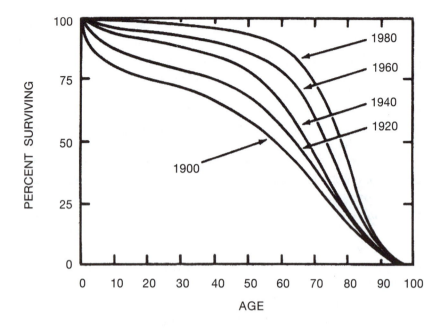

Figure 4–3 The Rectangularization of Survival Curves in the 20th Century. *Source:* Copyright © 1981, James F. Fries.

to 73 years, a truly remarkable increase. Note, however, two facts evident in these curves. First, the shape has become more rectangular over the years, with a longer period, up to age 70, having very little mortality, then an ever-steeper decline, with most deaths occurring between the ages of 70 and 85 years. Second, the successive curves all end at about the same point, with only a few individuals (about 1.5%) surviving to age 100. Life expectancy at ages above 85 has changed little. The natural limits to life expectancy are suggested by these curves.

Since 1980, life expectancy from birth has continued to increase and now averages 75 years for the entire population, approximately 79 years for women and 72 years for men. However, the term *life expectancy from birth* can be misleading. It is affected most strongly by reductions in infant mortality and in premature death at younger ages and has relatively little to do with longevity or the limits of life. The compression-of-morbidity proofs focus instead on life expectancy from advanced ages, age 65 or age 85. Further, the compression paradigm implies that a slowing of the increase in life expectancy would occur first in those groups, especially women, who already had the greatest life expectancies. This is because more complete elimination of premature deaths would reveal the natural life span—absent disease and accident—of a population. Rates of increase in life expectancy from such advanced ages as 65 or 85 in the United States have been nearly imperceptible over the past 20 years.

Figure 4–4 graphically represents female life expectancy for 1978 through 1995 from age 65 on. The rise has been from 18.4 years in 1978 to 18.9 years in 1995, an increase of about one half of a year (Kranczer, 1966). In contrast, the 1982 Social Security midrange projections suggest that an increase of more than 2.5 years should have occurred by 1995. In 1987, when the earlier projections began to look unrealistic, new projections suggesting more moderate future gains were made. By 1995, however, only the lowest projection of 1987 appears to be reasonably close to the mark.

Even more striking, life expectancy from age 85 on has been completely flat over the past two decades. The life expectancy of both sexes combined was 6 years in 1979 and 6 years again in 1995. Men slightly increased life expectancy from age 85—5.1 years in 1980 to 5.3 years in 1995; women were constant at 6.4 years in both 1980 and 1995 (Kranczer, 1966). Thus, one approximation of the maximum attainable age for a population—the

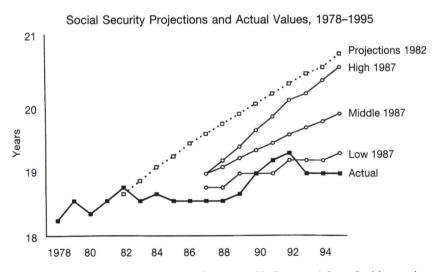

Figure 4–4 Female Life Expectancy from Age 65. *Source:* Adapted with permission from J.F. Fries, *Living Well,* © 1993, J.F. Fries, Addison-Wesley Publishing Company.

age at which life expectancy does not increase over time—suggests a population limit for both sexes combined of approximately 85 years, similar to some estimates projected by other methods.

Figure 4–5 illustrates some of the problems with future projections of the number of very old people, which are heavily dependent on the assumptions used. In the year 2050, the number of individuals aged 85 years or older in the United States is variously estimated at from 9.9 million to 48.7 million, a fivefold difference. The numbered projections in the figure represent the major projection studies funded by the National Institute on Aging, and they show a similar disparity. Discussion of these variations is beyond the scope of this article, but it is likely that the low projections of the Census Bureau are likely to prove the most accurate because they are based on current trends.

When we see statements that individuals aged 85 and older are the most rapidly growing group in the population, it must be recognized that these are only percentage increases, and that the coming increases will be fueled mostly by increasing numbers of births in successive years and by the number of individuals who avoid premature death and reach the ages of 65 or 85. It is the number of births 85 years earlier that drives the numbers.

It is this confusion that sometimes gives rise to the image of a future population full of senile old people. There will indeed be more people with Alzheimer's disease because of the larger numbers of very old people (probably three to four times as many as now), but because longevity from age 85 will change little, the typical person will *not* face an increased risk of Alzheimer's disease in 2050, even *without* discoveries in terms of prevention or treatment.

Only about 3% of projected increases in numbers of individuals over 65 or over 85 will be due to projected increases in life expectancy. At current rates, life expectancy from age 65 will increase perhaps 1.5 years by the year 2050, with increases from age 85 less than one third of this. Thus, from age 65 or 85, the increase in life expectancy is likely to be less than 10% above current figures. The average age of death of women alive at age 65 may increase from the current level of 83.9 years to 85.4 years.

TRENDS IN MORBIDITY

Data on changes in the morbidity and disability of our population are few. In general, it appears that morbidity at given ages is slowly decreasing

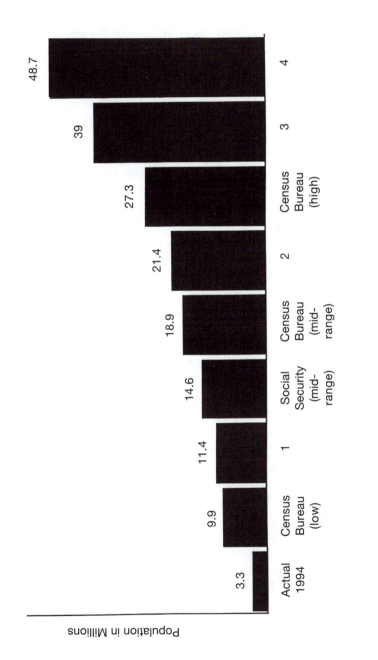

Figure 4–5 U.S. Population Projections: Number of People 85 and Older in 2050

and that "active life expectancy" is slowly increasing, but there is not a clear consensus as to whether cumulative lifetime disability is decreasing or increasing (Rogers, Rogers & Belanger, 1990).

How much decrease in morbidity over the past 20 years should have been expected as a result of primary prevention? On a national basis, changes in health behaviors have been inconsistent. In the United States in recent years, smoking frequency has decreased, but the frequency of obesity has increased, and sedentary lifestyles remain the norm (Lewis et al., 1997). Thus, relatively little progress toward morbidity compression from reduction in health risks should have been expected. The possible national gains in health from major changes in lifestyle risk factors have occurred much more slowly than they might have. To observe the potential compression of morbidity as it might have been, we need to look instead at particular populations practicing healthy living to see what could be.

PROOF POSITIVE

The compression of morbidity can now be directly studied due to the development of large longitudinal databases of elders. Comparison of "more favored" and "less favored" groups allows compression of morbidity to be most easily documented. If some groups of individuals have less total lifetime disability than do others, then lessons learned from study of such groups should be applicable to populations.

There are a number of ways to define "favored groups" for study. The four independent variables used to define "favored" status in major formal studies are socioeconomic status, educational level, the diligent practice of aerobic exercise, and reduction in multiple health risks, including exercise, smoking behavior, and body weight. The postulate is that the favored group will have decreased lifetime morbidity as compared with the less favored group, and that this advantage will be preserved, despite taking into account the greater longevity of the favored group. Let us review some of these studies.

J.S. House and colleagues (1990) at the University of Michigan found huge differences in functional status scores at all ages between lower, lower-middle, upper-middle, and upper socioeconomic classes, but the more favored classes showed rapidly deteriorating functional status at ages 75 and over, with disability rates beginning to converge with those of the lower socioeconomic classes. Thus, the more favored populations here led more "rectangular" lives, with disability postponed until a final terminal collapse. Paul Leigh and this author, using data from the epidemiologic follow-up to the National Health and Nutrition Survey, found that lifetime cumulative disability over age 50 was 60% less for persons with 16 or more years of schooling, as compared with those who had 11 or fewer years of schooling. If a higher level of education is an appropriate surrogate for the effect of good health practices—and it appears to be—then extending such practices, we concluded, will result in less rather than more lifetime disability (Leigh & Fries, 1994).

Our group has also studied long-distance running and the occurrence of disability in an ongoing study now 12 years in duration. We studied 451 members of a runner's club and 330 community controls who initially averaged 59 years of age, with appropriate controls for selection bias. After 8 years of longitudinal study, the runners had one third the disability of those in the control group, both at the outset of the study (0.026, compared with 0.079) and after 8 years, and steadily increased to 0.071 for runners, compared with 0.242 for nonrunners. Differences persisted after adjusting for age, sex, body mass, baseline disability, smoking history, history of arthritis, other comorbid conditions and other variables. Rates of disability progression, adjusted for these variables, were only one third the rate in the exercising groups, compared with the control group. These large differences in disability persisted through age 80, and the runners then began to develop disability at an accelerated rate, converging toward the level of the comparison population. Thus, older people who engage in vigorous aerobic activities have slower development of disability than do members of the general population. This is probably related to increased aerobic activity, strength, fitness and increased organ reserve (Fries et al., 1994).

Figure 4–6 shows the progression of disability over time in study participants. Physically active individuals had very low disability levels throughout our study period from 1984 to 1992. Physically active individuals similar to our study group are known to have an increase in life expectancy of approximately 2 years (Paffenbarger et al., 1994). Thus, the additional morbidity accumulated during those additional 2 years of life will constitute only a small percentage of the huge differences in lifetime morbidity between exercising and nonexercising groups.

Over the past 10 years, we have been following a group of 1,741 individuals who attended the University of Pennsylvania in 1939 and 1940. Yearly data were collected on disability and other morbidity from 1986 through 1994, from average ages of 67 to 75 years. From these data, we can

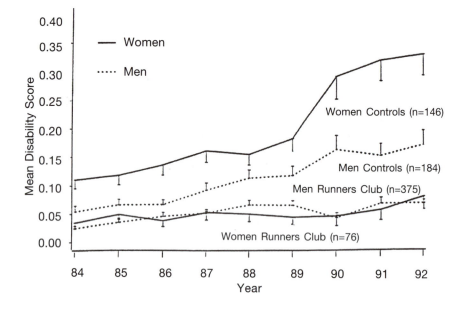

Figure 4–6 Development of Disability in Runners and Controls from 1984 through 1992, at Ages from 59 through 67 years. *Source:* Reprinted with permission from J.F. Fries, et. al., Running and the Development of Disability with Age, *Annals of Internal Medicine*, Vol. 121, pp. 502–509, © 1994, American College of Physicians.

estimate the cumulative disability for each individual through age 75, and for deceased subjects we could estimate total lifetime disability. Thus, we can directly test the compression-of-morbidity hypothesis. We divided these patients into three risk-factor strata (low, moderate and high risk) based on cigarette smoking, body mass index (obesity) and exercise scores as first reported in 1962 and again in 1986. The onset of disability was postponed by approximately 7 years in the low-risk stratum, as compared with the high-risk stratum (as shown by the maximum disability line in Figure 4–7). Cumulative disability was twice as great in the high-risk stratum, as compared with the low-risk. Mortality rate differences between strata suggest an ultimate extension of longevity of about 1–2 years in the low-risk stratum, as compared with the high-risk.

Thus, modifiable health-risk behaviors, as determined in mid-life and late adulthood, strongly predict subsequent lifetime disability. Importantly, morbidity in the final year of life is also decreased by half in those with better health habits. Thus, morbidity is postponed and compressed in

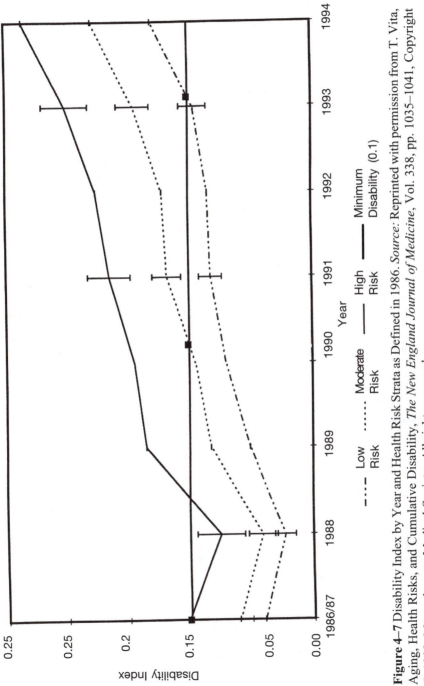

Figure 4–7 Disability Index by Year and Health Risk Strata as Defined in 1986. *Source:* Reprinted with permission from T. Vita, Aging, Health Risks, and Cumulative Disability, *The New England Journal of Medicine*, Vol. 338, pp. 1035–1041, Copyright © 1998, Massachusetts Medical Society. All rights reserved.

those with better lifestyles. Such studies of "favored groups" provide data on what might be.

Experimental data on the results of lifestyle and self-management interventions are also becoming available. Randomized trials of behaviorally based interventions document positive effects both on morbidity and on health care costs. Patient education interventions have decreased morbidity in populations with arthritis (Fries, Carey, & McShane, 1997) and Parkinson's disease (Montgomery, Leiberman, Singh, & Fries, 1994) as well as in healthy elders (Fries, Harrington, Edward, Kent, & Richardson, 1994). Importantly, reduction of morbidity from nonfatal conditions (such as osteoarthritis) is especially beneficial, as without extension of life expectancy, there is no morbidity offset due to longer life.

Informal study of less-favored groups is similarly instructive. Over the past several years, the author has been tabulating the composition of patients admitted to a medical service, using hospitalization as an indicator of morbidity. Four groups were readily identified: those young individuals with such self-destructive behaviors as drug overdose, morbid obesity or intravenous drug use; those older adults experiencing the consequences of such poor health habits as liver failure from alcoholism or emphysema from cigarette smoking; those at very old ages with such complications of terminal frailty as bed sores, aspiration pneumonia and weak host defenses; and, finally, those who are hospitalized for diseases such as leukemia or pancreatic cancer, for which there are no known modifiable risk factors. This last group accounts for fewer than 10% of hospitalizations. Illness resulting from self-destructive behavior accounts for 90% of hospital admissions and is largely preventable.

Another way to look at the aging process is to consider its "plasticity." How much of the aging process is preventable? A great deal. Over a lifetime, most basic abilities show growth in early years, plateau in early adulthood, and show decline by 1.5% per year after age 30. This course is represented by the lower line of Figure 4–8 and holds for cardiac output, running speed and many other mental and physical abilities. This is the bad news of aging—the declines. However, cardiac output, running speed, memory, bone density, reflex time and many other abilities may be improved—by almost everyone, at any age. Improvement comes from training and practice. This is the good news. On the other hand, lack of training or practice may accelerate the process of decline.

Training and practice can optimize an ability, at any age, until a personal maximum is reached. By these means, quality of life is improved and

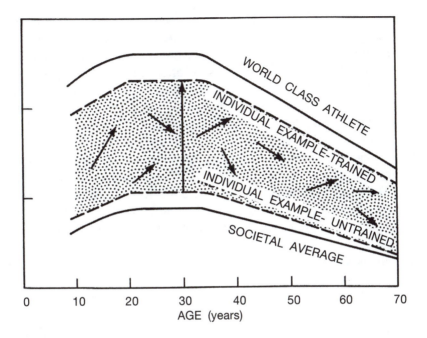

Figure 4–8 Maximum Performance with Age. *Source:* Copyright © 1981, James F. Fries.

morbidity decreased. Largely, the requirement is for individual action—healthy lifestyles to prevent disease and physical and mental exercise to improve abilities.

CONCLUSION

A better future is possible. However, national policies for reduction in cumulative lifetime disability are multifactorial and complex. There is no single or simple solution. Primary prevention approaches include exercise, smoking cessation, dietary changes and weight control. Vitamin E, low-dose aspirin, estrogens, calcium, vitamin D and other supplements may play a role. Improvement in the quality of the air and reduction in hazards of the immediate environment (from stairs to bathtubs to hospital beds) may require social interventions. Secondary prevention opportunities abound, including reduction in stroke associated with atrial fibrillation, the many approaches to secondary prevention of cardiovascular events and patient self-management of chronic illness. Diabetic leg ulcers, amputations, retinopathy and nephropathy usually may be postponed or prevented by a combination of personal and medical actions, many of which are quite inexpensive. Rehabilitation activities can often reduce morbidity. It is time to bring together the established pieces of the puzzle toward a comprehensive strategy for the reduction of morbidity (Fries, 1997).

Data that the cumulative amount of disability in average human life may be very substantially reduced are now strong and perhaps even conclusive. The outlines of necessary policy initiatives and national priorities can be seen quite clearly. These encouraging results, however, should not be used to excuse inattention to the most massive medical and social need of our time, that of caring for our expanding aging population. Even the most conservative projections indicate that, in half a century, we will have some 10 million individuals over age 85, three to four times the present number. Over the next several decades, the sheer numbers of persons in our aging populations will stress available resources.

The national morbidity burden may be thought of as a product of two factors: the number of people at particular age levels and the average amount of morbidity per individual at those ages, summed over all ages. We have little means of dealing with the first factor; the individuals who will make up the increased older populations of the next decades are already alive and growing older daily. The second factor, however, best considered as "cumulative lifetime disability," appears to be substantially modifiable. By decreasing the cumulative lifetime morbidity in the typical life, we may, in substantial part, offset the national disability increases to be expected from the increasing numbers of elders.

Common sense tells us that if one gets a chronic problem later in life, he or she will not have it as long. The evidence indicates that even simple changes in health risk factors can delay the onset of morbidity by 8 years. It is time to employ our current knowledge to improve our national health.

REFERENCES

Crimmins, E.M. (1990). Are the Americans healthier as well as longer-lived? *J Insurance Med, 22*, 89–92.

Fries, J.F., Carey, C., & McShane, D.J. (1997). Patient education in arthritis: Randomized controlled trial of a mail-delivered program. *J Rheumatol, 24(7)*, 1378–1383.

Fries, J.F., Harrington, H., Edward, R., Kent, L.A., & Richardson, N. (1994). Randomized controlled trial of cost reductions from a health education program: The California Public Employee's Retirement System (PERS). *Am J Health Promotion, 9*, 79–92.

Fries, J.F., Koop, C.E., Beadle, C.E., Cooper, P.P., England, M.J., Greaves, R.F., et al. (1993). Reducing health care costs by reducing the need and demand for medical services. *N Engl J Med, 329*, 321–325.

Fries, J.F., Singh, G., Morfeld, D., Hubert, H.B., Lane, N.E., & Brown, B.W. Jr. (1994). Running and the development of disability with age. *Ann Intern Med, 121*, 502–509.

Fries, J.F. (1980). Aging, natural death, and the compression of morbidity. *N Engl J Med, 303*, 130–136.

Fries, J.F. (1990). Compression of morbidity: Near or far? *Milbank Mem Fund Q, 67*, 208–232.

Fries, J.F. (1997). Can preventive gerontology be on the way? (Editorial) *Am J Public Health, 87*, 12.

Gruenberg, E.M. (1997). The failure of success. *Milbank Mem Fund Q, 55*, 3–34.

House, J.S., Kessler, R.C., Herzog, A.R., Mero, R.P., Kinney, A.M., & Breslow, M.J. (1990). Age, socioeconomic status, and health. *Milbank Mem Fund Q, 68*, 383–411.

Kranczer, S. (Oct–Dec 1966). Mixed life expectancy changes. *Stat Bull.*

Leigh, J.P., & Fries, J.F. (1994). Education, gender and the compression of morbidity. *Int J Aging Hum Dev, 39*(3), 233–246.

Lewis, C.E., Smith, D.E., Wallace, D.D., Williams, O.D., Bild, D.E., & Jacobs, D.R. (1997). Seven-year trends in body weight and associations with lifestyle and behavioral characteristics in black and white young adults: The CARDIA Study. *Am J Public Health, 87*(4), 635–642.

Manton, R.G. (1982). Changing concepts of mortality and morbidity in the elderly population. *Milbank Mem Fund Q, 60*, 183–244.

Montgomery, E.B. Jr., Leiberman, A., Singh, G., & Fries, J.F. (1994). Patient education and health promotion can be effective in Parkinson's disease: A randomized controlled trial. *Am J Med, 97*, 429–435.

Paffenbarger, R.S., Jr., Kampert, J.B., Lee, I.M., Hyde, R.T., Leung, R.W., & Wing, A.L. (1994). Changes in physical activity and other lifeway patterns influencing longevity. *Med Sci Sports Exerc, 26*(7), 857–865.

Rogers, A., Rogers, R.G., & Belanger, A. (1990). Longer life but worse health? Measurement and dynamics. *Gerontologist, 30*(5), 640–649.

Verbrugge, L.M. (1984). Longer life but worsening health? Trends in health and mortality of middle-aged and older persons. *Milbank Mem Fund Q, 62*, 475–519.

Vita, A.J., Hubert, H.B., & Fries, J.F. (1998). Aging, health risks, and cumulative disability. *N Engl J Med 338*:1035–1041.

CHAPTER 5

Do Physical Activity and Physical Fitness Avert Premature Mortality?

I-Min Lee and Ralph S. Paffenbarger, Jr.

Over the past two decades or so, evidence has been accumulating to indicate that an inverse relationship exists between physical activity and the risk of such chronic diseases as coronary heart disease, hypertension, non–insulin-dependent diabetes mellitus, certain site-specific cancers such as colon cancer and possibly breast cancer, and osteoporosis. Moreover, the proposed biologic mechanisms that enable an individual to benefit from physical activity appear highly plausible and make a case for a causal relation. If physical activity indeed reduces the risk of developing these chronic diseases, it is logical to surmise that premature mortality—from any cause—can be averted or at least delayed by physical activity. Conversely, physical activity can be expected to enhance longevity. This chapter will review the epidemiologic data on the association between physical activity and longevity to summarize the current state of knowledge.

EARLY OBSERVATIONS

The concept that physical activity and physical fitness promote health and longevity certainly is not new. In ancient China, circa BC 2500, are found perhaps the earliest records of organized exercise used for health promotion by Hua T'o (Keys, 1980). The Greek physicians Hippocrates and Plato (circa BC 460–370), and later, Galen (circa BC 200 to 129) also believed in the importance of a physically active lifestyle for well-being

Source: Adapted with permission from R.S. Paffenbarger and I. Lee, Do Physical Activity and Fitness Avert Premature Mortality? *Exercise and Sport Sciences Reviews*, Vol. 24, pp. 135–171, Lippincott-Williams & Wilkins, © 1996.

and in its usefulness in treating disease and disability (Keys, 1980). Later, in eighteenth-century Italy, Ramazzini noted the well-being of foot messengers ("runners") as contrasted to the ill health of such sedentary workers as cobblers and tailors (Ramazzini, 1940).

Beginning in the nineteenth century, investigators attempted to measure the benefits associated with physical activity more objectively, using numerical quantification. In some of the earliest such observations made about occupationally related physical activity and mortality, Smith noted, in 1864, that the mortality rate among British tailors was much higher than that among agricultural laborers. Meanwhile, across the Atlantic, in 1923, when Sivertsen and Dahlstrom classified men in Minnesota according to occupational physical activity, they observed that death rates declined with increasing activity on the job (Sivertsen & Dahlstrom, 1922). Furthermore, investigators noted that the average age at death increased in a gradient fashion with physically more demanding occupations.

With respect to nonoccupational forms of physical activity, rowing is one of the oldest sports having formal rules and organization. Thus, early in its history, this sport provided an opportunity for investigators to study mortality associated with vigorous physical activity. Nineteenth- and early twentieth-century studies of oarsmen from Cambridge, Oxford and Harvard showed that the life expectancy of these men tended to exceed that of the general population (Hartley & Llewellyn, 1939; Prout, 1972). Studies of other athletes—college men excelling in such different sporting activities as track and field, cricket or football and cross-country skiers—also showed that these men lived longer.

THE ASSOCIATION OF PHYSICAL ACTIVITY WITH AVOIDANCE OF PREMATURE MORTALITY

Studies examining the association of physical activity or physical fitness with total mortality generally have been prospective cohort in design. These studies have used two different strategies. Investigators have first classified men according to physical activity or fitness categories, then have examined all-cause mortality rates within each category. Secondly, investigators have analyzed mortality rates according to categories of men who did or did not change their physical activity or fitness profile over time. Sample studies belonging to the first category will now be discussed, ordered by date of publication and with related studies grouped together.

Study of U.S. Railroad Industry Employees, 1962

In this study, Taylor et al. (1962) wanted to test the hypothesis that men in physically active occupations experience lower rates of coronary heart disease than do those in sedentary occupations. Investigators chose the U.S. railroad industry for study because conditions in this industry discouraged men from shifting from one occupation to another. Investigators enrolled white men working as clerks (deemed most sedentary) and switchmen or section men (deemed physically most active). Additionally, men had to have worked for 10 years by 1951 and still be employed in 1954. Subjects were followed for mortality from 1955 to 1956. Only deaths occurring between the ages of 40 and 64 were included in the study. The age-adjusted death rates per 1,000 were 11.83 for clerks, 10.29 for switchmen and 7.62 for section men, with the differences statistically significant.

Study of British Civil Servants, 1978

Morris and co-workers (Chave et al., 1978; Morris, Everitt, Pollard, Chave, & Semmence, 1980) have pioneered research on the relationship between physical activity and the risk of developing coronary heart disease, laying the groundwork for much of what is known today. Their findings, with observations dating as far back as the 1940s, were derived from the study of London bus drivers and conductors, postal service workers and civil servants (Chave et al., 1978; Morris et al., 1973; Morris, Heady, Raffle, Roberts, & Parks, 1953). These data indicated that physical activity, whether occupational or leisure-time, was inversely associated with coronary heart disease risk. Furthermore, no benefit was found for total energy expenditure; only energy expended in vigorous sporting activities was associated with reduced incidence of coronary heart disease. Men engaging in such vigorous sporting activities experienced less than half the coronary heart disease rates of those who did not take part in such activities. This held true within categories of men without and with other risk factors for coronary heart disease (cigarette smoking, hypertension, high body mass, short stature and parental history of premature cardiovascular mortality).

In the above investigators' study of British civil servants, observations also were made for all-cause mortality. This particular analysis involved

17,944 male, executive-grade civil servants, ages 40–65 years. Between 1968 and 1970, these men were asked on a Monday morning to fill out a 5-minute-by-5-minute diary of their physical activities on the preceding Friday and Saturday. Men were not forewarned, so they presumably reported on their usual pattern of physical activities for a typical weekday and a typical weekend day. Coding of these 7-page physical activity diaries was carefully done without knowledge of the medical history of the civil servants. Men were classified as not having or having engaged in vigorous sports and recreation. The men were followed until 1977; during follow-up, 268 deaths occurred. Because subjects were civil servants, their morbidity and mortality experience could be traced with a high degree of completeness through the National Health Service Central Register and the Civil Service Medical Advisory Service.

For men reporting no vigorous exercise, 8.4% died during follow-up, as compared with 4.2% of men who reported vigorous exercise. Men who reported vigorous exercise tended to smoke less; of those who did smoke, fewer cigarettes were smoked. For coronary heart disease mortality, at least, when nonsmokers and smokers were examined separately, vigorous exercise was associated with lower mortality in each group. Furthermore, there was no evidence that the increased coronary heart disease mortality among men not reporting vigorous exercise was because of disability or ill health. Were this the case, as these unhealthy men died over time, the inverse association would disappear with the passage of time. When investigators divided the follow-up period into the first 3 years, the next 3 years and subsequent years, the same inverse association was noted for all three periods.

Study of Men and Women in Eastern Finland, 1982

This is one of the few studies in this review that includes women (Salonen, Puska, & Tuomilehto, 1982). Study subjects were a random sample of the population living in two counties of Eastern Finland, an area with extremely high morbidity and mortality from cardiovascular disease. Included were 3,978 men (ages 30–59) and 3,688 women (ages 35–59) who were free of cardiovascular disease in the 12 months preceding the baseline survey and who had data on the variables being studied. Baseline information on risk factors was collected via a self-administered question-naire in 1972. At the same time, blood pressure and serum cholesterol were measured. Investigators assessed physical activity at work and during leisure using two multiple-choice questions. For the purpose of this analysis, subjects were dichotomized into those having low or high physical activity at work and during leisure. Subjects were followed after baseline through 1978, during which time 172 men and 75 women died. Mortality follow-up presumably was complete as deaths were traced from the national death certificate data register.

Low physical activity at work predicted increased mortality during follow-up among both men and women. The relative risks for dying, adjusted for age, cigarette smoking, diastolic blood pressure, serum cholesterol and body mass index were 1.9 for men with low physical activity and 2.2 for women with low physical activity. Low physical activity during leisure time also predicted increased mortality.

The Harvard Alumni Health Study, 1986, 1993 and 1995

In 1986, Paffenbarger, Hyde, Wing, and Hsieh made one of the first rigorous attempts to quantify added years of life from being physically active. Investigators used data from the Harvard Alumni Health Study. This is an ongoing, prospective cohort study of the predictors of chronic disease in men matriculating as undergraduates from Harvard University between 1916 and 1950. The men provided information on their sociodemographic characteristics, personal and family medical history, and health habits via mailed questionnaires. The initial baseline questionnaire was mailed to alumni in 1962 or 1966; since then, data have been periodically updated by the same method. Additionally, information on the medical history and health habits of these men during their youth, obtained from a standardized medical examination at the time of college entry, also was available from college archives. Deaths in this cohort have been traced using information from the Harvard Alumni Office, with mortality follow-up that is more than 99% complete.

In this particular study of added years of life, investigators enrolled 16,936 men, ages 35–75 years, who were free of self-reported, physician-diagnosed coronary heart disease at baseline. On the baseline questionnaire, men were asked about the number of flights of stairs climbed daily, the number of city blocks walked daily, the types of sports or recreational activities engaged in, and the time spent on each of these activities. Although investigators did not inquire specifically about occupational activity, alumni were unlikely to have expended much energy on the job, apart from walking and climbing stairs. Investigators quantified physical activity as follows: Walking seven city blocks rated 56 kilocalories, whereas climbing seven flights of stairs rated 28 kilocalories. Sports and recreational activities were classified as light (5 kilocalories per minute of energy expenditure) vigorous (10 kilocalories), or mixed (7.5 kilocalories per minute). Investigators then summed kilocalories per week from blocks walked, flights climbed and sports or recreational activities carried out to obtain an index of weekly energy expenditure. Physical activity then was related to all-cause mortality between 1962/1966 and 1978. A total of 1,413 men died during the 12–16 years of follow-up, encompassing 213,715 person-years.

Table 5–1 shows that the age-adjusted mortality rates among alumni generally declined with increasing physical activity, although this benefit appeared to taper off after 3,500 kilocalories per week. When investigators examined men of ages 35–49, 50–59, 60–69 and 70–84 years separately, the inverse association held within each age stratum. Furthermore, the inverse relation was significant, regardless of the absence or presence of other factors predictive of mortality: cigarette smoking, hypertension, weight-for-height, weight change since college, early parental death and college athleticism.

Subsequent analyses of Harvard alumni examined all-cause mortality in relation to physical activity in 1977. The eligible men for this study were 10,269 individuals aged 45–84 in 1977 who were free of self-reported,

Table 5–1 Rates and Relative Risks of All-Cause Mortality (1962/1966–1978) in the Harvard Alumni Health Study, According to Physical Activity in 1962/1966

Physical Activity (kcal/week)	No. of Deaths	Mortality Rate (/10,000)	Relative Risk
<500	308	93.7	1.00 (referent)
500-999	322	73.5	0.78
1000-1499	202	68.2	0.73
1500-1999	121	59.3	0.63
2000-2499	89	57.7	0.62
2500-2999	62	48.5	0.52
3000-3499	42	42.7	0.46
>3500	203	58.4	0.62

Source: Reprinted with permission from R.S. Paffenbarger and I. Lee, Do Physical Activity and Physical Fitness Avert Premature Mortality?, *Exercise and Sport Sciences Reviews*, Vol. 24, pp. 135–171, © 1996, Lippincott-Williams & Wilkins.

physician-diagnosed cardiovascular disease, diabetes, cancer and chronic obstructive pulmonary disease at that time. Men were followed from 1977 to 1985, with 476 dying in 90,650 person-years. Findings were congruent with those from earlier analyses; however, a benefit continued to be observed with energy expenditure of greater than or equal to 3,500 kilocalories per week. In addition, men were classified according to the intensity of their sports or recreational activities, being categorized as engaging in light (< 4.5 mets, or multiples of resting metabolic rate) or moderately vigorous (≥ 4.5 mets) activities. In age-adjusted analyses, light activities were not significantly related to all-cause mortality rates, but moderately vigorous activities were.

In a further attempt to clarify the role of intensity in averting premature mortality, investigators launched a more detailed scrutiny of the intensity of physical activities carried out by these Harvard men. Specifically, they sought to answer the question, Is a set amount of energy expended in vigorous activities associated with a benefit equivalent to that of the same amount of energy expended in nonvigorous activities? This study involved 17,321 men, ages 30–79 who were free of self-reported, physician-diagnosed cardiovascular disease, cancer and chronic obstructive pulmonary disease at baseline (1962/1966). Additionally, subjects had to provide data on physical activity and other potentially confounding factors of interest.

Investigators assessed physical activity at baseline and again in 1977. The energy expended on walking and stair climbing was estimated as described earlier. For sports and recreational activities, investigators assigned a multiple of resting metabolic equivalent rate (MET score) to every activity (Ainsworth, Haskell, & Leon, 1993). The energy expended on each activity was estimated by multiplying its MET score with body weight in kilograms and hours per week of participation. Investigators then summed kilocalories per week from blocks walked, flights climbed and activities carried out to provide an index of total energy expenditure per week. The investigators further divided total energy expenditure in two components: that derived from vigorous activities that require six or more METs and that derived from nonvigorous activities requiring less than six METs. (Because walking speed was not ascertained in 1962/1966 and 1977, all walking was deemed nonvigorous, whereas stair climbing was considered vigorous.) Men then were classified into five categories each of vigorous and nonvigorous energy expenditure. The investigators followed men for mortality after return of the 1962/1966 questionnaire through 1988. A total of 3,728 men died in these 384,681 person-years of observation. In relating vigorous and nonvigorous energy expenditure estimated in

1962/1966 to all-cause mortality from 1962/1966 through 1988, investigators found that vigorous expenditure, but not nonvigorous, significantly predicted decreased mortality. When investigators allowed for physical activity to be updated in 1977, findings were unchanged.

The Alameda County, California Study (Human Population Laboratory), 1987

In this study, (Kaplan, Seeman, Cohen, Knudsen, & Guralnik, 1987) were interested in whether factors associated with increased mortality risk among older men and women were the same as those for younger individuals. Investigators used data from the Alameda County Study, a prospective cohort study of the predictors of mortality among a random sample of 6,928 adult residents of Alameda County, California. In this analysis, the investigators restricted the study population to 4,174 men and women who were age 38 and older at baseline, 1965, so that these individuals would be at least 55 at the end of the 17-year follow-up.

Study subjects completed a questionnaire on demographic, behavioral, social and psychologic characteristics in 1965. Physical activity was assessed based on frequency and presumed intensity of leisure-time participation in active sports, swimming, long walks, physical exercise, gardening, and hunting and fishing. Based on these data, investigators classified men and women as inactive or active. Subjects were followed until 1982, for 17 years. By that time, 1,219 had died.

After adjusting for age, self-reported health status and factors predictive of mortality in this cohort (cigarette smoking, alcohol intake, weight-for-height, hours of sleep, regular breakfast and snacking), physical inactivity was a significant predictor of mortality among those in the age groups 38–49, 50–59, 60–69, and over 70. Indeed, when crude survival curves were plotted by age group over the 17 years, the differential in mortality between inactive and active subjects was more marked in the oldest than in the youngest age group.

Study of Finnish Men, 1987

This group of Finnish men represents one cohort belonging to the Seven Countries Study (Keys, 1980). For this analysis, investigators restricted the study population to 636 healthy Finnish men, ages 45–64 at baseline in

1964. Physical activity was assessed at baseline, with men being interviewed regarding their leisure-time and occupational habits. Leisure-time physical activity covered habitual walking, bicycling and cross-country skiing. Occupational physical activity was classified as sedentary and light (mainly sitting), moderate (for example, shopkeeping or truck driving), heavy (mainly farming) or very heavy (mainly lumberjacking). Investigators then classified men into two categories of overall physical activity: low (60.7%) or high (39.3%), with the latter category consisting of men whose work involved heavy or very heavy activity and who also walked 5 or more kilometers per day on a regular basis, cycled more than 150 kilometers per month for 6 or more months a year, or cross-country skied 200 or more kilometers every winter. These men were then followed for 20 years until 1984, with 287 deaths observed.

Investigators first compared men with low and high physical activity, according to cigarette habit, in the first and second 10 years of follow-up. Smoking, as expected, increased mortality risk. Physical inactivity was found to predict increased mortality, but only in the first 10 years of follow-up, with the benefit disappearing in the second 10 years. This was confirmed when investigators plotted crude survival curves over 20 years for the two physical activity groups. There was a distinct advantage of the high physical activity group for perhaps the first 16 years, with the two survival curves merging after that. This led investigators to hypothesize that physical activity can reduce premature mortality but cannot extend life span (at the end of the 20-year follow-up, the oldest of these Finnish men was 85, perhaps close to the life span).

Investigators also estimated, for men who had died, the additional years lived by men with high physical activity. At baseline, the mean age of men in the low and high physical active groups was 54.9 and 55.2 years, respectively. At the end of the 20-year follow-up, 44.6% and 46.0%, respectively, of men in the low and high physical activity groups had died. Their mean ages at death were 67.4 and 69.1 years, respectively. After adjustment for differences in age, cigarette smoking, systolic blood pressure, serum cholesterol and body mass index, the more active men had survived for an additional 2.1 years.

The Lipid Research Clinics Mortality Follow-up Study, 1988

The original purpose of the Lipid Research Clinics Prevalence Study, conducted between 1972 and 1976, was to describe the lipid profile of men and women from 10 different centers in North America (Ekelund et al., 1988). Participating subjects were examined up to two times. Subsequently, investigators started the Lipid Research Clinics Mortality Follow-Up Study, examining the relation between factors ascertained at the second visit and, later mortality among participants, aged 30 years and over, who were examined at this visit.

In this study of physical fitness, investigators were interested primarily in cardiovascular disease mortality, but they also provided data on all-cause mortality. They enrolled 3,755 white men, 3,106 healthy and 649 with cardiovascular disease, ages 30–69 at baseline, with valid exercise test data. (Women were excluded because the small number of deaths precluded meaningful analyses.) Physical fitness was assessed at the second visit, using a submaximal treadmill exercise test. Men were then classified as unfit or fit, according to the amount of time they spent on the treadmill. Additionally, they were categorized into quartiles of fitness, by heart rate at stage 2 of the exercise test. Investigators followed men for mortality until 1983 or 1984, an average of 8.5 years. During this time, 45 fatalities from cardiovascular disease occurred among 3,106 healthy men and 46 deaths occurred among 649 men with cardiovascular disease. Mortality follow-up was 99% complete.

Among healthy men, physically unfit men experienced 1.8 times the mortality of fit men during follow-up after taking into account differences in age, cigarette smoking, systolic blood pressure and high-density and low-density lipoprotein cholesterol (Table 5–2). For men with preexisting cardiovascular disease, the corresponding relative risk was 2.9. Over the 8.5-year follow-up, the curves for the least and most fit men continued to diverge, suggesting that the benefit of fitness was unlikely to be artifactual, resulting from early mortality among men with subclinical illness who were unfit.

The Aerobics Center Longitudinal Study, 1989

This study represents the largest one to date of physical fitness and all-cause mortality (Blair et al., 1989). Additionally, it is one of the few studies in this review that includes women. For this analysis, investigators enrolled 10,244 men and 3,210 women, ages 20–60, who received a preventive medical examination between 1970 and 1981 at the Cooper Institute for Aerobics Research in Dallas. Subjects were predominantly white and

Table 5–2 Relative Risks for All-Cause Mortality (1972–1984) in the Lipid Research Clinics Mortality Follow-up Study, According to Physical Fitness in 1972–1976

Physical Fitness	Relative Risk (95% CI)
Healthy men	
High physical fitness	1.0 (referent)
Low physical fitness	1.8 (1.2–2.6)
Men with cardiovascular disease	
High physical fitness	1.0 (referent)
Low physical fitness	2.9 (1.7–4.9)

Source: Reprinted with permission from R.S. Paffenbarger and I. Lee, Do Physical Activity and Physical Fitness Avert Premature Mortality?, *Exercise and Sport Sciences Reviews*, Vol. 24, pp. 135–171, © 1996, Lippincott-Williams & Wilkins.

of middle to upper socioeconomic status. As part of their medical examination, men and women underwent a maximal treadmill exercise test. Investigators used total treadmill time, specific for each sex and age group, to classify subjects into quintiles of physical fitness; then they followed subjects through 1985, or for an average of over 8 years, during which 240 men and 43 women died in 110,482 person-years. Mortality follow-up was 95% complete.

Table 5–3 presents the age-adjusted mortality rates for men and women, according to their physical fitness category. There was a strong inverse association between fitness level and all-cause mortality in men. Although the number of deaths was small, the pattern appeared similar in women. The least fit men had a more than threefold increased risk of mortality than did the most fit men. The least fit women had a more than fourfold increase than did the most fit women. The largest mortality differential occurred between the least fit and the next-to-least fit. The inverse associations persisted after additional adjustments for cigarette smoking, systolic blood pressure, serum cholesterol, serum glucose, body mass index and parental history of coronary heart disease. Furthermore, investigators noted that the inverse association between physical fitness and mortality held within categories of each of these risk factors.

The Seventh-Day Adventist Mortality Study, 1991

Subjects of the Seventh-Day Adventist Mortality Study (Lindsted, Sonstad, & Kuzma, 1991) comprised 27,530 members of the Seventh-Day

Table 5–3 Relative Risks of All-Cause Mortality (1970–1985) in the Aerobics Center Longitudinal Study, According to Physical Fitness Assessed in 1970 to 1981

Physical Fitness	No. of Deaths	Mortality Rate (/10,000)	Relative Risk (95% CI)
Men			
Quintile 1 (least fit)	75	64.0	3.44 (2.05–5.77)
Quintile 2	40	25.5	1.37 (0.76–2.50)
Quintile 3	47	27.1	1.46 (0.81–2.63)
Quintile 4	43	21.7	1.17 (0.63–2.17)
Quintile 5 (most fit)	35	18.6	1.00 (referent)
Women			
Quintile 1 (least fit)	18	39.5	4.65 (2.22–9.75)
Quintile 2	11	20.5	2.42 (1.09–5.37)
Quintile 3	6	12.2	1.43 (0.60–3.44)
Quintile 4	4	6.5	0.76 (0.27–2.11)
Quintile 5 (most fit)	4	8.5	1.00 (referent)

Source: Reprinted with permission from R.S. Paffenbarger and I. Lee, Do Physical Activity and Physical Fitness Avert Premature Mortality?, *Exercise and Sport Sciences Reviews*, Vol. 24, pp. 135–171, © 1996, Lippincott-Williams & Wilkins.

Adventist Church in California who filled out a questionnaire on demographic, medical and lifestyle characteristics in 1960. For this analysis of physical activity and all-cause mortality, investigators limited the study population to 9,484 men aged 30 and over at baseline. Physical activity at work and during leisure was assessed using a single multiple-choice question on the baseline questionnaire. Men then were classified as inactive, moderately active or highly active. Investigators followed men for mortality through 1985, observing 3,799 deaths in those 26 years. Mortality follow-up was more than 93% complete.

Between 1960 and 1985, 798 (38.5%) of 2,072 inactive men died, as did 2,495 (43.0%) of 5,803 moderately active men and 506 (31.4%) of 1,609 highly active men. Mean ages at baseline of men in the three groups were 51.6, 54.7 and 49.9 years, respectively. Moderate physical activity was associated with greater benefit among Seventh-Day Adventist men than were high levels. Moreover, at higher attained ages, the impact of physical activity on decreased mortality began to disappear. Investigators hypothesized, as did Pekkanen et al. (1987) in their study of Finnish men, that physical activity served to postpone mortality of Seventh-Day Adventist men but could not extend life span.

THE ASSOCIATION OF CHANGES IN PHYSICAL ACTIVITY WITH THE AVOIDANCE OF PREMATURE MORTALITY

To date, only two studies have investigated all-cause mortality in relation to changes in physical activity or fitness. With regard to coronary heart disease, Paffenbarger et al. had examined, in an earlier study, the risk of heart attack associated with continuities and changes in physical activity during college and in middle life (Paffenbarger, Wing, & Hyde, 1978). Investigators reported on the importance of contemporary physical activity: Only men who continued to be active during their middle years experienced lower risk, regardless of their physical activity status during college years.

The Harvard Alumni Study, 1993

The population for this study has been previously described. Briefly, this analysis involved 10,629 Harvard alumni, ages 45–84 in 1977, who were free of self-reported, physician-diagnosed cardiovascular disease, diabetes, cancer and chronic obstructive pulmonary disease at that time. Men provided information via questionnaires on their physical activities in either 1962 or 1966 and again in 1977. Based on these data, investigators estimated an index of total energy expenditure for each man at each of the two times. Furthermore, each reported activity was classified according to intensity (Ainsworth et al., 1993). Men were followed from 1977 to 1985, with 476 dying in those 90,650 person-years. Mortality follow-up in this cohort was more than 99% complete.

Table 5–4 examines the association between changes in physical activity and all-cause mortality. With respect to energy expenditure, men who changed from being inactive to active had about the same mortality rate as did men who were active at both time points, with these two rates somewhat lower than that among men who were inactive at both times. Turning to intensity of physical activity, men who did not engage in any moderately vigorous activities in 1962 and 1966 but did so in 1977 had a 23% lower mortality than did those who never reported such activities, the difference being statistically significant. Meanwhile, men who habitually engaged in moderately vigorous activities had a 29% lower mortality, which was also statistically significant. These analyses were adjusted for

Table 5–4 Rates and Relative Risks of All-Cause Mortality (1977–1985) in the Harvard Alumni Health Study, According to Changes in Physical Activity between 1962/1966 and 1977

Physical Activity	1962/ 1966	1977	No. of Deaths	Mortality Rate (/10,000)	Relative Risk (95% CI)
Energy Expenditure					
>2000 kcal/wk	No	No	221	54.6	1.00 (referent)
	Yes	No	85	60.3	1.10 (0.78–1.50)
	No	Yes	69	46.6	0.85 (0.65–1.13)
	Yes	Yes	83	44.8	0.82 (0.63–1.08)
Activities at	No	No	139	61.7	1.00 (referent)
>4.5 METs	Yes	No	26	70.7	1.15 (0.73–1.71)
	No	Yes	131	47.4	0.77 (0.58–0.96)
	Yes	Yes	116	43.8	0.71 (0.55–0.96)

Source: Reprinted with permission from R.S. Paffenbarger and I. Lee, Do Physical Activity and Physical Fitness Avert Premature Mortality?, *Exercise and Sport Sciences Reviews*, Vol. 24, pp. 135–171, © 1996, Lippincott-Williams & Wilkins.

differences in age, cigarette smoking, hypertension and body mass index. When men of ages 45–54, 55–64, 65–74 and 75–84 were examined separately, similar risk reductions for each age group were observed among men taking up moderately vigorous activities, although the reductions were no longer significant because of the smaller number of deaths.

The Aerobics Center Longitudinal Study, 1995

The population for the Aerobics Center Longitudinal Study also has been described previously. Extended follow-up of this population (Blair et al., 1995) has enabled investigators to examine changes in physical fitness in relation to all-cause mortality rates. The present analysis involved 9,777 men aged 20–82 who received two preventive medical examinations between 1970 and 1989. Of these men, 6,819 were healthy, whereas 2,958 had a variety of chronic conditions (referred to hereafter as *unhealthy*). The interval between examinations ranges from 1 to 18 years, with a mean of 4.9 years. As described previously, physical fitness was assessed with a maximal treadmill exercise test. Investigators used total treadmill time from the first examination, specific for each age group, to classify men into quintiles of physical fitness. Because previous findings showed that mortality among the least fit men was substantially higher than that among men in the second quintile, in this analysis, unfit men were those belonging to quintile 1; all others were considered fit. Follow-up for mortality occurred after the second examination through 1989, with a mean follow-up of 5.1 years. Among healthy men, 103 men died, among those unhealthy, 120 died in a total of 47,561 person-years.

Among all men, the lowest age-adjusted mortality rates occurred among men who were fit at both examinations, whereas the highest rates occurred among those who were unfit at both examinations (Table 5–5). Men who changed in fitness, whether from unfit to fit or vice versa, experienced intermediate mortality rates that were similar for the two changed groups. Investigators next examined men aged 20-29, 30–49, 50–69 and 70 and up separately and observed the same pattern in each age group. They then examined healthy and unhealthy men separately and adjusted additionally for baseline fitness level, cigarette smoking, systolic blood pressure, blood cholesterol, glucose tolerance, family history of coronary heart disease and interval between examinations. For healthy men, each 1-minute improvement in treadmill test time from the first to the second examination was associated with an approximately 10% reduction in mortality—statistically significant—over follow-up. For the unhealthy men, the corresponding risk reduction was about 6%. However, that reduction achieved only borderline significance.

Finally, investigators compared the magnitude of benefit associated with favorable changes in various predictors of mortality. After adjusting for the variables listed above, as well as for health status, this magnitude was largest for favorable change in physical fitness (approximately 60% risk reduction), followed by cessation of smoking (approximately 50% risk reduction). Favorable changes in systolic blood pressure, blood cholesterol or body mass index were not associated with appreciable reductions in risk of dying during follow-up.

Table 5–5 Rates and Relative Risks of All-Cause Mortality (1970–1989) in the Aerobics Center Longitudinal Study, According to Changes in Physical Fitness between 1970 and 1989

| Physical Fitness | | No. of Deaths | Mortality Rate | |
1st Exam	2nd Exam	(/10,000)	(95% CI)	Relative Risk
Unfit	Unfit	32	122.0	1.00 (referent)
Unfit	Fit	25	67.7	0.56 (0.41–0.75)
Fit	Unfit	9	63.3	0.52 (0.38–0.70)
Fit	Fit	157	39.6	0.33 (0.23–0.47)

Source: Reprinted with permission from R.S. Paffenbarger and I. Lee, Do Physical Activity and Physical Fitness Avert Premature Mortality?, *Exercise and Sport Sciences Reviews*, Vol. 24, pp. 135–171, © 1996, Lippincott-Williams & Wilkins.

DISCUSSION

All of the studies reviewed above describe significant inverse associations between physical activity or physical fitness and all-cause mortality, suggesting that physical activity or fitness may avert premature mortality and enhance longevity. Biologically, it appears reasonable to expect physical activity or physical fitness to postpone mortality. Available data show that exercise training benefits the cardiovascular system. In rats, physical training induced lower heart rates and increased the resistance of heart muscle to ventricular fibrillation (Noakes, Higginson, & Opie, 1983; Williams, Schaible, Bishop, & Morey, 1984). Monkeys fed an atherogenic diet and exercised fared better than did sedentary controls fed the same diet: Their heart rates were lowered, and favorable changes in lipid profile occurred; atherogenic changes in the aorta and other arteries were less severe (Helmrich, Ragland, Leung, & Paffenbarger, 1991). Similar benefits are seen in humans: Physical activity increases oxygen supply to the heart, decreases oxygen demand and improves electrical stability (Blomquist & Saltin, 1983; Clausen, 1977, Saltin, 1990). It also increases collateral coronary artery formation and increases the diameter and dilating capacity of coronary arteries (Fuster, Badimon, Badimon, & Chesebro, 1992; Hambrecht et al., 1993; Richardson, Davies, & Born, 1989). Moreover, physical activity reduces the tendency for platelet aggregation and increases fibrinolytic activity (Bourey & Santoro, 1988; Kestin et al., 1993; Rauramaa et al., 1984). Physical activity further induces favorable changes in lipid profile, decreases blood pressure, increases insulin sensitivity and improves glucose tolerance (Dépres & Lamarche, 1994; Gordon & Rifkind, 1989; Hardman, Hudson, Jones & Norgan, 1989; Haskell, 1984; Lie, Munda, & Erikssen, 1985; Rauramaa, 1984; Tipton, 1991; Wood, Stefanick, Williams, & Haskell, 1991).

Whereas the above mechanisms represent favorable events that can stave off mortality from atherosclerotic, hypertensive and metabolic diseases, physical activity also appears capable of inducing changes in the immune and endocrine systems that can prevent cancer. Data from both animal and human studies consistently show that moderate amounts of physical activity enhance various components of the immune system, including natural killer cells, cytotoxic T lymphocytes and cells of the monocyte-macrophage system (Hoffman-Goetz, 1994; Nieman, 1994; Pedersen & Ullum, 1994; Shephard, Verde, Thomas, & Shek, 1991; Woods & Davis, 1994; Woods et al., 1994). Because the immune system is responsible for eliminating tumor cells from the body, it is plausible for physical activity also to reduce mortality from cancer. Additionally, various hormones are necessary for the development of male and female reproductive cancers (Gittes, 1991; Henderson, Ross, & Pike, 1993; Ross et al., 1986). In females, physical activity can delay the onset of menarche, reduce the number of ovulatory cycles and lower estrogen and progesterone levels, potentially reducing breast cancer incidence and premature mortality from this disease (Bernstein et al., 1987; Shangold, 1984; Warren, 1980). Similarly, in males, physical training can lower testosterone levels, potentially reducing prostate cancer incidence and mortality (Hackney, Sinning, & Brout, 1988; Wheeler, Wall, Belcastro, & Cumming, 1984).

What is the magnitude of benefit conferred by physical activity or fitness on all-cause mortality? Comparing those most active or fit with those least so, mortality rates have been found to be 17% (Slattery, Jacobs, & Nichaman, 1989) to 78% (Blair et al., 1989) lower among most active or fit individuals, with most investigators observing death rates that were perhaps between one quarter and one half lower. This magnitude translates to a benefit that is on par with other established predictors of mortality. Looked at from another perspective, middle-aged individuals might expect to gain, on average, some 2 years of life from being physically active (Paffenbarger et al., 1986, and Pekkanen et al., 1987). However, physical activity does not appear to extend life span; its benefit appears to come from postponing mortality (that is, from making the survival curve more rectangular) (Linsted et al., 1991 and Pekkanen et al., 1987). It is encouraging to note that even older individuals do benefit from a physically active life and that the process of healthy aging can begin at any age.

Of particular public health significance is this question, What physical activity regimen should be recommended to enhance longevity? In view of the many sedentary adults living in the United States today (Siegel et al., 1991), it seems sensible as an initial step to adopt this recommendation from the Centers for Disease Control and Prevention and the American College of Sports Medicine: "Every U.S. adult should accumulate 30 minutes or more of moderate-intensity physical activity on most, preferably all, days of the week."

Because available data indicate a dose-response relation and because several studies suggest that intense or vigorous activities are more beneficial, we further propose, as the next step, that healthy people should engage in more intense activities. Of course, we recognize that there are those—for example, the infirm and the aged—for whom that next step is ill advised. We emphasize the importance of gradually increasing the amount (intensity and duration) of physical activity, because high-intensity activities can precipitate acute myocardial infarction, with the risk especially severe among those habitually sedentary (Mittleman et al., 1993; Siscovick, Weiss, Fletcher, & Lasky, 1984; Thompson, Funk, Carleton, & Sturner, 1982; Willich et al., 1993).

To conclude, physical activity, as well as physical fitness, is inversely related to all-cause mortality in men and women. This association is likely to be causal; moreover, there appears to be a dose-response relation. The most active or fit individuals experience mortality rates that are, perhaps, one quarter to one half lower than are the rates among the least active or fit. The benefit of physical activity appears to be in averting premature mortality, rather than extending life span.

This chapter reprinted and adapted with permission from:

Holloszy, John O. M.D., ed. *Exercise and Sports Sciences Reviews*, Williams and Wilkins: Baltimore. 1996: Volume 24.

REFERENCES

Ainsworth, B.E., Haskell, W.L., & Leon, A.S., et al. (1993). Compendium of physical activities: Classification of energy costs of human physical activities. *Med Sci Sports Exerc, 25,* 71–80.

Bernstein, L.R., Ross, R.K., Lobo, R.A., Hanisch, R., Krailo, M.D., & Henderson B.E. (1987). The effects of moderate physical activity on menstrual cycle patterns in adolescence: Implications for breast cancer prevention. *Br J Cancer, 55,* 681–685.

Blair, S.N., Kohl, H.W. III, Barlow, C.E, Paffenbarger, L.W. Jr., Gibbons, L.W., & Macera, C.E. (1995). Changes in physical fitness and all-cause mortality: A prospective study of healthy and unhealthy men. *JAMA, 273,* 1093–1098.

Blair, S.N., Kohl, H.W. III, Paffenbarger, R.S., Jr., Clark, D.G., Cooper K.H., & Gibbons, L.W. (1989). Physical fitness and all-cause mortality: A prospective study of healthy men and women. *JAMA, 262,* 2395–2401.

Blomquist, C.G., & Saltin, B. (1983). Cardiovascular adaptations to physical training. *Ann Rev Physiol, 45,* 169–189.

Bourey, R.E., & Santoro, S.A. (1988). Interactions of exercise, coagulation, platelets, and fibrinolysis: A brief review. *Med Sci Sports Exerc, 20,* 439–446.

Chave, S.P.W., Morris, J.N., Moss, S., & Semmence, A.M. (1978). Vigorous exercise in leisure time and the death rate: A study of male civil servants. *J Epidemiol Community Health, 32,* 239–243.

Clausen, J.P. (1977). Effect of physical training on cardiovascular adjustments to exercise in man. *Physiol Rev, 57,* 779–815.

Deprés, J.P., & Lamarche, B. (1994). Low-intensity endurance exercise training, plasma lipoproteins and the risk of coronary heart disease. *J Int Med, 236*, 7–22.

Ekelund, L.G., Haskell, W.L., Johnson, J.L., Whaley, F.S., Criqui, M.H., & Sheps, D.S. (1988). Physical fitness as a predictor of cardiovascular mortality in asymptomatic North American men: The Lipid Research Clinics Mortality Follow-up Study. *N Engl J Med, 319*, 1379–1384.

Fuster, V., Badimon, L., Badimon, J.J., & Chesebro, J.H. (1992). The pathogenesis of coronary artery disease and the acute coronary syndromes. *N Engl J Med, 326*, 242–250, 310–318.

Gittes, R.F. (1991). Carcinoma of the prostate. *N Engl J Med, 324*, 236–245.

Gordon, D.J., & Rifkind, B.M. (1989). High-density lipoprotein—The clinical implications of recent studies. *N Engl J Med, 321*, 1311–1316.

Hackney, A.C., Sinning, W.E., & Brout, B.C. (1988). Reproductive hormonal profiles of endurance-trained and untrained males. *Med Sci Sports Exerc, 20*, 60–65.

Hambrecht, R., Niebauer, J., & Marburger, C., et al. (1993). Various intensities of leisure time physical activity in patients with coronary artery disease: Effects on cardiorespiratory fitness and progression of coronary atherosclerotic lesions. *J Am Coll Cardiol, 22*, 468–477.

Hardman, A.E., Hudson, A., Jones, P.R.M, & Norgan, N.C. (1989). Brisk walking and plasma high-density lipoprotein cholesterol concentration in previously sedentary women. *Br Med J, 299*, 1204–1205.

Hartley, P.H.S., & Llewellyn, G.F. (1939). The longevity of oarsmen: A study of those who rowed in the Oxford and Cambridge boat race from 1829–1928. *Br Med J, 1*, 657–662.

Haskell, W.L. (1984). Exercise-induced changes in plasma lipids and lipoproteins. *Prev Med, 13*, 23–36.

Helmrich, S.P., Ragland, D.R., Leung, R.W., & Paffenbarger, R.S. Jr. (1991). Physical activity and reduced occurrence of non–insulin-dependent diabetes mellitus. *N Engl J Med, 325*, 147–152.

Henderson, B.E., Ross, R.K., & Pike, M.C. (1993). Hormonal chemoprevention of cancer in women. *Science, 259*, 633–638.

Hoffman-Goetz, L. (1994). Exercise, natural immunity, and tumor metastasis. *Med Sci Sports Exerc, 26*, 157–163.

Kaplan, G.A., Seeman, T.E., Cohen, R.D., Knudsen, L.P., & Guralnik, J. (1987). Mortality among the elderly in the Alameda County Study: Behavioral and demographic risk factors. *Am J Public Health, 77*, 307–312.

Kestin, A.S., Ellis, P.A., Barnard, M.R., Errichetti, A., Rosner, B.A., & Michelson, A.D. (1993). Effect of strenuous exercise on platelet activation state and reactivity. *Circulation, 88*, 1502–1511.

Keys, A. (1980). *Seven countries: A multivariate analysis of death and coronary heart disease.* Cambridge, MA: Harvard University Press.

Lie, H., Munda, R., & Erikssen, J. (1985). Coronary risk factors and incidence of coronary death in relation to physical fitness: Seven-year follow-up study of middle-aged and elderly men. *Eur Heart J, 6*, 147–157.

Lindsted, K.D., Sonstad, S., & Kuzma, J.W. (1991). Self-report of physical activity and patterns of mortality in Seventh-Day Adventist men. *J Clin Epidemiol, 44*, 355–364.

Lyons, A.R., & Petrucelli, R.J. (1978). *Medicine: An illustrated history.* New York: Harry N. Abrams.

Mittleman, M.A., Maclure, M., Tofler, G.H., Sherwood, J.B., Goldberg, R.J., & Muller, J.E. (1993). Triggering of acute myocardial infarction by heavy physical exertion: Protection against triggering by regular exertion. *N Engl J Med, 329*, 1677–1683.

Morris, J.N., Chave, S.P.W., Adam, C., Sirey, C., Epstein, L., & Sheehan, D.J. (1973). Vigorous exercise in leisure-time and the incidence of coronary heart disease. *Lancet, 1*, 333–339.

Morris, J.N., Everitt, M.G., Pollard, R., Chave, S.P.W., & Semmence, A.M. (1980). Vigorous exercise in leisure-time: Protection against coronary heart disease. *Lancet, 2*, 1207–1212.

Morris, J.N., Heady, J.A., Raffle, P.A.B., Roberts, C.G., & Parks, J.W. (1953). Coronary heart-disease and physical activity of work. II. Statement and testing of provisional hypothesis. *Lancet, 2*, 1111–1120.

Nieman, D.C. (1994). Exercise, upper respiratory tract infection, and the immune system. *Med Sci Sports Exer, 26*, 128–139.

Noakes, T.D., Higginson, L., & Opie, L.H. (1983). Physical training increases ventricular fibrillation thresholds of isolated rat hearts during normoxia, hypoxia, and regional ischemia. *Circulation, 67*, 24–30.

Paffenbarger, R.S. Jr., Hyde, R.T., Wing, A.L., & Hsieh, C. (1986). Physical activity: All-cause mortality and longevity of college alumni. *N Engl J Med, 314*, 605–613.

Paffenbarger, R.S. Jr., Hyde, R.T., Wing, A.L., & Hsieh, C. (1986). Physical activity and longevity of college alumni. *N Engl J Med, 315*, 400–401.

Paffenbarger, R.S. Jr., Wing, A.L., & Hyde, R.T. (1978). Physical activity as an index of heart attack risk in college alumni. *Am J Epidemiol, 108*, 161–175.

Pedersen, B.K., & Ullum, H. (1994). NK cell response to physical activity: Possible mechanisms of action. *Med Sci Sports Exerc, 26*, 140–146.

Pekkanen, J., Marti, B., Nissinen, A., Tuomilehto, J., Punsar, S., & Karvonen, M. (1987). Reduction of premature mortality by high physical activity: A 20-year follow-up of middle-aged Finnish men. *Lancet, 1*, 1473–1477.

Prout, C. (1972). Life expectancy of college oarsmen. *JAMA, 220*, 1709–1711.

Ramazzini, B. (1940) *DeMorbis Artificum Diatriba* [The Latin text of 1713, revised, trans and notes by W.C. Wright]. *Diseases of workers* (pp. 281–285, 295–301). Chicago: University of Chicago Press.

Rauramaa, R. (1984). Relationship of physical activity, glucose tolerance and weight management. *Prev Med, 13*, 37–46.

Rauramaa, J., Salonen, J.T., & Kukkonen-Harjula, K., et al. (1994). Effects of mild physical exercise on serum lipoproteins and metabolites of arachidonic acid: A controlled randomized trial in middle-aged men. *Br Med J, 288*, 603–606.

Richardson, P.D., Davies, M.J., & Born, G.V.R. (1989). Influence of plaque configuration and stress distribution on fissuring of coronary atherosclerotic plaques. *Lancet, 2,* 941–944.

Ross, R., Bernstein, L., Judd, H., Hanisch, R., Pike, M., & Henderson, B. (1986). Serum testosterone levels in healthy and young black and white men. *J Natl Cancer Inst, 76,* 45–48.

Salonen, J.T., Puska, P., & Tuomilehto, J. (1982). Physical activity and risk of myocardial infarction, cerebral stroke and death: A longitudinal study in Eastern Finland. *Am J Epidemiol, 115,* 526–537.

Saltin, B. (1990). Cardiovascular and pulmonary adaptation of physical activity. In C. Bouchard, R.J. Shephard, T. Stephens, J.R. Sutton, and B.D. McPherson (Eds.), *Exercise, fitness, and health: A consensus of current knowledge* (pp.187–203). Champaign, IL: Human Kinetics.

Shangold, M.M. (1984). Exercise and the adult female: Hormonal and endocrine effects. *Exerc Sport Sci Rev, 12,* 53–79.

Shephard, R.J., Verde, T.J., Thomas, S.G., & Shek, P. (1991). Physical activity and the immune system. *Can J Sport Sci, 16,* 169–185.

Siegel, P.Z., Brackbill, R.M., Frazier, E.L., Mariolis, P., Sanderson, L.M., & Waller, M.N. (1991). Behavioral risk factor surveillance, 1986-1990 MMWR. *Morbidity Mortality Weekly Rep, 40*(SS-4), 1–23.

Siscovick, D.S., Weiss, N.S., Fletcher, R.H., & Lasky, T. (1984). The incidence of primary cardiac arrest during vigorous exercise. *N Engl J Med, 311,* 874–877.

Sivertsen, I., & Dalstrom, A.W. (1922). The relation of muscular activity to carcinoma: A preliminary report. *J Cancer Res, 6,* 365–378.

Slattery, M.L., Jacobs, D.R. Jr., & Nichaman, M.Z. (1989). Leisure time physical activity and coronary heart disease death: The US Railroad Study. *Circulation, 79,* 304–311.

Smith, E. (1864). Report on the sanitary conditions of tailors in London. *Rep Med Officer* (pp. 416–430). London: The Privy Council.

Taylor, H.L., Klepetar, E., Keys, A., Parlin, W., Blackburn, H., & Puchner, T. (1962). Death rates among physically active and sedentary employees of the railroad industry. *Am J Public Health, 52,* 1697–1707.

Thompson, P.D., Funk, E.J., Carleton, R.A., & Sturner, W.Q. (1982). Incidence of death during jogging in Rhode Island from 1975 through 1980. *JAMA, 247,* 2535–2538.

Tipton, C.M. (1991). Exercise, training, and hypertension: An update. *Exerc Sport Sci Rev, 19,* 447–505.

Warren, M.P. (1980). The effects of exercise on pubertal progression and reproductive function in girls. *J Endocrinol Metab, 51,* 1150–1157.

Wheeler, G.D., Wall, S.R., Belcastro, A.N., & Cumming, D.C. (1984). Reduced serum testosterone and prolactin levels in male distance runners. *JAMA, 252,* 514–516.

Williams, R.S., Schaible, T.F., Bishop, T., & Morey, M. (1984). Effects of endurance training on cholinergic and adrenergic receptors of the rat heart. *J Mol Cell Cardiol, 16,* 395–403.

Willich, S.N., Lewis, M., Lowel, H., Arntz, H.R., Schubert, F., & Schroder, R. (1993). Physical exertion as a trigger of acute myocardial infarction. *N Engl J Med, 329*, 1684–1690.

Wood, P.D., Stefanick, M.L., Williams, P.T., & Haskell, W.L. (1991). The effects on plasma lipoproteins of a prudent weight-reducing diet with or without exercise, in overweight men and women. *N Engl J Med, 325*, 461–466.

Woods, J.A., & Davis, J.M. (1994). Exercise, monocyte/macrophage function and cancer. *Med Sci Sports Exerc, 26*, 147–156.

Woods, J.A., Davis, J.M., Kohut, M.L., Chaffar, A., Mayer, E.P., & Pate, R.P. (1994). Effects of exercise on the immune response to cancer. *Med Sci Sports Exerc, 26*, 1109–1115.

CHAPTER 6

The Case for Preventing Decline in the Aging Brain

Zaven S. Khachaturian

The prevalence of many chronic disabilities, especially brain disorders, increases nearly exponentially with age, almost doubling every 5 years. As a greater proportion of the population survives beyond the age of 85, increasing numbers of individuals will be at risk for a neurologic disorder in general and, in particular, some form of dementia. It is estimated that by the year 2050 there will be more than 14 million people affected by some form of cognitive dysfunction or dementia, requiring care and, often, institutionalization. If nothing is done to delay or prevent the onset of late-life neurodegenerative diseases, these demographic trends in the age distribution of the U.S. population foretell a major public health disaster for the beginning of the twenty-first century.

Although aging is considered to be one of the most important and consistent risk factors for most late-life neurologic disorders, age per se does not cause these disorders. Contrary to the widely shared misconception, many older people remain healthy, continue to be creative and productive, and function well and independently into late life. Unfortunately a fraction of older people suffer from one or more health problems. Among these disorders of later life, those relating to the aging brain have the most profound effects on a person's dignity, quality of life and ability to maintain independent function. The medical, psychologic, social and scientific problems associated with the aging brain include several different domains of the function of the central nervous system, including cognition, attention, sleep, language, vestibular/balance, incontinence, motor and sensory processes, the neuroimmune system and behavioral/psychiatric disorders.

Source: Copyright © 1998, Zaven S. Khachaturian.

The rising cost of long-term care in recent years has made the economics of health care one of the most important problems in the array of major public health concerns. Neurologic disorders of late life—especially dementias, with their long clinical course—are perhaps the most significant disabilities requiring various forms of long-term care. The burden of care on the families of these patients is not just emotional stress and physical hardship, but financial cost as well. It is estimated that the total annual direct and indirect cost of care for neurologic disorders to the country as a whole is between $100 billion and $150 billion. The cost of the disability most immediately affects patients and their families, but ultimately the disease has major economic impact on society as a whole by reducing or impairing potential productivity. The lack of any means to cope with this pending national public health disaster is a major source of concern for public policy. The discovery of safe and effective treatments for these disorders is an urgent public health challenge.

In this chapter, the spotlight has been placed on only one of many disorders of the aging brain—Alzheimer's disease. This is because Alzheimer's is a convenient template for other disabling conditions. The arguments and the case being made for Alzheimer's disease apply equally well for the other neurodegenerative diseases of late life.

Alzheimer's disease is the most common type of dementia among people aged 65 and older. It is currently estimated that Alzheimer's affects approximately 4 million Americans in the mild, moderate and severe forms of the disease. Ongoing population studies may soon provide more accurate estimates of the number of people at different stages of the disease. Slightly more than half of people with Alzheimer's receive care at home, and others are in residential facilities.

The disease puts a heavy economic burden on the families and on society. A recent study estimated that the cost of caring for one Alzheimer's disease patient with severe cognitive impairments at home or in a nursing home, excluding indirect losses in productivity or wages, is more than $47,000 a year. The overall cost of Alzheimer's disease to families and to society is staggering, due to the very long clinical course of the disease, which can span from 2–20 years, with an average duration of 8–10 years. It is projected that this duration of disability will increase substantially as the baby boomers, healthier and better-educated cohorts, come of age. The annual economic toll of Alzheimer's disease in the United States in terms of health care expenses and lost wages of both patients and their caregivers is estimated at $80–$90 billion.

Alzheimer's is a progressive brain disorder, and in most people the first symptoms appear after age 60. However, in a small percentage of cases with a strong family history of the disease, they can appear at earlier ages. Impossible to detect in its early stages, Alzheimer's handiwork gradually becomes apparent as a slow but steady decline in cognitive functioning occurs and begins to interfere with the activities of daily living. The changes in memory, behavior, personality and thinking abilities cannot be reversed. The only viable long-term solutions are to prevent the disease before it starts or to slow down its progression.

First symptoms often include loss of recent memory, faulty judgment and alterations in personality. Often, people with Alzheimer's think less clearly and forget the names of familiar people and common objects. Later in the disease, they may forget how to do simple tasks like washing their hands. Eventually, people with Alzheimer's disease lose all ability to remember and come to depend on other people for everyday care. Finally, the disease becomes so debilitating that patients are bedridden and likely to develop co-existing illnesses. Most commonly, people with Alzheimer's disease die from pneumonia or some other medical condition resulting from being bedridden for a long time. The course of this disease varies from person to person, as does the rate of decline.

Research into the basic biology of the aging nervous system is critical to understanding what goes wrong in the brain of a person with Alzheimer's disease. The inherent plasticity of the healthy normal central nervous system allows repair and continued function normally throughout the life span. If abnormalities in function occur, they are due to specific causes that can be identified, described, understood and eventually controlled. *In the absence of a disease, the human brain often can function well into the tenth decade of life and beyond.* Understanding how nerve cells lose their ability to communicate with one another and the reasons that some nerve cells die is at the heart of scientific efforts to discover the cause of Alzheimer's disease.

It is a given fact that a gradual decline in one or more brain functions does occur in some individuals as they age. However, the rate, the severity and the age at which the decline is observed varies from one person to another. In the mild-to-moderate ranges of decline, such loss of function-ing is often attributed to normal aging. While the phenomenon of dimin-ished capacity in some older individuals, based on longitudinal studies of functional capacities, is not in dispute, the explanation of aging per se as an underlying causal factor must be questioned. Any decline in brain functioning, whether mild, moderate or severe, must be due to some failure or disruption within the brain.

The human brain is made up of billions of nerve cells, called *neurons*, that share information with one another through a large network of biologic and chemical signals. Even more numerous are glial cells, which surround, support and nourish neurons. Except for its actual small size measured in millionths of an inch, a neuron resembles an uprooted tree. Each neuron has a cell body (the tree trunk), an axon (branches) and many dendrites (roots). The nucleus, which contains deoxyribonucleic acid, has the genetic code or the blueprints for regulating all the activities of a cell. The axon, which extends from the cell body, sends messages to other neurons. Dendrites, which also branch out from the cell body, receive messages from axons of other nerve cells or from specialized sense organs. Axons and dendrites collectively are called *neurites*.

Neurons communicate with each other and with sense organs by producing and releasing chemicals. Inside the cell, another set of chemical messages serves as an intercom system in regulating the internal housekeeping activities of the cell. Some of the incoming messages, after being processed internally, are transmitted as a traveling shift in ion concentrations, which can be measured as an electrical charge or a nerve impulse. This charge (positive and negative ion shifts) travels down the nerve cell until it reaches the end of the axon. Here, the nerve impulse triggers the release of neurotransmitters. There are many different types of neurotransmitters, which serve as keys to unlock different types of locks.

The availability of many different neurotransmitter or chemical messaging systems allows different parts of the brain to communicate in different languages. Thus, each part of the brain can carry out many tasks at the same time, each requiring operations in different time domains. These chemicals carry messages from the axons across synapses (gaps between nerve cells) to the dendrites or the cell bodies of other neurons. Synapses are specialized ports of communications between nerve cells. It is estimated that the typical neuron has hundreds and thousands of synapses.

Neurotransmitters carrying messages bind to specific receptor sites on the receiving end of dendrites of adjacent nerve cells. A receptor and its neurotransmitter work as a lock-and-key combination. A specific neurotransmitter can stimulate only a particular type of receptor. Receptors are proteins on the surface of the cell that recognize and bind to chemical messengers from other cells. The molecular structure of receptors determines the unique physical and chemical traits of cells.

When a receptor is activated, it undergoes a reversible structural change that activates other proteins in the membrane of the cell. Thus, a relay of activity is initiated. The end of this long and complex chain of events, which lasts only thousandths of a second, is the instruction to the cell "to do its thing." This may involve turning a gene on or off, or releasing small amounts of neurotransmitter to stimulate the next cell. Some neurotransmitters inhibit nerve cell function; others stimulate them.

In this way, signals travel back and forth across the brain in fractions of a second. Millions of signals flash through the brain all the time. Groups of neurons in the brain are organized to perform specific jobs, such as carrying signals from the eye to different parts of the brain. Some of these groups of neurons are exclusively dedicated to one specific task, and other neurons become members of different groups and perform multiple tasks. The parts of the brain that are involved in higher cognitive functions, such as memory, language, thinking and creativity, tend to rely more on the eclectic groups of neurons. For example, the brain's cerebral cortex is a large collection of neurons all over the surface of the brain. Some of these nerve cells are involved in thinking, learning, remembering and planning.

The complex operations of the brain can be carried out with great efficiency throughout the life span of a person, as long as a disease process, toxins or trauma do not cause damage to the neurons of the brain. There are many examples of individuals who have lived well beyond the tenth decade with their brains in perfect operating order. The survival of nerve cells in the brain depends on the healthy functioning of three dynamic mechanisms all working in harmony—communication, metabolism and repair.

The communication or transmission of information within and between nerve cells is critical to the survival and normal function of a neuron. In many neurologic disorders, it is often the loss of one or more of several chemical messengers or the loss of receptors that leads to disruptions in cell-to-cell communication and results in abnormal brain function.

Another critical factor necessary to ensure the normal function and survival of the neuron is metabolism, an efficient use of energy in which glucose and oxygen are transformed into more useable (slow-release) forms of fuel. Efficient metabolism in neurons requires proper circulation and perfusion of the cell with an adequate blood supply of nutrients, oxygen and glucose. Glucose is the only source of energy available to the brain under normal circumstances. Depriving the brain of oxygen or glucose causes nerve cells to die within minutes.

The ability of the neuron to synthesize new proteins and lipids (oily molecules that make up the membrane of a neuron) and to degrade or get rid of used proteins and lipids is the other feature essential to ensure neuron survival. Unlike most other cells in the body, neurons live a very long time. Brain neurons are built to last more than 100 years. In the adult, when neurons die (due to disease or injury), they are not replaced. To prevent their own death, living neurons constantly maintain and remodel themselves. If cell cleanup and repair slow down or stop for any reason, the nerve cell cannot function properly.

It is not clear when and why some neurons start to die and some synapses stop working. Research shows that such neurologic disorders involve changes or abnormal functioning in one or more of these three mechanisms.

In degenerative disorders of the brain such as Alzheimer's disease, communication between some nerve cells breaks down, and they eventually die. In Alzheimer's disease, the death of many neurons in specific parts of the brain underlies decline in cognitive functioning as the disease progresses from mild to severe forms. Alzheimer's disease destroys neurons, particularly in parts of the brain that help code memories—the hippocampus and cortex. As nerve cells in the hippocampus stop functioning properly, short-term memory fails, and the person's ability to do familiar tasks begins to decline. The disease inflicts its greatest damage in areas of the cerebral cortex responsible for such functions as language and reasoning. As the disease runs its course, personality changes are accompanied by emotional outbursts; language skills and judgment decline, and the frequency of disturbing behavior such as wandering and agitation increases.

THE PROMISE OF EARLY DETECTION

The long path leading to the dysfunction, destruction and death of neurons involves a cascade of events and may take as long as 40–60 years before the merciful end. The scientific challenge for the future is to detect this molecular and biochemical mischief early in its history and prevent or slow down these destructive processes. Several lines of research have begun to provide strong evidence that the neurodegenerative changes associated with Alzheimer's disease may begin up to 40 years before the first clinical symptoms appear. Although ethical concerns present difficulties, early detection is crucial to effective intervention.

There is an urgent need to develop the technologies required for early and accurate detection of Alzheimer's disease and the discovery of biologic markers of the disease. These technologies and markers are needed *not only* for diagnosis of presymptomatic cases, but also to track the progression of the disease and to evaluate the efficacy of agents in clinical trials. To learn about early changes in the development of the disease, it is important to follow presymptomatic people at risk for Alzheimer's disease: the oldest old, those with a first-degree relative with Alzheimer's disease, those with a genetic predisposition to the disease and identical twins of affected individuals.

Recent studies have demonstrated that combining information from brain imaging with that of genetic predisposition or risk for the disease through apolipoprotein E (APOE) genotyping promises to become a powerful tool for early detection. Brain imaging technologies, such as magnetic resonance imaging (MRI) and positron emission tomography (PET), enable investigators to study the brain of living patients, following them longitudinally to evaluate disease progression and the effect of therapeutic interventions. However, to realize the maximum potential of these technologies, they must be improved. Higher resolution for both PET and MRI, as well as the development of new ligands for PET scanning, are required. The PET is a device that allows researchers a way to measure the amount of sugar being used by different parts of the brain, thus measuring metabolic activity or energy utilization by the brain. The MRI is a different imaging instrument that allows scientists to obtain structural or anatomic pictures of the brain by capturing the different magnetic characteristics of the different elements that make up the brain tissue, such as water, phosphor or oxygen.

It has become apparent that there may be different forms of Alzheimer's disease. Heterogeneity in Alzheimer's, which is the result of genetic influences, is evident in its many variable manifestations, such as age of onset, duration, clinical course, types and patterns of neurologic and psychiatric symptoms, neuropathologic lesions and response to treatment. The biologic basis for this heterogeneity will probably be found in the interaction between genetic and other factors.

GENETICS

Genes are basic units of heredity that can direct almost every aspect of the construction, operation and repair of living organisms. Each gene is a set of chemical instructions that tells a cell how to make one of the many unique proteins in the body. Every human cell has thousands of genes arranged on the chromosomes like beads on a string. Genes are made up of four chemicals (bases) arranged in various patterns along the strands of DNA. In each gene, the bases are lined up in a different order, and each sequence of bases directs the production of a different protein. Even slight changes in a gene's DNA code can make a faulty protein, and a faulty protein can lead to cell malfunction and possibly disease.

There are two types of Alzheimer's disease: familial Alzheimer's disease, in which Alzheimer's follows a certain inheritance pattern, and sporadic (seemingly random) Alzheimer's disease, which follows no obvious inheritance pattern. During the last several years, researchers have identified four chromosomes associated with Alzheimer's disease. Almost all familial Alzheimer's disease known so far is early-onset, and many cases involve defects in genes located on three of the four chromosomes.

Recent research on the genetic basis of Alzheimer's disease has yielded some of the most important findings in the broader field of neurodegenerative disease. It is now known that a family history of Alzheimer's disease in a first-degree relative increases the odds of developing the disease several times. Recent studies have found mutations on three chromosomes—14, 1 and 21—that play a key role in causing early-onset Alzheimer's. However, these mutations affect only a small fraction of the total Alzheimer's population.

The emphasis on familial Alzheimer's began to shift in 1992, when researchers found an increased risk for late-onset Alzheimer's disease with inheritance of the apolipoprotein E4 (APOE4) allele on chromosome 19. An allele is one of two or more alternate forms of the same gene. APOE is a protein that helps carry blood cholesterol throughout the body. APOE is found in neurons of healthy brains, but it also is associated with the plaques and neurofibrillary tangles found in the brain with Alzheimer's disease.

The relatively rare APOE2 may protect some people against the disease; it seems to be associated with a lower risk for Alzheimer's disease and later age of onset. APOE2 also appears to protect people with Down syndrome from developing Alzheimer's disease. APOE3 is the most common version found in the general population; researchers believe it plays a neutral role in Alzheimer's disease. Scientists are most interested in APOE4 because it is linked to an increased risk of the disease. The APOE4 form in Alzheimer's disease patients is not limited to those with a family history of Alzheimer's disease. In addition, people who carry two copies of APOE4 are more likely to get Alzheimer's disease than are those with one copy. How APOE4 increases a person's susceptibility to Alzheimer's disease is not yet known, but it also appears to lower the age of onset of Alzheimer's disease, perhaps because APOE4 speeds up the disease process in some unknown way.

Whatever its role in Alzheimer's disease, the mere inheritance of an APOE4 gene does not predict Alzheimer's disease with certainty. As of now, no predictive test for Alzheimer's disease exists. Even with current knowledge about APOE, scientists cannot predict whether or when any person might develop Alzheimer's disease, no more than a doctor can predict whether a person with high cholesterol will have a stroke. However, many researchers believe that inheriting an APOE4 gene in association with poor memory performance in older people that gradually worsens over time may be a predictor for Alzheimer's disease.

The discovery of the APOE gene as a major risk factor for Alzheimer's disease has been one of the most important discoveries in the field of Alzheimer's disease research because it opened doors for many new lines of research. The APOE discovery has led to epidemiologic studies showing that the age of onset can vary by as much as 20 years, depending on which form of the APOE gene a person carries. The findings of a relationship between APOE and Alzheimer's disease provide a crucial biologic marker for epidemiologic studies for sorting patients into homogenous groups. It also opens the door to previously unforeseen opportunities for developing technology for early detection and identifying people at risk. The discovery of the APOE as a major risk factor reinforces expectations and strengthens the hope that biologic interventions for delaying the onset of Alzheimer's disease can be found.

Another important challenge is to exploit emerging genetic information in developing new and more effective interventions. Genetic analysis someday could help scientists find people with probable Alzheimer's disease to include in clinical trials of promising treatments. Because of the increased risk signs of Alzheimer's disease, those who have a particular genetic mutation may be among the first volunteers to be studied in clinical trials of experimental drugs. It may follow that having multiple risk-factor genes may increase a person's likelihood of developing Alzheimer's disease. With each new finding, researchers gain more clues about basic mechanisms in Alzheimer's disease and move closer to understanding the disease and designing treatments that slow its progression, delay its onset or even prevent it.

CELL DYSFUNCTION AND DEATH

One of the most important early discoveries in Alzheimer's research was finding a link between cognitive loss and a specific biochemical deficit in the brain. These early studies of neurotransmitter chemistry led to the development of current strategies for treating the symptoms of Alzheimer's by replacing missing chemicals. Now, as result of these early investigations conducted some 20–25 years ago, there are two drugs available as treatments for Alzheimer's disease, and soon there will be additional choices for patients and their physicians.

The prospects of developing prophylactic treatments in the near future are more promising than ever. While work on the neurochemistry of treatment was proceeding, significant advances were also being made in unraveling the molecular details of the hallmark neuropathologic lesions of Alzheimer's disease—senile plaques, tangles and neuronal synapse loss. Now we have many important clues as to how these abnormal proteins are formed, how they might affect nerve-cell function, what role they might play in destroying nerve cells and how drugs might be developed to correct this molecular mischief.

A key factor in Alzheimer's disease is the loss of contacts, or synapses, between nerve cells. The symptoms of Alzheimer's disease are an expression of and are caused by the loss of function of an ever-increasing number of neurons. At first, these losses appear to have no immediate impact on behavior in the same way that the loss of a few soldiers at the beginning of a battle does not appear to be of significance to the conduct of a long campaign. However, as the losses mount, it becomes obvious that the war will be lost because there are not enough soldiers remaining. There is now strong evidence that the process of gradual pruning of the connections of neurons may start up to 20–40 years before the first clinical signs of the disease appear. Since the late 1970s, a rich array of scientific evidence has emerged to explain the proximal cause of cell dysfunction and cell death in Alzheimer's disease. Current hypotheses include the accumulation of proteins that disrupt cell functioning, the abnormal processing of proteins essential to cell functioning, disruption in cell energy metabolism, deregulation of calcium homeostatic mechanisms, and exposure to toxins and inflammatory reactions.

EXPERIENTIAL AND ENVIRONMENTAL FACTORS

Epidemiologic studies have uncovered three major risk factors for Alzheimer's disease: aging, genetic predisposition and head trauma. These three risk factors meet the generally accepted epidemiologic criteria for causality. Each of these risk factors is accompanied by a plausible biologic explanation; their effects are strong and consistent, and have been replicated. Although different epidemiologic studies report varying prevalence rates, almost all find an exponential increase as a function of increasing age. Therefore, aging is well established as a strong risk factor. In addition, health histories, head trauma, dietary habits, occupation, low levels of formal education and exposure to toxins have also been linked to Alzheimer's disease as factors increasing risk.

These observations of potential risk factors, derived from epidemiologic studies, may provide new clues to the mechanisms of the disease by linking genetic and nongenetic risk factors, such as life experience, to changes in the brain. By pinpointing selective risks and understanding their interactions with genetic factors, intervention may be possible to delay or even prevent Alzheimer's disease. Preliminary studies have provided some important clues to the roles of these variables in causing Alzheimer's disease, but better tools and larger populations must now be used.

INTERVENTIONS: BIOLOGIC APPROACHES

The first-generation drugs, which work to increase the strength of nerve signals, have demonstrated that the expression of symptoms can be delayed by 6–9 months. It is anticipated that second-generation compounds, which will probably improve the quality of the signals and, thus, the ability of nerve cells to communicate, will provide longer delays. As more is learned about the neurobiology of Alzheimer's disease, there will be greater reliance on new and more efficient techniques to design specific molecules aimed at correcting a particular cellular dysfunction. Some of the important therapeutic targets and the most promising leads in delaying or preventing the onset of symptoms include:

- neurotransmitter replacement
- amyloid processing
- drugs to combat inflammatory reactions in the brain
- drugs to mimic the combined effects of estrogen and growth-promoting factors to repair and restore function in damaged or dying nerve cells
- gene therapy
- restoration of energy metabolism
- correction of phosphorylation, calcium hemostasis, estrogen replacement, antioxidants or vitamin supplements
- herbal medicines such as Ginkgo biloba.

The development of treatments in the future should be targeted at strategies that will prevent premature cell death by terminating the initiating events or by interrupting the underlying process to ensure the survival of nerve cells and stimulate or restore function in the surviving nerve cells. Current strategies adopted by most biotechnology and pharmaceutical companies focus primarily on developing symptomatic treatments for the middle and late stages of the disease. Treatment usually begins after the degenerative process has progressed to the point of little doubt about the diagnosis. Unfortunately, by that time, most of the nerve cells that might benefit from the treatment are either dead or too impaired to regain function. These traditional approaches may provide some very temporary symptomatic relief (measured in months only), but they will not provide long-term solutions.

INTERVENTIONS: BEHAVIORAL
APPROACHES TO TREATMENT

One of the most critical dilemmas in Alzheimer's disease research is the struggle for a balance between biologic and psychosocial research. There is a sharp contrast between the excitement generated by rapid progress in the biomedical arena and frustration with the slow pace of progress in developing well-tested practical strategies to reduce the burdens of care. Though work continues to determine the neurobiologic basis of Alzheimer's disease, this work remains a promissory note for those many who are the caregivers for a family member afflicted with the disease. These caregivers share the excitement of progress, but they also experience the pain and frustration of their daily reality.

During the last few years, research on the behavioral, social and environmental aspects of Alzheimer's disease has been making impressive progress. Further advances will enhance some of the now-available practical interventions, providing families with help they so desperately need. It has been clearly established and widely accepted that the consequences of the disease are very difficult but vary by social, structural and environmental characteristics. The stresses have been demonstrated to be enormous, with implications for the health of primary caregivers. Although individual experiences are varied, the families of patients suffer substantial negative consequences from the disease, including financial burdens.

Investigators have moved beyond the establishment and general characterization of care and management issues to a more refined analysis of the circumstances and reverberations leading to requirements for care and management. The goal is to provide carefully delineated targets and timetables for interventions and for the development of interventions and supportive services that will maintain patients and their families in dignity and independence for as long as possible. A better understanding of psychosocial problems during the long course of the disease has provided guidelines for helping families. The experiences of families, the study of environmental and social factors influencing requirements for care and information about behavioral disturbances in home and institutional settings have contributed to this understanding.

CONCLUSION

The current national commitment to discovering a solution to Alzheimer's disease, which now costs the country an estimated $100 billion a year, is very modest—about $80 per person suffering from the disease, or $1 for every $310 that Alzheimer's disease is now costing society. The current level of annual support for Alzheimer's disease research at the National

Institutes of Health is about $320 million, compared with $2.7 billion for cancer, $1.5 billion for acquired immune deficiency syndrome, and $1 billion for heart disease—all public health problems of comparable cost and concern to the American people. Reaching the ambitious goal of "a world without Alzheimer's" will take an unprecedented level of financial commitment from both the public and private sectors.

The public health objective must be to slow the rate of deterioration in cognitive performance by discovering treatments that will allow people to continue to function independently for an additional 5, 10 or 20 years. The ultimate goal is to reduce: the duration of disability, the numbers of persons affected by Alzheimer's disease, and thus the cost of long-term care. With nearly 500,000 new patients every year, it is anticipated that by the year 2050, more than 14 million individuals—up from 4 million today—may be affected by Alzheimer's disease and may require medical care and institutionalization. A delay of 5 years in the onset of the symptoms of Alzheimer's disease will reduce the number of people affected by half, thus reducing cost of care significantly.

At present, the delay to develop safe and effective drugs for prevention is not so much due to the lack of scientific know-how, but because of inadequate interest and investment in the overall discovery efforts. It is imperative to expand research aimed at finding strategies for prevention. Recent population-based studies provide encouragement that it might be within the grasp of scientists to delay the onset of disabling symptoms and to allow patients to continue functioning independently for longer periods.

However, action must be taken quickly. In 20 years, attempts will be too little and too late. It can take up to 2 years for researchers to obtain support from funding sources, if the time from idea to receipt of the check is included. If an application is not funded after the first submission, the researcher can revise and resubmit it for the next round, delaying the research for another year. Additionally, most grants are limited to an average duration of 3 years, which is too short a time for a chronic, end-of-life condition such as Alzheimer's disease.

Though support for Alzheimer's research is not increasing substantially in the United States, the cost of conducting research continues to rise with technologic advances. Among the most expensive of the new research resources are the large colonies of transgenic and gene-targeted mice. Such mice must be observed for up to 2 years to assess an age-dependent process, especially relevant to studies of Alzheimer's disease and related degenerative disorders. Simply put, though progress has been made nationally, the research enterprise is in jeopardy because of inadequate resources to support the necessary work.

The decision making and the administrative structure for supporting research simply cannot meet the needs of the rapidly evolving scientific world because of limited funds for research. The process now in general use nationwide for identifying cutting-edge ideas, creative investigators and new scientific opportunities is strained. Although the most important breakthroughs in science have often come from unconventional thinkers, the current decision-making system does not accommodate the risks associated with truly imaginative ideas. It is necessary to have a quickly responding and flexible system that supports rapid decision making and can handle unexpected opportunities and breakthroughs.

Research funds are not available to begin new initiatives or to attract new investigators into the field of Alzheimer's disease research just at the moment when their expertise is most urgently needed. The National Institute on Aging, which supports nearly 70% of Alzheimer's disease-related research, can fund only 20–25% of the new applications it considers each year.

Since 1978, remarkable progress has been made in understanding Alzheimer's disease. The nature and the quality of these discoveries have gradually enhanced the credibility and prestige of Alzheimer's disease research in the eyes of the wider scientific community. Now there is a rich array of new ideas and opportunities for making quantum leaps in advancing knowledge toward causes, early detection, treatment and care. The time is ripe to launch a well-coordinated initiative to accelerate the process of developing the needed knowledge. The success of this venture is virtually assured because all essential elements are at hand: The goal is well defined, the good ideas exist, the necessary human capital is available and the scientific infrastructure is in place.

CHAPTER 7

Biotechnology: Molecular Engineering for Healthy Aging

Ronald W. Eastman

Tara Lipinsky became an Olympic ice-skating champion at the age of 15. Strom Thurmond announced that he would serve in the United States Senate until the completion of his current term in 2002, when he will be 100 years old. Why are these accomplishments extraordinary? It is extraordinary when anyone rises above the physical and mental demands of sports and politics, and does so at the highest competitive level with a mastery that outshines others. It is truly extraordinary that the difference in age between these two champions is greater than the average human life span in any country in the world.

Tara Lipinsky became a champion at a very early age. By today's standard, Strom Thurmond remains a champion at a very old age. Biotechnology offers a means for changing the standard, for extending the length of time we can execute our equivalent of a triple axel and for allowing each of us to contribute to the growth of our society as extensively as the good senator from South Carolina. The promise of biotechnology to extend healthy aging, which should not be confused with extending lifespan, is derived from molecular engineering.

At the mention of technology today, most of us think instantly of Silicon Valley and the chip revolution. There is no question the chip revolution has dramatically changed the way we learn, communicate and play. However, the biology revolution that is now called *biotechnology* has far greater potential to change our world. It will take longer because the human body is extremely complex. However, the results, derived through molecular engineering, will have an increasingly extraordinary impact on human life.

There can be no more noble or necessary mission than understanding the mechanics of human life. This understanding must start at the cellular level because humans, like all living things, are constructed of and controlled by cells. It is estimated that there are more than 100 trillion cells in our bodies. These cells are organized into at least 15–20 different major cell types, such as fibroblasts (one type of skin cell) and osteoblasts (one type of bone cell). More than 100,000 genes, each with a specific responsibility for driving a bodily function, are crammed into the nucleus of every cell. Also, let us not forget that our genes are mysteriously organized on 23 pairs of chromosomes. Where does a cell biologist start?

Interestingly, the term *cell* was not coined until 1665, when an English scientist by the name of Robert Hooke discovered them when looking at cork through a microscope. It took more than 170 years before we realized that all living organisms are made of cells. For this discovery, we can thank two German biologists, Matthias Schlieden and Theodore Schwann. Another 100 years passed before James Watson and Francis Crick, two young and clever scientists at Cambridge University, identified the molecular structure of the backbone of cells—DNA. This discovery in 1953 opened a large window through which it was possible to study cellular biology and which was, perhaps, the most enabling discovery behind the development of biotechnology.

Biotechnology can be thought of as the application of cell biology. It consists of converting what we know about how life operates at the cellular level into the discovery of products and services that will improve the human condition. Most biotechnology is focused on the detection, prevention and treatment of human disease, but biotechnology is also pursued to improve our understanding and use of the animal and plant world around us.

In name, biotechnology is only a generation old. In practice, it has existed for more than 8,000 years and traces its origins to the discovery of how to make bread, cheese, wine and beer. Each of these dietary "necessities" is the product of biotechnology in its purest sense—using a living organism, in this case, single-celled yeast, to create a product.

Today, biotechnology has evolved into the exploration and utilization of cells and their molecular components to combat cellular malfunction. By understanding what is happening at the molecular level of human biology, we improve our chances of actually treating the cause of disease, as opposed to its symptoms. This is the great promise of biotechnology, and it must be pursued vigorously for we still do not have an appropriate therapeutic response to more than 50% of all known diseases.

The first company formed specifically to commercialize products using biotechnology was Genentech, an acronym for "genetic engineering technology." Founded in 1976, Genentech was a pioneer in a field that now includes more than 1,300 companies in the United States and approximately half that many companies in Europe. In the United States, biotechnology companies employ more than 120,000 people and invest more than $8 billion in research and development each year. On average, biotechnology companies invest more than $70,000 in research and development expense per employee. It is worth noting that this is 10 times higher than the average spent by all companies in the United States on research and development (Ernst & Young, 1996, 1997, 1998).

Biotechnology companies, together with their academic and governmental collaborators, have already invented approximately 100 drugs that are now being used to treat almost 100 million patients around the world (Biotechnology Industry Organization, 1996). It is estimated that at least 700 additional drugs are currently being clinically tested (UBS Global Research, January, 1998).

However, the process of discovering and testing new drugs is enormously challenging. The mission that biotechnology companies pursue is time-consuming, capital-intensive, and thanks to the complexity of human biology, risky. According to a January 1996 report by the Boston Consulting Group, it costs, on average, $300–500 million to get one new medicine from the laboratory to patients in the United States. The Tufts University Center for the Study of Drug Development calculated that it takes 15 years, on average, for an experimental drug to travel from the lab to patients in the United States. Further, only 5 in 5,000 compounds that have been identified as therapeutically promising ever get to the stage of human testing, and only 1 of those 5 ever gets approved (Pharmaceutical Researchers and Manufacturers Association, PhRMA, 1997). There are, of course, some products that get developed, approved and commercialized faster and at considerably less expense, but the overwhelming majority do not.

The funding of biomedical research, especially given its inherent risks, is a critical issue. There may be no research effort that is more capital-intensive than biomedical research. In 1997, more than $36 billion was spent for biomedical research in the United States. However, that represented less than 20% of the total dollars spent for all research and development. Population growth and aging trends will require a substantially increased investment in biomedical research. This must mean greater funding for the National Institutes of Health (NIH), which, together with other federal agencies, today account for only a third of total biomedical research and development.

Industry, which includes biotechnology as well as large pharmaceutical companies, contributes more than 50% of the costs of biomedical research and commercializes much of the research conducted by government and academic laboratories. To maintain this level of investment, regulatory and financial conditions that serve to stimulate rather than suffocate discovery and innovation are required. Finally, all of those dedicated to biomedical research need their discoveries respected and protected with patents in a way that is commensurate with the risk of making them. As it is, only 5% of biotechnology companies have products, and only 2% have profits. Clearly, biotechnology companies still have a considerable way to go to generate the revenues and profits they need to be self-sustaining and to fully deliver on the promise of the revolution in modern biology.

As society ages, the research and product development challenges facing biotechnology become more daunting. Every day more than 6,000 Americans now celebrate their 65th birthday. As we enter the 21st century, nearly 33 million Americans, or 13% of the population, will be 65 or older. At the turn of the last century there were only three million Americans or 4% of the population 65 and older. At that time, around when Strom Thurmond was born, the average age at death was 47. Today the average is 75, and it continues to rise.

More Americans are living longer and enjoying it more, in part because of advances already made in drugs, medical care and our basic understanding of how nutrition and exercise affect our health. A recent survey found that 89% of Americans between the ages of 65 and 74 say they have no disabilities. The survey also found that 40% of those 85 and older claim to be fully functional. In fact, today there are at least 1.4 million fewer disabled older people in the United States than there would have been if the health status of the elderly population had not improved since 1982 (Rowe, 1997). Nevertheless, alghouth 13% of the population is over the age of 65, they consume more than one third of our health care costs. Biotechnological innovation is necessary if we are to outpace the graying of our population.

In 1997 a survey by PhRMA found that 91 companies are developing 178 drugs for the treatment of the debilitating and costly diseases that can make aging a poor reward for our contributions in life. In addition, more than 400 medicines are being tested for heart disease, stroke and cancer, the three leading causes of death among older Americans.

It is important to note that all of these drugs are either in clinical trials or are awaiting approval by the Food and Drug Administration (FDA). Obviously, many more are in various stages of development. Drugs that are in clinical trials or awaiting approval include:

- Seventeen that target Alzheimer's disease, which affects 4 million Americans and is a leading cause of nursing home admissions;
- Nine that target depression, which affects 15–20% of older Americans and results in 6000 suicides a year;
- Twenty-one that target diabetes, which claims the lives of more than 40,000 older Americans each year; and
- Twenty-four that target arthritis, which affects nearly half of all Americans age 65 and older.

When we add to this the 96 medicines targeted at heart disease and stroke and the 316 medicines targeted at cancer, we can see that there is a veritable war being fought against the diseases associated with aging (PhRMA, 1997). However, we must remember that, on average, only one in five of the drugs undergoing clinical testing will ever be approved by the FDA.

Most biotechnology product development to date has been disease focused. That is, drugs have been identified and designed that modify a particular biologic characteristic of a particular disease. This has already brought us great advances in certain diseases, with cardiovascular disease being the most prominent among age-related diseases. However, as a whole, diseases associated with aging, such as Alzheimer's, cancer, osteoporosis and macular degeneration, are not well understood or well treated. The cost to society in suffering, death and lost productivity is incalculable.

In recent years, a parallel and new approach to product development has been launched. This approach treats aging, not the associated diseases of aging, as the biologic problem. It now appears that there are common biologic mechanisms that are both fundamental to aging and play a causal role in numerous age-related diseases. This is a new biologic frontier that biotechnology is just beginning to explore and that holds extraordinary promise for improving healthy aging—adding life to life.

Humans have no doubt pondered aging and its physical effects since its first impact on human activity. Along the way, sages, scientists and the proverbial snake-oil salesmen have offered countless explanations and remedies for aging. Today, cell and molecular biologists are delivering with remarkable speed a significantly improved understanding of how and why we age and suffer from the physical complications of aging.

Why has it taken so long? Have we been complacent, ignorant or both? After all, we all age. So does every organ in our body. Our muscles will waste away, and fat will accumulate. Our vision will decline as our lenses thicken. Our skin will lose its elasticity and heal more slowly when damaged. Our bones will lose their density and become more susceptible to breaking. Our ears become less able to distinguish between high- and low-pitched sounds. The prognosis is perfectly predictable: We, all of us, will become handicapped and a burden to ourselves and to society.

It has taken considerable time to achieve breakthroughs in our under-standing of the biology of aging because, again, human biology is enor-mously complex and human aging no less so. Perhaps because few have considered aging a disease, a biologic process that is alterable, the number of scientists who have been attracted to studying it is still small. Nonethe-less, it is also likely that the sheer complexity of the task remains our primary impediment to greater achievement in research on aging.

This is changing with recent findings that indicate that aging and the diseases associated with it are not just the products of accumulated insults or wear and tear to the body. They are the combination of these insults, wear and tear, and, perhaps most significantly, genetically programmed changes in the body.

How are we programmed to age? We certainly have not fully answered this provocative question. We do know that in *C. elegans*, a laboratory roundworm whose genetic structure is relatively similar to humans, the manipulation of any one of eight genes can extend this species' life span. In one instance, the life span was extended fourfold, or the equivalent of 340 human years!

Closer to home, we now know that the manipulation of a single human gene results in Werner's syndrome. Werner's is one of several premature aging syndromes that results in the early onset of such diseases as athero-sclerosis, osteoporosis, cataracts and cancer. Premature aging syndromes invariably result in premature death. In other words, our health and longevity appear in part governed by genetic programming.

Biotechnology is helping us explore the dynamics of normal human aging at the cellular level. This research will enable us to manipulate the molecular mechanisms that program or control aging in order to detect, prevent and treat the diseases associated with aging. My favorite example of the relatively few biotechnology companies pursuing the common biologic mechanisms of aging and the diseases associated with it is, of course, Geron, where I serve as chief executive officer.

Geron focuses on telomeres, structures at the ends of our chromosomes that act as a molecular "clock" of cellular aging. It also focuses on telomerase, an enzyme that resets the "clock" and can confer cellular immortality. Geron has shown that when telomeres, which shorten with each cell division, reach a certain short length, cells stop dividing and become senescent. Nondividing senescent cells can have a destructive impact on surrounding tissue. This can be seen in organs throughout our bodies—our skin, eyes, bones and blood vessels. Further, the destructive impact of senescent cells in these tissues contributes to such age-related diseases and conditions as reduced wound healing, macular degeneration, osteoporosis and atherosclerosis.

Our reproductive cells, such as spermatagonial cells, have achieved the ability to divide indefinitely. They do so by maintaining their telomere length. Each time our reproductive cells divide, a single complex enzyme called *telomerase* actually rebuilds the telomere. Maintaining telomere length prevents cellular senescence, which in reproductive cells allows us to pass on our full genetic code, generation after generation. Telomerase then can be thought of as an "immortalizing" reproductive enzyme.

Telomerase is not detectable in most normally dividing cells. It appears to be repressed or rendered biologically inactive in early human development in all but the reproductive cells and cells of highly proliferative tissues, such as the gut. Thus, our normally dividing cells have no means to rebuild their telomeres with cell division and will eventually senesce.

Geron has also discovered that telomerase plays a role in cancer. The company has shown that for most cancerous tumors to attain life-threatening size or for cancer to metastasize throughout the body, cancer cells must become immortal. They have already undergone numerous mutations to become cancerous. Without becoming immortal, however, they would simply divide themselves to death. It turns out that telomerase is abnormally reactivated in most cancers. Telomerase gets turned back on in certain cancer cells, thereby conferring replicative immortality. In other words, the problem with these cancer cells is that *they do not age.*

Geron and its collaborators have shown telomerase to be present in all of the more than 20 cancers that it has studied, including breast, prostate, lung, colon and bladder cancer. Further, it has been demonstrated in the laboratory that if telomerase is blocked in cancer cells, telomeres resume the process of becoming shorter with each new cell division, leading to the death of the cancer cell. The company is actively searching for chemical compounds that can be turned into drugs that will inhibit telomerase in human cancer cells. It is difficult to imagine a more promising molecular target for fighting cancer, given that telomerase is detectable in all cancers and appears to be necessary for cancer cells but not for most normal cells. That is, telomerase inhibition could be a universal and safe cancer treatment.

On January 16, 1998, Geron and its collaborators at the University of Texas Southwestern published in *Science* what is arguably the most significant advance to date in our understanding of the mechanisms that regulate aging at the cellular level (Bodnar et al., 1998). These scientists demonstrated that putting telomerase back into normally dividing skin and eye cells allowed these cells to maintain their telomere length and to divide indefinitely. Further, the addition of telomerase did nothing to otherwise alter these cells. In effect, telomerase put aging on hold in these cells, just as it does in reproductive cells. The promise of this finding is that if telomerase can be added back to or turned on in cells in the body, we can postpone the onset of various debilitating age-related conditions like skin wrinkling and macular degeneration. Considerable effort is still required to realize the full potential of this advance, but it is an excellent example of how biotechnology, through molecular engineering, holds promise for postponing and effectively treating the diseases associated with aging.

Geron is certainly not alone in its pursuit of treatments that will increase our health span. Alteon, Inc. is attempting to block and tear down the build-up of glucose with its advanced glycostatin end product technology. This technology appears to have applications in diabetes, atherosclerosis and Alzheimer's disease, in which complications result from the formation of abnormal glucose–protein complexes. Alteon is already in late-stage clinical trials with one drug.

Such companies as Aeiveos Sciences Group LLC, MRx Biosciences, Inc., Jouvence Pharmaceuticals, Inc. and LifeSpan BioSciences, Inc. are also searching for genes that contribute to or control aging and even longevity. Their search often starts in lesser organisms, such as yeast or fruit flies, where genes can more readily be manipulated and tested for their role in aging (UBS, 1996). The findings can then be extrapolated to humans. Others are looking at premature aging syndromes like progeria and Werner's syndrome. The former affects children, the latter young adults. Both result in an early and dramatic onset of various age-related diseases that cause premature death. Identifying the genes responsible for these diseases may also provide clues and targets for effective molecular engineering to combat the destructive effects of normal aging.

We cannot close this brief look at how biotechnology is attempting to detect, postpone and treat age-related diseases without recognizing that biologic questions are not the only ones that must be answered. Many important social, ethical, legal and financial issues face us in this biologic revolution. As valuable as knowing how we work is, it is not an end that justifies every means. We must constantly be mindful of this. It is an end, however, that can and will be achieved.

In closing, we are on the threshold, thanks to the promise of biotechnology, of dramatically extending healthy aging. It has taken considerable time to get here, largely because human biology at the cellular level is very complex. Now that we are here, society should reject the notion that diseases associated with aging are inevitable. They are not, and society should demand greater progress in demonstrating this. The social and economic return to society of accelerated progress in eliminating age-related diseases warrants making it our leading health care priority. In fact, the National Institute on Aging should be the NIH Institute with the greatest level of funding. How can we, given the increasing incidence of age-related disease in our growing aging population, demand anything less?

REFERENCES

Biotechnology Industry Organization. (1996). *Industry update.* Washington, DC.

Bodnar, A., et al. (1998, January 16). Extension of life-span by introduction of telomerase into normal human cells. *Science, 279,* 349–352.

Ernst & Young. (1996, 1997). *Annual reports on the biotechnology industry.* San Francisco, CA.

Pharmaceutical Researchers and Manufacturers Association (PhRMA). (1997*). New medicines in development for older Americans.* PhRMA Survey. Washington, DC.

Rowe, J.W. (1997, October 17). The New Gerontology [Editorial]. *Science, 278,* 367.

UBS Global Research (1996, January 26). *Biotechnology in Europe.* Zurich, Switzerland.

PART TWO

Gerontologizing the Practice of Health Care

CHAPTER 8

The Future of Geriatrics: A Call to Action

Robert N. Butler

Theories of aging are determinant, stochastic or a combination. All have made an appearance at one time or another on the stages of history whenever there was reflection on aging and longevity. But how many of our contemporary students have even an inkling of this extraordinary terrain—the fascinating topics of aging and longevity? Biology textbooks in our secondary schools and even in our colleges and medical schools present little on these subjects to intrigue or even inform the student.

Medical students may only dimly recognize that the three great antecedents of all diseases are (1) genes ("bad" genes); (2) the environment, broadly defined to include the quality of our air and water, as well as what we eat and what we do, and (3) aging. The Gompertzian curve holds that after 30 years of age, the force of mortality increases exponentially every 7 years. Yet we have devoted little conceptual, procedural or financial energy to the understanding of the biology of aging. More specifically, we have overlooked the increasing vulnerability to disease and dysfunction that comes with the processes of aging.

Indeed, at the moment, the National Institute on Aging's (NIA) grant holdings are unbalanced. Perhaps no more than $50 million, if that, is devoted to the study of anything close to the basic biology of aging. Nearly 40–45% of the holdings are devoted to Alzheimer's disease. Many people studying Alzheimer's disease have little understanding of gerontology. As important as the disabilities of age are, especially the dementias, it was never the intention of the NIA to become the National Institute on Alzheimer's Disease. This author supports every nickel that is being spent on Alzheimer's disease and would, indeed, encourage more. Notwithstanding, there is an unhealthy imbalance within the Institute. That balance must be rectified by

113

a broader and larger amount of absolute funds devoted to academic geriatrics, basic biogerontology and the relevant social and behavioral sciences.

No one can possibly escape the fact that we have experienced a revolution in longevity in this century, with nearly 28 years of added life expectancy in the United States—perhaps 20% of it from the base age of 65 and above. This is an extraordinary human accomplishment that is not a function of biologic evolution but of social evolution. That being the case, it is amazing that we have spent so little in the way of resources on the development of academic gerontology and geriatrics in American medicine.

How can we be so passive, given the fact that there are increasing demands being placed on geriatrics? This is due to the rising number of older persons, especially the frail, the old and elderly women; the extraordinary epidemiologic relationship between aging and disease; spectacularly rising health care costs; and, finally, the negative attitudes often held about older people and aging in general, due to our personal fears about growing old.

We have yet another reason to promote the development of gerontology and geriatrics—the very fact that in this century there has been at least some increase in our understanding of aging. The great Eli Metchnikoff introduced the word *gerontology* in 1906, and the American physician Ignatz Nascher introduced the term *geriatrics* in 1909. In the 1940s, American gerontology was recognized and institutionalized by the creation of the Gerontological Society of America and the American Geriatrics Society. Pressure mounted for the development of the NIA, which was founded in 1975.

Despite the enormous growth in our knowledge of gerontology and geriatrics, however, interest in geriatrics in the United States has been slow to develop. Unlike medical schools in the United States, the medical schools of Great Britain all have a department of geriatrics. The Scandinavian countries have medical schools with departments of geriatrics, and Japan is following suit. The author was instrumental in the creation in 1982 of the first Department of Geriatrics and Adult Development in the United States. Why do we have only two departments of geriatrics in the entire country? Why don't we have more? Are these embarrassing questions? Are the answers peculiarly American, functions of our obsessive preoccupation with youth? Are the answers due to the opposition of traditional medicine, especially academic internal medicine, which, undoubtedly, fears the further splintering of its field?

The author's views have been that America should *not* create a new practice specialty of geriatrics, but that it should develop an academic and consultative specialty that would integrate and mainstream geriatrics *within* primary-and specialty-care medicine, not just internal medicine. Geriatricians must also be made medical directors of nursing homes and must be available at continuing care retirement communities and naturally occurring retirement communities.

Divisions of geriatrics could be present in any number of different primary care or specialty departments, not just in departments of medicine. Moreover, geriatrics requires a superordinate position to give it influence on all primary care and specialty education and to bring together a variety of disciplines.

As a supraspecialty, geriatrics must go beyond classic internal medicine and classic psychiatry and must work closely with other health fields, such as social work, nursing, physical therapy and clinical pharmacy, in providing clinical services and education.

How can this happen today if geriatrics is buried within another department or specialty—however well-intentioned psychiatry, internal medicine, neurology and some other departments may be? It must be recognized, of course, that there are outstanding divisions of geriatrics in departments of medicine in perhaps 15 schools and that there are important units of geriatric psychiatry within departments of psychiatry. This author does not oppose divisions of geriatrics within psychiatry, medicine, neurology and surgery, but rather favors them.

However, every medical school must have a strong and powerful geriatrics component that is separate, standing on its own and, therefore, central to the organization of the school. Geriatrics should be seen as a *perspective* concerned with a stage of life that calls for an interdisciplinary approach and interspecialty collaboration. Geriatrics must transcend any one primary care or specialty group (comparisons have been made to pediatrics).

The United States has a shortage of primary care physicians. Seventy percent of physicians in the United States are specialists, and only 30% are primary care doctors, compared to the 50:50% ratio in most industrialized nations. There are outstanding general internists and family physicians who do practice primary care medicine, and some have learned and applied some of the principles of geriatrics. However, academic internal medicine has become very fragmented and in general, is devoted to organ-specific diseases. It is not as attentive to the complex, multicausal conditions found in older patients.

In contrast, let us examine Mount Sinai Hospital's Geriatric department's outpatient services as an example of what knowledge and skills are needed. These are geared to patients with an average age of 80+, who have multiple, complex interacting acute and chronic, as well as psychosocial and physical pathologies. Half of patients have psychiatric disabilities of one sort or another. Perhaps nearly as many have neurologic signs and symptoms, and a substantial number require rehabilitative support. The entire medical faculty is composed of board-certified internists with certificates of competence in geriatrics. Because the goals of geriatrics are comprehensive assessment and individualized care and treatment with a view to maintaining or restoring *function*, an interdisciplinary (team) model is used in the clinical services, collaborating extensively with nursing, social work and psychology. There is also access on a consultative basis to specialists such as psychiatrists, cardiologists, orthopedists, gyne-cologists, psychiatrists, physical therapists, neuropsychologists, and phar-macists. A neurologist and psychiatrist have joint appointments.

So what are the obstacles to the development of academic geriatrics in America? The list is simple enough. First, there is the disease of academic stasis, somewhat endemic and difficult to prevent or treat. Second, there is a shortage of model programs and teachers, even though there are perhaps 20 significant medical and psychiatric geriatrics programs at various of the 126 medical schools in the United States, compared to virtually none in 1975. Third, geriatrics is not a high-paying procedural specialty. The Physician Payment Review Commission (of which the author was a member) has not yet succeeded in altering the balance of payment to physicians so that reimbursement for the primary care physician's work in evaluation and management is augmented while payments to procedural and surgical specialists are reduced. These days, of course, this must be done in a budget-neutral manner.

Finally, there has not been the kind of general federal support for geriatrics that there was for cardiology (as an example) through the National Heart Institute (NHI). During the NHI's first 22 years of exist-ence, it trained some 16,000 cardiologists. Had that not happened, one wonders whether the field of academic cardiology would be as strong as it is today. Would this country have had the dramatic reductions in deaths from heart disease and stroke that have been seen over the last two decades? Unfortunately, there is no comparable development in academic geriatrics.

How can medical education be changed and a framework in which academic geriatrics and gerontology can become a respected and important part of academic medicine in the United States be developed? Money is an important, indeed, crucial factor. This author has testified before several Senate committees and called for a *federal geriatrics initiative*, with an eye toward a true effort to mobilize Medicare's Graduate Medical Education funding and the Department of Veterans Affairs funding to further support the development of medical school education by strengthening our postgraduate programs. To do this means, in part, redirecting the power base from the hospital director, who controls residency funds, to committees that would at least include the dean of the medical school, as well as the hospital director, representatives of long-term care (nursing home and home care program affiliates) and, where appropriate, a representative administrator from Veterans Affairs. The latter is emphasized because the majority of medical schools have affiliations with the Department of Veterans Affairs hospitals. It is time for the NIA and the Department of Veterans Affairs to be given major responsibility and funding so that they may contribute to the building of academic geriatrics.

The private sector should also contribute its share, as it has in other fields, by establishing endowed chairs, departments and divisions. Here, the goal is to ensure that every student graduates from medical school with a decent introduction to gerontology and, of course, team-based functional diagnosis and clinical care.

The private sector, foundations and individuals, can contribute on a proactive basis, a policy that the author has tried to implement at the Mount Sinai School of Medicine. Some foundations, such as the Brookdale, Commonwealth Fund, Hartford and Dana, have shown outstanding leadership in supporting geriatrics. With the assistance of the Alliance for Aging Research, the Commonwealth Fund is working to develop a physician-scientist program in aging. Philanthropists are generally older people and, thus, are more aware of the problems associated with aging in their own families. If they are given a sense that something positive can be done, philanthropists will contribute to special endowments for research fellowships, research laboratories and young faculty development, as well as funding for clinical services and endowed chairs, departments and divisions. A national campaign is in order.

The American Board of Internal Medicine, the American Academy of Family Practice and the American Board of Neurology and Psychiatry now offer examinations for certificates of competence in geriatrics. However, care must be taken in counting the numbers of geriatricians in the United States. The 7,000 physicians who have passed examinations to obtain a certificate of competence in geriatrics do not constitute either a subspecialty group or a cadre of academic geriatricians. Most gained their opportunity to take the examinations under the grandparent clause and, therefore, were not required to take a 2-year fellowship in geriatrics.

Although it is required now that medical residencies provide a rotation in geriatrics in teaching hospitals, this does not mean that every medical intern and resident actually goes through such a rotation. This situation should be rectified. Another problem with residency or postgraduate education is the failure of programs to provide a longitudinal experience for medical interns and residents so that they may better appreciate the nature of unfolding medical and social conditions of patients. In addition, there is the failure to provide experience at a wide variety of sites, including long-term care institutions, home care programs and hospices, so that the medical intern and resident can appreciate the spectrum or continuum of care required as needs change over time. Moreover, medical schools must be moved beyond their limited hospital base. The twenty-first century demands the creation of multisite medical schools, as well as multisite residency training programs.

It is clear that this country is now at a point in the cycle of development in gerontology and geriatrics where the gerontologic knowledge already existing could be made even more profound and remarkable. This is a point where the biologic cycle is propelling the baby boomers, who now constitute one third of the entire population, toward old age. The clock is running. The integration of the content of geriatrics in all primary care specialties is essential so that all students in the medical, nursing and allied health professions can be properly prepared to care for a growing older population. This must also include continuing education to update all providers.

The power base of medicine must shift from preoccupation with organ-specific and procedure-specific medicine—the importance of which, nonetheless, should not be denied—toward a new balance of power shared with primary care, health promotion, disease prevention and rehabilitative medicine. The energy that is centered in the dean's office and the offices of medicine and surgery chairs must be influenced by both the public and the private sector, which should also play a large part in raising endowment and operational funding for programs.

Consumers—older people and their families—are beginning to speak up, insisting on better integrated and more gerontologically oriented care. It is hoped that the baby boomers will get the message and also help lead the charge, for otherwise they are a generation at risk when they grow old.

A federal geriatrics initiative joined by private efforts of individual philanthropists, foundations and corporations (in general) must begin with the development of an outstanding cadre of academic and consultative geriatricians as its first of many goals. In addition, general internal medicine and family practice should take leadership in the primary care of older patients. Rehabilitation medicine, psychiatry and neurology should also play major roles in providing the best of care. Indeed, to effectively respond to the needs of older people, all primary care and specialty Medicare providers must be prepared. Academic medicine, in general, must exert imaginative and proactive leadership. Academic medicine should be challenged to become the engine to advance geriatrics in this country.

CHAPTER 9

The Past, Present and Future of Gerontologic Nursing

May L. Wykle and Patricia E. McDonald

Time present and time past are both perhaps in time future, and time future contained in time past.

—T.S. Eliot (1936)

In the Hebrew Bible (*Deuteronomy* 31:2) Moses stated, "I am an hundred and twenty years old this day: I can no more go out and come in." Although Moses was 120 years old when he died, "his eye was not dim, nor his natural force abated" (*Deuteronomy* 34:7). The latter passage portrays a gentleman who still had strength and keen vision when he died, yet the former passage implies that the same individual no longer felt able to maintain mobility and was vulnerable in his community.

The Bible has more to say about old age. Psalm 90:10 indicates that 70 years of age is more or less promised if we lead healthy lives, but vitality may be compromised, at best, as people become more defenseless in the face of aging. Finally, *Ecclesiastes* 12:3 speaks about elders in terms of their physical frailties, suggesting trembling, bowed souls with few teeth and dimmed vision.

Though a spiritual focus on old age is ancient, the scientific focus on aging and quality of life is a relatively new phenomenon driven, perhaps, by the fact that so many people are now living to be old. The British physician, Howell (1976), argued that "although geriatrics has only recently been acknowledged as a special branch of medicine, human interest in old age is eternal." The first attempt at a statistical approach to longevity was made by Barnard Van Oven in 1853 (Howell, 1976), who provided a series of tables showing the names of 1,500 men and women who had attained ages from 100 to 110; 331 between 110 and 129, and 47 who were said to have exceeded even that age.

After 35 years in medical practice, Van Oven was convinced that a vast number of those who attained a very old age passed through life remarkably free from disease; many were never ill, never took medicine, retained the powers of body and mind until the latest period and seemed to sink suddenly into death without passing through any period of "decay and decrepitude." Hope for today and tomorrow's elders springs eternal as attempts to prolong the "good life" prevail. Rowe and Kahn (1998) contend that losses in physical function are not an inevitable part of advancing age. These researchers cite the MacArthur Foundation Study, which demonstrates how lifestyle choices made while young, perhaps more than heredity, determine health and vitality in old age.

Centenarians, those people who live to be 100 years old or more, are becoming commonplace in today's world, with the expectation of 100,000 by the beginning of the twenty-first century. The graying of America is a phenomenon of the twentieth century that is without precedent. By the year 2030, one of every four Americans will be 60 years of age or older. Life expectancy has increased dramatically since 1900, reaching a high of 75.7 years; and people who reach the age of 65 can expect to live well into their eighties (Department of Health and Human Services, 1991).

IMPORTANCE OF GERONTOLOGIC NURSING

The older population has not only increased in size, but it has also aged. Americans are living longer lives due to advances in medical technology and the provision of better health care, social care and long-term care for older adults. As people get older, they often need continuous care, particularly with the onset of chronic disease and disability. In addition, as age advances, problems caused by chronic illness increase, and elders' perceptions of their health decrease (Van Nostrand, 1992). It is not unusual for a person over age 65 to have three to five chronic illnesses. The aging of the older population has important nursing implications. These include the need for extended care among the growing number of frail members of society, as well as care provided to impaired older adults living in the community. It is estimated that 46% of all registered nurses will be providing direct care to elderly people at the turn of the century (Buckwalter et al., 1997).

The development of gerontologic nursing parallels the increase in longevity. Nursing was the first professional group to develop standards of gerontologic care and the first to provide a certification mechanism to ensure specific professional expertise through credentialing (Ebersole & Hess, 1998). Nursing has also been credited largely for the rapid advance of gerontology as a profession over the past 25 years. Nurses have been on the front lines of elder care, providing hands-on care, supervision, administration, program development, teaching and research.

The core goal of gerontologic nursing is to touch older persons in ways that minimize impending threats to their ability to live as independently as possible for as long as they can; to assist elders in selecting options for their preferred type and site of care; to help them to live in comfort and with dignity, and to achieve a peaceful death.

Nursing homes, once viewed as the primary setting for the provision of long-term care, are now believed to be just one place on a continuum of long-term care service options in the community (Dunkle & Kart, 1997). A number of options, including board and care homes, respite care, foster care, home care, hospice, protective services and adult day care, are synonymous with long-term care. Though an estimated 1.7 million elders are currently in nursing homes (Dunkle & Kart, 1997), most old people do not end up in nursing homes. Only a reported 5% of elders are institutionalized at any one time. Yet we all want to receive quality nursing care, should we ever need to enter a nursing home.

A body of research has developed that suggests that informal family caregivers may prevent or delay institutionalization of frail and vulnerable older adults living in the community. Estimates have further indicated that 10% of frail elders who live at home are as functionally impaired as those in institutions. It is believed that the needs of this group are best met with a proper balance between formal and informal supports, including the services of gerontologic home health nurses (Dunkle & Kart, 1997).

Gerontologic nurses are adept in handling the chronic illnesses associated with age, particularly heart disease, cancer and cerebrovascular disease or strokes, the three diseases that cause the greatest proportion of mortality and loss of function among elders (Kart, 1997). Hypertension, arthritis, diabetes, visual and hearing impairment and Alzheimer's disease are also prevalent among older adults. Older people frequently report having several of these chronic conditions. Differences in the number of reported illnesses exist by gender, family income, race and place of residence. In general, those reporting the highest number of chronic illnesses are females, those with incomes below $15,000, nonwhites and rural residents.

Health promotion, which should be an integral part of nursing, holds promise for improving the health of people as they age. Those who remain active and exercise, eat nutritious meals and have a positive psychological outlook on life are likely to experience better health. Moreover, older people often show significantly improved physical performance with practice (Rowe & Kahn, 1998). Even in late life, modifying certain risk behaviors into healthy ones can improve health and reduce the likelihood of disability (Department of Health and Human Services, 1991).

Ebersole and Hess (1988) argue that aging is inextricably tied to history and culture. Thus, views of aging are varied as humankind experiences changes in the anticipated life span. Today, scientists believe that, biologically, we can expect to reach the age of 120 or even 130. Certainly, expected longevity changed dramatically between the beginning of the twentieth century and its end. As the demographics on aging are becoming more remarkable, the world searches for strategies to ensure the well-being of aging people. Gerontologic nursing has an important role to play in both finding and implementing solutions.

THE HISTORY OF GERONTOLOGIC NURSING

Florence Nightingale (1980) has been characterized as the "original geriatric nurse" because she dared to accept a position as superintendent in an institution comparable to today's nursing home. Nightingale, credited with being the founder of modern-day nursing, cared for residents who were primarily governesses and ladies' maids from wealthy English families, in what was known as the Institution for the Care of Sick Gentlewomen in Distressed Circumstances. During that time, family members were solely responsible for their elders, and nursing for gentlewomen, such as the kind Nightingale provided, was unheard of.

In England, Marjory Warren, a physician, accepted responsibility for the care of old people housed in dingy, overcrowded, dark wards. Within 12 years, she changed the scene into one of bright, cheerful and amply furnished wards filled with a flurry of activity for patients. This concept of reenablement and rehabilitation had never before been applied to people who were old and ailing. Doreen Norton (1988), a British gerontologic nurse, has remarked that this move must rank as one of the great revolutions in medical history.

The first article on *nursing* old age and disease was published in 1904 in the *American Journal of Nursing* (Buckwalter et al. 1997). Nurses began to recognize that nursing care specific to older adults was needed. These nurses were concerned that the old-age homes and poor houses needed nursing services for their residents (Ebersole & Hess, 1998), and these homes were forerunners of today's long-term care institutions. As far back as 1925, the *American Journal of Nursing* considered geriatric nursing as a possible specialty in nursing, stating that older patients require a different kind of care. The first geriatric textbook for nurses, however, was not published until 25 years later. Some 12 years later, in 1966, the American Nurses Association (ANA) created a division of gerontologic nursing. Standards of practice for gerontologic nursing were established 4 years later by the ANA and revised in 1973.

There were several pioneer nurses who advocated for certification in geriatric nursing practice, a demand that was eventually adopted by the ANA. The first issue of the *Journal of Gerontological Nursing* was published in 1975. For the first time, gerontologic nursing had its own specialty journal, thus opening the way for nurse practitioners and researchers to disseminate and share knowledge about the care of elders. The 1970s witnessed exponential growth in the number of books and journals in the area of gerontologic nursing, and the first gerontologic nursing academic track was funded in 1975 by the division of nursing at the University of Kansas School of Nursing. The early 1970s was a period of growth in gerontologic nursing programs at the masters level as well, and in 1979 the ANA Council on Long-Term Care Nurses was established.

During the early 1980s, much more emphasis was placed on the psychologic health of older adults. Spearheading this development was Mary Harper of the National Institute of Mental Health. The first geropsychiatric specialty at the master's level was established at Case Western Reserve University's School of Nursing in 1983. Another milestone in reaffirming the importance of gerontologic nursing was the establishment in Cleveland in 1983 of the first endowed chair in gerontologic nursing anywhere in the world.

Also during the 1980s, gerontologic nurses developed an organized voice. In 1984, the National Gerontological Nurses Association was established to provide gerontologic nurses with influence in policy making and to disseminate research as well as practice innovations. In the early 1990s, the ANA redefined long-term care to include a life span approach that was potentially more useful for planning continuums of care.

According to Ebersole and Hess (1998), the foundation of gerontologic nursing as we know it today was largely built by a small cadre of nurses who understood the special needs and necessary care of persons who are aging. Many of the advances in the basic care needs of elders have been fostered by gerontologic nurse researchers.

THE SHORTAGE OF GERONTOLOGIC NURSING EDUCATION

Although geriatric courses are being added to nursing curricula, many schools of nursing do not offer a specialty in aging. When they do, the lack of consideration for the diversity of the aging population has prevented adequate curriculum development. Yet, many of the needs of the aged and the special nature of their care require the most devoted and most sophisticated nurses.

Unfortunately, even today, gerontologic nursing courses are not required in all basic schools of nursing, yet it is recognized by many disciplines as a specialty. There is still a need for gerontologic nurse practitioners and clinical nurse specialists, particularly as the number of elderly people continues to grow. Because almost half of the patients in acute care and a high number in home- and community-based health settings are over the age of 65, nursing must step up and equip all of its students with the skills and knowledge derived from an evidence-based practice of providing quality care for elders.

Fueled by the National Institutes of Health and with help from the National Institute on Aging and the Administration on Aging, research in geriatrics has increased dramatically during the last three decades. At the same time, the National Center for Nursing Research, later changed to the National Institute for Nursing Research, has added status to and recognition of nurses as health care researchers. Current research is directed toward studies of the aging population in institutions and in the community, and from the perspectives of women's and minority aging and family caregiving. Nevertheless, there is a great need for increased funding for research in gerontology nursing.

Another reason for the shortage of gerontologic nurses is that the specialties of geriatrics and gerontology have lacked prestige and have been seen by prospective nurses and physicians as unrewarding areas in which to work. Some even regard it as drudgery. Thus, gerontologic nursing has not attracted large numbers of candidates from the potential pool of health care professionals. One commonly shared myth is that some of the least prepared, unskilled registered nurses work in nursing home settings because they are unable to manage in larger medical centers. In fact, because health care for the elderly population requires long-term management of chronic multisystem diseases that are strongly affected by psychologic, social and economic factors, advanced preparation and certification in gerontologic specialties is not only recommended, but imperative.

Society lags far behind in the development of a positive attitude toward the health care and treatment of elders. So, too, the nursing profession must gain a healthier appreciation for this very important yet frequently neglected area of health care in primary and community-based care, in managed care, in hospitals and nursing home settings and in academic practice. Nurses in gerontology should seek to encourage their colleagues, effectively generating enthusiasm in sharing new developments in nursing and inspiring new leaders, new models and new pathways based on innovative research findings that enlighten clinical practice. Only then will advances in the science of gerontology and gerontologic nursing be made available that can be supported by societal, political and health care strategies.

Whereas attitudes toward gerontology may be changing, many nurses still maintain a negative stereotype about the care of elders in community-based and institutional settings, where the greatest challenge remains that of assisting frail elders to reach maximum levels of productive functioning. The numerous needs of older adults and the special nature of their care require the most devoted and competent nurses. Qualified gerontologic nurses are at a premium at all levels of education, particularly at the baccalaureate, master's and doctoral levels of preparation. Advanced practice nurses form the backbone of care for elders in community-based and institutional settings.

One way to increase awareness of geriatric nursing as a subject needing special study is to implement educational models like those done 21 years ago by Fiedler et al. (1977). Preclinical medical and pharmacology students participated in a geriatric medical education program by working in a nursing home. The student-run health services clinic at the 110-bed facility succeeded in leading the student participants beyond their initial preoccupation with "physical complaints"—from "the smell of urine" to "the lack of trained staff"—to a genuine interest and regard for the psychologic, social and economic issues experienced by the nursing home residents and their effects on health. Students felt challenged by the variety and complexity of health problems in the nursing home geriatric population. Moreover, they noted that the isolation and loneliness of elders were as important as their diseases. Although suffering from severe medical problems, seemingly insignificant aspects of life were highly appreciated by the nursing home residents, and opportunities for increased socialization (getting new glasses or receiving foot care, for example) were frequently reported to most positively affect their lives. Based on this model, nursing programs could place beginning students in nursing homes or other extended care facilities, enabling them to gain clinical experience.

Expanded interdisciplinary initiatives can also be promoted in educational models such as the Robert Wood Johnson Teaching Nursing Home Project to improve the care to older institutionalized adults as well as those in other gerontologic settings. For example, students often have visions of less-than-optimal care from uninterested and uncaring institutional staff. As in the study by Fiedler et al. (1997), these medical students became conscious of the value of nurses' insights about nursing home residents based on daily, long-term observations in comparison with their own somewhat naive appraisals after brief encounters, gaining newfound respect for the role of nursing. Likewise, the student participants were encouraged to assume greater responsibility for care in future contacts with residents, and more in-depth comprehensive services were provided. Models of geriatric nursing education hold great promise for students in improving attitudes toward aging, as they learn that appropriate care for elders with such complex needs requires a coordinated effort by many health and social service providers.

GERONTOLOGIC NURSING TODAY

The current scope and practice of gerontologic nursing is expanding. A gerontologic nurse may function in the role of a generalist or a specialist. The generalist draws upon the expertise of the specialist in assessment; in identifying nursing diagnoses, and in planning, implementing and evaluating care to older adults in a variety of traditional settings—acute care hospitals, home health services, community-based care such as assisted living, and care in the nursing home. Graduate nursing programs must also prepare nurses to be credentialed as geriatric nurse practitioners, geropsychiatric specialists, gerontologic nurse clinical specialists, geriatric case managers for acute and long-term care settings, nurse administrators in acute and long-term care, and as gerontologic faculty (Ebersole & Hess, 1998).

Some of the issues being addressed today by geriatric nurses are nursing's unique perspective and subsequent role in patient-care situations, nursing's unique focus in conducting geriatric research, and the factors that differentiate nursing students who have completed excellent, well-designed rotations in geriatrics from those who have not. In addition, undergraduate programs contain an inadequate amount of studies in gerontology (Whall, 1996). Of even more concern is the fact that there are no national gerontologic nursing curriculum standards, resulting in high variability in course content from program to program. Another issue is the fact that the proportion of content dedicated to elder care on state board examinations is inadequate, in view of the numbers of elders that nurses will be dealing with in the next century. Whall (1996) contends that the development of content recommendations regarding elder care in nursing is relatively new. She has further noted that gerontologic nursing curricula at all levels of nursing throughout the United States vary tremendously, and for the most part they do not meet the National League for Nursing's standards. This organization has put forward 19 recommendations, including rationale and required action for research, education and practice in gerontologic nursing.

FUTURE DIRECTIONS IN GERONTOLOGIC NURSING

In the spirit of expanded interdisciplinary initiatives in gerontologic nursing, geriatric nurses should continuously seek to identify effective and compassionate models of practice that are competitive in the health care marketplace. For example, marketing advance-practice nursing skills to potential partners and employers has been an area of expansion in the care of older adults. There is a need for models that provide adequate staffing as well as evidence-based practice. Many nursing models seem to substantially improve health care delivery to older persons, and some reflect innovative approaches for integrating nationally agreed-upon "best practices" into nursing education, practice, research and public education (Mezey & Fulmer, 1997). Other models address the need to ease the transition of patients as they move between hospital, home and nursing home. Still other models replicate geriatric care that has been proven successful in other countries.

To attract nurses to the field of gerontologic nursing, the most gratifying aspects of care should be emphasized. There are untapped opportunities for clinical experiences with the young-, middle- and oldest-old in the community (Wykle & Musil, 1995). Further, the community may have a variety of organizations, such as "senior citizen" organizations and "golden age" centers, where students can observe and interact with well elders. Development of these settings as viable clinical sites is most likely to occur when the needs of families in the community drive the clinical services provided. Well-elder clinics in housing and shopping centers could be used as clinical sites for more advanced students. The development of ethnic sites in which culturally sensitive geriatric nursing care can be delivered to diverse populations is particularly critical.

One way to extend the base of academic clinical support is to allow master's and doctoral students to supervise beginning students working in agencies. An educational model that has been used in medical education for a number of years would be appropriate in nursing education as well. The idea is that new students shadow older students, providing a "learning-by-watching" model, but also affording early mentorship experiences for older students. In addition, qualified directors of nursing in nursing homes could serve as mentors of gerontologic nursing students to expand the geriatric faculty base (Wykle & Musil, 1995).

There is an expanded body of research on innovative ways to provide nursing care to older adults that improves health, promotes productive aging and maintains high quality of life. Nurses may test new concepts and approaches to the difficult care needs of older people, as well as models that offer promise in improving access and coordination of services. Nurse-run primary care clinics or well elder care clinics will become commonplace in the future, providing counseling and health education for elders and their family members. Nursing opportunities to disseminate information to elders via the Internet will be readily available. Also, home care agencies for elder care and outreach nurses will flourish in the coming century's marketplace. In the decades to come, the growth of the aging population, coupled with longer life expectancy, will increase the demand for long-term care services. Competent nurses will be prepared to address the transition and flow of elderly patients between health care settings, with a focus on patient function, comfort, dignity and cultural competence.

Over the past three decades, the cost of medical care has risen faster than prices in general, with nursing home costs being no exception. In 1993, health care expenditures in the United States approached $1 trillion, with an estimated 33% of this amount spent on elder care (Abrams, Beers, & Berkow, 1995). At present, 11% of the older adults are now 85 years old and over, and these individuals may require institutionalization or may have other complex care needs. The financial implications of providing care for the rapidly increasing elderly population is cause for concern within both political and professional ranks, particularly among geriatric physicians and gerontologic nurses, but Abrams, Beers and Berkow (1995) believe that data from geriatrics-oriented research on the delivery and organization of health services are encouraging. These data include favorable cost-benefit analyses of preventive care in older persons and biomedical developments promising improved diagnosis and treatment.

Major reforms in the financing and organization of health services, such as managed care, are occurring and will continue to occur in this country, and they undoubtedly affect the role of gerontologic nurses. We face substantial redesign of Medicare, imminent cutbacks in Medicaid, continued expansion of managed care, unregulated acceleration of community-based care and a reimbursement environment that focuses on costs at the expense of quality. Mezey and Fulmer (1997) hold that government and industry leaders are already feeling the backlash from changes in health care that older consumers perceive to be precipitous, insensitive, unfeeling and not in their best interests.

We believe that the role of gerontologic nursing in the restructured health care system of the twenty-first century should be a dominant one, with nurses providing primary health care and support for informal caregivers (Wykle, 1996). The geriatric nurse will be instrumental in keeping the nation healthy as it ages and will be heavily engaged in an educative and preventive mode.

The leadership role of the gerontologic nurse will be as the "hub in the wheel," managing and coordinating all providers instrumental in promoting the health of older adults. The nurse will be a major patient advocate for optimal quality of life and care for all elderly people. These nurses will become experts in providing culturally competent care and will be sensitive and responsive to the needs of a growing number of elders. In order to accomplish this expanded role, gerontologic nurses should be heavily involved in decision making and in formulating effective health care policy. Nurses can shape and restructure the health care system as well as gerontologic nursing practice. The twenty-first century gerontologic nurse truly will participate in collaborative, interactive and interdisciplinary models of care.

It is believed that the nursing home of the future will be community-oriented and without walls. Gerontologic nurses will become autonomous contractors of nursing services for a caseload of clients with chronic illnesses. They also will be community-based and assigned to catchment areas. Gerontologic nurses in the twenty-first century ideally will manage nursing clinics but will still function in acute care settings, managing the critical illness of elders.

REFERENCES

Abrams, W.B., Beers, M.H., & Berkow, R. (Eds.). (1995). *The Merck manual of geriatrics* (2nd ed.). Rahway, NJ: Merck & Co.

Buckwalter, K., Ebersole, P., Fulmer, T.T., McDowell, J.B., Whall, A.L., & Wykle, M.L. (1997). Nursing. In S.M. Klein (Ed.), *A national agenda for geriatric education* (1–26). New York: Springer Publishing Co.

Department of Health and Human Services. *Healthy People 2000: National health promotion and disease prevention objectives.* (1991). DHHS Publication No. (PHS) 91–50213. Washington, DC: U.S. Public Health Service.

Dunkle, R.E., & Kart, C.S. (1997). Long-term care. In C.S. Kart (Ed.), *The realities of aging: An introduction to gerontology* (5th ed., pp. 437–464). Boston: Allyn & Bacon.

Ebersole, P., & Hess, P. (1998). *Toward healthy aging: Human needs and nursing response* (5th ed.). St. Louis, MO: Mosby.

Eliot, T.S. (1936). *Historical items: Collected poems* (p. 213). New York: Harcourt Brace & Company.

Fiedler, K., Kaufman, A., Johnston, T., Benevidez, G., Greenberg, J., Szalay, E., & Clements, M. (1997). Undergraduate medical education in geriatrics: Nursing home experience. *J Fam Pract, 4,* 869–871.

Howell, T.H. (1976). Aspects of the history of geriatric medicine. *Proc Roy Soc Med, 69,* 445–449.

Kart, C.S. (1997). *The realities of aging: An introduction to gerontology* (5th ed.). Boston: Allyn & Bacon.

Mezey, M., & Fulmer, T. (1997). The John A. Hartford Foundation Institute for Geriatric Nursing. New York: New York University, School of Education, Division of Nursing. [Brochure].

Mikulencak, M. (1993, July/August). The 'graying of America': Changing what nurses need to know. *Am Nurse*, 1.

Musil, C.M., & Wykle, M.L. (1995). Psychiatric mental health content for gerontological nursing education. In T.T. Fulmer & M. Matzo (Eds.), *Strengthening geriatric nursing education* (pp. 85–98). New York: Springer Publishing Co.

Nightingale, F. (1980). Historical items. *Oklahoma Nurse*, 6.

Norton, D. (1988, April). Wartime and the beginnings of geriatric nursing. *Geriatr Nurse Home Care*, 26–28.

Rowe, J.W., & Kahn, R.L. (1998). *Successful aging.* New York: Pantheon Books/Schocken Books.

Smith, J. (1752). *The Pourtrait of old age* (3rd ed.). London.

Van Nostrand, J. (1992). Health data on older Americans: United States, 1992. *Reviews of New Reports.* Centers for Disease Control and Prevention/National Center for Health Statistics (PHS) 93–1411.

Whall, A. (1996). Gerontological nursing in the 21st century: Is there a future? In E.A. Swanson & T. Tripp-Reimer (Eds.), *Advances in gerontological nursing: Issues for the 21st century.* New York: Springer Publishing Co.

Wykle, M.L. (1996, April). *Nursing leadership in the 21st century.* A report of ARISTA II Healthy People: Leaders in Partnership. Indianapolis, IN: International Center for Nursing Scholarship (under the auspices of the Sigma Theta Tau International Leadership Institute).

Wykle, M.L., & Musil C.M. (1995). Expanding clinical experiences. In T.T. Fulmer & M. Matzo (Eds.), *Strengthening geriatric nursing education* (pp. 37–47). New York: Springer Publishing Co.

CHAPTER 10

The Geriatric Evaluation and Treatment Unit:

A Model Site for Acute Care of Frail Elderly Patients, Education and Research

Howard M. Fillit and Myron Miller

Geriatric inpatient units have been an integral component of geriatric care for more than 50 years (Matthews, 1984). A growing number of geographically based hospital inpatient geriatric units are emphasizing different aspects of geriatric care, including acute care, geriatric assessment, geriatric rehabilitation and geriatric psychiatry (Epstein et al., 1987). The Mount Sinai Medical Center Geriatric Evaluation and Treatment Unit is an example of an acute-care geriatric inpatient unit that represents a structured approach to the complex, interdisciplinary problems of hospitalized frail elderly patients whose health care needs often extend beyond the treatment of a single acute medical illness. Because many of the patients have multiple chronic illnesses, the goal of geriatric care is often the restoration and maintenance of function essential to the preservation of a reasonable quality of life.

The traditional medical ward may not have the expertise or resources to provide comprehensive and efficient care for such frail elderly patients with multiple complex interdisciplinary needs. For this reason, there is growing recognition of the need for geriatric inpatient units in hospitals throughout the United States (Matthews, 1984).

Let us consider two 90-year-old women. One is essentially healthy, living with her spouse at home. During the flu season, she becomes

Source: Reprinted with permission from H. Fillit and M. Miller, The Geriatric Evaluation and Treatment Unit: A Model Site for Acute Care of Frail Elderly Patients, Education, and Research, *The Mount Sinai Journal of Medicine*, Vol. 60, No. 6, pp. 475–481, © 1993.

superinfected with pneumonia and is admitted to a traditional hospital bed. She is given the standard 14 days of antibiotic therapy and goes home. She does well on a traditional medical ward.

The other 90-year-old woman lives in a fourth-floor apartment in a building without elevators. She has become deconditioned, has fallen in her apartment several times and has developed a fear of falling. She has mild cognitive impairment of unknown etiology. She rarely ventures outside and has not been to the doctor in 6 months, despite her long history of multiple chronic illnesses. When this patient becomes ill with the flu and pneumonia, she also develops delirium.

On her admission to a hospital, several additional health care problems are noted that may affect her outcome, including hypertension, diabetes, congestive heart failure, malnutrition, dehydration, urinary incontinence of recent onset and a stage-I pressure sore. As a result of the agitation secondary to delirium and the history of falls, she has orders for physical restraints. The patient, already incontinent of urine, now develops functional fecal incontinence. In the face of the restraints, she becomes more agitated, climbs out of bed and fractures her hip. The stage-I pressure sore soon becomes a stage-IV pressure sore, complicated by osteomyelitis and requiring 6 weeks of intravenous antibiotics. Her malnutrition contributes to impaired wound healing and causes a secondary immunodeficiency, which predisposes her to sepsis secondary to her osteomyelitis. A vitamin B-12 deficiency goes undiagnosed, yet may contribute to her progressive cognitive impairment.

Even if she does recover from her acute illness, she may be sent home without maximal comprehensive nursing, medical and social services, only to return to the emergency room in a few weeks with more severe malnutrition and a worsening pressure sore or a fall. Her hospital length of stay is prolonged by the complications she suffers, as well as the complex discharge planning that she needs.

UNIT OPERATION AND STAFF

The unit is modeled as a hospital specialty unit, much like the cardiac care unit or the stroke unit. The demographics of unit patients encompass frail elders who have complex medical and nursing problems, and functional and psychosocial impairment. Although a majority of patients are currently admitted via the emergency room or the geriatric clinic, an increasing number are admitted specifically for geriatric assessment and acute geriatric care from the other units of the hospital and private practitioners. These referrals are greatly encouraged, as the unit is a service for the benefit of all frail elderly medical patients at Mount Sinai Hospital. Although the unit team necessarily functions in the traditional "service" model (the unit attending physician being the attending physician during the patient's stay), the input of each patient's primary care physician is actively sought and appreciated, and patients discharged from the unit are always returned to their primary care physician with a report from the unit to ensure continuity of care after discharge. Only about 10% of unit cases come from, or are discharged to, nursing homes.

Although the unit is not a high-technology unit, it does provide intensive, interdisciplinary acute care to medically complex patients. Medical care is supervised by attending physicians who are board-certified in internal medicine with added qualifications in geriatric medicine. In addition to addressing the traditional medical problems that result in the acute hospital admission, the geriatricians provide geriatric specialty care, including, for example, evaluation for reversible causes of falls or urinary incontinence; investigation of the etiology of cognitive impairment; management of decubitus from a medical perspective; or recognition and treatment of malnutrition. The geriatrics fellow is responsible for the conduct of comprehensive geriatric assessment during the hospital stay. Medical house staff members are responsible for traditional primary medical care.

Consultants play an important role in the unit. Because about 50% of our frail elderly patients have a psychiatric co-morbidity—most commonly dementia, depression/or delirium—a liaison psychiatrist with board certification in geriatric psychiatry is an integral unit team member. The impact of psychiatric co-morbidities on medical care is manifest by such events as patient refusal to cooperate with radiologic tests, drug noncompliance and falls. The comorbidities of dementia and delirium result in an approximate doubling of hospital length of stay (Fulop, Strain, Vita, Lyons, & Hammer, 1987; Torian, Davidson, Sell, Fulop, & Fillit, 1992). Thus, the presence of the geriatric psychiatrist not only improves quality of care, but may ensure efficient care and reduce length of stay. Other specialists, including a geriatrics neurologist, geriatrics physiatrist and a nutritionist, also participate on the unit team.

The unit is staffed by nurses with special training in geriatric nursing. The unit has one of the highest nursing-to-patient ratios in the hospital because the average patient carries a high score on the scoring system employed throughout the hospital to determine nursing staffing on individual units (Torian et al., 1992). In fact, the unit nursing care acuity is almost equal to that in the cardiac care unit.

Social care is critically important in the unit (Fillit et al., 1992). Most hospitalized frail elderly have significant psychosocial problems that have an important effect on health care outcomes. The unit social worker has special training in geriatric social work. In contrast to the social worker on the traditional medical ward, the geriatrics unit social worker functions following a "screening" rather than "consultation" model, so every patient is seen by the social worker within 24 hours of admission to ensure effective social counseling and efficient discharge planning from day one of admission. Because family members are often essential to the posthospitalization care of the frail elderly person, as caregivers or as case managers, the unit holds frequent family conferences. House-staff are asked to participate in these family conferences and are often enlightened to discover the great efforts families often make to meet their frail elderly family members' health care needs. These conferences also assist in improving quality of care and reducing length of stay by facilitating discharge planning.

THE PROCESS OF GERIATRIC ASSESSMENT IN THE UNIT

Comprehensive and efficient acute geriatric care is provided through the process of geriatric assessment combined with traditional medical care. Comprehensive geriatric assessment is a method of geriatric care that employs the team approach to the evaluation and management of the hospitalized frail elderly patient with complex interdisciplinary health care needs and is accomplished through the use of an organized, efficient set of "instruments" to ensure that the assessment process is structured and quantitative and does not prolong hospital length of stay.

There are four essential components of comprehensive geriatric assessment: Physical health, functional health, mental health and social health. Assessment of a geriatric patient's physical health typically includes taking a geriatric medicine history, a physical examination and such laboratory tests as gait/falls/mobility and incontinence assessments. Assessing functional health involves the patient's ability to perform the activities of daily living—feeding themselves, taking baths and so on—as well as the instrumental activities of daily living, which include such areas as money management and transportation.

A comprehensive geriatric assessment will also address an elderly patient's mental health, including a cognitive assessment to determine whether dementia or deliriums are present and an effect assessment to determine whether such mental disorders as depression are involved. Lastly, the comprehensive assessment will examine the patient's social health: economic condition, the presence or absence of caregivers and their ability to give care, whether or not the patient has a health care proxy and whether or not the patient has done needed estate planning.

Geriatric assessment in the unit is conducted by the unit fellow and is facilitated and organized by the *Handbook for Geriatric Assessment* (Fillit, 1998). The admission comprehensive geriatric assessment is completed within 48 hours of admission and summarized by the fellow in a "Geriatric Assessment" admission note in the patient's medical record. The results of the assessment process are discussed with house staff, students and other team members.

Frail elderly patients may benefit from admission to the unit for inpatient comprehensive geriatric assessment when an outpatient assessment would require numerous clinic or office visits over the course of several weeks or months, during which time the patient might progressively deteriorate as a result of unresolved problems and be at great risk for further morbidity or even mortality. Thus, an important concept regarding admissions for "geriatric assessment" under Medicare is that of multiple diagnoses in frail elderly patients for whom the diagnostic sum is greater than its parts. That is, whereas no single diagnosis alone might justify the admission of an individual patient, a multitude of diagnoses might equal an "acute" admission because the sum of the complex problems results in a geometric increase in morbidity. Although obvious risks are associated with hospitalization, these might be outweighed by the benefits of a relatively quick and comprehensive evaluation of complex problems.

Medicare does not provide a diagnosis-related group (DRG) for geriatric assessment. Therefore, the performance of geriatric assessment for Medicare beneficiaries must be an efficient and comprehensive process that does not prolong hospital length of stay. Although these patients clearly require hospital admission to the unit for geriatric assessment, they may not have traditional diagnoses normally employed by internists for acute care under Medicare. However, many DRGs of the Medicare Prospective Payment system can be employed for admitting these frail patients. In addition to the usual acute-care diagnoses, a number of DRG diagnoses are applicable, such as change in mental status, Alzheimer's disease or senile dementia, dementia, urinary incontinence, sleep disorders, cachexia, malnutrition, or weight loss. Diagnosis alone is not the sole criterion for approval of admission. The most important aspect of a successful Medicare admission for "geriatric assessment" is the documentation in the admitting note of the medical record, which clearly explains the acuity of the patient's illness, particularly from an expert geriatric medicine perspective.

IS THE UNIT COST EFFECTIVE?

Several research studies have demonstrated that geriatric assessment units provide high-quality comprehensive geriatric care while saving the health care system money (Rubenstein, Stuck, Siu, & Weiland, 1991). With proper targeting, geriatric assessment units clearly have the capacity to improve a variety of hospital outcomes, including reduction in mortality for patients when followed for up to 1 year. Much of the cost savings have come from a reduction in nursing home utilization during the year after admission to the geriatric unit.

However, the Mount Sinai unit is a mixed-use acute-care geriatric unit that functions to meet the needs of our local hospital health system. As with other special care units such as those for stroke or cardiac care, the actual cost-effectiveness of this geriatrics unit has not been demonstrated. However, data on length of stay are available. In 1987, the average length of stay was approximately 28 days. Subsequent studies (Fillit et al., 1992) revealed the important contribution of hospital "social stays" to total length of stay in the unit. These studies demonstrated that a minority of frail elderly with prolonged hospital lengths of stay that included up to 70% alternate-level-of-care days ("social care") markedly prolonged total length of stay on the unit. By 1989, the average length of stay reduced to approximately 16 days and now averages about 15 days. Major reductions in hospital length of stay were achieved through focused team efforts at discharge planning, including intensive social work intervention (Fillit et al., 1992). These data are consistent with other hospital reports of length of stay for frail elderly patients in this age group (average age 83 years) who commonly have psychiatric co-morbidity and social problems (Safran & Eastwood, 1990). The decrease in length of stay achieved by the reduction in alternate-level-of-care stays and other mechanisms was estimated to save over $3 million per year in hospital costs. Thus, our hypothesis is that acute geriatric care in the unit provides a win-win situation: improvement in quality of care accompanied by a reduction in hospital length of stay, compared with an equivalent "control" group of hospitalized frail elderly patients given acute care on traditional medical wards.

EDUCATION AND CLINICAL RESEARCH IN THE UNIT

The unit serves as the primary site for training in geriatrics for the house staff from the Department of Medicine. In this model, house staff members play an integral role in the provision of primary acute care while learning the principles of geriatric medicine through the supervision and assistance of fellows and faculty of the Department of Geriatrics. The education of medical students is also an important function of the unit. A geriatrics rotation is required of all medical students attending the Mount Sinai School of Medicine. Approximately 20% of students receive their clinical training on the unit. In addition to significant didactic training, medical students learn to perform complete geriatric assessments on aged patients under the direct supervision of the unit geriatrics fellow. The unit has been demonstrated to be a successful site for education in geriatrics, both improving clinical skills and increasing knowledge (Fields, Jutagir, Adelman, Tideiksaar, & Olson, 1992).

There are three components to the body of knowledge in geriatric medicine taught in the unit: (1) how normal development (aging) affects the practice of geriatric medicine; (2) the altered presentation of disease in geriatric patients; and (3) specific diseases and syndromes particularly prevalent in old age. Although the effects of aging on organ function begin, in general, around the age of 30 or 40 years, they usually do not become clinically significant until the age of about 75 or 80 years. This knowledge becomes critically important in the provision of acute care to patients over the age of 75 years.

Geriatric medicine encompasses diseases (such as Alzheimer's disease) and syndromes (such as falls) that occur almost exclusively in old age and are rare in traditional "middle age" medicine. These geriatric syndromes often have multifactorial, sometimes reversible causes. Falls provide a good illustration (Tideiksaar, 1990). Falling is connected with a high mortality rate in the elderly population. Approximately 20% of people over the age of 80 years who fall and break a hip are dead within 1 year. In a young population, the most common cause of falling might be syncope.

However, the most common cause of falling in old age is simple deconditioning.

Teaching on the unit is provided by geriatrics fellows and attending physicians on a daily basis through bedside rounds and through formal talks and conferences. Specialists in geriatric psychiatry, neurology and physiatry also make weekly specialty teaching rounds. A syllabus with articles on geriatric medicine from the *New England Journal of Medicine*, the *Annals of Internal Medicine, the Journal of the American Geriatrics Society* and other geriatric medicine subspecialty journals, as well as traditional textbooks on geriatric medicine (Brocklehurst, Tallis, & Fillit, 1992), expose house staff members to the literature of geriatric medicine and help prepare them for the questions on geriatric medicine in the American Board of Internal Medicine Certification Examination.

The unit has been successfully employed as a site for clinical research in acute geriatric care. Research on length of stay in frail elderly patients has demonstrated the significance of alternate-level-of-care or "social care" stays in prolonging total hospital length of stay of these patients and has demonstrated the critical importance of intense social work intervention to prevent lengthy social stays (Fillit et al., 1992).

Studies of the impact of dementia on ethical decisions have demonstrated that the majority of acutely ill frail elderly medical patients and their families opted for resuscitation rather than forgo life-sustaining technologies, but that for the demented elderly patients, families tended to choose "do not resuscitate" orders more frequently for their demented family member than the patients themselves might (Torian, Davidson, & Fillit, 1992).

Studies of the impact of dementia on acute medical care in the frail elderly population have demonstrated the interesting finding that, whereas the most common cause of admission to hospital for frail elderly patients without dementia was, as expected, cardiovascular disease, the most common cause of admission to hospital for medically ill demented patients was infectious disease (Torian et al., 1992). These studies also demonstrated the impact of dementia on hospital length of stay and costs, and the gross underreporting of dementia as a DRG diagnosis in medically ill patients. Other studies have compared the utility of two assessment instruments in the evaluation of cognitive impairment in acutely ill, hospitalized frail elderly patients (Fields et al., 1992).

Studies of malnutrition and immunologic function in the hospitalized frail elderly patients have shown that more than 40% of patients admitted to the unit were malnourished, that the sensitivity of detection of malnutrition in these patients could be increased by employing anthropometry and that the rate of immunodeficiency in the unit population was high—43% of patients demonstrating lymphopenia and impaired delayed skin test hypersensitivity (Lansey, Waslien, Mulvihill, & Fillit, 1993). These data emphasize that malnutrition is the most common (though often unrecognized) cause of acquired immunodeficiency in the elderly population (Fillit, 1991).

The two oldest known patients with acquired immune deficiency syndrome (AIDS) induced by human immunodeficiency virus (HIV) have been reported. In one case, a 92-year-old man suffered an HIV infection from a transfusion at the age of 87 years (Fillit, Fruchtman, Sell, & Rosen, 1989). The other case was an 89-year-old woman with HIV-AIDS secondary to heterosexual transmission (Rosenzweig & Fillit, 1992). These two cases emphasize the occult nature of HIV-AIDS in elderly patients with typical geriatric syndromes of dementia and cachexia.

CONCLUSION

Geographically based inpatient geriatric units are an increasingly common organizational approach throughout the world for the care of hospitalized frail elderly patients with complex, multidisciplinary acute care needs. The unit provides comprehensive, efficient quality care to these patients by bringing together, in a geographically based unit, specialists from a multiplicity of disciplines to provide needed services in a coordinated manner. To accomplish its goals, the unit employs experts in geriatric medicine, nursing, social work, psychiatry and other disciplines in a team approach to comprehensive assessment. The education of medical students, medical house staff and geriatrics fellows is a critical function of the unit. The unit also serves as a site for research in improving the care of hospitalized frail elderly patients.

REFERENCES

Brocklehurst, J.C., Tallis, R.C., & Fillit, HM. (1992). *Textbook of geriatric medicine and gerontology* (4th ed.). London: Churchill Livingstone.

Epstein, A.M., Hall, J.A., Besdine, R., Cumella, E. Jr., Feldatein, M., McNeil, J., & Rowe, J.W. (1987). The emergence of geriatric assessment units: The "new technology of geriatrics." *Ann Int Med, 106,* 299–303.

Fields, S.D., Fulop, G., Sacks, C., Strain, J., & Fillit, H.M. (1992). A comparison of two instruments for screening for cognitive impairment. *Int Psychogeriatry, 4*, 93–102.

Fields, S.D., Jutagir, R., Adelman, R.D., Tideiksaar, R., & Olson, E. (1992). Geriatric education. Part I: Efficacy of a mandatory clinical rotation for fourth year medical students. *J Am Geriatr Soc, 40*, 964–969.

Fillit, H., Fruchtman, S., Sell, L., & Rosen, N. (1989). AIDS in the elderly. *Geriatrics, 44*, 65–70.

Fillit, H. (1998). *Handbook for geriatric assessment*. Available on request.

Fillit, H.M., Howe, J., Fulop, G., Sachs, C., Siegal, P., Sell, L., Miller, M., & Butler, R.N. (1992). Studies of hospital social stays in the frail elderly and their relationship to the intensity of social work intervention. *Soc Work Health Care, 18*, 1–22.

Fillit, H.M. (1991). Reversible acquired immune deficiency in the elderly: A review. *Age, 14*, 83–89.

Fulop, G., Strain, J.J., Vita, J., Lyons, J.S., & Hammer, J.S. (1987). Impact of psychiatric co-morbidity on length of hospital stay for medical/surgical patients: A preliminary report. *Am J Psych, 144*(7), 878–882.

Lansey, S., Waslien, C., Mulvihill, M., & Fillit, H. (1993). The role of anthropometric assessment for malnutrition in the hospitalized frail elderly. *Gerontology 39*, 346–353.

Matthews, D.A. (1984). Dr. Marjory Warren and the origin of British geriatrics. *J Am Geriatr Soc, 32*, 253–258.

Rosenzweig, R., & Fillit, H. (1992). Probable heterosexual transmission of AIDS in an aged woman. *J Am Geriatr Soc, 40*, 1261–1264.

Rubenstein, L.Z., Josephson, K.R., Weiland, G.D., English, P.A., Sayre, J.A., & Kane, R.L. (1984). Effectiveness of a geriatric evaluation unit: A randomized clinical trial. *N Engl J Med, 311*, 1664–1670.

Rubenstein, L.Z., Stuck, A.E., Siu, A.L., & Weiland, D. (1991). Impacts of geriatric evaluation and management programs on defined outcomes: Overview of the evidence. *J Am Geriatr Soc, 39*, 8s–16s.

Safran, D.G., & Eastwood, E.A. (1990). *Transitional care: The problem of alternate level of care in New York City*. New York: United Hospital Fund of New York.

Tideiksaar, R. (1990). Falls and gait disorders. In W.E. Abrams, R. Berkow (Eds.), *The Merck manual of geriatrics*. West Point, PA: Merck Sharp and Dohme Research Laboratories, 52–68.

Torian, L.V., Davidson, E.J., & Fillit, H.M. (1992). Decisions for and against resuscitation in an acute geriatric medicine unit servicing the frail elderly. *Arch Int Med, 152*.

Torian, L.V., Davidson, E.J., Sell, L., Fulop, G., Fillit, H. (1992). The effect of senile dementia on acute medical care in a geriatric medicine unit. *Psychogeriatry, 4*, 231–239.

CHAPTER 11

Creativity and Healthy Aging

Gene D. Cohen

When an adult is described as having various problems with health, work, or social interaction, one often hears the question, How old is he? However, when an adult does something unusual from a creative vantage point, inquiries about age seldom occur. Herein lies the kernel of an important message for aging research, practice and policy: Creativity in later life is underrecognized, underreported and underutilized. There is no denying the magnitude of disease and disability associated with aging. Something that is considerably overlooked—if not denied—is the opportunity and frequency of creative growth and expression among older adults. To the extent that the nature, prevalence, and capacity for creativity in later life are misunderstood or ignored, research, services and policies addressing the needs and potential contributions of current and future older adults will suffer.

In the mid-1970s, developments in gerontology and geriatrics led to the delineation of late-life changes that reflected illness rather than "normal" aging, that is, the inevitable concomitants of aging per se. Thus, unless a negative change in an older person is perceived as a problem—as opposed to an unavoidable decrement associated with growing old—the opportunity and responsibility to intervene are overlooked. Modern geriatrics, however, has begun to demonstrate strongly the benefits of preventive strategies among older people, and a growing array of clinical interventions along the continuum of primary, secondary and tertiary prevention is becoming available and widely accepted within all aspects of health care.

Just as it is important to differentiate changes associated with aging from those caused by illness in later life, it is important to recognize that change

Source: G.D. Cohen, The Aging Brain and Creativity, *The Brain in Human Aging*, pp. 184–199, © 1988, Springer Publishing Company, Inc., New York 10012, used by permission.

can occur in two directions—positive as well as negative—independent of age. Unless this ongoing potential for positive, even creative, growth with advancing years is appreciated, important opportunities for maintaining independence and developing new strategies to cope with loss will be overlooked. The costs will be high in both emotional and fiscal terms, and the enormous potential that older persons hold will be poorly tapped as a national resource.

Developing new skills adds to one's ability to adapt with aging, thereby promoting the maintenance of independent functioning. Recognizing the capacity to learn new strategies in the face of loss expands rehabilitation potential for older adults and focuses intervention not only on treating problems, but also on fostering new strengths; this practice would greatly enhance the possibility of restoring function and well-being. At a societal level, the role of older persons as a resource has historically been apparent in the wide spectrum of their contributions, ranging from the sharing of wisdom (e.g., on the Supreme Court) to volunteerism, to helping with the family (be it with finances or babysitting). The better health, higher level of education, and larger number of individuals with ample assets among today's older population as compared to earlier elderly cohorts speaks to the greater collective role that those aged 65 and older can play in contemporary society.

Examples of creativity in later life abound. Though it is easier to illustrate this by looking at well-known people, they merely punctuate the point. Picasso remained prolific as a painter until he died in his nineties (from March through October at age 86 he created 347 engravings); Verdi composed his opera *Falstaff* at age 80; Freud wrote the *Ego and the Id* at age 67; Edison was still inventing up to his death in his eighties; Benjamin Franklin achieved heroic stature internationally as a diplomat in his seventies; Eubie Blake, the outstanding talented pianist and composer of ragtime music and show tunes, continued to be in great demand as a performer well into his nineties, giving his last concert one week before his ninety-ninth birthday and receiving the Medal of Freedom earlier that year; Grandma Moses, who lived to 101, turned to painting at the age of 78, when arthritis prevented her from continuing with needlework (by age 79, she had had 15 one-person shows throughout the United States and Europe). The list goes on, as does the variation in the ways creativity is expressed among older adults.

WHAT IS CREATIVITY?

Creativity is not an easy concept to define. Therefore, the nature of what is new or innovative can vary enormously. Not only a new theme, but a variation on that theme can be creative; so, too, can be different approaches to expressing that theme. Not surprisingly, the famous are easier to cite as examples of creative achievement in later life. However, many an act of "ordinary" older individuals could well fit most definitions of creativity. The remarkable adjustments and "new" strategies adopted by so many older widows following the deaths of their spouses support this conclusion.

Many speak of creativity as reflecting a special intelligence. Here, too, we confront complexity, as when Howard Gardner argues that "there is persuasive evidence for the existence of several relatively autonomous human competencies," which he refers to as *human intelligences*. The six intelligences he defines are: linguistic, musical, logical-mathematical, spatial, bodily kinesthetic, and personal. Gardner (1983) goes on to assert that:

> It is appropriate to question whether personal intelligences—
> knowledge of self and others—should be conceived of as being at
> the same level of specificity (and generality) as other intelli-
> gences.
> . . . Perhaps it makes more sense to think of knowledge of self
> and others as being at a higher level, a more integrated form of
> intelligence, one more at the behest of the culture and of histori-
> cal factors, one more truly emergent, one that ultimately comes to
> control and to regulate more "primary orders" of intelligence.

Gardner (1983) also discusses the views of the British psychologist N.K. Humphrey in emphasizing how knowledge of the social world involves creative capacities. Of Humphrey, he asserts:

> He makes the bold claim that the chief creative use of human
> intellect lies not in the traditional areas of art and science but
> rather in holding society together. He points out that social
> primates are required to be calculating beings, to take into
> account the consequences of their own behavior, to calculate the

likely behavior of others . . . all in a context where the relevant evidence is ephemeral, likely to change, even as a consequence of their own actions. Only an organism with highly developed cognitive skills can make do in such a context. The requisite abilities have been worked out over the millennia by human beings and passed on with great care and skill from the elder to the younger individuals.

It is important to note that, in this case, the creative situation of the "elder" is discussed not only in terms of transferring personal knowledge to younger individuals, but from a developmental perspective where, with aging, one might acquire more fully developed personal knowledge.

THE "ULYSSEAN ADULT"

In leading up to his definition of creativity, John A.B. McLeish (1976) discusses the view of Abraham Maslow on creativity. Maslow separated creativity into two types: "special talent creativity" and "self-actualizing creativeness." McLeish elaborates:

> First, "special talent creativity—the creativity of the gifted inventor, scientist, poet, sculptor, architect, novelist and so on; and second, "self-actualizing creativeness," which Maslow defined as owing itself much more to creative changes in the personality and a tendency to do anything creatively—that is *living* creatively.

McLeish then offers his own definition of creativity:

> The process by which a person employs both conscious and unconscious domains of the mind to combine various existing materials into fresh constructions or configurations that, in some degree, cause significant changes in the self-system of the person concerned, or significantly alter the environment surrounding the person.
>
> When, therefore, in our own time we saw a man or woman in the later years who maintains the questing spirit, and who does so with courage and resourcefulness in a wide variety of circum-

stances, many of them terribly, even tragically adverse, such a man or woman may well be seen as Ulyssean. The quest, the courage, and the resourcefulness may be exhibited on a human stage of immense proportions or in total solitariness and obscurity.

As but one example, McLeish then goes on to list 125 noted scientists from all fields who were richly creative in their later years.

A research team led by V. Bullough formed the hypothesis that achievement is related to the ability to survive so that, with greater longevity, people have the opportunity to bring their work to greater fruition and maturity. To test it, Bullough and his colleagues (Bullough, Bullough, & Mauro, 1978) studied intellectual and creative achievers in two historical periods of significant intellectual and creative achievement—eighteenth-century Scotland and fifteenth-century Florence. The fifteenth century was known as the Renaissance and the eighteenth century as the Enlightenment.

The researchers examined the age at death of 375 eminent eighteenth-century Scottish achievers and 158 eminent fifteenth-century Florentine achievers. The significance of the subject's age becomes even more so when we consider that, in eighteenth-century Scotland, the median age of death of those in the general population who survived their first year was around 40; the median age of death among the achievers, however, was over 70, with 21% of the achiever group living to beyond 80. For the fifteenth-century group, there are no census data, but it is known that for those in the general population who survived their twenty-first birthday, death came at around 30. For the achievers studied, the average age of death was 61, with 31% living beyond 70 years of age.

CREATIVITY AND AGING

To expand recognition and understanding of the nature and prevalence of creativity in relation to aging, consider the following four categories (which are not mutually exclusive):

- creativity that continues with aging
- creativity that commences with aging

- creativity that changes with aging
- creativity that occurs in conjunction with loss associated with aging

Creativity That Continues with Aging

Perhaps the most commonly recognized and cited, this category includes the likes of Picasso, Verdi and Shaw. Some may object that these older geniuses are the outliers, that they do not represent the norm. Never mind that creative genius, at any age, is outside the norm. The point is not that everyone over age 65 can and should be a Picasso, but that aging does not preclude either productivity or the display of great creative accomplishment. Moreover, creative capacity after age 65 is considerably more common than the myth-carriers would have one believe. Note, for example, the folk artists discussed in the next section, who often commence their creative works after age 65.

Creativity That Commences with Aging

In 1980, the Corcoran Museum of Art in Washington, DC exhibited the works of black artists identified in a study of 50 years of folk art in the United States. What had not been described about these artists, but struck me on attending the exhibit, was that, of the 20 artists in the show, 16 (80%) were age 65 or older and 30% were aged 80 or older. Moreover, most of these artists had only begun their work or first reached their mature phase after age 65. Bill Taylor, whose work was featured on the cover of the exhibit catalog, had been born a slave. He created his first painting at the age of 85.

Upon further examination of folk art in America, it becomes apparent that, independent of racial or ethnic background, folk art is dominated by older artists. Remember that Grandma Moses started painting at age 78. That an entire field of art should be dominated by older artists argues that these individuals cannot be stereotypically dismissed as outliers or *Ripley's Believe It Or Not* cases. Folk art also provides a bridge for appreciating that marked creative potential in later life resides not just with the Picassos but with a broad range of individuals.

Creativity That Changes with Aging

The writings of Carl Jung and, especially, of Erik Erikson have established the concept that individuals pass through several psychologic stages of development as they age. It should not come as a surprise, then, that creative orientations also evolve over time. Consider the eighteenth-century Scotsman, James Hutton. As a young man, Hutton developed an interest in chemistry, later entered the legal profession, then moved into medicine, where he earned an MD degree. From medicine, Hutton went on to devote himself to agriculture and eventually focused on geology. In this field, in his seventh decade, Hutton (Baily, 1967) made some historic discoveries and developed seminal theories that he set forth in a major two-volume work, *Theory of the Earth*, published in 1795, as he approached his seventieth birthday.

Known as the father of modern geology, Hutton originated one of the most fundamental principles of geology—uniformitarianism—which explains the formation, features, and aging of the earth's surface. The effect of his ideas on the learned world at that time has been compared with earlier revolution in thought brought about when Copernicus and Galileo (whose master works were completed and published when each of them was about 70) proposed that the sun, not the earth, was the center of the solar system.

Creativity That Occurs in Conjunction with Loss Associated with Aging

Ancient Greek mythology tells about the Theban, Tiresias, who suffered the misfortune of viewing the goddess Athena while she was undressing to bathe. In a burst of rage, Athena blinded Tiresias. But Zeus took pity on the mortal and replaced Tiresias' loss of outer vision with great insight and prophetic powers that grew over the years and facilitated long life for the seer. One is reminded of the poet and physician William Carlos Williams, who, following a stroke in his sixties, turned full time to his verse, writing about an "old age that adds as it takes away" (Foy, 1979). Williams was posthumously awarded the Pulitzer Prize in poetry for *Pictures from Brueghel and Other Poems*, which he published at 79.

Leon Edel (Edel, 1979), in studying artists as they age, looked at the rage of William Butler Yeats in the poet's later years. Edel saw Yeats as manifesting a "controlled rage," in part a response to his perceived "loss" of youth, as Edel described:

> When he went to Stockholm to receive the Nobel Prize, Yeats looked at the medal that came to him with Sweden's bounty; it

showed a young man listening to the Muse. Yeats thought, "I was good-looking once like that young man, but my unpracticed verse was full of infirmity, my Muse old as it were; and now I am old and rheumatic, and nothing to look at, but my Muse is young. I am even persuaded that she is like those angels in Swedenborg's vision and moves perpetually 'towards the day-spring of her youth.' Let us remind ourselves that when the angels of Swedenborg kissed, the kiss was a burst of flame."

Returning to the earlier point about widows, the concomitance of loss and creative adaptation can again be observed. Certain well-known widows highlight the phenomenon for those lacking fame but not accomplishment. The image of Eleanor Roosevelt has provided a mirror for many women losing a spouse in their later years.

Again, this capacity has enormous relevance for aging policy, practice, and research. The ability to respond creatively to loss in later life suggests a new avenue for maintaining independence and achieving rehabilitation, one that involves a synergistic linkage between therapeutic practice and the development of new skills that promote adaptation. The application of this concept can be even broader. Awareness of the potential for new creative orientations psychodynamically mobilized in response to disease or disability identifies a new pathway toward maximizing overall functioning and mental health in later life. Tapping into this creativity—be it continuing, commencing, or changing with age (either in or apart from a response to loss)—offers important opportunities for innovative clinical practice, new directions in research, and creative social policies relevant to older adults and the family as a whole.

It is my hope that institutions of learning, psychologists, counselors, and the community at large will recognize and respond to the opportunities offered by our older citizens by putting in place programs and attitudes that nurture their vast and changing creative forces. Through such a shift in perspective, we can hope to more readily associate "creativity" with "aging" in the generations to come.

REFERENCES

Baily, E.B. (1967). *James Hutton: The founder of modern geology*. New York: Elsevier Science.

Bullough, V., Bullough, B., & Mauro, M. (1978). Age and achievement: A dissenting view. *The Gerontologist, 18*(6), 584–587.

Cohen, G.D. (1988). *The brain in human aging.* New York, Springer.

Cohen, G.D. (1993). How old is too old? *The American Journal of Geriatric Psychiatry, 1*(2), 91–93.

Cohen, G.D. (1994). Creativity and aging: Relevance to research, practice, and policy. *The American Journal of Geriatric Psychiatry, 2*(4), 277–281.

Edel, L. (1979). Portrait of the artist as an old man. In D.D. Van Tassel (Ed.), *Aging, death, and the completion of being.* Philadelphia: University of Pennsylvania Press.

Foy, J.L. (1979). *Creative psychiatry.* New York: GEIGY Pharmaceuticals.

Gardner, H. (1983). *Frames of mind.* New York: Basic Books.

McLeish, J.A.B. (1976). *The Ulyssean adult: Creativity in the middle & later years.* New York: McGraw-Hill Ryerson Limited.

CHAPTER 12

New Models of Health Care for Elders at Risk

Chad Boult and James T. Pacala

Most elders are healthy, but a minority have chronic conditions that require frequent, intensive and expensive care. As a result, 5–10% of the older population consistently incurs 60–70% of its annual health care expenses (Freeborn, Pope, Mullooly, & McFarland, 1990; Gornick, McMillan, & Lubitz, 1993; Gruenberg, Tompkins, & Porell, 1989). This dense concentration of morbidity and use of health-related services is unfortunate for those who are affected, but it offers hope for effectively focusing resources where they will do the most good. This chapter describes currently available methods for identifying high-risk elders, those whose chronic conditions place them at risk for developing health-related crises and for needing expensive health care. We then discuss several options for reducing risk, presenting the available data about the outcomes and cost-effectiveness of these approaches. The conclusion makes recommendations for implementing these interventions within today's (and tomorrow's) systems of health care for older persons.

In a capitated environment, organizations bearing financial risk for the health care of older populations have strong incentives to identify high-risk people as promptly as possible and then provide them with special care designed to maintain or improve their health and avert future health-related crises. Such an investment strategy is feasible because most older people do not change health care systems often; disenrollment from Medicare health maintenance organizations (HMOs) averages less than

Source: Reprinted from C. Boult and J.T. Pacala, New Models of Health Care for Seniors at Risk, in *New Ways To Care for Older People*, Calkins et al., eds., © 1998, Springer Publishing Company, Inc., New York, 10012, used by permission.

8% per year (Nelson et al., 1996). If successful, this strategy of identification and intervention would lead to healthier aging, better quality of life, higher levels of satisfaction with care and lower total costs for many high-risk older people. We should recognize, however, that early detection may not be cost effective for all high-risk conditions and that not everyone desires intervention.

Nevertheless, these incentives—coupled with the availability of pooled capitation dollars—are nudging health care organizations to invest in innovative systems of care for high-risk elders. As we look across these innovations, a few common elements emerge: targeting services to those most likely to benefit; developing well-trained interdisciplinary teams of professional caregivers; performing focused, standardized assessments; providing proactive, goal-oriented, protocol-driven care; calling patients by telephone to follow up on recommended regimens and promoting elders' and their families' involvement in their own care. As comprehensive health care systems incorporate these innovations, the available evidence about their cost-effectiveness warrants a hard look.

IDENTIFYING HIGH-RISK ELDERS

The initial challenge is to anticipate which high-risk people would be appropriate recipients of more intensive interventions, i.e., those whose health-related problems are likely to lead to expensive crises that could be ameliorated by special care. Geriatric professionals currently use three complementary approaches to identify these people: periodic screening of the population by mail or telephone, recognition by clinicians, and analysis of administrative data (see Figure 12–1, top). None of these approaches is sufficient as a single method for monitoring risk. Surveys are superficial, incomplete (<100% response rates), and only moderately accurate; only elders with whom astute clinicians have personal contact can be recognized as high-risk; and administrative data reflect primarily the past and are not readily accessible. The ideal monitoring system would integrate data from all three sources.

Many screening tools for estimating older persons' general risk of health crises have been created and used in ambulatory (Brody, Johnson, & Ried, 1997; Coleman et al., 1998; Freedman, Beck, Robertson, Calonge, & Gade, 1996) and hospitalized (Reuben et al., 1992; Sager et al., 1996) populations. The most extensively studied and widely used general screen-

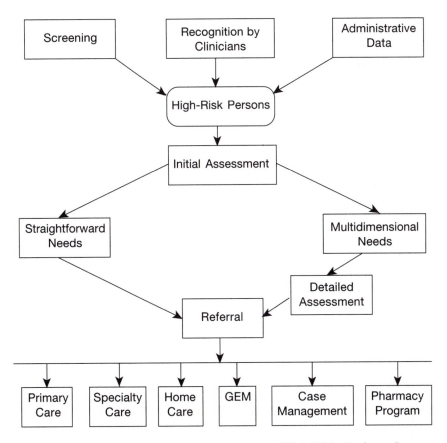

Figure 12–1 Identification and Management of High-Risk Seniors. *Source:* Courtesy of AAHP Foundation.

---

ing instrument consists of eight questions that are asked by mail or by telephone (see list in Appendix 12–A) (Boult et al., 1993). Elders' responses are entered into the formula, which produces an estimate of the probability of repeated admission (P_{ra}) to a hospital in the future. P_{ra} values above a predetermined threshold indicate a high-risk status and a need for further evaluation.

Longitudinal studies have shown that elders' risk status often changes over time; 15–20% of functionally disabled older persons regain their independence within a year. It is important, therefore, to know whether risk scores, which are based on elders' present and past characteristics, predict future events accurately. Prospective testing of the P_{ra} instrument in three diverse populations has confirmed that high-risk elders use twice as many health-related services as low-risk elders during the 1–4 years after they complete the eight questions (see Table 12–1) (Boult et al., 1993; Pacala, Boult, & Boult, 1995; Pacala, Boult, Reed, & Aliberti, 1997). The P_{ra}'s test-retest reliability has also been shown to be high ($r = 0.78$) (Boult, Boult, Pirie, & Pacala, 1994). The extensive testing to which the P_{ra} has been subjected, coupled with its brevity and accompanying high response rates (85–90%), distinguishes it from many similar screening instruments.

Recommended in 1996 by the HMO Workgroup on Care Management to be used as the "primary indicator of risk" for Medicare managed care plans (Aliberti et al., 1996), the P_{ra} instrument has been widely adopted. By June 1998, licenses for its use had been obtained by more than 170 health care organizations in the United States.

The implementation of a risk-monitoring program, even if limited to the use of an eight-item questionnaire, is a multifaceted challenge that should be preceded by careful planning and budgeting. At a minimum, it requires an ongoing system of data collection, entry, management, analysis, and reporting. Organizations that are willing to make necessary investments in hardware, software and personnel may wish to conduct their own screening programs. Others may wish to contract with data management companies that will conduct parts or all of the screening process for them. Resources are also required to design, initiate and sustain risk-monitoring systems that include referral "hot lines" (by which clinicians can identify patients whom they recognize as high risk) and "data scans" (by which administrative databases are scanned electronically (Coleman et al., 1998) to identify elders who have ominous diagnoses, medication profiles, or

Table 12–1 Predictive Accuracy of P_{ra} Screening Instrument

	Low Risk	High Risk	Ratio of Utilization (High/Low)
		Annual Hospital Days	
National Medicare Population	2.6	5.2	2.0
Minnesota Medicare-Medicaid Population	2.4	4.5	1.9
		Annual Costs	
Medicare HMO Population (costs for non-capitated care)	$1,331	$2,756	2.1

Source: C. Boult and J.T. Pacala, New Models of Health Care for Seniors at Risk, in *New Ways to Care for Older People*, Calkins et al., eds., © 1998, Springer Publishing Company, Inc., New York 10012, used by permission.

patterns of using health-related services—emergency rooms, for example—frequently).

On a cautionary note, it should be acknowledged that the widely held belief in the cost-effectiveness of "targeting" (focusing intensive interventions on the high-risk minority of the older population) is supported so far by the results of only a few positive studies in which high-risk elders were selected and treated. Several of these are described in the following sections. The weight of the evidence supports the value of targeting, but as yet insufficient definitive studies have directly compared the outcomes of interventions provided to targeted older populations against untargeted older populations.

ASSESSING HIGH-RISK ELDERS

Following their identification, high-risk elders should next receive some sort of special care if their health careers are to be favorably altered. The next logical step, a brief *initial* assessment, is intended to determine the level of complexity of the identified person's needs. A brief semistructured initial assessment interview can be conducted by a physician, a nurse practitioner, or an experienced gerontologic nurse, either in person or by telephone. One suggested set of interview questions is shown in Appendix 12–B (Aliotta et al., 1997).

As a result of the brief initial assessment interview, some elders will be found to be not at high-risk after all, that is, they are false positives from the risk-identification process, or to have problems that cannot be modified. Others will be found to have straightforward needs that can be met easily. Still others, those with high but potentially modifiable risk, will have complex needs requiring more in-depth evaluation before effective plans of action can be established.

The *full* assessment of this last group is best completed by a team: either interdisciplinary or multidisciplinary. Team members with expertise in the care of older adults (typically, a geriatrician, a nurse and/or a social worker) meet with the person individually to evaluate in greater depth the issues that were identified during the risk-identification and initial assessment processes. This comprehensive geriatric assessment (CGA) is a diagnostic process intended to determine the person's medical, psychosocial, and functional capabilities and limitations in order to develop an overall plan for treatment and long-term follow-up (Rubenstein, Stuck,

Siu, & Wieland, 1991). Brief standardized instruments are frequently used to evaluate functional ability, cognition, affect, intuition, mobility and other major health-related domains (see Appendix 12–C).

In *inter*disciplinary teams, care planning occurs when the team members meet after their individual data-gathering encounters to establish priorities and take responsibility for specific next steps. In *multi*disciplinary teams, each professional prepares an evaluation and a set of recommendations that are then integrated into a plan of care by one of the team members.

Recent work has begun to identify the conditions on which teams might best focus their efforts, i.e., the conditions that often lead to the greatest losses and costs—and for which treatment is the most effective. For example, impairments in vision, hearing, and lower extremity strength and affect have been found to be precursors of falls, incontinence and functional dependency (Tinetti, Inouye, Gill, & Doucette, 1995). Validated instruments are available to detect these and other sentinel conditions such as poor nutrition and cognitive impairment (Solomon, 1988), and evidence-based guidelines are becoming available for effective treatment. To improve further the health care of high-risk elders, initial and comprehensive assessment programs of the future should attempt to set priorities and plan interventions based on the emerging evidence about what is most likely to be most beneficial.

MANAGING HIGH-RISK ELDERS

As systems of health care become more sophisticated, the number and range of interventions available to high-risk elders will grow. Several of the better tested and more promising interventions to which assessment could lead are described on the following pages.

Geriatric Evaluation and Management

CGA is more likely to improve functional status if it is linked to control over patient management (Applegate & Burns, 1996; Burns, 1994). The expanded process is called geriatric evaluation and management (GEM). A meta-analysis of 28 CGA and GEM programs of five types confirmed that effective programs target those elders who are likely to benefit from it and then deliver an intervention that combines assessment with sustained treatment by an interdisciplinary team (Rubenstein, Bernabei, & Wieland, 1994; Stuck, Siu, Wieland, & Rubenstein, 1993).

Though some of the most successful outcomes from GEM have been observed in inpatient settings (Rubenstein et al., 1984), the cost of such interventions is high, encouraging the delivery of GEM in less expensive outpatient settings. Individual controlled trials of outpatient GEM have demonstrated the potential to improve diagnostic accuracy (Silverman et al., 1995; Tulloch & Moore, 1979), functional ability (Williams, Williams, Zimmer, Hall, & Podgorski, 1987; Yeo, Ingram, Skurnick, & Crapo, 1987), and satisfaction with care (Englehardt et al., 1996), to increase use of home services (Rubin, Sizemore, Loftis, Adams-Huet, & Anderson, 1992; Rubin, Sizemore, Loftis, & Loret de Mola, 1993; Williams et al., 1987; Yeo et al., 1987), and to decrease mortality (Toseland et al., 1996), health care costs (Rubin et al., 1992; Tulloch & Moore, 1979; Williams et al., 1987), anxiety (Silverman et al., 1995; Toseland et al., 1996), depression (Burns, Nichols, Graney, & Cloar, 1995; Toseland et al., 1996), stress for caregivers (Silverman et al., 1995), and use of emergency rooms (Engelhardt et al., 1996) and hospital services (Rubin et al., 1992; Tulloch & Moore, 1979; Williams et al., 1987). Unfortunately, the *overall* results of most published studies of outpatient GEM have been inconsistent and disappointing.

The characteristics most common among the GEM programs that have produced positive results are:

- Small, close-knit teams of clinicians who are trained and interested in geriatrics
- The targeting of patients who are neither too healthy nor too sick to benefit
- The use of carefully selected standard assessment instruments
- Treatment for several months according to well-established principles of geriatrics
- Effective communication with patients, families, and primary care physicians.

It appears that only a small percentage (perhaps 20%) of elders initially identified as high-risk have treatable conditions that are so complex that the benefits of sustained team management outweigh the personal and financial costs. The other 80% have needs that are either straightforward, unresponsive to present treatments, or best managed by their own primary care physicians—or they do not wish to accept care from a GEM team.

Case Management

Another intervention, to which referrals of high-risk elders are frequently made, often as a result of a risk-monitoring program and an assessment, is case management (CM). Case managers, whose backgrounds are usually in nursing or social work, arrange social and health-related services and coordinate them across a wide range of settings (Kodner, 1993). Many high-risk elders who are not appropriate recipients of GEM (and most who are) may benefit from CM.

A 1994 survey found that all large Medicare HMOs offer some form of CM that includes many, and often all, of the following processes: case finding, assessing clients' needs, planning their care, implementing plans, and monitoring the care provided (Pacala, Boult, Hepburn, et al., 1995). Most HMOs reported that their CM programs were designed to reduce the use of hospitals, to increase the satisfaction of their enrollees and providers, and to optimize the functional ability of their enrollees. Although many HMO executives reported decreased hospitalization among enrollees who received CM, few provided data to support their claims. Nevertheless, most said they were committed to continuing or expanding their CM programs (Pacala, Boult, Hepburn, et al., 1995).

Program types can be characterized broadly as either low-volume and high-intensity (in which the case managers carry case loads of 60 or fewer clients, see them frequently, and both provide and arrange services for them) or high-volume and low-intensity (in which the case managers arrange services for 100 or more clients, but see them infrequently). Unfortunately, CM programs are extremely heterogeneous, and many are structured loosely. The case managers receive variable amounts of training, the criteria for offering CM to clients may be subjective, and the services provided may not consistently focus on activities that are likely to yield maximal benefit. Some programs emphasize cost containment more than risk reduction.

In a study of older people who were hospitalized with congestive heart failure (CHF), CM proved very useful. Before discharge, the patients received intensive structured education about CHF from a nurse and a dietitian. Their discharge arrangements and postdischarge services, which were arranged and coordinated by a social worker, included home care and telephone follow-up. During the 90 days after discharge, the recipients of CM had 56.2% fewer hospital admissions, slightly lower costs of care, and twice as much improvement in quality-of-life scores as recipients of usual care (Rich et al., 1995).

The benefits of CM would likely be maximized by adherence to the following principles: systematic targeting, clear roles and treatment protocols, proactive follow-up and significant patient self-management. Case managers and their supervisors state that effective case management results from: clear role definitions; a team approach with good communication; formulation of specific, realistic individual plans of care; physicians' cooperation; strong organizational support; and enrollees' and family members' familiarity with and acceptance of CM (Pacala & Boult, 1996).

Interdisciplinary Home Care

A related approach for some high-risk elders is to provide comprehensive services through interdisciplinary home care (IHC), an integrated system for providing medical and supportive care at home. The integration of medical and social aspects of care distinguishes IHC from other forms of home care in which communication between physicians and home care providers is usually limited to the sharing of written notes. IHC attempts to minimize morbidity and mortality and maximize elders' ability to live in the community as long as possible. These services are usually initiated, coordinated, or even partly provided by case managers.

Working in teams with physicians, therapists and aides, home care nurses typically monitor elders' ability to live independently, suggest changes in supportive and therapeutic services, evaluate home safety, educate patients and their families, and reinforce the principles of self-care. Home health aides provide personal care and homemaker services. Occupational and physical therapists provide rehabilitative services as needed. Occasional home visits by physicians, thought not at first glance cost-effective, can often obviate the need for the expensive, labor-intensive, uncomfortable, and sometimes disorienting transportation of frail elders to physicians' offices.

IHC has been evaluated in several controlled clinical trials and, unlike traditional forms of home care (Hedrick & Inui, 1986), has been found to be more effective and efficient than other treatment options (see Table 12–2) (Challis, Darton, Johnson, Stone, & Traske, 1991; Cummings et al., 1990; Melin, Hakansson, & Bygren, 1993; Mitchell, 1978; Zimmer, Groth-Juncker, & McCusker, 1985). Overall, it appears most consistent in reducing rates of hospitalization and satisfying elders' informal caregivers.

Despite these convincing data, the medical and supportive components of home care in the United States are rarely well integrated. Home health services for Medicare beneficiaries are used for long-term supportive care much more than for medical management, and there is a large geographic variation in the use of these services (Welch, Wennberg, & Welch, 1996). For example, five southern states average more than nine home care visits per Medicare enrollee, whereas 14 other states average fewer than three visits per enrollee.

Pharmacy Program

Older persons with chronic conditions are often also at high risk for having adverse effects from taking too many medications, too-high doses, the wrong medications, or medications that interact—or they may simply not take their medications correctly. The involvement of pharmacists in their care has taken several forms. In some programs, pharmacists are members of interdisciplinary assessment teams, or they provide face-to-face consultations when a medication problem has already been noted by others (Hatoum & Akhras, 1993). In other programs, they perform medication audits (chart reviews without seeing patients) and provide information to primary providers about potential drug interactions, side effects, and criteria for dosing. For high-risk elders, personal pharmacist-patient consultations have been reported to be cost-effective methods for reducing medication problems (Borgsdorf, Miano, & Knapp, 1994; Der, Rubenstein, & Choy, 1997). Written suggestions to health care providers have been less successful (Wagner et al., 1994).

THE NEED FOR ENHANCED GERIATRIC SKILLS

In the primary care of older high-risk outpatients, the lack of geriatrics training possessed by many of today's physicians—in practice and in training—continues to obstruct cost-effective care. A long-term solution is

Table 12-2 Studies of Geriatric Home Care

Author	Year	Country	Intervention	Design	Significant Results* Associated with Inter-disciplinary Home Care	Control
Mitchell	1978	U.S.	Home care by interdisciplinary team	Quasi-experimental (n = 318)	Better functional ability; lower rate of hospital admissions (12% vs. 28%)	NH care
Zimmer et al.	1985	U.S.	Home care by interdisciplinary team	RCT** (n = 167)	More home services; higher satisfaction by informal caregivers	Physician care
Cummings et al.	1990	U.S.	Home care by interdisciplinary team	RCT (n = 419)	Higher satisfaction by informal caregivers; lower six-month mean hospital costs ($3,000 vs. $4,246)	Usual care in Veterans Administration
Challis et al.	1991	U.K.	Home care by interdisciplinary team	Quasi-experimental (n = 214)	Better morale and affect	NH care or day hospital
Melin et al.	1993	Sweden	Home care by interdisciplinary team	RCT (n = 183)	Better functional ability; fewer drugs; fewer unre-solved diagnoses; 67% fewer mean nursing home days	Home care by usual caregivers

*p<.05
**Randomized controlled trial

Source: Reprinted from C. Boult and J.T. Pacala, New Models of Health Care for Seniors at Risk, in *New Ways to Care for Older People*, Calkins et al., eds., © 1998, Springer Publishing Company, Inc., New York, 10012, used by permission.

to improve the geriatrics education of medical students and residents. In the near future, primary care could be improved and continuing education of practicing family physicians and general internists could be provided through practice guidelines and quick access to consulting geriatricians by telephone or by two-way video communications (which would allow consultants to interview and "examine" patients from afar). However, the present shortage of geriatricians challenges the dissemination of even this high-efficiency model. Addressing the shortage of geriatric expertise, which is projected to increase in the coming years (Reuben et al., 1992), will be crucial in planning all systems of health care for the high-risk older persons of the future (Health Resources and Services Administration, 1995).

RECOMMENDATIONS

Many organized systems of health care now monitor the risk status of their elder populations and provide high-risk members with some form of case management. Far fewer offer interdisciplinary home care, GEM, or other proactive interventions, partly because of lack of evidence of cost-effectiveness and partly because of shortages of geriatricians and gerontologic nurse practitioners. In the years ahead, the evolution of new systems of care will be influenced by data, vision and market forces. The data available now about outcomes of interventions for high-risk older persons support most strongly the implementation of interdisciplinary home care and structured case management for congestive heart failure. Additional data about the cost-effectiveness of GEM, CM and pharmacy programs will become available in the next few years. New methods for delivering these (and other) forms of care will probably evolve and be even more effective than the best programs of today. Ultimately, mature systems of health care will likely incorporate such "elements of success" into a coordinated array of services for high-risk older persons. The needs of this population may be met most effectively and efficiently by comprehensive delivery systems that offer most (if not all) of the successful elements and programs described above.

Organized systems that invest in special programs for high-risk elders will need to learn to integrate those programs so that high-risk older adults are not overwhelmed and do not fall through the cracks. Care will probably be most cost-effective when it is coordinated and continuous, proactive and comprehensive. Fragmentation of care, the Achilles heel of our present system of care for persons with complex needs, should be avoided. When elders become acutely ill, develop chronic illnesses, or acquire disabilities, the new systems should be able to provide efficient, seamless, appropriate care with a minimum of iatrogenic complications. The cornerstone of such systems will likely be good primary care, in which one provider, collaborating with other professionals and services, oversees all of a person's care. The evolving infrastructure of the new systems should be planned to attain these goals.

Decisions about implementing programs for high-risk elders will also reflect executives' vision of their organizations' mission. Those who equate future success with an ability to enhance health and thereby to contain costs are likely to invest in proactive preventive programs for high-risk (and for low-risk) elders. Those who seek more immediate financial returns are likely to invest more heavily in marketing, utilization management, and programs that reduce the costs of acute illness. Ultimately, market forces will probably determine the future. To the extent that elders and their families, through political and commercial channels, demand high-quality, health-sustaining care, the prevention-oriented organizations will be rewarded for their investments.

Infrastructural Changes

The ability to implement many of the programs designed for high-risk elders will depend on increased access to coordinated teams of clinical specialists (e.g., geriatricians, gerontologic nurse practitioners, social workers, therapists, and other technicians), improved processes for educating primary care physicians about geriatrics, better alignment of incentives, and new integrated clinical information systems.

Many of the interventions described earlier rely on teams of professionals with expertise in geriatrics. The creation of effective interdisciplinary teams requires time, training, communication and revision of many traditional roles. Professionals from different disciplines must learn each other's language, values, background, skills, and work habits. They must learn to respect, appreciate and rely on each other. Attainment of such collaborative relationships will require commitment, resources, explicit training in team development and patience—from our medical education system and from our health care organizations.

Establishing a cadre of skillful primary care physicians will also be a challenge. Many current physicians, nurses and other providers will need new knowledge, skills and attitudes to practice effectively in the systems of the future. Traditional curricular components, such as courses, readings and conferences, should be upgraded and provided while newer, more effective methods such as on-line decision support, evidence-based practice guidelines, telephone consultation with geriatricians and two-way interactive video case conferences are refined. Much greater emphasis on the care of chronically ill older persons is also needed in the curricula of most health professional schools and residency programs (Health Resources and Services Administration, 1995).

Comprehensive, integrated information systems will be required to facilitate many of the processes embedded in these systems of the future: the screening of populations, the monitoring of individuals' risk levels, and the sharing of up-to-date clinical information among providers. Basic clinical information that is accessible on-line to providers at widely dispersed sites of care will be essential to coordinate care effectively.

As systems of care become larger and more complex, it will also become increasingly important to create and maintain incentives that encourage all of the participants to strive toward the goals of the organization. For example, hospitals must be rewarded rather than penalized for supporting successful organizational initiatives to reduce hospital days. Physicians should be allowed sufficient time, training and resources for organizing, planning and coordinating the care of their complex frail older patients—and be rewarded to the extent that their efforts lead to desirable health outcomes and more appropriate use of resources. Realigning incentives in large complex organizations is a long, tedious and often contentious process, but one that will determine the ultimate success of implementing most of the interventions described in the preceding pages. Underlying the success of this realignment process is the need to link—if not merge—several diverse cultures: management, health care, science, and finance. The challenges will be at least as great as the potential rewards.

Nevertheless, better models for identifying and caring for high-risk elders must be developed and implemented soon. Readers of this book do not need to be reminded of the coming demographic wave of "new" elders or of the burdens faced by a financially compromised health care system.

These facts are undisputed. They point us urgently to the revision of current standards and systems and to new and more appropriate ways to help elders achieve healthier aging. The interdisciplinary approaches to assessment and treatment discussed in this chapter offer a starting point toward that goal.

REFERENCES

Aliberti, E., Aliotta, S., Boult, C., et al. (1996). *Identifying high-risk Medicare HMO members: A report from the HMO Workgroup on Care Management.* Washington, DC: Group Health Foundation.

Aliotta, S., Boult, C., Butin, D., et al. (1997). Planning care for high-risk Medicare HMO members. Washington, DC: AAHP Foundation.

Applegate, W., & Burns, R. (1996). Geriatric medicine. *JAMA, 275*(23), 1812–1813.

Borgsdorf, L.R., Miano, J.S., & Knapp, K.K. (1994). Pharmacist-managed medication review in a managed care system. *Am J Hosp Pharm, 51,* 772–777.

Boult, C., Boult, L., Morishita, L., Smith, S.L., & Kane, R.L. (1998). Outpatient geriatric evaluation and management (GEM). *J Am Geriatr Soc, 46*(3), 296–302.

Boult, C., Dowd, B., McCaffrey, D., Boult, L., Hernandez, R., & Krulewitch, H. (1993). Screening elders for risk of hospital admission. *J Am Geriatr Soc, 41,* 811–817.

Boult, L., Boult, C., Pirie, P., & Pacala, J.T. (1994). Test-retest reliability of a questionnaire that identifies elders at risk for hospital admission. *J Am Geriatr Soc, 42,* 707–711.

Brody, K.K., Johnson, R.E., & Ried, L.D. (1997). Evaluation of a self-report screening instrument to predict frailty outcomes in aging populations. *Gerontologist, 37,* 182–191.

Burns, R. (1994). Beyond the black box of comprehensive geriatric assessment. *J Am Geriatr Soc, 42,* 1130.

Burns, R., Nichols, L.O., Graney, M.J., & Cloar, F.T. (1995). Impact of continued geriatric outpatient management on health outcomes of older veterans. *Arch Intern Med, 155,* 1313–1318.

Challis, D., Darton, R., Johnson, L., Stone, M., & Traske, K. (1991). An evaluation of an alternative to long-stay hospital care for frail elderly patients: Its costs and effectiveness. *Age and Aging, 20*(4), 245–254.

Coleman, E.A., Wagner, E.H., Grothaus, L.C., Hecht, J.A., Buchner, D.M., & Savarino, J. (1998). A comparison of models to predicting hospitalization and functional decline in older health plan enrollees: Are administrative data as accurate as self-report? *J Am Geriatr Soc, 46*(4), 419–425.

Cummings, J.E., Hughes, S.L., Weaver, F.M., et al. (1990). Cost-effectiveness of Veterans Administration hospital-based home care: A randomized controlled trial. *Arch Intern Med, 150,* 1274–1280.

Der, E.H., Rubenstein, L.Z., & Choy, G.S. (1997). The benefits of in-home pharmacy evaluation for older persons. *J Am Geriatr Soc, 45,* 211–214.

Engelhardt, J.B., Toseland, R.W., O'Donnell, J.C., Richie, J.T., Jue, D., & Banks, S. (1996). The effectiveness and efficiency of outpatient geriatric evaluation and management. *J Am Geriatr Soc, 44*, 847–856.

Freeborn, D.K., Pope, C.R., Mullooly, J.P., & McFarland, B.H. (1990). Consistently high users of medical care among the elderly. *Med Care, 28*, 527–540.

Freedman, J.D., Beck, A., Robertson, B., Calonge, B.N., & Gade, G. (1996). Using a mailed survey to predict hospital admission among patients older than eighty. *J Am Geriatr Soc, 44*, 689–692.

Gornick, M., McMillan, A., & Lubitz, J. (1993). A longitudinal perspective on patterns of Medicare payments. *Health Aff, 12*, 140–150.

Gruenberg, L., Tompkins, C., & Porell, F. (1989). The health status and utilization patterns of the elderly: Implications for setting Medicare payments to HMOs. *Adv Health Econ Health Serv Res, 10*, 41–73.

Hatoum, H.T., & Akhras, K. (1993). 1993 bibliography: A 32-year literature review of the value and acceptance of ambulatory care provided by pharmacists. *Ann Pharmacother, 27*, 1106–1119.

Health Resources and Services Administration. (1995). A national agenda for geriatric education: White papers. Washington, DC: U.S. Government Printing Office.

Hedrick, S.C., & Inui, T.S. (1986). The effectiveness and cost of home care: An information synthesis. *Health Serv Rev, 20*, 851–880.

Kodner, D.L. (1993). *Case management: Principles, practice and performance*. Brooklyn, NY: Institute for Applied Gerontology.

Melin, A., Hakansson, S., & Bygren, L. (1993). The cost and effectiveness of rehabilitation in the home: A study of Swedish elderly. *Am J Public Health, 83*, 356–362.

Mitchell, J.B. (1978). Patient outcomes in alternative long-term care settings. *Med Care, 16*, 439–452.

Nelson, L., Gold, M., Brown, R., Ciemnecki, A.B., Aizer, A., & Cybulski, K.A. (1996). Access to care in Medicare managed care: Results from a 1996 survey of enrollees and disenrollees. Washington, DC: Physician Payment Review Commission, selected external research series #7.

Pacala, J.T., & Boult, C. (1996). Factors influencing the effectiveness of case management in managed care organizations: A qualitative analysis. *J Care Manage, 2*(3), 29–35.

Pacala, J.T., Boult, C., & Boult, L. (1995). Predictive validity of a questionnaire that identifies elders at risk for hospital admission. *J Am Geriatr Soc, 43*, 374–377.

Pacala, J.T., Boult, C., Hepburn, K., et al. (1995). Case management of older adults in health maintenance organizations. *J Am Geriatr Soc, 43*, 538–542.

Pacala, J.T., Boult, C., Reed, R.L., & Aliberti, E. (1997). Predictive validity of the P_{ra} instrument among older recipients of managed care. *J Am Geriatr Soc, 45*, 614–617.

Reuben, D.B., Wolde-Tsadik, G., Pardamean, B., et al. (1992). The use of targeting criteria in hospitalized HMO patients: Results from the demonstration phase of the hospitalized older persons evaluation (HOPE) study. *J Am Geriatr Soc, 40*, 482–488.

Rich, M.W., Beckham, V., Wittenberg, C., Leven, C.V., Freedland, K.E., & Carney, R.M. (1995). A multidisciplinary intervention to prevent the readmission of elderly patients with congestive heart failure. *N Engl J Med, 333*, 1190–1195.

Rubenstein, L.Z., Bernabei, R., &Wieland, D. (1994). Comprehensive geriatric assessment into the breach. *Aging Clin Exp Res, 6*(1), 1–3.

Rubenstein, L.Z., Josephson, K.R., Wieland, D., English, P.A., Sayre, J.A., & Kane, R.L. (1989). Effectiveness of a geriatric evaluation unit: A randomized controlled trial. *N Engl J Med, 311*, 1664–1670.

Rubenstein, L.Z., Stuck, A.E., Siu, A.L., & Wieland, D. (1991). Impacts of geriatric evaluation and management programs on defined outcomes: Overview of the evidence. *J Am Geriatr Soc, 39S*, 8S–16S.

Rubin, C.D., Sizemore, M.T., Loftis, P.A., Adams-Huet, B., & Anderson, R.J. (1992). The effect of geriatric evaluation and management on Medicare reimbursement in a large public hospital: A randomized clinical trial. *J Am Geriatr Soc, 40*, 989–995.

Rubin, C.D., Sizemore, M.T., Loftis, P.A., & Loret de Mola, N. (1993). A randomized, controlled trial of outpatient geriatric evaluation and management in a large public hospital. *J Am Geriatr Soc, 41*, 1023–1028.

Sager, M.A., Rudberg, M.A., Jalaluddin, M., et al. (1996). Hospital admission risk profile (HARP): Identifying older patients at risk for functional decline following acute medical illness and hospitalization. *J Am Geriatr Soc, 44*(3), 251–257.

Silverman, M., Musa, D., Martin, D.C., Lave, J.R., Adams, J., & Ricci, E.M. (1995). Evaluation of outpatient geriatric assessment: A randomized multi-site trial. *J Am Geriatr Soc, 43*, 733–740.

Solomon, D.H. (1988). Geriatric assessment: Methods for clinical decision-making. *JAMA, 259*, 2450–2452.

Stuck, A.E., Siu, A.L., Wieland, G.D., & Rubenstein, L.Z. (1993). Comprehensive geriatric assessment: A meta-analysis of controlled trials. *Lancet, 342*, 1032–1036.

Tinetti, M.E., Inouye, S.K., Gill, T.M., & Doucette, J.T. (1995). Shared risk factors for falls, incontinence and functional dependence: Unifying the approach to geriatric syndromes. *JAMA, 273*, 1348–1353.

Toseland, R.W., O'Donnell, J.C., Engelhardt, J.B., Hendler, S.A., Richie, J.T., & Jue, D. (1996). Outpatient geriatric evaluation and management: Results of randomized trial. *Med Care, 34*(6), 624–640.

Tulloch, A.J., & Moore, V. (1979). A randomized controlled trial of geriatric screening and surveillance in general practice. *J Coll Gen Pract, 29*, 733–742.

Wagner, E.H., Lacroix, A.Z., Grothaus, L., et al. (1994). Preventing disability and falls in older adults: A population-based randomized trial. *Am J Public Health, 84*(11), 1800–1806.

Welch, H.G., Wennberg, D.E., & Welch, W.P. (1996). The use of Medicare home health services. *N Engl J Med, 335*, 324–329.

Williams, M.E., Williams, T.F., Zimmer, J.G., Hall, W.J., & Podgorski, C.A. (1987). How does the team approach to outpatient geriatric evaluation compare with traditional care: A report of a randomized clinical trial. *J Am Geriatr Soc, 35*, 1071–1078.

Yeo, G., Ingram, L., Skurnick, J., & Crapo, L. (1987). Effects of a geriatric clinic on functional health and well-being of elders. *Gerontol, 42*(3), 252–258.

Zimmer, J.G., Groth-Juncker, A., & McCusker, J. (1985). A randomized controlled trial of a home health care team. *Am J Public Health, 75*, 134–141.

Appendix 12–A*
P$_{ra}$ Screening Questions

1. In general, would you say your health is:
   - ❏ Excellent
   - ❏ Very good
   - ❏ Good
   - ❏ Fair
   - ❏ Poor

2. In the previous 12 months, have you stayed overnight as a patient in a hospital?
   - ❏ Not at all
   - ❏ One time
   - ❏ Two or three times
   - ❏ More than three times

3. In the previous 12 months, how many times did you visit a physician or clinic?
   - ❏ Not at all
   - ❏ One time
   - ❏ Two or three times
   - ❏ Four to six times
   - ❏ More than six times

4. In the previous 12 months, did you have diabetes?
   ❏ Yes   ❏ No

5. Have you ever had

   A. Coronary heart disease?
   ❏ Yes   ❏ No   ❏ Don't know
   B. Angina pectoris?
   ❏ Yes   ❏ No   ❏ Don't know
   C. A myocardial infarction?
   ❏ Yes   ❏ No   ❏ Don't know

*Copyright © Regents of the University of Minnesota. School of Public Health, Center on Aging, Room D351 Mayo (Box 197), 420 Delaware Street, SE, Minneapolis, MN 55455. All rights reserved. Do not copy or reproduce without permission

   D. Any other heart attack?
      ❏ Yes   ❏ No   ❏ Don't know

6. Is there a friend, relative, or neighbor who would take care of you
   for a few days, if necessary?
      ❏ Yes   ❏ No   ❏ Don't know

7. Are you
      ❏ Male   ❏ Female

8. What is your date of birth?

Appendix 12–B
Initial Assessment Interview
Questions and Problem Labels

ASSESSMENT DOMAIN 1: COGNITIVE FUNCTION

Suggested Questions	*Problem Labels*
1. Please spell your whole name.	Cognitive deficit
2. What is your address, including zip code?	
3. What is your date of birth?	
4. How old are you?	

ASSESSMENT DOMAIN 2: DIAGNOSES/MEDICAL CONDITIONS

Suggested Questions	*Problem Labels*
1. Please tell me the names of your health problems.	
2. *For each condition named*: How often do you feel sick because of _____?	High medical risk
3. *For each condition named*: Have you been treated overnight in the hospital for _____?	Medically unstable
a. How many times were you admitted to the hospital for this problem?	
b. When was the last time?	

ASSESSMENT DOMAIN 3: MEDICATIONS

Suggested Questions	*Problem Labels*
1. Please tell me the names of your prescription medications and how often you take them.	Polypharmacy

Source: Courtesy of AAHP Foundation.

2. Do you take them the way your doctor wants you to take them? (If no, Why not?)

Fails to obtain medications or fails to take as prescribed

3. Is there someone who helps you take the medicines the way your doctor wants you to, or do you handle that yourself?

4. Please tell me the names of your medications for which you do not need a prescription.

Polypharmacy

ASSESSMENT DOMAIN 4: CARE ACCESS

Suggested Questions	Problem Labels
1. What is the name of your primary care physician (PCP)?	Lacks primary care physician
2. How often do you see your PCP?	Not keeping or not scheduling appointments appropriately
3. What do you do if you get sick before your scheduled appointment?	
4. Do you have an appointment scheduled with a specialist?	
5. Are you scheduled for any surgery or special procedures?	
6. How many times were you treated in the emergency room in the past year?	Overuses or under-uses emergency room or hospital services
7. How many times were you hospitalized in the past year?	
8. Do you have an advance directive?	Lack of advance planning

ASSESSMENT DOMAIN 5: FUNCTIONAL STATUS

Suggested Questions	Problem Labels
1. Are you able to take care of all your personal needs by yourself?	ADL or IADL deficit

2. Do you need help with/Who helps you with:
   a. preparing your meals? eating?
   b. taking a bath?
   c. getting dressed?
   d. getting to the toilet?
3. Are you able to move about your home   Mobility problem
   without help? (Do you use a cane or walker?)
4. Do you need help/Who helps with:
   a. walking outside?
   b. getting to the doctor's office?
5. Do you need help with/Who helps with: IADL deficit
   a. housework?
   b. food shopping?
   c. managing your money?
6. How many falls have you had in the past   Falls
   year? Have you had a serious injury from
   a fall?
7. Do you have problems seeing? (If yes,   Visually impaired
   Do problems seeing make it hard to follow
   your doctor's instructions?)
8. Do you have hearing problems? (If yes,   Hearing impaired
   Do hearing problems make it hard to
   follow your doctor's instructions?)

ASSESSMENT DOMAIN 6: SOCIAL SITUATION

Suggested Questions	*Problem Labels*
1. Who lives in the house with you?	Isolated
2. Does that person help you with:	Dependent;
a. personal care?	unreliable
b. medications?	caregiver
c. preparing meals?	
d. housework?	
e. food shopping?	
3. Do you need more help with those items than you have?	Inadequate support

ASSESSMENT DOMAIN 7: NUTRITION

Suggested Questions	*Problem Labels*
Has your weight changed in the past six months?	Malnourished

1. *If there has been a weight loss:*
   a. Have you been trying to lose weight?
   b. How much weight have you lost?
   c. Have you discussed this weight loss with your doctor?
2. *If there has been a weight gain:*
   a. Have you been trying to gain weight?
   b. How much weight have you gained?
   c. Have you discussed this weight gain with your doctor?

ASSESSMENT DOMAIN 8: EMOTIONAL STATUS

Suggested Questions	*Problem Labels*
1. Do you often feel sad or blue?	Depressed
2. Do you often feel anxious or on edge?	Anxious

Appendix 12–C
Examples of Brief Standardized Instruments
Used in Comprehensive Geriatric Assessment

Domain	Topics Often Assessed	Instrument
Personal	Demographics, occupation, education, religion, living situation, finances	
Emotional	Depression	GDS
Functional	Ability to perform ADL, IADL	Katz, OARS
Nutrition	Poor nutrition	NSI Checklist
Cognition	Cognitive dysfunction	MMSE
Medications	Polypharmacy, non-adherence	
Psychosocial	Relationships, interactions, activities, support	SNS
Environment	Safety, convenience	
Services	Community and home services used or needed	
Gait	Risk of falls	Get Up and Go
Preferences	End-of-life care	
Medical history	Conditions, lifestyle, prevention	CAGE
Physical exam	Medical diagnoses	

Source: Courtesy of AAHP Foundation.

CHAPTER 13

Geriatric Assessment and Managed Care

Howard M. Fillit, Jerrold Hill, Gloria Picariello,
and Samuel Warburton

Comprehensive geriatric assessment is considered by most geriatricians to be an important and effective form of secondary and tertiary preventive care for the frail elderly (Fillit & Picariello, 1997; Rubenstein, Wieland, Bernabei, 1995; Stuck, Siu, Wieland, & Rubenstein,1993). In traditional fee-for-service (FFS) medicine, comprehensive assessment of older patients is often highly individualized and is provided at the site of care by a multidisciplinary team. Targeting of this relatively complex, costly, and time-consuming process to individuals who have the potential to benefit from subsequent interventions is crucial to its success.

Outside of academic medicine and private philanthropy or government funding, however, most medical practice sites under Medicare FFS reimbursement cannot afford the time and personnel required for multidisciplinary geriatric care. Although Medicare now pays for some preventive services (influenza and pneumonia vaccines, as well as mammography), it does not provide reimbursement for comprehensive geriatric assessment. Thus, prior to the recent growth of Medicare managed care organizations (MCOs), the application of multidisciplinary geriatric care has been limited. In this chapter, we describe how two strategic elements of traditional geriatric assessment—identifying high-risk members and targeting them to comprehensive geriatric case management programs—are being adapted and effectively implemented by MCOs. We discuss how recent changes in the structure and funding of Medicare managed care are likely to impact MCOs and the physicians with whom they contract.

THE DRIVING FORCES OF MANAGED CARE

The principal forces driving managed care of older patients in the United States are Congress and the Health Care Financing Administration (HCFA)

Source: Reproduced with permission frcm *Geriatrics*, Vol. 53, Number 4, April 1998, pp. 76–89. Copyright by Advanstar Communications, Inc. Advanstar Communications, Inc. retains all rights to this material.

through the Medicare program. Medicare managed care programs have been growing fairly rapidly, with relatively low disenrollment rates in most regions, suggesting general satisfaction of members (Riley, Ingber, & Tudor, 1997).

The Congressional Balanced Budget Act of 1997 mandated that Medicare MCOs no longer be termed *risk contractors* but rather *coordinated care plans*. This change in terms (to *Medicare+Choice Coordinated Care Plans*) signals a change in emphasis in the program. In addition to health maintenance organizations (HMOs) operated by an insurance company or a health system, provider service organizations can now contract directly with HCFA. Regardless of their structure, coordinated care plans offer the opportunity to apply the principles of geriatric medicine to large populations of older persons.

The economic and clinical forces of managed care are promoting innovative approaches to caring for patients aged 65 and older (HMO Workgroup on Care Management, 1997). MCOs have the potential to organize care and practice effective population-based medicine. For example, disease management programs generally include the identification of high-risk members and the targeting of coordinated care to those individuals (Roglieri et al., 1997).

Targeting allows the resources of the multidisciplinary geriatric team to be provided to individuals with the most potential to benefit. Including persons who are "too healthy" or "too sick" can be nonproductive or futile. In traditional FFS medicine, targeting is rarely performed and is rather subjective, inefficient and highly variable. It is generally done for individual patients, based on the individual practitioner's judgment.

Medicare MCOs perform population-based targeting through "high-risk screening" or "health-risk appraisal." Health-risk assessments are often used to identify MCO members requiring primary, secondary or tertiary preventive health interventions. High-risk members can then be triaged to interventions such as geriatric case management (HMO Workgroup on Care Management, 1997).

CASE FINDING: SELF-REPORT VERSUS ADMINISTRATIVE DATA

Self-Reported Data

Older individuals at high risk for health outcomes can be identified effectively by self-reported health risk assessments that take into consideration the unique health problems of this population (Coleman et al., 1998; Mukamel, Chou, Zimmer, & Roethenberg, 1997; Pacala, Boult, Reed, & Aliberti, 1997). Such instruments have demonstrated impact on health and utilization outcomes when they have been integrated into a comprehensive geriatric assessment program (Stuck et al., 1993).

Some instruments (health-risk appraisals) attempt to gather large amounts of data on individuals' health status. Others (high-risk screening instruments) are brief and attempt only to identify members at high risk for adverse health outcomes and increased utilization of service. A limited number of specific clinical variables have been shown to predict increased medical utilization and adverse health outcomes (Mukamel et al., 1997; Pacala et al., 1997). Such variables as prior hospitalization, advanced age, number of medications and self-reported health status have been incorporated into scoring algorithms.

Self-reported data can be obtained by telephone, in person or through the mail. Person-to-person methods are generally prohibitively expensive and time-consuming, although they may be the most reliable method for obtaining some data. Telephone methods for screening large populations are also expensive and more time-consuming than mailings, although additional, more reliable information can be obtained if necessary. Mailings have considerable advantages in terms of cost and efficiency, although they also have drawbacks. In the authors' experience, mailed self-reported health risk appraisals proved to be expensive, and a significant segment of the population failed to respond to the survey (Fillit, Picariello, & Warburton, 1997). The health status of nonresponders is generally worse than that of responders (Mukamel et al., 1997).

Administrative Data

Most Medicare HMOs gather information about patients from such sources as insurance claims, pharmacy records and encounters with primary care physicians. These administrative data have been employed for health-risk assessment of populations (Coleman et al., 1998; Mukamel et al., 1997; Newhouse, Buntin, & Chapman, 1997), as well as for assessing quality of health care (Iezzoni, 1997). Administrative data are readily available in most Medicare HMOs and are relatively inexpensive to obtain. HCFA is now implementing a system of health-risk-adjusted payment rates for Medicare+Choice Coordinated Care Plans that uses administrative data on patient diagnoses.

The authors developed a health-risk assessment instrument based on administrative data obtained during 1997 on more than 50,000 members of our Medicare HMOs. A regression model based on diagnosis and cost information from medical and pharmacy claims over a 6-month baseline period was used to predict medical costs for the subsequent 6 months. Linear regression was used to estimate relationships between the independent variables measured at baseline and costs measured at follow-up. The regression model was then used to predict each member's costs for the follow-up period.

Members were ranked by predicted cost, and those exceeding the ninetieth percentile were selected as the "high-risk" group. In the follow-up period, high-risk members (approximately 6%) accounted for 27% of medical costs and 28% of hospital days; their average cost, number of hospital days and rate of death were nearly five times that of all members. The prevalence of chronic diseases and use of multiple medications were much higher in the high-risk group compared with all members.

When the relative predictive value of this model was compared with that of the self-reported health status data, it was found that:

- Administrative data and self-reported health data were equally powerful as predictors of future utilization of health care resources.
- The response rate to the self-reported health survey was only 56% of members, whereas the administrative data model captured close to 100% of members, with a utilization history at a much lower cost.
- Nonresponders to the self-reported health assessment had higher utilization, confirming that nonresponders among the elderly population are at higher risk.

Some Caveats

Administrative data probably represent the best method for identifying high-risk members among existing populations with utilization histories. However, these are the drawbacks:

- Administrative data are generally not available for newly enrolled members. Thus, brief self-reported health assessments are most useful for newly enrolled members in an MCO.

- Some common geriatric health problems cannot be identified by administrative data. These include an individual patient's smoking history, alcohol use, cognitive and emotional state, falls and nutritional status, and perceived health status. Therefore, when MCOs seek to target disease management programs to such problems, they must employ self-reported health assessments.
- Administrative data cannot replace self-reported health risk appraisals in their potential to promote wellness in healthy older patients who may not generate utilization data.
- In some MCOs, administrative data can be compromised in quality, timeliness and availability.

Thus, the optimum result is obtained when self-reported survey data and administrative data are considered together as part of an overall strategy to manage the care of older individuals.

CASE MANAGEMENT AND THE OLDER PATIENT

Primary care physicians in Medicare FFS generally do not have the time, resources, financial incentives or, in some cases, the knowledge to effectively practice multidisciplinary geriatric care. Conversely, in an MCO, an older patient who is identified as at high risk is likely to be triaged to geriatric case management programs (HMO Workgroup, 1998; Mukamel et al., 1997). It is through these programs that MCOs have adapted and implemented multidisciplinary geriatric assessment.

Geriatric care managers use the details from self-reported health assessments and administrative-data instruments for managing the care of individual members. The results are also sent to the primary care physician. Under various risk-sharing capitated arrangements of many MCO models, physicians have the financial incentive to focus on preventing iatrogenesis, functional decline and institutionalization of their older patients (Fillit & Capello, 1994).

Role of the Physician

The managed-care model of geriatric case management does not necessarily match the traditional academic format of multidisciplinary teams at the primary site of care. Such models are expensive, have demonstrated limited impact on outcomes (Stuck et al., 1993) and are clearly impractical in the wider world of primary care practice in most settings.

In MCOs, geriatric case management programs can be situated in a health plan, an independent practice association network office or the offices of large multispecialty group practices. They can enable primary care providers to practice multidisciplinary geriatric care by providing knowledge, additional personnel and seamless access to the geriatric continuum of care (from home care to skilled nursing assistance to hospitalization, for example) as determined by the individual patient's needs (Rich et al., 1995; Stuck et al., 1995).

The primary care physician is crucial to the success of comprehensive case management and should quickly receive the health-risk assessments of older patients identified as medically at risk. Any further patient assessment conducted by mail or telephone by geriatric case managers should also be provided to the physician prior to the patient's next office visit.

In some cases, health-risk assessments may obtain patient information that requires timely intervention. For example, it is clinically (and perhaps medicolegally) important for the physician to know that on the health-risk appraisal a patient has answered "yes" to the question, Have you fallen recently? Such a response indicates a need to evaluate the patient's risk factors for falls and to develop strategies to prevent further falling.

The purpose of a preventive health visit is to prevent unnecessary deterioration, functional decline and adverse health events in a patient with preexistent, often multiple chronic illnesses. The authors have previously described how this can be conducted in the primary care office by employ-ing the principles of geriatric assessment (Fillit & Capello, 1994) and have developed a practical guide for these purposes (Fillit, Picariello, & Warburton, 1997). In brief, the assessment should address the common problems of frail older patients, including their medical conditions, assessment of their mental (cognitive and emotional) function, a functional assessment and a social assessment.

Often, in productive partnerships between MCO case managers and the primary care physician, the case manager may perform the functional and social assessments, and some aspects of the medical and mental assess-ments. Finally, the physician's assessment is communicated to the case manager for coordination of any further assistance that may be needed (for example, such community services as home care).

Efficacy of Case Management

Studies indicate that significant cost savings reflecting improvements in the quality of care can be realized by combining high-risk screening with targeted geriatric case management (Aliotta, 1996; Mukamel et al., 1997). However, true "clinical trials" of geriatric case management as an intervention (either in managed care or in traditional Medicare FFS) are lacking.

There is also great variability in the content, substance and emphasis of geriatric case management programs, which affects their efficacy. Some programs may be conducted primarily by telephone, whereas others might include home visits. Some programs may focus on working with older patients or their caregivers to teach self-management skills, whereas others may depend on primary care physicians to implement suggested plans of care or to make a substantial investment in working with other providers to achieve shared goals.

It is the view of the authors that one of the most important factors determining the success of any geriatric case management program is the knowledge of the geriatric case managers in the principles of geriatric medicine. This knowledge allows them to effectively participate in the assessment and coordination of geriatric care for a high-risk, frail older person.

FINANCIAL RISK AND CASE MANAGEMENT

Knowledge of the health status of a Medicare managed care population is essential, not only for providing preventive services but also for assessing an MCO's financial risk under the current payment system. Because the 5% of members at risk for high utilization and adverse health outcomes account for 62% of hospital costs (Freeborn, Pope, & Mulloly, 1990; Riley, Lubitz, & Prihoda, 1986), the proportion of high-risk members in the Medicare risk plan will have a profound impact on the health plan's profitability.

Medicare pays a fixed capitation payment for each member that reflects the average cost to Medicare under FFS for a beneficiary with the same demographics (age, sex and whether the member is in a nursing home, is working or is on welfare). Plans with a high proportion of high-risk members (adverse selection) face the possibility of financial losses because the expected cost for these members exceeds the capitation payments (Gruenberg, Kaganova, & Hornbrook, 1996). Likewise, plans with a low proportion of high-risk members (favorable selection) may more easily profit.

Obviously, the ability to predict medical costs based on knowledge of health status enables the health plan to produce more accurate financial forecasts and to focus resources for cost management to specific members and subpopulations with high expected costs.

HCFA also views knowledge of health status as essential for establishing a payment system for Medicare Coordinated Care Plans that will result in savings to the Medicare program and provide financial incentives for plans to enroll and manage high-risk patients. Under the current system:

- There is considerable evidence (Brown, Clement, Hill, Retchin, & Bergeron, 1993; Hill & Brown, 1990) that the Medicare program is losing money because Medicare risk plans on balance are experiencing favorable selection.

- Medicare risk plans have an incentive to encourage healthier beneficiaries to enroll and to discourage enrollment of high-risk beneficiaries.

In the Balanced Budget Act of 1997, Congress included a requirement that HCFA adopt a health-risk-adjusted payment methodology for Medicare Coordinated Care Plans by January 1, 2000. If properly designed, such a system would decrease payments to plans with favorable selection and increase payments to plans with adverse selection. In addition, if substantially higher payments are provided for high-risk beneficiaries, all plans would realize greater financial incentives to enroll and effectively manage high-risk Medicare patients.

CONCLUSION

The challenge—and the opportunity—for Medicare+Choice Coordinated Care Plans is the widespread application of the principles and practice of geriatric medicine. Although geriatric medicine has flourished in some large academic centers, most communities in the United States lack its two important components: a substantial base of knowledgeable providers and effective systems of geriatric care.

Medicare+Choice Coordinated Care Plans and the provider groups with which they contract manage the care of large populations of older individuals and have powerful clinical and financial incentives to practice geriatric medicine. By realigning financial incentives to encourage care at the site of lowest acuity (for example, home care versus long-term care), capitation can be a positive force for the adoption of the principles and practice of geriatric medicine (Boland, 1997).

The success of medical management in these MCOs depends to some extent on the ability to identify high-risk members and to efficiently target them to comprehensive geriatric case management programs working in partnerships with primary care physicians. In many communities, MCOs are working in innovative partnerships with provider groups and primary care physicians to provide the added resources and personnel necessary for the practice of geriatric care.

We expect the new risk-adjustment methodology for compensating MCOs as mandated by the Balanced Budget Act of 1997 to further encourage enrollment of frail elders in MCOs. As the number of high-risk Medicare enrollees grows, it will become increasingly important for MCOs to develop effective geriatric case management programs based on the promotion of health and the prevention of functional decline.

REFERENCES

Aliotta, S.L. (1996). Components of a successful case management program. *Managed Care Q, 4*, 38–45.

Boland, P. (1997). The power and potential of capitation. *Managed Care Q, 5*, 1–9.

Brown, R.S., Clement, D.G., Hill J.W., Retchin, S.M., & Bergeron, J.W. (1993). Do health maintenance organizations work for Medicare? *Health Care Finance Rev, 15*, 7–23.

Coleman, E.A., Wagner, E.H., Grothaus, L.C., Hecht, J., Savarino, J., & Buchner, D.M. (1998). Predicting hospitalization and functional decline in older health plan enrollees: Are administrative data as accurate as self-report? *J Am Geriatr Soc* (in press).

Fillit, H., & Capello, C. (1994). Making geriatric assessment an asset to your primary care practice. *Geriatrics, 49*, 27–35.

Fillit, H.M., & Picariello, G.P. (1997). *Practical geriatric assessment.* London: Greenwich Medical Media (distributed by Oxford University Press).

Fillit, H.M., Picariello, G.P., Warburton, S.W. (1997). Health risk appraisals in the elderly: Results from a survey of 70,000 Medicare HMO members. *J Clin Outcomes Meas, 4*, 23–29.

Freeborn, D.K., Pope, C.R., Mulloly, J.P., et al. (1990). Consistently high users of medical care among the elderly. *Med Care, 28*, 527–540.

Gruenberg, L., Kaganova, E., & Hornbrook, M.C. (1996). Improving the AAPCC with health-status measures from the MCBS. *Health Care Finance Rev, 17*, 59–75.

Hill, J.S., & Brown, R.S. (1990). Biased selection in the TEFRA HMO/CMP Program. Princeton, NJ: Mathematica Policy Research, Inc.

HMO Workgroup on Care Management. (1997). Identifying high-risk Medicare members. *Case Manager, 8*, 57–61.

HMO Workgroup on Care Management. (1998). Essential components of geriatric care provided through health maintenance organizations. *J Am Geriatr Soc, 3*, 1831–1839.

Iezzoni, L.I. (1997). Assessing quality using administrative data. *Ann Int Med, 127*, 666–674.

Mukamel, D.B., Chou, C., Zimmer, J.G., & Roethenberg, B.M. (1997). The effect of accurate patient screening on the cost-effectiveness of case management programs. *Gerontologist, 37*, 777–784.

Newhouse, J.P., Buntin, M.B., & Chapman, J.D. (1997). Risk adjustment and Medicare: Taking a closer look. *Health Affairs, 16*, 26–42.

Pacala, J.T., Boult, C., Reed, R.L., & Aliberti, E. (1997). Predictive validity of the P_{ra} instrument among older recipients of managed care. *J Am Geriatr Soc, 45*, 614–617.

Rich, M.W., Beckham, V., Wittenberg, C., Leven, C.L., Freedland, K.E., & Carney, R.M. (1995). A multidisciplinary intervention to prevent the readmission of elderly patients with congestive heart failure. *N Engl J Med, 333*, 1190–1195.

Riley, G.F., Lubitz, J., Prihoda, R., et al. (1986). Changes in the distribution of Medicare expenditures among aged enrollees. *Health Care Finance Rev, 7*, 53–63.

Riley, G.F., Ingber, M.J., & Tudor, C.G. (1997). Disenrollment of Medicare beneficiaries from HMOs. *Health Affairs, 16*, 117–124.

Roglieri, J.L., Futterman, R., McDonough, K.L., et al. (1997). Disease management interventions to improve outcomes in congestive heart failure. *Am J Managed Care, 3*, 1831–1839.

Rubenstein, L.Z., Wieland, D., & Bernabei, R. (Eds.). (1995). *Geriatric assessment technology: The state of the art.* Milan, Italy: Editrice Kurtis.

Stuck, A.E., Siu, A.L., Wieland, D., & Rubenstein, L.Z. (1993). Comprehensive geriatric assessment: A meta-analysis of controlled trials. *Lancet, 142*, 1032–1036.

Stuck, A.E., Aronow, H.U., Steiner, A., et al. (1995). A trial of annual in-home comprehensive geriatric assessments for elderly people living in the community. *N Engl J Med, 333*, 1184–1189.

CHAPTER 14

Older, Sicker, Smarter, and Redefining Quality: The Older Consumer's Quest for Service

Bruce Clark

My family and I live in the country outside of San Francisco and own four horses, two dogs, one goat, three chickens and two birds. Fortunately, we have great veterinarians. They make house calls, remind us when our animals need their shots, are easy to reach on the phone, generally have appointments at convenient times for us, seldom keep us waiting and treat every one of our beloved beasts with tender, loving, personal care. In fact, Cherpie, our $5 parakeet, is taking medicine for a common upper-respiratory affliction, and we've received no fewer than three phone calls from the vet to check on her progress over the past 2 weeks.

Now my wife, son and I are relatively happy with our health plan; we are not planning to switch any time soon. However, we cannot make any of the same claims about our health plan that I just made about our veterinarians. We are lucky if we can reach a live voice without being put on hold; we take whatever appointment is available, whether or not it is convenient for us; we never know (and are never told) how long we will be waiting for the doctor once we arrive for our appointments; and Saturday—forget it. House calls and "TLC" are not even among our expectations. Face it, our animals have the "preferred plan."

Oddly enough, customer service is rarely emphasized in health care, particularly at the level of the provider, and even more surprisingly, it is rarely demanded by the consumer. Money-back guarantees, 100% satisfaction, no-waiting-in-line policies, no-questions-asked returns and on-time commitments are all expectations we readily apply to our involve-

---

Source: Except where otherwise noted, adapted with permission from B. Clark, Older, Sicker, Smarter, and Redefining Quality, *Healthcare Forum Journal,* © 1998, The Healthcare Forum.

ment with retailers, airlines, hotels, banks and restaurants. However, we are complacent about applying them to our health care interactions.

It is unlikely that consumers do not want good customer service from health care providers. How, then, do we explain the low expectations we have been conditioned to hold with regard to customer service and medical care? One answer certainly lies in the emphasis we have put on child-oriented and acute care medicine over the past two generations. As a youthful society, America concentrated her efforts on finding quick and easy solutions to the traumas and ills of the young. Emergency care became a science; pediatrics and obstetrics practices flourished and the scourges of youth—smallpox, polio and the like—were conquered. All of this is very good news, but these advances did little to prepare American medicine for the different needs of today's largest consumers of health care.

About 27% of our current population is over the age of 50 (U.S. Bureau of the Census, 1997). By the time this author reaches 50 years of age in the year 2001, there will be 80 million Americans over the age of 50 (U.S. Bureau of the Census, 1997), and it is projected that we will consume about 70% of health care services based on consumer expenditures.

As this group lives longer and moves into older age, they will have more time to contract and manage chronic conditions. (Today, the average 65-plus individual must deal with three or four chronic conditions, according to the National Center for Health Statistics). The future of health care in America will be dominated by how we learn to respond to and manage this vast population of elders with multiple chronic conditions who will be living well into their eighties by the year 2030.

As we move into this new arena, it is key for providers of health care services to ask themselves: What do these older consumers want? What demonstrates quality care and customer service in their eyes?

QUALITY, BY WHOSE DEFINITION?

Over the past 12 years, the total focus of Age Wave has been the older consumer. We have conducted hundreds of mature-market programs, research projects and focus groups for retailers, banks, drug, automotive and financial services companies and, especially, hospitals and managed care organizations. Today, all of these businesses are obsessed with quality—especially quality in health care.

Do we agree on what "quality" is? When I give lectures, I sometimes ask health care executives to define *quality*. Their answers are fairly consistent: They point to measures such as provider network access, provider credentials, access to the best technology and, certainly, outcomes.

When I talk to elders about quality, I hear very important differences. Whereas they acknowledge the importance of the above, they identify quality in human and relational terms: Did the doctor listen? Was the phone call returned? Was the receptionist hurried or impolite? Was the appointment honored? When I was wandering in the hospital finding my way from the clinical lab to X-ray, did someone put down what they were doing and guide me or did they just point down the hall and return to their more "important" task?

For older consumers, who tend to measure the quality of their health care experience in terms of face-to-face services and personal exchanges, the dignity, care and respect they receive in their health care experience will often outweigh even extraordinary outcomes.

In a study recently conducted of health care issues among seniors *(Age Wave Health Services Senior Health Beacon™, 1998)*, 58% of the more than 3,400 mature men and women surveyed nationwide indicated that the responsiveness of their health plans to their individual needs was "extremely important" in their selection of a health plan.

Clearly, liability issues are also strongly influenced by service perceptions. Seventy-five percent of all malpractice cases stem from patients' *feelings* about the care that they received. These findings confirm that in the eyes of the older consumer, the quality of the care involved in an artfully replaced hip or the early diagnosis of a tumor can all but be undone by a rude billing clerk, an unreturned phone call or a disrespectful physician.

BABY BOOMERS EXPECT MORE

If that is the case, why has there been no groundswell of opposition to poor service in health care. Again, the answer may lie in the demographics. The current 65-plus population tends to be somewhat reverential toward doctors and the health care system. Importantly, however, the aging of the baby boomers is bringing about a change in this attitude. The first of the massive demographic wave of Americans born between 1946 and 1964 started turning 50 in 1996. Today, every 8 seconds, another baby boomer turns 50 (Dychtwald & Flower, 1989). This group of people tends to live in dual-income households and to consider time as a precious resource. They grew up with the convenience of fast food, do-it-yourself books and stores, and customer-friendly services.

When it comes to health care, maturing baby boomers can be distinguished from previous generations by the following six characteristics:

- *They are more concerned about a healthy lifestyle and healthy aging.* The number of adults who smoke decreased by 40% between 1965 and 1993 (U.S. CDC, 1994). The per capita consumption of beef and butter dipped by 21% between 1970 and 1992, and the amount of chicken consumed per person grew by 65% during this same period (U.S. Bureau of the Census, 1992) . This population wants a "collaborative" health care provider to help them age well.
- *They crave information and will go to any lengths to get it.* Health information is no longer the exclusive purview of the physician. Baby boomers pour over self-help publications and search for health information on the Internet, videos, and audiotapes. It is estimated that about 38% of Internet users seek out health-related information. *Prevention* magazine has a circulation of more than 3.4 million and is available at the supermarket, right next to the *National Inquirer*.
- *They demand convenience along with excellent service.* Other industries have bent over backward to accommodate the increase in both working women and working hours. In 1993, 58% of women (and 66% of the general population) was in the labor force, up from 38% of women (and 60% of the general population) in 1960 (U.S. Bureau of the Census, 1992). Meanwhile, full-time workers spent 138 hours more per year working in 1989 than they did in 1969 (Girl Scouts of America, 1996). Except for health care, nearly every American industry, from banks to auto repair, has modified its hours of operation to accommodate these systemic changes,
- *They expect evidence of quality and expertise.* Consumers are gaining access to comparative information about their health plans through "report cards" that appear in such publications as *Consumer Reports* and *Newsweek*. At the same time, employers are demanding that health plans supply Health Plan Employer Data and Information Set scores on a variety of measures, including member satisfaction. Tomorrow's health care consumers will expect and demand this kind of "proof" of good outcomes.

- *They refuse to accept advice at face value.* Baby boomers include the generation of women who grew up with such educational, self-help books as *Our Bodies, Ourselves* and fought for reproductive freedom and natural childbirth. Women and men alike embraced myriad social movements and challenged authority, including the physician's authority. The very public recognition of this fact is evidenced by *Fortune's* cover story in 1996 on Andy Grove, chief executive officer of Intel, and his exhaustive search—which included more than 15 experts and numerous information sources—for the best medical protocol and treatment alternatives in his battle against prostate cancer.

- *They are willing to explore alternative therapies.* In 1990, Americans made 425 million visits to providers of such unconventional therapies as chiropractors and massage therapists, *exceeding the 388 million visits to conventional physicians* who provide primary care (Eisenberg, 1993). These statistics suggest that so-called alternative therapies are more mainstream than is conventional medical care.

Even this abbreviated snapshot shows that, though these "new" older patients may not have the same expectations as their predecessors (having one family doctor for most of their lives), they nonetheless have other, higher expectations of their health plans. Providers who succeed in this new environment will be those who consistently meet or exceed those expectations.

SHOOTING THEMSELVES IN THE FOOT

Most people agree that managed care is here to stay. How can managed care plans respond to the needs and expectations of the fastest-changing and fastest-growing population segment?

At Age Wave Health Services, Inc., we work a great deal with Medicare health maintenance organizations (HMOs), which now cover 16%—6.5 (HCFA, 1998) million people—of the 65-plus population. This group is growing so quickly that this author predicts risk-based plans, including hospital-based and point-of-service plans, will cover nearly half of the older population by the year 2003.

Older adults switch from other Medicare arrangements to HMOs because HMOs often provide better benefits, such as prescription drugs and vision care. Elders also say they like the availability of preventive care, 24-hour telephone advice and member activities.

However, it is in the area of customer service that managed care companies can build—or destroy—their growth opportunities with mature consumers. Our *Age Wave Health Services Senior Health Beacon* (1998) research shows how managed care plans—which purport to be aggressively seeking enrollees in their Medicare HMOs—consistently shoot themselves in the proverbial foot by not meeting the quality and service expectations of their target audience. From this research and earlier studies in which we hired elderly men and women to telephone HMOs and ask for information about a Medicare HMO, we encountered not just weak customer service but, in some cases, no service at all:

- Twenty-six percent of the "shoppers" had to leave a voice-mail message or call back.
- Forty-eight percent did not receive the material they requested within four weeks.
- Only 14% received a follow-up call.

It costs a Medicare HMO between $500 and $1,500 to acquire a member; yet, 10% of these new members disenroll—many because of poor communication and interaction. It doesn't take a financial wizard to see the cost that poor service extols.

WHO IS DOING IT RIGHT?

Although nearly every other service industry has reshaped itself over the past two decades to become proactive in the delivery and promise of good customer relations and service, health care continues to resist. The health care industry remains the last bastion of opposition to the business model that regards the consumer as a critical partner for success.

There are, however, a few signs of change. In my lectures and interactions with health care executives across the country, I am beginning to see an interest in proactive, groundbreaking customer relations, but I have come upon only a handful of applications in the health care marketplace.

One of these is Oxford Health Plans, an HMO that is really listening and responding to its customers. Though this company has stumbled recently, due to widely publicized accounting and information-systems problems, it continues to maintain an unusual level of customer loyalty. After surveys showed that 75% of members wanted nontraditional treatment options, it added several thousand chiropractors, nutritionists, massage therapists, yoga instructors and acupuncturists who provide services at substantial discounts. How does its intense focus on customer service impact the bottom line? The Norwalk, Connecticut-based HMO has grown to 1.5 million members since its birth in the mid-1980s.

Another health care industry anomaly is Lake Forest Hospital, located in a suburb of Chicago. Since 1989, this 250-bed facility has been offering a "money-back guarantee" with its services, including its surgical cases. Although the physicians initially panicked, in the day-surgery unit, where this customer service program was initiated, only 10 of the more than 3,100 annual day-surgery cases resulted in "guaranteed service" payouts in 1992. These payouts represented less than .0004% of revenues; the program's impact on revenues was considerably greater. The money-back guarantee is just one component of a full-fledged, customer-service and employee awareness program that focuses on listening to its patients and addressing their needs.

When it comes to combining care and technology, we are currently witnessing a literal explosion of exciting innovations in health care service that is creating empowered patients and better service. In April 1998, the West Jersey Health System in Voorhees, New Jersey, provided 300 diabetes patients with personal computers to track blood sugar levels, diet and activity from the convenience of their homes. Via these Internet-connected computers, patients share information with providers who monitor progress and provide on-line advice. The goal of the program is to give patients and their providers greater control and more precise management while reducing costs.

Innovative approaches to helping seniors and their families realize their wish to navigate long-term chronic care needs from home are gaining attention among America's 38 million caregivers. Louisville-based *CAREtenders* provides a full spectrum of services to persons in need and to their caregivers, including care managers who work with family members and physicians to coordinate in-home care plans, in-home aides to support care and household needs and a unique adult day care program called *Almost Family* for seniors who require respite care but want to return home each evening. Another model for senior independent living that is serving as a national prototype in the reshaping of long-term care is the *On Lok*

Senior Health Services program based in San Francisco. Since 1979, this combination adult day-care and residential program has focused on the needs of the frail elderly. With six locations across the city, *On Lok* manages the care needs of hundreds of frail seniors who would otherwise require expensive institutional care.

ARE WE REALLY PREPARED TO CARE FOR AN AGING SOCIETY?

As important as these quality and service issues are, health care has an even deeper layer of issues to address as we look toward the new millennium. I was introduced to one of these issues recently in an unforgettable way.

It was the call I had always dreaded. I was on vacation when my brother, a physician in southern California, reached me with disturbing news. My 81-year-old and otherwise remarkably healthy father was in the hospital in intensive care with a fast-moving, serious pulmonary inflammation. My brother is not one to be unduly alarmed, so I took his advice and flew home. Sunday, February 18, 1995 was the last day I spent with my father. It was a time I have ever since felt fortunate to have.

*I experienced two important revelations about health care that day. The first was the truly amazing competence and efficiency of the clinical team treating my father. The pulmonologist, cardiologist and intensive care unit nurses could not have impressed me more. Beyond their professionalism, which engendered great trust, I sensed something even deeper. I sensed that they cared deeply about my father and about our family on this dramatic day.

The second revelation was brought on by what the hospital staff did following my father's death that Sunday evening—absolutely nothing. From the moment he died and the doctors and nurses went on to other pressing duties, the caring and excellent service we had been receiving vanished. No visit from a chaplain. No piece of paper that provided details on what to do next. No information on how you might expect to feel over the coming days. No invitation to my mother to join a bereavement support group. Nothing.

As I was driving home that evening, it struck me that the hospital had missed an important opportunity, if not an obligation, to help us and other patients and their families navigate through life's most dramatic moments.

Source: Adapted with permission from *Chief Executive Officer* (Winter 1998): 1 & 4 (Chicago: American College of Healthcare Executives, 1998).

This service requires little time or infrastructure to deliver but can yield lifelong loyalty to the hospital by the family.

I have been privileged to help numerous companies over the past 12 years to develop a new understanding of the business opportunities to be found in serving older consumers. These companies—from the retail, financial services and consumer products industries—realize the critical importance of developing a binding relationship with their customers in order to succeed, yet few have the opportunity to connect with a customer as deeply and personally as those of us in health care have every day.

My personal experience is less a critique than an observation. There is no doubt in my mind that the vast majority of people who make health care their profession do so because they are motivated by a desire to care for people. Clearly, the pace, pressure and demands on medical care providers today have dramatically increased. However, an important opportunity exists for health care organizations to make a real difference in the lives of millions of people touched by death and serious illness by giving people the direction and the resources to provide the guidance and support they would like to give.*

Allowing patients and families to navigate the end of life in a sensitive and supportive setting transcends the temporal concept of service. One program that sets a uniquely high standard in this important, emerging field is called Commonweal. Located in Bolinas, California, Commonweal offers transformational education programs in an intensive retreat setting for persons with life-threatening illness and their families. Featured in the Bill Moyers' PBS television special, *The Healing Mind*, the program now offers special workshops for organizations that want to learn from Commonweal's more than two decades of experience. Another trailblazer in this field of services is the York Health System in York, Pennsylvania. Though many hospitals offer limited bereavement and support services for families experiencing the loss of a loved one, few have programs as comprehensive and well coordinated. This program has a full-time be-reavement coordinator who acts as a case manager after a patient dies. In addition to a wide array of materials, programs and consultation services support groups, the nurses hired by the 500-bed facility go through a special training program to sensitize them to the grief process and to introduce them to the tools they will have to provide the necessary support.

In 1997, approximately 2.2 million Americans died (U.S. Dept. of Health and Human Services, 1998). Most of them died in a hospital or hospice without a plan in place to deal with their needs or with the needs of

---

Source: Adapted with permission from *Chief Executive Officer* (Winter 1998): 1 & 4 (Chicago: American College of Healthcare Executives, 1998).

their families. This raises an even larger issue. How prepared are we to address the needs of the vast population entering the new disease and care paradigm of the twenty-first century?

AN EPIDEMIC IS UPON US

We are heading toward an era of epidemic levels of chronic disease in America. There are more than 34 million people today over the age of 65. That number will increase to nearly 70 million by the year 2030. What will their health care profiles be? Today, the average person over 65 years old has four or more chronic diseases. Though vascular disease and cancer represent two thirds of all deaths in our elder population (U.S. CDC/ National Center for Health Statistics, 1994), it is the deterioration of soft tissues, the clogging of arteries, the loss of sensory functions and the management of pain, compliance and self-care solutions that will dramatically test our current delivery system in the years to come.

Although we have developed a truly wondrous system for acute care in America, we have little infrastructure for cost-effective, easily accessed chronic care. In particular, we have a dramatic need to increase the number of care providers who are trained and familiar with the diseases of aging. Today, we have 128 medical schools in this country but only two departments of geriatrics. We have 42,000 pediatricians but fewer than 7,500 geriatricians. Less than one half of one percent of nurses are trained as geriatric nurse practitioners, yet elders, representing 13% of our population, account for more than 50% of the hospital patient days (U.S. CDC/ National Center for Health Statistics, 1994). Rather than a system that coordinates with the "elder care network" (senior centers, respite care, meals-on-wheels, hospice, adult day care, wellness programs and other senior-oriented sites), we have a system that is fundamentally disconnected and seems more concerned about turf and reputation than coordination.

EMPOWERING PEOPLE

A simple recommitment by health care organizations is needed to help patients and families access the information and expert advice they need. We should make our hospitals and health plans the first place consumers turn to for health information. Here are a few ways to work toward that goal:

- Distribute guides to credible Web sites for health information
- Provide written support materials to families who have just experienced the loss of a loved one
- Help patients and families alike to link to the many support groups, even Internet chat rooms, concerned with such issues as Alzheimer's care, breast cancer, prostate cancer, end-of-life care and bereavement
- Make sure that all providers are knowledgeable about the caregiving resources available in their community
- Most importantly, familiarize staff with the elder care network of services available in most communities

WHERE WE GO FROM HERE

We are living civilization's dream—to grow older people. Older Americans see not only their children grow and flourish, but their grandchildren and great-grandchildren as well. Today, 10% of the individuals over 65 have children that are at least 65 years old. Yet, we also are at an important crossroads. The decisions we make over the next few years will determine whether we can successfully transform our approach to health service and care into a system that values the consumer in a new way. This new health care system will provide new levels of service, access and quality. Perhaps of greatest importance, this new system will better serve the chronic care and end-of-life needs of an aging population.*

REFERENCES

Dychtwald, K. & Flower, J. (1989). *Age wave: The challenges and opportunities of an aging America*. Los Angeles: Tarcher.

Eisenberg, D. (1993, January). Unconventional medicine in the United States. *N Engl J Med*.

Girl Scouts of America. (1996). *Environmental scanning report, 1994–96*.

---

*Source: Adapted with permission from *Chief Executive Officer* (Winter 1998): 1 & 4 (Chicago: American College of Healthcare Executives, 1998).

Graves, E.J. & Owings, M.F. *Summary: National Hospital Discharge Survey*. Advance data from vital and health statistics: no. 291. Hyattsville, MD: National Center for Health Statistics. Available at: http://www.cdc.gov/nchswww/products/pubs/pubd/ad/ad.htm (6/25/98).

U.S. Bureau of the Census. Population Division, release PPL-91. *United States population estimates, by age, sex, race and Hispanic origin, 1990 to 1997*. Available at: http://www.censu.gov/population/estimats/nation/intfile2-1.txt (25 June 1998).

U.S. Bureau of the Census. Current population report. Series P25-1130. *Population projections of the United States by age, sex, race, and Hispanic origin: 1995 to 2050*. Available at: http://www.census.gov/population/projections/nation/nas/npas0105.txt

U.S. Bureau of the Census. (1992, 1994, 1997). *Statistical Abstract of the United States: 1992 (112th ed.), 1994 (114th ed.), 1997 (117th ed.)*. Washington, DC.

U.S. CDC/National Center for Health Statistics. (1994). *Vital Health Stat [10], 190*, 106.

U.S. Dept. of Health and Human Services. (1998, 19 June). Centers for Disease Control and Prevention. National Center for Health Statistics. *Monthly vital statistics report, 46* (11).

PART THREE

Making Healthy Aging a Key Priority of Healthcare Financing

CHAPTER 15

The Political Economy of Health Care for the Elderly Population

Uwe Reinhardt

Throughout the industrialized world, the care of elderly people has become a major focus of domestic policy. Economic and technical progress since the end of World War II has vastly enhanced standards of living and the effectiveness of health care. Both have combined to extend average life expectancy in these nations beyond the projections policy makers might have made only decades ago. At the same time, general economic progress also has depressed the net reproduction rates in the industrialized world. As a result, elders have come to represent an ever-larger proportion of the population in these nations, a trend that will accelerate more sharply in the decades ahead. Increasingly, therefore, the fruits of economic and medical progress are being discussed as mixed blessings. In the United States, for example, the impending retirement of the baby boom generation sometime after the year 2010 is now being viewed with the apprehension normally reserved for an impending hurricane.

Much of this apprehension stems from two widely held beliefs often perpetuated by the media and in the political arena. The first is the notion that caring for a nation's frail elders is primarily an economic drain; that is, the net effect of such care is a decrease in our gross domestic product (GDP) without some compensatory gain of similar merit. The second belief is that the workers contributing to the care of the elderly population *own* all of the resources they generate, making social health services that derive from them an act of charity toward the people who benefit.

In this chapter, policy makers are invited to challenge both points of view. A just system of care for elderly people is of paramount importance to this country precisely because neither of these perspectives is true.

The first point—that our social systems for elder care are a fiscal drain that "buys" nothing valuable in return—ignores the indisputable value of what economists term the *public good*. Though intangible, the public good and one of its prime components—social peace—are real, measurable assets to a nation, something Europeans have long acknowledged in their Principle of Solidarity. Far from luxurious acts of charity, the European nations recognize social welfare programs as insurance against the more expensive possibilities of social unrest and its myriad outcomes.

The second issue—that workers own all that they produce and are therefore providing a "gift" of any services they themselves do not consume—also ignores a critical point: that these workers have already benefited from the investment that earlier generations made in *them* through education and training. Returning some of the profits of their labors to these older generations can and should be viewed as an appropriate return on the investments these earlier workers made to the social programs, including public education, from which the current population of workers benefits.

To support these arguments and to provide a comprehensive overview of the complex issues of caring for elderly citizens, this chapter will explore the provision of health care to the elderly from a macroeconomic perspective. To provide a backdrop for that discussion, the chapter will begin with the experience of other nations in the Organization for Economic Cooperation and Development (OECD), with whom the United States competes in the international economy and against whose economic record it assesses its own. Although the average age of the population in many of these nations is somewhat higher than that of the American population, these nations manage to offer older citizens far more effective protection against the financial inroads of ill health than is afforded elders in the United States. However, they devote a much lower percentage of their GDP to total national health spending than does the United States, without visibly negative effects on the general health of the populations. These data might pique the curiosity of hard-pressed policy makers in the United States. Something useful might possibly be learned from these nations' style of managing health care for their elderly citizens.

Against this international backdrop, the focus will then return to the United States by exploring a question that runs through the entire debate on Medicare reform, namely, Is Medicare perhaps too generous a program? If so, who is too generous?

Finally, a macroeconomic primer will be offered on the general political economy of sharing the nation's GDP among the gainfully employed, who may imagine themselves to be producing the entire GDP, and those who are either too young or too old to be gainfully employed. The challenge for policy makers in the early twenty-first century will be to effect that sharing with civility.

HEALTH CARE FOR ELDERLY PEOPLE IN OTHER COUNTRIES

As American policy makers contemplate the current and future burden of financing Medicare (and Social Security), they might be surprised to learn that, by international standards, the United States actually is a relatively young country (see Figure 15–1). Only in the year 2015 will the United States attain the age structure of the population that is already

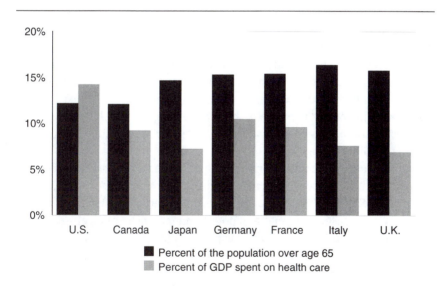

■ Percent of the population over age 65
▦ Percent of GDP spent on health care

Figure 15–1 The Lack of Relationship Between Aging and Total National Health Spending, Selected Countries, 1996. *Source:* Adapted with permission from G.F. Anderson, In Search of Value: An International Comparison of Cost, Access, and Outcomes, *Health Affairs,* Vol. 16, No. 6, pp. 163–171, Copyright © 1997, The People–to–People Health Foundation, Inc., All Rights Reserved.

manifest in Europe today. If misery loves company, the United States has ample company in this regard.

One should think that the European economies would break under the enormous economic burden imposed upon them by their elderly populations. To be sure, total taxes take a much higher percentage of the GDP in Europe than they do in the United States. Of the industrialized nations represented in the OECD, only Australia, Switzerland and Japan channel as low a proportion of their GDP though the public sector as does the United States. It is also the case that the European economies are plagued by high unemployment and sluggish economic growth, which can be attributed in part to the high marginal tax rates faced by private-sector decision makers in those countries. On the other hand, the highly rigid labor laws in those countries probably contribute even more than do high taxes to their high unemployment rates. These labor laws, which make it very difficult to trim a firm's work force in tune with economic conditions, literally convert employed labor to a fixed cost.

Remarkably, spending on health care by itself cannot explain these countries' relatively sluggish economic performance. Figure 15–1 also shows total national health spending as a percentage of the GDP in selected nations. This figure shows that the United States devotes a much larger share of its GDP to health care than do other countries in the OECD, in spite of the fact that some 40 million Americans do not have health insurance at any point in time. Other things being equal, the uninsured must exert at least some downward pressure on health spending in the United States, as health care for the low-income uninsured is effectively rationed to them by price and ability to pay.

Standard economic theory predicts that relative income and wealth drive international differences in health spending—which can explain a good part of the relatively higher spending on health care in the United States— and such is the case. Differences in per-capita income explain close to 80% of the observed differences in per-capita health spending across nations. However, even after adjustment for relative differences in per-capita income, the United States tends to spend about $1,000 more per capita on health care than do other nations, in spite of the relatively younger age of the population.

Research has never established concretely just what additional health care and health benefits Americans actually receive for their higher per-capita outlays on health care, other than the faith that the United States health system is "the best in the world." Certainly, that higher spending does not reflect itself in the traditional health statistics—such as life expectancy or infant morality—by which nations typically compare themselves. On the contrary, on some of these indicators, the United States actually does not rank highly (e.g., Schieber, Pouillier, & Greenwald, 1994). Total national health spending measures only the slice of the GDP that society has ceded to the providers of real health care resources in return for whatever real resources the providers have devoted to patients. Cross-national comparisons of health spending per capita tell little about what real health care benefits that spending actually buys. Conceivably, two nations identical in all real respects might devote exactly the same set of real health care resources (labor, equipment and so on) to patients, yet might cede vastly different slices of their GDP to the providers of these real resources. There is mounting research evidence that this is not merely a theory (Pauly, 1993; Reinhardt, 1987).

Just how tenuous the relationship between the financial and the real resource flow in health care actually is can be inferred from a recent, in-depth cross-national study undertaken by the management-consulting firm McKinsey & Company (1996). With the help of an advisory board of distinguished economists and clinicians, these investigators sought to explain international differences in the use of real resources and in the money flow in health care. Table 15–1 illustrates one such comparison. In that display, the McKinsey researchers tried to explain the factors that made 1990 per-capita health spending in the United States exceed the comparable German number by roughly $1,000. Although the precise

Table 15–1 Sources of Differences in Per-Capita Health Spending
1990 U.S. Dollars, Purchasing Power Parity

	Additional Health Spending Per Capita in the U.S. Relative to Other Countries	
	U.K.	GERMANY
Spending in Country	**$1,113**	**$1,473**
Medical inputs used	$388	($390)
Prices of inputs	$686	$737
Administration	$437	$360
Other	($185)	$259
Spending in the U.S.	**$2,439**	**$2,439**

Source: Courtesy of McKinsey Global Institute, 1996, Los Angeles, California.

magnitudes of these estimates may be subject to debate, the general thrust of the study seems on the mark.

According to the McKinsey study, Americans actually tend to receive about 15% fewer direct patient-care resources per capita than do Germans. That assessment is consistent with earlier cross-national studies. Schieber et al. (1994), for example, have shown that most nations in the OECD have more hospital beds and physicians per capita than does the United States, and their citizens receive commensurately more bed days and physician visits per capita than do Americans. Europeans in general also use vastly more pharmaceutical products than do Americans. On the other hand, the McKinsey study also confirms what has long been known about the American health system, namely, that American patients must support a much more costly public and private bureaucracy than do their counter-parts in other countries. If "health care bureaucrats" include not only the civil servants who administer our public health programs but also the huge corps of administrative and marketing personnel in the private health care economy, the U.S. health system probably ranks as the most bureaucratic health system anywhere in the world.

The researchers at McKinsey & Company prefer to interpret the ob-served cross-national difference in the use of direct patient-care resources as a difference in patient-care productivity, and that may well be so. An alternative interpretation, however, might be that at least some of the higher use of patient-care resources in Germany—longer length of stays in hospitals, extensive stays in convalescent health spas, a larger number of physician visits per capita and a higher consumption of pharmaceutical products per capita—add comfort that is enjoyed by patients but that is not measurably reflected in the clinical outcome data used in the study.

Be that as it may, the important point that stands out in the McKinsey study is that, relative to German patients, American patients are made to hand over to the providers of health care much larger sums of money per unit of real health care resources received by American patients than do German patients. That circumstance and lower spending on administration go a long way in explaining why Germans—and Europeans in general—are able to care rather well for a larger proportion of elderly people without ceding to the providers of health nearly as large a slice of the GDP as Americans do. If the McKinsey researchers are right and Europeans really could increase the productivity of the patient-care resources they use without lowering the clinical quality of care and patient satisfaction, they probably could lower the percentage of GDP spent on health care even further.

With the exception of Japan, elders in the other nations of the OECD do not have separate health insurance programs specifically for them. Instead, they are fully integrated into the overall health insurance and health care delivery systems of those countries. Usually, the out-of-pocket spending on health care at point of service is small outside the United States. Although France has always imposed on patients systematic cost sharing at point of service through the so-called *ticket moderateur*, that cost sharing is limited for chronically ill, very sick, and poor patients. For an elderly patient in Germany, on the other hand, all physician services, hospital services, prescription drugs, appliances, dental care and so on are fully covered, although there are now copayments, for more elective dental care and for prescription drugs. These may well be raised somewhat as part of the health-reform measures now being contemplated by the German government. There is more heavy cost sharing for elective stays in Germany's famous health spas, although not if these stays are certified by a physician as genuine rehabilitation following a hospital episode. Finally, there is some cost sharing for transportation costs—for example, for the taxi fares to physicians' offices or pharmacies reimbursed under the statutory German health insurance system.

The generosity of the standard benefit package elsewhere in the OECD must be noted in considering the relative generosity of the Medicare program. To elders in the United States, Medicare has been a genuine blessing, which is why they are so fiercely protective of it in the political arena. It is, alas, not a program to boast about at international gatherings of health-policy experts.

HOW GENEROUS IS MEDICARE, AND TO WHOM?

In the past, the annual growth in Medicare spending per enrollee has not consistently outpaced private-sector spending per capita and, in the later 1980s, actually fell below the growth in private-sector spending (see Figure 15–2). However, the Congressional Budget Office (CBO) currently projects Medicare spending to continue to grow substantially faster than private-sector spending in the foreseeable future. The CBO expects total Medicare spending to grow from $203 billion in 1996 to $501 billion in

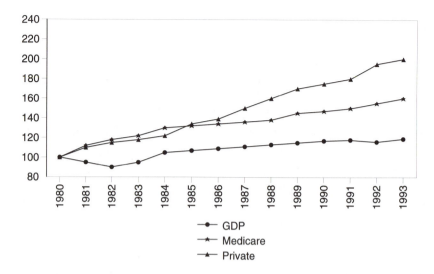

Figure 15–2 Trends in Per-Enrollee Expenditures for Medicare and Private Health Insurance and Gross Domestic Product per Capita, 1980–1983. *Source:* Physician Payment Review Commission analysis of information compiled from the Health Care Financing Administration and the Congressional Budget Office. *Note:* Values have been adjusted for inflation and are expressed in 1980 dollars. Reprinted from *Annual Report to Congress*, 1996, Physician Payment Review Commission.

2007 at an effective average and annual compound growth rate of 8.6%. It expects private-sector health spending to grow from $549 billion in 1996 to $972 billion in 2007, which represents an average compound growth rate of only about 5.3% (Congressional Budget Office, 1997).

In 1996, total Medicare spending, net of the premiums contributed by elders themselves, amounted to 2.4% of the GDP. (For Part B of Medicare, which covers physician services and lab tests, the elderly cover with monthly premiums of about $40 per elderly, roughly 25 percent of the total Part B budget.) The CBO estimates that, by the year 2010, total Medicare spending net of premiums paid by beneficiaries will have risen to 4.1%. It is expected to be 7.1% by the year 2030 (O'Neill, 1997). Although these bites on the GDP certainly are not trivial, the general public probably is not aware that these huge outlays actually cover less than half of total health spending on the elderly population (see Figure 15–3). Though other public programs—notably, Medicaid—pick up another 18%, roughly 37% comes from private sources, much of it in the form of out-of-pocket spending by elders. These out-of-pocket outlays include the premiums paid under Part

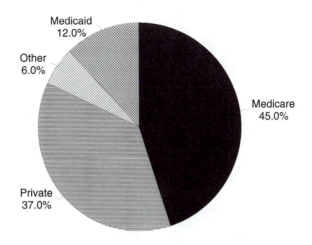

Figure 15–3 Sources of Finance for Health Care Spending on the Elderly, United States, 1987. *Source:* Reprinted from D. Waldo, S.T. Sonnenfeld, D.R. McKusick, and R.H. Arnett, Health Expenditure by Age Group, 1977 and 1987, *Health Care Financing Review*, Vol. 10, No. 4, pp. 111–120.

B of Medicare, premiums for private Medigap policies, the considerable cost sharing at point of service that Medicare visits on its enrollees, and spending on prescription drugs and other items that Medicare does not cover at all. The typical American who obtains private insurance coverage on the job probably would consider Medicare's benefit package unacceptably limited. By international standards the Medicare benefit package is downright harsh.

In the debate on Medicare reform, it is often noted with some pride that, so far at least, Medicare has been a "one-class" insurance system that stands ready to bestow, on rich and poor alike, identical health services for given medical conditions. It is argued that this feature of Medicare is worth preserving. However, if the more relevant yardstick of a "one-class" insurance system—the degree to which the program actually protects the elderly from the financial consequences of illness—is adopted, Medicare comes across as harshly regressive—much harsher and more regressive, surely, than health insurance for the elderly population anywhere else in the OECD. That judgment is underscored by much of the work of Marylin Moon (1996), of which Figure 15–4 is representative. An insurance program that produces the data shown in Figure 15–4 cannot claim the label *egalitarian*. Instead, it rests on a quite peculiar ethical platform.

Income

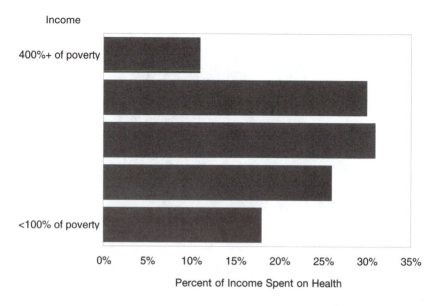

Poverty status definitions: poor = <100% of poverty; near poor = 100–125%; low income = 125–200%; middle income = 200–400%; and high income = 400% or more.

Figure 15–4 Total Out-of-Pocket Health Spending by the Noninstitutionalized Elderly as a Percentage of Family Income, 1996.

Figure 15-4 should give pause to those who believe that Medicare may be excessively generous. Medicare certainly cannot be judged as excessively generous with regard to the bulk of the elderly population in this country, whose income is rather modest. Medicare might be judged generous to the 25% of the elderly with income about $35,000, who probably could contribute more toward the cost of their care than they now do. It certainly is needlessly generous with regard to the relatively few wealthy older people—for example, retired corporate executives, who could afford to pay fully for their own health care and who are known to extract from the program a multiple of what they contributed to it during their work lives, including accumulated interest on those contributions.

Finally, as noted earlier, in terms of the money it turns over to the providers of health care for real resources devoted to patients, the Medicare program can also be judged to be quite generous vis à vis those providers. That is certainly so by international standards but it is increasingly true also by the standards of the financial rewards that private managed care organizations within the United States now pay the providers of health care.

There remains the question of what burden Medicare imposes on the overall economic welfare of society, however generous or miserly one may judge that program to be. Do resources devoted to a nation's elderly people necessarily come at the expense of capital formation and future economic growth, which is defined as annual increases in real (inflation-adjusted) GDP per capita? That question is explored further on, after a brief primer on the composition and distribution of that penultimate barometer of our economy, the GDP.

ON THE POLITICAL ECONOMY OF SHARING THE GDP

Of all the yardsticks by which national prowess and the performance of American presidents are assessed, none seems as important as the GDP. Although formal economic analysis employs rather subtle and sophisticated definitions of *efficiency*, in public discourse, the term typically is meant to be simply "GDP efficiency." In the vernacular, policies that increase the GDP that a nation's population manages to extract from itself within a given year are "GDP-efficient." Policies that detract from GDP are "GDP-inefficient."

Alas, although the GDP is ubiquitously cited in public discourse, it probably is less well understood than it ought to be. In particular, many users of the statistic seem not to appreciate the tenuity between that narrow economic statistic and the intangible something one might call *economic welfare, standard of living* or, in short, *national well-being*. This is so, even in elevated company, and there may be merit in examining briefly the content of the GDP and the process by which it is distributed among the citizenry.

GDP and "National Well-Being"

Formally, a nation's GDP is the money value, calculated at market prices, of all of the final goods and services that have been produced during a year within a nation's geographic boundaries and that have been traded in the marketplace. The measure includes the goods and services produced or put in place by a government for the rest of society. That part of GDP (about 19%) includes the valuable output produced by, say, the Federal Aviation Administration, the National Institutes of Health, the Centers for Disease Control, the Federal Bureau of Investigation, the judicial system and the armed forces, to mention but a few. The government's contribution to GDP also includes long-lived capital goods (public schools and universities, roads, airports, military hardware, and so on) procured and put in place by government on behalf of the citizenry (about 3% of GDP) (The Economic Report of the President, 1996, Table B-16).

The "final goods and services" that make up the GDP fall into two broad categories: (1) consumption (that is, items that are used up in the same year in which they are produced) and (2) gross investments (that is, the structures, equipment and knowledge gained through research and development that will be used over several future years to enhance the productivity of human labor). If generous caring for the elderly population detracts from a nation's economic growth, it will be through the split of the GDP between consumption and capital formation.

In 1994, for example, the U.S. GDP was about $7 trillion. Of that total, Americans devoted roughly 84% to consumption and 17% to the creation of productive capital goods (structures, equipment, research and development, and so on) that will support the production of GDP for many years.

The Role of Nonmarket Output

The phrase "and traded in the marketplace" is crucial in the definition of the GDP, because that measure excludes the production of a myriad of highly valuable goods and services that citizens exchange outside the formal marketplace. In the United States, these "nonmarket" products produced by the economy do not always receive the respect they deserve in debates on domestic policy.

For example, the important services that are exchanged in the home among generations are not counted in GDP, yet it is generally agreed that these services are crucial to the well-being and progress of a nation. If in country A both child care and elder care were purchased predominantly in the marketplace, those services would be counted as part of the GDP. If in country B child care was typically rendered by grandparents who live with and are cared for by their children, these services would not be counted in country B's GDP. In other words, country A would register a higher GDP than would country B, even if they were identical in all other respects. In fact, however, the actual standard of human well-being in country B might well be much higher than that in country A.

The GDP also excludes another very important public good that is produced by a nation: the highly valued, intangible something called social peace. In economics, *a public good* is defined as "one whose consumption by one person does not detract from the consumption of that good enjoyed by other persons." Clean air is a public good, as is the control of contagious diseases. The ability of citizens to walk safely through their nation's capital very literally is part of a nation's social peace, as is the sense of well-being generated by a fail-safe system that protects one's family from the devastating financial inroads that can come with bad luck. This includes the "bad luck" of living longer than one had anticipated in one's younger years, when provisions were made for the proverbial golden age, the bad luck of serious illness or the bad luck of having one's life's savings wiped out somehow by a general economic calamity or an imprudent investment decision.

Social Peace as a Policy Goal

In Canada and, especially, in Europe, the concept of social peace is openly cited in debates on public policy. It is viewed as a highly valued part of national output and given considerable deference in debates on domestic policy, in the sense that some economic growth is consciously traded away in these nations for the sake of a rather airtight social safety net. That sentiment finds its most explicit expression in the much cited-Principle of Solidarity that has constrained health policy in those nations for a century and that often leads these nations to pursue policies American policy makers would regard as much too GDP-inefficient. To illustrate, it is evident that American policy makers consider universal and comprehensive health-insurance coverage for all children prohibitively GDP-inefficient. Presumably, that is why American policy makers have shied away from that otherwise desirable policy so far. By contrast, Europeans would not even contemplate reducing their comprehensive and universal health-insurance coverage of children for the sake of superior economic growth. It would violate the Europeans' Principle of Solidarity, a principle whose faithful observance by public policy is deemed vital for the production of social peace.

One should not think that the European penchant for social peace springs from pure altruism; part of it springs from political pragmatism. Econo-mists refer to *pure altruism* as a "positive externality in consumption," which means that person A derives happiness from seeing person B consume more of certain goods or services (such as food and health care). However, there are also "negative externalities in consumption," among them, social envy. Social envy is the tendency among human beings to resent it when certain basic consumables—such as health care—are highly unequally distributed. Because social envy can beget social unrest, it is closely linked to the nation's production of social peace, a link commonly overlooked by economists—certainly by American economists. To the European mind, for example, it is a manifestation of social unrest when citizens cannot walk safely within their own neighborhoods or within their nation's capital. They view it as a negative output of an economy, like air pollution.

The presumed link between social envy and social peace has long driven social policy in many countries of the OECD. Thus, when Chancellor Otto von Bismarck introduced the concept of social insurance to Germany in the late nineteenth century, he was probably less motivated by a Prussian aristocrat's innate compassion for the working class than by the theory that social insurance, by directly enhancing the well-being of the toiling masses, would indirectly protect the propertied classes from the inroads of social unrest.

Even if social envy does not lead to outright social unrest, however, it can nevertheless color the overall satisfaction that a nation's citizens derive from their health system. American providers of health care and American politicians regularly proclaim that the American health system is the "best in the world." They must find it sobering that cross-national opinion surveys, based on large national samples, are not consistent with that assessment. Table 15–2, taken directly from the most recent survey of this sort, indicates that a higher proportion of American respondents declared themselves to be dissatisfied with their health systems than did Canadian and German respondents, even though, in 1994, Americans were

Table 15–2 Ratings of Health Care Systems in the United States, Canada, and Western Germany, 1988, 1990, and 1994

	United States		Canada		West Germany	
	1988	*1994*	*1988*	*1994*	*1990*	*1994*
On the whole, the health care system works pretty well, and only minor changes are necessary to make it work better	10%	18%	56%	29%	41%	30%
There are some good things in our health care system, but fundamental changes are needed to make it work better	60	53	38	59	35	55
Our health care system has so much wrong with it that we need to completely rebuild it	29	28	5	12	13	11
Not sure	1	2	1	a	11	4

aLess than 0.5%

Sources: Reprinted with permission from R.J. Blendon et al., *Health Affairs*, Vol. 14, No. 4, p. 222, Copyright © 1995, The People-to-People Health Foundation, Inc., All Rights Reserved.

relatively more positive about their system than they were in 1988, when private health-insurance premiums increased at double-digit rates. Although many factors can explain the relatively more negative assessment Americans accord their health system—among them, culturally conditioned differences in expectations and perceptions—it may be significant that a higher percentage of American respondents considered themselves "unfairly treated" by their health system, had "problems paying doctor and hospital bills last year," "could not get needed medical care last year," and, moreover, felt that "the health system involves too much bureaucracy," (Blendon et al., 1995) a feature of the American health system already remarked upon earlier, in connection with the McKinsey study. Policy makers in other countries appear to be highly sensitive to that intangible aspect of "national well-being," which may explain why they are more reluctant than are American policy makers to embrace the idea of rationing health care by price and ability to pay, even if economists certify the latter approach to be more GDP efficient

In spite of the importance we accord it in our debates on domestic policy, the GDP actually is a highly truncated and systematically biased yardstick of a nation's economic well-being, and it is therefore justly criticized (Cobb, Halsead, & Rowe, 1995). For better or for worse, however, that statistic now is the central score in the game by which we assess the performance of our nation and of our politicians. Therefore, the impact that material requirements of the elderly population might have upon the growth of the GDP over time must be determined. To explore that question, let us examine more closely the process by which GDP is shared among members of society and what effect different ways of sharing might have on GDP efficiency.

Distributing the Nation's GDP among Young and Old

Economics professors find it useful in their teaching to depict the GDP as a giant national pie that is baked by some members of society, then sliced up and distributed among all members of society. In the United States, fewer than half of the population actually produces the GDP of any given year (The Economic Report of the President, 1996, Tables B-30 and B-31). These pie bakers, of course, contribute more than their time and brawn to the production process. The most important contribution they make actually comes from the "human capital" that, with considerable help from the rest of society, they have obtained through education and training. These human pie bakers are further supported, of course, by a vast array of physical capital goods, the bulk of which are owned by "private capitalists" (although government owns a sizable array of capital goods as well).

These "private capitalists" are made up of individuals who own those capital goods outright, as proprietors of their own business firms. They also include individuals who own capital goods indirectly, as investors in mutual funds, private pension funds or other savings institutions that finance the acquisition of productive capital by producers. The financial institutions to which the indirect capitalists entrust their savings hold ownership rights in the revenue streams yielded by the capital goods that these institutions finance. The indirect capitalists, in turn, claim the bulk of the financial institutions' earnings through such legally enforceable financial contracts as pension contracts, life insurance policies or savings accounts. In this way, perhaps unwittingly, millions of American workers and older people are actually bona fide capitalists.

Very broadly speaking, distribution of the GDP among members of society can be thought of as a two-phased process. In the first phase—the purely economic phase—generalized claims to the GDP are distributed among those who actually can take credit for baking the pie: gainfully employed Americans who bring to the process their time, brawn and human capital; and the direct or indirect capitalists who "lend" these employed Americans the physical capital goods used in production. In the second phase of distributing GDP—the purely political phase—the government redirects the claims to the GDP made by those who take credit for baking the GDP pie to others, through the process of taxation and transfer payments.

Figure 15–5 provides details on the first phase of this distribution. Here, it is best to think of the GDP pie as the total amount of revenue booked by all of the "vendors" of the goods and services that are represented in the GDP. First, the "vendors" carve out a slice equal to about 12% of the GDP as a so-called capital consumption allowance to make good for the wear and tear of productive physical capital used in the production of GDP. Next, the private "vendors" are required to hand over to the government a slice equal to about 9% of total GDP in the form of excise and other indirect business taxes that are not based on earned income. The remainder of the GDP pie, usually about 80% or so, is called the *net national income*. It is the portion of the GDP that is available for distribution to those who actually take credit for baking the GDP pie.

Chief among the owners of productive inputs are, of course, the roughly 127 million gainfully employed Americans. Together, they received ap-

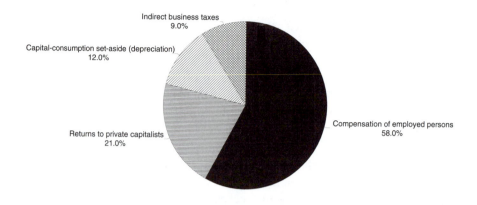

Figure 15–5 The Distribution of Gross Domestic Product, United States, 1994. *Source:* Economic Report of the President, February, 1996. Reprinted from Health Care Financing Administration.

proximately 58% of the GDP in 1994 in the form of pretax wages and salaries, including employer-paid fringe benefits. The bulk of their share actually is a return on the human capital they carried into the production process. We shall explore later whether these employed Americans actually deserve full return on that human capital, given that its creation was probably financed by the preceding generation rather than these employees themselves.

The remaining 21% or so of the GDP pie in 1994 was paid to direct and indirect private capitalists, who were issued those claims in the form of pretax interest, pretax rental income for leased property, proprietor's pretax income and pretax corporate profits. After paying taxes on corporate profits (close to 3% of GDP in 1994), the after-tax profits were either distributed by corporations to their shareholders in the form of dividends (about 2.9% of GDP in 1994) or retained by the corporations and reinvested on behalf of the corporate owners (about 1.7% of GDP in 1994).

Direct and indirect private capitalism plays a very important role in the distribution of GDP to the elderly population, whose investments in pension funds and other savings vehicles cast them in the role of capitalists. Elders' actual and potential role as private capitalists will be increasingly highlighted in the current debate on the reform of Social Security and Medicare because it is one mechanism by which elders can divert claims to GDP toward themselves without triggering the ire of younger, employed Americans. The alternative mechanism of transferring GDP to the elderly population is, of course, the redistribution of claims to the GDP through taxes and government transfers.

How large a fraction of GDP is actually involved in the second, tax-and-transfer stage, for "governments" at all levels? As noted earlier, American governments at all levels currently divert a bit less than one third of the nation's GDP to their budgets via taxes of all sorts, including the indirect business taxes mentioned earlier. However, not all of the government's total take goes to transfer payments proper. Close to two thirds of it (about 19% of the GDP) is used to produce, or to procure from the private sector, the goods and services that government itself contributes to the GDP. Only the remaining third (between 11% and 14% of GDP, depending on the precise categorization of items) ends up as transfers to all age groups in the United States. Included in these transfers are cash payments to Social Security recipients, retired civil servants and military personnel, the poor, the unemployed, poor and wealthy farmers and so on. These transfers also include the transfer of benefits in kind, such as the procurement of health care from the private sector on behalf of elderly and poor people through the Medicare and Medicaid programs, and similar programs in which government pays private entities for services rendered to its citizens under public programs.

At this point, a question arises. Is the tax-and-transfer mechanism supporting the elderly population merely a neutral substitute for transferring GDP through private capitalism or does it have unique drawbacks?

THE ELDERLY POPULATION'S CLAIM ON GDP, SOCIAL EQUITY AND GDP EFFICIENCY

Hidden beneath the typically technical debate over the reform of Social Security and Medicare are two assertions. The current allocation of GDP to the nation's elders, with its heavy reliance on taxes and transfers, is not only GDP-inefficient (and might be judged unfair to future generations) but it is also unfair among contemporaries (Peterson, 1997).

The Issue of Fairness

The argument that a tax-and-transfer policy of caring for the elderly population is unfair is part of the more general taxpayers' revolt that has driven American domestic policy in recent years (and is apt to drive domestic policy in other countries as well). Many gainfully employed Americans and the private capitalists whose productive resources have produced the GDP in any given year tend to think that, as a matter of principle, they have a right to all of the GDP produced by their resources. Many of them question government's authority to divert what they consider their justly earned claims on GDP to people who did not contribute directly (through work) or indirectly (through ownership of capital) to the baking of the GDP pie. It is an argument not easily dismissed.

Conveniently overlooked in this argument, however, is that gainfully employed people receive the returns of human capital that were not of their own making. This human capital was predominantly financed by members of the preceding generation. If intergenerational fairness is the issue, the question may be how the generation that substantially financed the succeeding generation's human capital ought to be compensated for that investment.

The Issue of GDP Efficiency

The issue of GDP efficiency arises from the widely held theory that government's claim on a nation's GDP in general tends to detract from the economy's GDP efficiency and economic growth. That theory has two distinct aspects. The first is straightforward supply-side theory. The second involves the hypothesis that resources devoted to the elderly population will be shifted into added consumption at the expense of capital formation.

The core of the first argument, supply-side theory, is that taxes and transfers impose on the economy what economists call a *deadweight loss*. This loss arises from the distortions that taxation introduces into the economic incentives faced by decision makers in the private sector. High marginal income-tax rates, for example, are thought to discourage work effort as they effectively subsidize the enjoyment of leisure. High marginal income-tax rates are also thought to discourage savings, as well as investments in productive capital goods. Income taxes discourage savings, it is thought, because they reduce the after-tax reward to foregoing consumption. They are thought to reduce investment in capital goods because they reduce the after-tax reward to that form of risk taking. Reduction of this deadweight loss through across-the-board tax cuts is one of the major objectives of supply-side economics.

There is surface appeal to the second argument, namely, that a nation's support of the elderly population comes at the expense of capital formation. At its extreme, this theory conjures up the image that tax-supported spending is financed by taxpayers through reductions in savings and capital formation rather than through reductions in consumption. There is, of course, no reason to make so extreme an assumption. Income and payroll taxes displace both consumption and savings. Indeed, it is instructive to note that nations in the OECD with relatively high marginal tax rates on income and as a percentage of the GDP tend to save and invest a larger fraction of their GDP than does the United States.

Even so, the second argument should not be dismissed entirely. Many factors other than mere tax rates drive cross-national differences in savings and investment rates. It certainly is plausible to argue that, other things being equal, tax-and-transfer mechanisms can have an additional impact on economic growth when they redistribute income among income classes with inherently different propensities to consume and save. If claims to the GDP are taken from individuals with a high propensity to save (high-income taxpayers, for example) and given to individuals with a high propensity to consume (elderly or poor people, for example), the overall proportion of the GDP allocated to the production of long-lived capital goods is apt to shrink. It would be the price, in terms of GDP efficiency, that is paid for the sake of social solidarity.

Privatizing the Financing of Health Care for the Elderly Population

Evidently, the objections to the current and future allocation of GDP to the elderly population are not due to the size of that allocation. They are based strictly on the heavy reliance currently placed on taxation to effect that allocation. Presumably, there would be no objection to that allocation if elders received their current claim on GDP chiefly as a return for "renting" physical capital goods owned directly or indirectly by elders to young workers to enhance their own productivity. Some reform proposals seek precisely that arrangement. The idea would be to phase out over time the tax-financed Medicare program as we know it and to replace it, for currently younger Americans, with a massive program of individually owned medical savings accounts to be built up during the individual's work years and made available to finance private health-insurance coverage in retirement.

Such a major shift toward private capitalism as a means to finance health care for the elderly population might offer two advantages. First, it might serve to reallocate GDP away from consumption and into investments in the capital goods that enhance labor productivity. As economist Herbert Stein has pointed out in connection with privatizing Social Security (Stein, 1997), this process of reallocation actually is more complex and less certain than may be imagined. Even so, a major shift toward financing the health care of the elderly population through private capitalism might well trigger some reallocation of GDP away from consumption and into capital formation. A second potential advantage of privatizing the financing of health care for the elderly population might be that younger generations would view the payments of "rentals" to elders (in the form of interest, dividends, rentals for space and so on) with less resentment than they do the payment of payroll taxes for Medicare. There surely is something to that argument as well.

However, this proposal to privatize the financing of health care for the elderly population also carries with it some major complications. For one, the proposal would eliminate the already limited degree of social solidarity now built into the Medicare program. Health care for the American elderly population in general would be even more extensively rationed by price and ability to pay than it is now. Furthermore, unless it were decided as a matter of policy to financially compensate chronically ill individuals in all income groups for their particular burdens, and unless such a compensation scheme were technically feasible if it were desired, privatizing the financing of Medicare would be likely to reallocate the financial burden of illness away from healthy elders onto the shoulders of the chronically sick elderly people. It is not clear that the American public would endorse that shift if it were fully understood.

Second, the ability to accumulate direct or indirect ownership rights in physical capital goods during their work years varies enormously across members of society. In the long run, the privatization of Medicare (and Social Security) would widen the distribution of income and wealth among the elderly population. Therefore, there would still have to be explicit transfers of claims to the GDP, not only from the young to the old, but also from better-off elders to their poorer contemporaries. Among the latter might be individuals whose earning power during their work years had been substantial but who, for some reason, mismanaged their investments in capital or simply met with bad luck.

Third, in fairness to the elderly population, such a policy ought to entail a much broader reexamination of intergenerational equity. It would require some revolutionary changes in the financial social contract between generations. If the allocation of GDP to a nation's elderly citizens is to be effected less through taxes and transfers and more through the ownership of private capital by elders themselves, it seems only fair that the financial contracts surrounding this arrangement be extended to the formation of human capital. Practically, this would mean the complete abolition of tax-financed higher education, including state-supported medical, business and law schools. Instead, the younger generation would borrow the entire cost of their education and training from private pension funds, thereby allowing the owners of pension contracts to amass legal claims on the returns to the human capital that higher education gives to students. A full exploration of the implication of such an approach for higher education in this country lies beyond the compass of this essay. Suffice it to observe that the effect of these implications would be monumental.

In the meantime, for Americans currently in or near retirement, there is little choice but to keep their faith in the social contract that is now in place for them and that surely will be honored by their children, even if grudgingly. To help ease their pain, it might help hard-pressed baby boomers to view payroll taxes they now pay for Medicare and Social Security as "rentals" for human and physical capital bestowed upon them by the elders who now benefit from these public social insurance programs. That will not do anything to alleviate the tax burden borne by the baby boomers, of course, but it might improve their mental health.

There is one additional question we might ask ourselves as we contemplate the burden that elderly Americans impose on the younger generation, namely, To what extent is that burden needless and self-inflicted?

The Price of Pluralism

Sooner or later at any conference on Medicare reform, after contemplation of the huge and partially uncontrollable cash flow triggered by health care for the elderly population, someone exclaims in exasperation, "Of course, if one were asked to design a health-insurance program for the nation's elders from scratch, no one in their right mind would ever put in place the crazy-quilt system we now have."

Crazy-quilt systems are the inevitable products of what we celebrate so exuberantly on other occasions in this country, namely, "incrementalism" and "pluralism." Unfortunately, it requires enormous resources and superb human capital to operate crazy-quilt systems. It also requires a high tolerance for waste.

Although Medicare seems to waste little money on sheer administration overhead—it pays out to the providers of health care a higher percentage of the dollars it takes in than does any other public or private health insurance program. Health care that is paid for is not necessarily health care worth paying for, and even worthwhile care may be purchased at needlessly high prices. The European data cited earlier suggest that at least some of the burden that Medicare imposes on the young could be reduced simply through better methods of procuring and producing health care for the old. Donald Berwick (1996), an American expert on quality improvement in health care, noted after observing that European hospitals that "seem at least as good as any comparable American facility" somehow operate at costs that are 25–40% lower than comparable American costs, "We stand to harvest lessons of immense value from the serious study of organizations and [health] systems far from our own. We can learn from the international diversity in approach to clinical care, professional roles, the organization of delivery, and financing. Improvement thrives everywhere, and good ideas do not end at any border."

That Medicare currently is not acting as a prudent purchaser on behalf of the nation's elderly is suggested by more than cross-national comparisons. It can be inferred also from the enormous, largely inexplicable regional variation in age- and sex-adjusted per capita spending within the Medicare program itself (e.g., Welch, et al., 1993). It surely would be very difficult to justify with an appeal to clinical science or geographic economic factors the remarkable differences in age-, sex- and price-adjusted average per capita cost under the Medicare program (Figure 15–6), which varies by a factor of more than two across counties in the United States (Moon, 1996). As is seen in Figure 15–6, under the current risk-contracting method, Medicare increased the premiums paid health maintenance organizations (HMOs) in counties that already enjoyed relatively high premiums in 1995 much more than it increased premiums for HMOs in counties that were paid relatively low premiums in 1995. It taxes the imagination to detect prudent purchasing in these numbers.

This remark is not intended to question the competence of the civil servants who administer Medicare. On the contrary, their technical sophistication is not likely to be exceeded anywhere in the world, nor is their

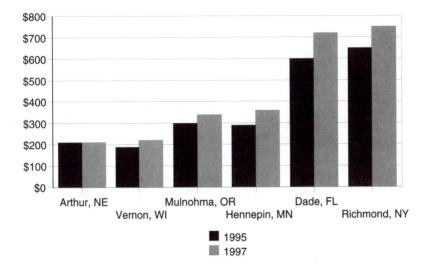

Figure 15–6 Adjusted Average Per Capita Cost (AAPCC) Medicare HMO Payment Basis—1995 and 1997 (Dollars per Member per Month). *Source:* HCFA, cited in Presentation by Coalition for Fairness in Medicare, 1997.

---

motivation to administer the program efficiently and fairly to both taxpayers and the elderly population. The problem is that the vast army of health care providers who book Medicare spending as revenue is highly sophisticated as well, as is the army of lobbyists that toils so hard on behalf of those providers to vitiate many of the efforts of the sophisticated civil servants who seek to administer Medicare fairly and efficiently.

Thus, jointly, this vast armada of truly sophisticated Americans has produced over time the cumbersome and needlessly expensive "crazy quilt" we all lament. Occasionally, that crazy-quilt system exhibits a truly astounding lack of sophistication—for example, in its disbursements for home care, for the services of skilled nursing facilities, for durable medical equipment and for risk contracts with HMOs. That sporadic lack of sophistication probably is unrivaled anywhere in the world.

It can be doubted, for example, that any health-insurance program in the world would blindly compensate private health care facilities for the work of physical therapists, for example, without some notion of a reasonable benchmark for the proper price for those services, including benchmark salaries for therapists. As the General Accounting Office of the U.S. Congress reported recently, however, Medicare does just that (General Accounting Office, 1996).

It can be suspected that, behind it all lies not a lack of competence all around but the working of our unique model of representative democracy. At the behest of the armada of sophisticated lobbyists who finance the costly campaigns of the typically sophisticated legislators writing Medicare legislation, these legislators frequently force the nation's sophisticated civil servants to do some very unsophisticated things, often against the better judgment of these legislators' own sophisticated staffers, then shrug it off with a paraphrase of comedian Flip Wilson, "The system made us do it!"

In fairness to Medicare beneficiaries, however, we should admit that the invoice for Medicare we pay on their behalf should properly be written as follows:

THE ALL AMERICAN MEDICARE BILL

For necessary health care proper		$ M
Plus: • Surcharge for incrementalism		$x\%$
• Surcharge for "pluralism"		$y\%$
• Fair return on PAC money		$z\%$
TOTAL		$[100+x+y+z]\%(\$M)$

A lively debate could be had on the relative and absolute sizes of surtaxes x, y and z; but surely no one would deny their significant role in driving the cost of the program. If Europe's health systems and the health systems in, for example, the states of Oregon or Minnesota are any guide, these surcharges might add up to 20% or more.

As we, the baby boomers who now administer the Medicare program, lament its burden and contemplate its reform, we might ask ourselves the following two pointed questions: Can we fairly blame frail and sick elderly Americans who need our help for the many surtaxes that our own folly adds to their health care bill? and, Do we have the genius to rise above the folly?

REFERENCES

Anderson, G.F. (1997). In search of value: An international comparison of cost, access and outcomes. *Health Aff, 16*(6).

Berwick, D. (1996, Spring). The globalization of health care. *Quality Connection, 5*(2), 2.

Blendon, R.J., Benson, J., Donelan, K., Leitman, R., Taylor, H., Koeck, C., & Gitterman, D. (1995). Who has the best health care system? A second look. *Health Aff, 14*(4), 220–230.

Cobb, C., Halsead, T., & Rowe, J. (1995, October). If the GDP is up, why is America down? *Atlantic Monthly,* 59–78.

Congressional Budget Office. (1997, January). *The economic and budget outlook: Fiscal years 1998–2007.* Appendix H, Table H-2, p. 127.

Economic Report of the President, transmitted to the Congress (1996, February). Washington, DC, Table B-16.

General Accounting Office, United States Congress. (1996). *Medicare: Early resolution of overcharges for therapy in nursing homes is unlikely.* Pub. No. GAO/HEHS-96-145.

McKinsey & Co. (1996, October). *Health care productivity.*

Moon, M. (1996). *Medicare now and in the future.* Washington, DC: The Urban Institute, p. 11.

O'Neill, J.E. (1997, March). *Opportunities and problems for Medicare in the competitive market place.* Princeton Conference on Medicare Reform, Princeton, NJ.

Pauly, M.V. (1993, Fall). U.S. health care costs: The untold story. *Health Aff,* 152–159.

Peterson, P.G. (1997, 28 February). *Medicare in the context of a balanced budget.* Presented at the Princeton Conference on Medicare Reform.

Rheinhardt, U.E. (1987). Resource allocation in health care: The allocation of life styles to providers, *Milbank Mem Fund Q, 65*(2), 153–176.

Schieber, G.J., Pouillier, J.P., & Greenwald, L.M. (1994, Fall). Health system performance in OECD countries, 1980–1992. *Health Aff, 13*(4), 100–112.

Stein, H. (1997, 5 February). Social security and the single investor. *The Wall Street Journal,* p. A-18.

Welch, W.P., Miller, M.E., Welch, H.G., Fisher, E.S., & Wennberg, J.H. (1993, 4 March). Geographic variation in expenditures for physicians services in the United States. *N Engl J Med, 328*(9), 621–627.

CHAPTER 16

Healthy Aging in the National Interest: The Politics of Research

Daniel Perry

America is burning a short fuse to the age boom. Our politicians, not exactly celebrated for long-range planning, must act now with unusual foresight to make the strategic investments that will make it possible to postpone and prevent the diseases of aging. To break old habits of partisanship and delay, Americans must let Washington know that healthy aging matters to them. If the public demands it, policies that promote longevity and independence will become central to American politics. The question is, Will that happen soon enough?

At best, the United States has only about 10 years to get its national act together in medical research and training. In 1998, Medicare outlays for hospital and medical services for some 33 million older Americans will come to $200 billion, or more than 10% of the federal budget. That is almost double the cost of Medicare as recently as 1990. Even with the deep cuts passed by Congress last year, the Medicare hospital trust fund will go bankrupt in 2007, 4 years before the first baby boomer turns 65. At the present rate of growth, it is estimated that medical costs for the oldest members of society will balloon six times that of current levels in today's dollars as the baby-boom generation grows older (Schneider & Guralnik, 1990).

Much of the nation's looming Medicare crisis might be defused by discoveries that would improve the health of older people. However, investments in research and training do not generate instant returns. It takes time and money to draw the best minds toward careers in science and to create incentives that keep researchers pursuing innovative solutions. When breakthroughs do come, they can take years to gain broad acceptance in the scientific community. Regulations that dictate when new drugs or processes can be made widely available are necessary for public safety but they, too, can slow the process by several years. The long lead time required for research breakthroughs demands that the public act now.

We are scarcely a dozen years from the time that baby boomers begin drawing old-age benefits from Medicare, yet we still have not committed the nation to an all-out research effort to find solutions to Alzheimer's disease, diabetes, stroke or frailty. Half of all patients soon will be people over age 65, but fewer than 3% of today's medical students choose to take courses in geriatrics (Reuben & Beck, 1994), the field of medicine that deals with the complex needs of older people. What is wrong with this picture?

DIFFERING TIME HORIZONS

In contrast, consider what is happening in Japan, where men live, on average, to 76.3 years, women live to age 83 and the average age within the entire Japanese population is 40. Japanese social planners are paying close attention to their demographic destiny. Western visitors sometimes hear of a successful Tokyo department store being managed according to a 500-year business plan. The tale is probably apocryphal, but it is characteristic of the Japanese love affair with long-range planning. An American executive will watch the daily gyrations of the stock market, paying close attention to the quarterly bottom line, whereas the Japanese executive will follow a plan for corporate growth that may not bear fruit for a decade or more.

In the 1980s, the Japanese Economic Planning Agency developed the "Golden Plan" to design health services for a larger older population—one-quarter of the population of Japan will be over 65 by the year 2020 (Bureau of Health and Social Welfare Services, 1993). More recently, the Japanese government stepped up funding for "longevity science" at a state-of-the-art national laboratory near Nagoya. Despite the economic reversals Japan has suffered in recent years, proactive investment in aging research and an improved geriatric health care system continue to take top priority.

Meanwhile, the American political attention span is decreasing. We tend to reward political leaders for finding short-term solutions that provide a quick fix for long-term problems. American politicians do not seem able to see much beyond the next election or, perhaps, the next opinion poll. Short-range perspectives prevent our leaders from asking very much of citizens in the near term, even if a little sacrifice now would produce a major social benefit in the future. Americans usually can be expected to do the right thing if the wolf is at the nation's door; just do not expect us to get too excited if the wolf is not expected to show up for another 20 years.

Though this is conventional wisdom, the impact of the graying of America has already been deeply felt in the domestic politics of the 1990s. Concern over the aging of the population is at least implicit in nearly all the domestic debates of the day: budget and spending priorities, medical savings accounts, health care reform, Social Security, Medicare, Medicaid and long-term care. Can we count on government programs born of the New Deal and the Great Society to sustain 76 million baby boomers through their old age without bankrupting the nation? Do these programs need some judicious tinkering, or must we start now with new ideas?

Since 1997, both Republican and Democratic party leaders have claimed credit for the passage of the Balanced Budget Act. A keystone of that legislation is a commitment to save $115 billion in Medicare spending between 1998 and 2002. This is actually a less drastic measure than it appears, as the largest part of the saving will not be realized until the year 2002, and most of the cuts are designed to fall first on hospital, skilled nursing and home care expenditures.

MISSING IN THE MEDICARE ACTION

The Balanced Budget Act relies on conventional means to control spiraling Medicare costs. The majority of savings will come from reducing reimbursements for providers of care. Though older Americans will be given a broader array of choices in selecting health care providers, managed-care options will be strongly encouraged to hold down costs. However, reliance on moving elders into managed care may not produce anything close to the savings anticipated in the new law. In addition, the consumer backlash against managed care and its manifestation in legislation could very well eliminate the cost reductions anticipated in the enactment of new options for Medicare services.

Although not included in the final bill signed by the President, the Senate had considered more dramatic reforms. These included raising the eligibility age for Medicare from 65 to 67 for future beneficiaries and means testing benefits such that people who are more affluent would be required to pay more for their own health care. These and other proposals, possibly including a major overhaul that converts Medicare to a voucher system, eventually may come back to Congress. In the meantime, a bipartisan commission is expected to make recommendations on future reforms to the Medicare program in early 1999.

What has been missing from the Medicare debate so far has been the realization that the soaring costs of health care for the elderly population cannot be controlled effectively unless older people are healthier and more independent for longer periods of their lives. There has been almost no attention paid to the potential for innovations that would produce a healthier, more productive and independent population of older Americans that, in turn, would reduce some of the need and demand for chronic-care services.

Until now, the debate in Washington on how to deal with the impending insolvency of Medicare has focused almost entirely on reducing expenditures and shifting costs from taxpayers to beneficiaries. There has been little or no emphasis on pursuing a strategy that would reduce need and lower demand for health services. Largely overlooked is a scientific investment strategy aimed at reducing demand among Medicare beneficiaries, especially the very old. The goal ought to be to foster more efficient treatment and more effective means to prevent or postpone chronic age-related diseases. It is a strategy that cries out for serious consideration by policy makers.

The most expensive users of federal health insurance are chronically disabled older people who require continuing outpatient, institutional or at-home care. According to the Health Care Financing Administration, the government agency that runs Medicare, the 11% of the patient population that requires the most intensive care accounts for more than three-quarters of all Medicare spending (Riley et al., 1986). Even a small improvement in reducing disability within this group would have an enormous impact on the program's total cost. Similarly, even a modest delay in the onset of age-related disability would relieve suffering for millions and effect huge savings in health care costs.

DELAYING CHRONIC DISEASE—IT WORKS!

The longer people live, the greater the chance that they will experience a geriatric problem—incontinence, immobility, loss of memory or loss of vision or hearing—that can rob them of their ability to live independently.

In the past, the conventional response of the health care system has been to spend more on nursing homes and other forms of "sick care." A more humane and cost-effective approach would be to coax from research more effective means to cure, prevent or postpone dysfunction until much later in life.

Scientists in aging-related research are working to reset the clocklike regularity with which risks of chronic aging-related diseases double approximately every 5 years after middle age. Except for rare exceptions, diseases such as dementias of the Alzheimer's type, osteoporosis or stroke are nearly unheard of in people younger than 40. At middle age, the risks for these diseases and a wide variety of other incurable and chronic afflictions double every 5–7 years.

Is it really feasible to talk about putting aging or aging-related diseases on hold? A growing chorus of research scientists say it is. The would-be generals in a war on aging-related disability are beginning to understand that a determined strategy of delay against the onset of chronic disease is both plausible and highly cost effective. Either by delaying the onset by 5 years or by effecting a 5-year "time out" in the progression of disease, the exponential portion of the curve would double one time less near the end of life. Such a change would ultimately eliminate half of all cases of many age-related diseases and half of the attendant cost and human misery.

Even a brief delay could translate into dramatic savings. It is estimated that postponing the onset of Alzheimer's disease in older people by just 5 years would, in the course of time, reduce its incidence by half, thus saving half of the cost of this terrible, terminal illness (Butler & Brody, 1995; Fillet & Butler, 1997). It is currently estimated that Alzheimer's disease alone costs the United States $100 billion each year (Khachaturian, 1997). A 5-year delay in the onset of major cardiovascular illness could save an estimated $69 billion annually; delaying diabetes by 5 years would save another $50 billion by cutting in half the number of people who would incur the age-related form of the disease during their lifetime. A 5-year postponement of nursing-home admissions would, in time, save $35 billion each year. Putting off the average age at which hip fractures are incurred by just 5 years would reduce the incidence by 140,000 in 1 year, saving another $5 billion (Alliance for Aging Research, 1995).

It is common these days for pharmaceutical companies to promote new medications for heart disease, especially the cholesterol-lowering agents called *statins*, by emphasizing prevention or delay of the risks of a coronary attack. There is evidence suggesting that hormone replacement strategies are effective in delaying the onset of osteoporosis, as well as heart disease in older women. Evidence also suggests that estrogen, Vitamin E and common antiinflammatory drugs may be extending the healthy years of life by protecting people from Alzheimer's disease for significant periods of time. Meanwhile, in the laboratory, our ability to reset the aging clock in humans appears to grow closer each day with new understanding of how telomeres, free radicals and genes work to control cell expression and cell life spans.

Epidemiologists are now noticing that Americans who entered their 70s and 80s within the last 15 years are experiencing lower rates of disability than anyone had expected. Writing in *Science*, John W. Rowe (1997) of the Mount Sinai Medical Center in New York states that we already are witnessing a compression of morbidity among Americans in old age. Rowe observes that 89% of people aged 65–74 report no disability and that, even among those over age 85, 40% are fully functional (Rowe, 1997).

HEALTH SPAN UNDER THE MICROSCOPE

Kenneth Manton and his colleagues at the Duke University Center for Demographic Studies have demonstrated that the health status of older Americans has been improving steadily since 1982 (Manton et al., 1997). According to a study reported last year in the *Proceedings of the National Academy of Sciences*, as many as 1.8 million fewer older Americans were disabled in 1995 than what had been expected based on trends in place just 15 years ago. These researchers say these lower disability rates in the elderly population translated into Medicare savings of between $25 billion and $33 billion in 1995 alone.

Reasons for these encouraging developments range from the current generation of elders' higher educational levels and economic status to improved nutrition. Certainly, the availability and value of such medical technologies as joint replacements, improved cardiac treatment and highly effective cataract surgery are all having an impact.

This suggests that an entirely different approach to the Medicare funding crisis is feasible—bringing the system into balance by accelerating the rate of the decline in disability in the later years that we are currently experiencing. Today, there are significantly fewer disabled older Americans than there would have been if the health status of older people had not improved since 1982. According to Manton and colleagues, disability in the elderly population has decreased, on average, 1.3% a year for the last 15 years (Manton et al., 1997). They calculate that if it were possible to increase that rate of decline to 1.5% annually, we could achieve a balance between payroll contributions from today's workers and Medicare outlays without raising taxes and without further cuts in benefits. In short, keeping older Americans healthier in the first place, by accelerating trends already in motion, is a realistic strategy, albeit one usually overlooked in the current Medicare debate.

The key to accelerating the decline in disability is research. Increasing our national investment in biomedical research shortens the timetable for discovering and making available new therapies that will make the 1.5% decline rate possible. Accelerating the pace of medical discovery will require raising the success rate of research grant applications at the National Institutes of Health (NIH) from the current 20% to 35–40% (Ullian, 1997). This, in turn, means increasing appropriations for medical research by 30–50% by the year 2000. Though many in Congress have called for significant increases in funding for the NIH, there should be a special effort made to target increased support for aging-related research in order to help balance the Medicare account. A coordinated NIH effort to stimulate research aimed at delaying dementia and frailty, for instance, could be the best possible investment Congress could make in response to the aging of the population. A wealth of research data shows that such an initiative would be extremely popular (Charlton Research Company, 1998).

Our lives have been enriched enormously by medical science. In the past few years alone, we have seen hundreds of new treatments come into use that can statistically reduce the need for chronic care in the elderly population: hip and knee replacements, laser-assisted cataract removal, hormone replacement therapy and the new "designer estrogens" for women, and antibiotics rather than surgery for peptic ulcers, to name a few. Insights first gleaned from research and now common knowledge among Americans of all ages include the benefits of exercise and better nutrition, a simple aspirin a day for cardiovascular health, the benefits of breaking the smoking habit and the life-saving potential of automobile seat belts.

The possibility of extending the human "health span" is very real. It could profoundly affect our approach to financing long-term health care. It is an idea beginning to be heard in Washington. Robert N. Butler, the founding director of the National Institute on Aging (NIA), recently told a gathering of health advocacy groups in the nation's capital that "the best way to moderate public costs of old age and improve the quality of life for older people is to foster research to keep older people as healthy and productive as possible, for as long as possible" (Butler, 1997).

In fact, it would be foolhardy *not* to expect dramatic improvements in health care for elders and others from the current national investment in biomedical research. Between the pharmaceutical and biotechnology industries and government funding of academia, the nation spends some $35 billion yearly in the hope of affecting better quality of life and improved health status for people of all ages. In addition to the advances cited here, there is a near certainty that amazing new insights will emerge from biomedical research with enormous potential to extend the human "health span." We must understand that technology will likely transform the amount and the quality of health care that is available to satisfy national needs. We should do nothing to hinder or delay the development of innovations in health technologies. Indeed, we should take steps to facilitate and accelerate discoveries that produce a healthier older population.

Democratic lawmaker Edward M. Kennedy frequently cites statistics from the Duke study, saying, "greater support for medical research may well be the key to achieving the goal of protecting Medicare by reducing disability rates" (Kennedy, 1997). Senator Kennedy flatly declares that "improving longevity cuts Medicare costs. Healthier senior citizens means healthier Medicare." At a legislative gathering of the leadership of the American Association of Retired Persons (AARP), the Republican Speaker of the House, Newt Gingrich, lectured the nation's largest organization of older Americans, urging them to use their political muscle to step up support for aging research. "There is no place we will get a bigger payback than in research into aging which allows people to not go to nursing homes, to remain in independent living, to have a sense of being able to take care of themselves," Gingrich asserted (Gingrich, 1998).

TRACKING THE POLITICS OF MEDICAL RESEARCH

On the strength of such powerful bipartisan endorsements, it might be assumed that biomedical research to ensure the health of older people has all the support in Washington that it needs. Sadly, this is not yet the case. Compared with the cost of treating medical problems, our nation seriously underinvests in research to prevent and postpone the effects of disease. Total annual spending for health care in the United States was $1.1 trillion in 1997. About one third of these costs were incurred by people over the age of 65, although that age group is still only 13% of the population (Administration on Aging, 1997). Even when public spending is combined with larger research contributions from private industry, the total for medical research is about *three cents* for each dollar spent on providing health services. It is a general rule of thumb in business to invest at least 7% of sales in research and development or risk losing to the competition. Such high-tech industries as electronics, information systems and biotechnology tend to have research budgets that are at least 10% of total income. For the United States to set aside just 3% for research from public and private sources combined is a serious underinvestment in the critical business of health care.

Most biomedical research supported by the federal government is done by the NIH. Important but smaller life-sciences research programs are carried out through the National Science Foundation, the Department of Veterans Affairs, the Food and Drug Administration and other agencies, but examining the NIH budget is the best way to judge the nation's commitment to medical research. The NIH budget for 1998 is $13.6 billion. It has increased slowly and steadily, but each year, a smaller percentage of promising proposals from scientists receives the NIH support needed to come to fruition. During the agency's high point in the 1970s, the NIH was able to fund about half of all promising research grants that were submitted. Scientific opportunities are now outstripping resources. Last year, only about one of every five applications ranked worthy of funding by the NIH were actually funded. The crunch today is due, in part, to increasing numbers of scientists seeking limited funds, but it has also become increasingly difficult for champions of medical research within the Congress to maintain the previously high level of support.

President Clinton's first budget to Congress in 1992 actually called for a decrease in the budget for NIH. Despite grumbling within the scientific community, the Clinton administration's budget requests for NIH and other research agencies have barely kept pace with inflation in recent years. Each year, Republicans and Democrats alike have added monies to appropriations legislation to keep NIH ahead of inflation, even as other nondefense programs have suffered.

Though it has been a struggle to maintain federal funding for all medical research, it has been a particular challenge to build and maintain momentum in support of aging research. Research into the basic biomedical aspects of aging accounts for a mere 6% of NIH funding (Lonergan, 1991). The majority of aging-related biomedical, behavioral and social science research funded by the NIH comes through the NIA (though studies of musculoskeletal, neurologic and other diseases are done through other institutes as well). The NIA was created by Congress in 1974 because the science of human aging was finally coming into its own. It was also a recognition of the growing power of the senior lobby, though the major part of that political power has rarely, if ever, been placed in service of the NIA or aging research. Whereas health care for older people has dominated much of American politics, funding for research at the NIA has remained static since 1992. In the mid-1980s, the NIA ranked tenth of the 11 Institutes of Health. Today, with a total of 18 institutes at the NIH, the NIA ranks in the middle in terms of budget size and annual increases voted by Congress.

At first glance, this is a puzzlement. Why would a system supposedly attuned to public opinion allocate over $2 billion annually to cancer research, $1.5 billion each to heart disease and AIDS research, but barely $0.5 billion to aging? After all, aging is the primary risk factor that predisposes all of us to cancer, heart disease, diabetes and much more. Unlike specific diseases, aging affects every living person. Even the very young will come face to face with the vicissitudes of aging sooner or later, first in their relations to grandparents and parents and ultimately, unless something worse happens, in their own experience. The government's funding system works as it does because it *is* highly attuned to public opinion and public action, and, at present, the public expresses its concerns in terms of specific diseases rather than in terms of the underlying basis of most diseases—the aging process itself.

THE CLOUT OF THE BABY BOOM GENERATION

Robert Butler, when he was director of the NIA, used the expression "the politics of anguish" to describe how fear of disease drives public opinion, which then translates into research dollars. Many people, at some level of awareness, fear the specter of cancer, a heart attack or acquired immune deficiency syndrome (AIDS) because it seems that these threats are all around us. Individuals may fear being disabled or being dependent on others but, in general, people do not live in fear of growing older. Nor should they. However, because aging is a phase of life and not a disease in itself, there has been little citizen advocacy mobilized to advance the cause of aging research—at least until now.

The baby boomers, who have put their unique stamp on every stage of life they have experienced so far, are presumably going to feel and act differently about their aging. Beginning at the stroke of midnight on December 31, 1995, they began turning 50 years old at a rapid clip. Before New Year's Day 1996 was finished, 10,000 boomers had entered the sixth decade of life. By the end of that year, some 3.4 million of them had turned 50 years old. It is probably safe to assume that most of them were duly solicited to join AARP, an experience met by many with mixed emotions. By the end of the 1990s, more than 12 million people will be added to the 50+ age bracket.

On three occasions since 1990, the Alliance for Aging Research has surveyed Americans on attitudes toward health and longevity. People have been asked whether they want to live to 100 years of age. Without qualification, about two thirds consistently report a desire to live to the century mark if it would be possible. Most baby boomers and younger people look forward to living a long time and believe that their own lifestyle choices will help improve their longevity odds. Our surveys show that even language that describes the phases of life is changing as this generation grows older. Three of five boomers believe that "middle age" does not even begin until age 50 or older, and 66% put "old age" at somewhere beyond 70; a third put it after age 85 (Alliance for Aging Research, 1991, 1992, 1996).

Baby-boomer attitudes about health and longevity were shaped early. Compared with earlier generations, boomers' childhoods were marked by general good health enhanced by the polio vaccine, antibiotics, fluoride and high standards of nutrition and hygiene. In youth and middle age, boomers have pursued wellness as a goal. Though there are obvious variations within any group so large, it is probably fair to say that this generation tends to be uncomfortable with physical decline, these people having enjoyed a relatively high level of health for most of their lives. They dread infirmity and worship the vigor and attractiveness of youth. Most likely, this is going to be a generation that does not want to grow old if that means being faced with physical and mental incapacity. It will be sobering, to say the least, when boomers begin to face higher odds of being diagnosed with a chronic, life-altering health condition. The average person between the ages of 49 and 59 will see her or his risk for hypertension, arthritis or diabetes triple. During the coming decade, millions of our most self-absorbed generation—the vanguard of what was once the youth culture—are about to take a trip through "Heart Attack Canyon," and some will be ambushed in "Stroke Valley." Coming to grips with chronic conditions that limit physical and mental performance will become a life-transforming experience. The large majority that continues to enjoy relatively good health will be almost constantly aware of the changes that come with aging. They, too, will swell the growing ranks of the worried.

WILL HEALTHY AGING FIND A CONSTITUENCY?

With their fixation on wellness and fitness, will the baby boomers finally turn sound strategies for disease prevention into a permanent national trend? Alternatively, will they be merely avid consumers of fad diets, untested antiaging tonics and quack cures? It is likely that some number will express enlightened self-interest in improving their personal experience with aging. What if they were to make common cause with researchers in demanding policies that would supercharge the quest for new knowledge? If such a group were organized and able to articulate a coherent demand for government research policies leading to cures, prevention or postponement of the major diseases of aging, how would Washington respond?

The power to influence the course of events in our democracy belongs to those who can articulate the authentic desires of a significant segment of the public. In recent years, the government and private industry have invested heavily to find cures, better prevention and treatment of human immunodeficiency virus/AIDS, breast cancer and research in women's health, despite ongoing fiscal austerity. Still other competitors for scarce research dollars—groups concerned with Parkinson's disease and children's health, for instance—have gained ground more recently, due to specific lobbying efforts.

In medical research, as in other fields, productive activity follows the money. Recent improvements in drug therapy for AIDS patients; growing demands for long-overdue research on women's health; and improved survival rates and prevention of heart disease, stroke and some cancers were all underwritten by the principle that money from government, industry and philanthropy sets the priorities for science and intensifies the search for answers. Gains in these areas have occurred in large measure because of the drive and effectiveness of activists who identified with these causes. In the language of marketing, these are the "influentials" or "early adopters," individuals with a personal interest in the outcome of the research who often succeed in making full use of the mass media and political channels to achieve their goals. More than scientists themselves, these lay activists succeed in setting the national agenda for the advancement of medical science.

Is it reasonable to assume that a cadre of early adopters will mobilize around healthy aging as others have helped to put AIDS, breast cancer and other diseases on the research fast track? Healthy-aging activists certainly could draw their inspiration from the knowledge that by stimulating scientific, social and medical discovery in the human aging process and in the alleviation of age-related disability, they would be advancing the greatest good for the greatest number of their fellow citizens. That greater good will be a palpable reality in the first few decades of the next century. Of course, the early adopters will have to see that future, even before it is obvious to the general population.

The question is open as to whether citizen activists for healthy aging will emerge in time to pave the way for the critical breakthroughs. Laboratory teams are hard at work, potentially unraveling the secrets of longevity, and the public is beginning to know it. Economic and social planners are becoming aware of how much the nation will need medical innovations that ensure the health of older people, extend their productive potential and reduce dependency and frailty to the shortest possible time. It is hoped that an abiding desire for healthy aging—for one's parents and for one's self—is riding the crest of the approaching age wave and will soon manifest itself in the public arena.

THE TIMES, THEY HAVE "A-CHANGED"

For the first time in many years, political and economic forces are in favorable alignment for investing in research to ensure healthy aging for more Americans. In early 1998, President Clinton erased years of a lukewarm stance with regard to the NIH by announcing plans for a twenty-first-century research fund that contains $31 billion in increases for nearly every federal research agency, including an 8.4% budget request for the NIH. A few days earlier, Vice President Gore revealed the administration's plans to increase cancer research by $4.7 billion over the next 5 years. Advocates are now scrambling in hopes of winning additional research dollars for scores of disease-specific causes. Skeptics point out that plans for steep increases in medical research will materialize only if Congress agrees to a $60 billion settlement of lawsuits against the tobacco industry—which is a big "if." Either way, the Clinton administration has discovered the political capital that comes from promising big increases in funding for medical research. They are not likely to forget that lesson any time soon.

Of course, the major reason for the current bright prospects for investment in research—health-related research in particular—is the rapid disappearance of the federal budget deficit. For a full generation, the onerous tide of budget red ink made government spending policies essentially a zero-sum game. Then a high-performing economy produced soaring tax revenues for both state and federal government. Revenues from income taxes at the federal level last year were up more than 20% at the close of 1997. Federal spending, apart from outlays for interest, fell to 17.2% of gross domestic product—the lowest level since 1966. Meanwhile, the nation simultaneously enjoys the lowest levels of inflation and unemployment in its history and the all-time longest-running stock boom in memory despite occasional market corrections.

Until very recently, proposals for investment in the nation's economy, educational and scientific infrastructure were soundly blocked by the argument that all available revenues had to be devoted to taming the runaway deficit. Now a different debate is beginning as policy makers begin to address what to do with the coming budget surplus. For the first time in years, it is possible to talk responsibly about spending money on investments that will pay dividends as the baby-boom generation ages.

Both Republican and Democratic leaders in Washington recognize the shift in the debate. President Clinton has said that we must apply any budget surplus to save Social Security first. The Republican chair of the Senate Budget Committee, Pete V. Domenici of New Mexico, has said that additional funds should be used to save Medicare first. The champions of healthy aging can make a solid case that relatively modest but targeted investments in promoting health and productive aging can meet both of these worthy goals and much more. Social Security will be on a firmer footing when older Americans are enjoying more productive years, as well as more years over all. That can best be achieved on a large scale by bringing about a further extension of the human health span through research. Declines in the incidence of age-related diseases could save multiple billions of dollars for Medicare. That, too, will come from research. Best of all, discoveries that are sure to arise from better scientific understanding of aging will give Americans what they most want—the health and personal independence that make long life worth living.

REFERENCES

Administration on Aging. Department of Health and Human Services. (1997). *A profile of older Americans: 1997.* Washington, DC.

Alliance for Aging Research & American Federation for Aging Research. (1995). *Putting aging on hold: Delaying the disease of old age.* Washington, DC: 5.

Alliance for Aging Research. (1991). *Americans view aging: Results of a national survey.* Washington, DC.

Alliance for Aging Research. (1992). *Health and longevity: Results of a national survey.* Washington, DC.

Alliance for Aging Research. (1996). *Perceptions about aging: Findings from a national survey on aging.* Washington, DC.

Butler, R.N. (1997, 17 March). Remarks at a press conference to release Duke University's Center for Demographic Studies' study, *Chronic disability trends in elderly United States populations: 1982–1994.*

Butler, R.N., & Brody, J.A. (1995). *Delaying the onset of late-life dysfunction.* New York: Springer.

Charlton Research Company. (1998 April). Research polls conducted for *Research!America.* Washington, DC: Charlton Research Company.

Fillet, H.M., & Butler, R.N. (Eds.). (1997). *Cognitive decline: Strategies for prevention (Greenwich Medical Media).* London: Oxford University Press.

Gingrich, N. (1998, 5 February). Remarks at the 1998 American Association of Retired Persons National Legislative Council Meeting.

Kennedy, E. (1997, 17 March). Press statement at the release of Duke University's Center for Demographic Studies' study, *Chronic disability trends in elderly United States populations:1982–1994.*

Khachaturian, Z.S. (1997, 5 June). *Prospects for preventing Alzheimer's disease.* Congressional testimony before Senate Committee on Labor and Human Resources, 2.

Lonergan, E. (Ed.). (1991). *Extending life, enhancing life: A national research agenda on aging.* Washington, DC: Institute of Medicine.

Manton, K., et al. (1997, March). Chronic disability trends in elderly United States populations: 1982–1994. *Proceedings of the National Academy of Sciences, 94,* 2595–2598.

Reuben, D., & Beck, J. (1994). *Training physicians to care for older Americans: Progress, obstacles, and future directions.* Washington, DC: Institute of Medicine, 3–8.

Riley, G., et al. (1986, Spring). Changes in distribution of Medicare expenditures among aged enrollees, 1969–1982. *Health Care Financing Rev, 7*(3).

Rowe, J.W. (1997, October). The new gerontology. *Science, 278*(17), 367.

Schneider, E., & Guralnik, J. (1990, 2 May). The aging of America: Impact on health care costs. *JAMA, 263*(17), 2335–2340.

The Bureau of Health and Social Welfare Services for the Aged and Ministry of Health and Welfare of Japan. (1993). *Health and welfare for the elderly. An outline of systems and trends.* Japan: 5.

Ullian, A. (1997, 17 March). Research-based solution to Medicare crisis. Task force on science, health care & the economy. Remarks at a press conference to release Duke University's Center for Demographic Studies' study, *Chronic disability trends in elderly United States populations: 1982–1994.*

CHAPTER 17

The Insurer's Role in Shaping a New Health Care Agenda

Patrick G. Hays

To many Americans, the term *health insurance* signifies a system of paying claims for medical expenses. Indeed, health insurers have done just that for more than seven decades. In recent years, though, insurers have assumed important new roles in the health care system. Instead of simply administering and paying for health benefits, today's insurers now form partnerships with physicians, hospitals, pharmacies and other health care providers to create coordinated, accountable health plans. These organized programs integrate a broad range of services across the spectrum of care delivery—from preventive efforts like immunizations to intensive hospital treatment to custodial care in nursing homes. Insurers use their extensive databases to identify population segments with unique health care needs and to develop customized programs for treating targeted conditions. Insurers also provide a core foundation of financial stability and risk management to support these new health plan ventures. By building innovative partnerships with providers, insurers are moving away from cost-based reimbursement for health care services toward a competitive marketplace that rewards quality, efficiency and innovation.

This revolution in health system design will prove critical in preparing our society for the twenty-first century. As the United States approaches the new millennium, it faces a challenging paradox: Medical science can cure more illnesses and injuries than ever before—and as a result, our citizens are living longer, healthier lives. Yet the current Medicare pro-

---

Note: The author is indebted to Tracey Noe of BCBSA's Washington, DC, office for her key assistance in developing this chapter.

gram—one of our nation's most critical safety nets—lacks the resources necessary to pay for the health care of an ever-larger elderly population. Medicare spending already outpaces its funding, and the relative number of working people available to pay Medicare taxes is diminishing. Moreover, Medicare's traditional payment system creates perverse incentives that encourage acute, inpatient, high-tech procedures instead of lower-cost, comprehensive care management approaches that emphasize improving the health and functional ability of older adults. Without major structural reforms, Medicare faces bankruptcy in the near future.

Today's insurers are contributing their unique skills to help bring Medicare out of the 1960s and into the twenty-first century by increasing beneficiaries' choices, using epidemiologic and outcomes research to improve the quality of care delivered to older people, and providing physicians incentives to intervene early, before their patients develop serious complications. During the past 3 decades, Medicare has largely succeeded in expanding access to health services for older Americans. However, the movement toward providing truly integrated, cost-effective elder care services has just begun—with insurers at the forefront.

HOLES IN THE SAFETY NET

Throughout the first half of the twentieth century, most Americans aged 65 and over had no health insurance, and medical expenses often left them impoverished. To address this problem, in 1965 the federal government established Medicare, a federally funded health insurance program for people who receive Social Security benefits and Medicaid, a joint federal-state health insurance program for people with low incomes. In 1972, Medicare was expanded to include people under 65 who receive disability benefits, as well as those with end-stage renal disease.

Medicare was originally designed to offer elderly and disabled people the same financial protection and access to health care that working people receive from their employers. Medicare's original benefit design was similar to that of most commercial insurance policies created during the 1960s. Medicare Hospital Insurance (Part A)—which automatically enrolls every citizen who turns 65—covers inpatient care, skilled nursing facilities, home health care and hospice care. Beneficiaries must pay an annual deductible ($764 in 1998), along with 20% of the bill for an inpatient stay longer than 60 days. Along with their Part A coverage, beneficiaries may choose to purchase Supplementary Medical Insurance (Part B), which covers physician office visits and other outpatient services in exchange for a monthly premium ($43.80 in 1998). Medicare Part B covers 80% of the bill for outpatient services after the beneficiary meets a $100 deductible. The beneficiary must pay the remaining 20%.

This kind of health insurance is known as *fee-for-service coverage*, because the patient must pay a separate fee and file a separate claim for each inpatient visit and for each procedure the physician performs. As these rules suggest, Medicare was designed to pay only claims for specific procedures and treatments. Until recently, the Medicare program did not provide incentives for health professionals to coordinate patients' use of multiple health services, to provide patients advice about healthy lifestyle choices, or to help patients manage chronic health problems.

It can be said with some certainty that, until now, Medicare has worked. More than 97% of Americans over 65 have health insurance coverage, along with more than 90% of people with end-stage renal disease (Vladeck & King, 1995). To support this growing enrollment, however, Medicare consumes an ever-larger portion of federal spending. Expenditures grew from $3.4 billion in 1967 to $194.3 billion in 1996. Moreover, the Medicare Part A Hospital Insurance Trust Fund has been operating at a deficit since 1995, when it paid out $36 million more in benefits than it received in tax contributions. Additionally, the ratio of working taxpayers to Medicare beneficiaries is shrinking quickly. In 1995, there were 3.9 workers paying taxes for each beneficiary receiving benefits, but by 2030, taxes from only 2.2 workers will support each beneficiary (Committee on Ways and Means, 1997).

Despite these substantial outlays, however, Medicare coverage is far from comprehensive. For example, it does not cover outpatient prescription drugs, long-term care services, vision screenings, hearing aids and other benefits that many older people need. Additionally, Medicare's deductibles are higher than those in many employer-sponsored plans. Many beneficiaries purchase supplemental "Medigap" policies from private insurers to cover these out-of-pocket expenses. All told, the average Medicare beneficiary spends $2,750 per year for noncovered services and Medigap premiums (Butler, 1996).

In recent years, many older Americans have expressed dissatisfaction with the gaps in traditional Medicare coverage. Though beneficiaries give the program high marks overall, they are frustrated with its limited benefits and high out-of-pocket costs, according to focus group research conducted by the Henry J. Kaiser Family Foundation, a national health care philan-thropic organization (Frederick/Schneiders Inc., 1995). Beyond these gaps in coverage, older adults recognize that Medicare has not kept pace with private-sector employers' recent innovations in health benefits. Many private employers now offer workers a choice of health plans with differ-ent levels of coverage for different contributions. Throughout the 1980s, insurers began creating managed care plans—including health mainte-nance organizations (HMOs), preferred provider organizations (PPOs) and point-of-service plans—to help employers offer their workers broader benefits while reducing health care costs. In these arrangements, patients agree to visit only the physicians and hospitals that participate in the health plan or to pay more when they see health care providers who are not members of the plan's network. Insurers that offer these managed care arrangements create incentives for health care providers to deliver cost-effective care. Instead of charging a separate fee for each procedure they perform, physicians participating in managed care plans often accept a monthly lump sum to cover the cost of all medically necessary care for each patient. Enrollment in these types of plans has skyrocketed during the last 2 decades, topping 160 million in 1998.

Although managed care plans are increasingly available to working people, Medicare beneficiaries until recently have had limited access to them. Along with this lack of choice, Medicare's focus on treating acute episodes of illness has not kept pace with older people's chronic health care needs. The average life expectancy for a beneficiary who enrolls in Medicare at age 65 is dramatically longer today than it was when the program was enacted. Today, healthy 65-year-old men can expect to reach age 80, and healthy 65-year-old women can expect to reach age 84. But Medicare's benefit design—which reimburses health professionals only for specific medical procedures, not for coordination of services and advice—does not account for the complex health care needs most older people experience as they age. The challenge for tomorrow's health care system is effectively managing chronic illness and addressing quality-of-life issues through evidence-based research and appropriate social/clinical interventions. As Dr. Robert Butler of New York's International Longev-ity Center recently wrote, "Medicare still remains in the shadow of the acute care model of employer-based health insurance; the program was designed as if its beneficiaries were adult male breadwinners. In reality, its beneficiaries are older people who are more likely than younger adults to have complex, interacting, acute and chronic physical and psychosocial problems and to need long-term care and outpatient drug therapy, neither of which is covered by Medicare" (Butler, 1996). (See Dr. Butler's two chapters in this book, Chapters 2 and 8.)

THE RISE OF ACCOUNTABLE HEALTH PLANS

Today's insurers are addressing these concerns about Medicare's rising costs, coverage limits and outdated benefit design by encouraging older people to join HMOs—coordinated health care systems that offer a broad range of health services in exchange for a prepaid fee. Medicare HMOs replace Part A and Part B and eliminate the need for supplemental Medigap policies. Instead of reimbursing beneficiaries for each health care service they use, the federal government pays HMOs directly to care for beneficiaries' needs.

HMOs allow each patient to develop a long-term relationship with a personal primary care physician, who oversees all aspects of the patient's care and coordinates referrals to specialists. This arrangement allows for greater continuity of care than is possible in the fragmented fee-for-service system, where multiple physicians may unwittingly prescribe conflicting modes of treatment.

HMO members agree to visit only physicians and hospitals that participate in the HMO's network and to obtain authorization from the HMO before being treated by an out-of-area provider, except in emergencies. These procedures help ensure that members receive only the most appropriate health care, while reducing costs for both members and the federal government.

In exchange for these restrictions, most HMOs that cover Medicare beneficiaries offer much broader benefits than does the fee-for-service program. Beyond the services traditionally covered under Medicare Part A and Part B, HMOs typically cover mammograms, Pap smears, routine foot care, hearing and vision screenings, cholesterol tests, immunizations and preventive dental services. HMOs also offer optional coverage for prescription drugs and comprehensive dental work.

To emphasize prevention and wellness, insurers offering Medicare HMOs invest in sophisticated computer systems that keep track of members' needed tests and screenings. The insurers share these data with participating physicians so they can develop customized care plans for each member. Managed care payment systems reinforce this emphasis on prevention. Because physicians are paid a lump sum to cover the entire cost of a patient's care, they have incentives to detect minor health problems early and prevent future complications.

Older adults have clearly demonstrated their preference for this coordinated approach: In 1985, about 300,000 of the 30 million people then covered by Medicare were enrolled in HMOs; today, about 5.5 million beneficiaries—or 15%—are HMO members, and an additional 80,000 beneficiaries join HMOs each month (Zarabozo & LeMasurier, 1996).

RESPONDING TO OLDER AMERICANS' NEEDS

Because HMOs are becoming more popular, insurers must develop innovative products and services to meet customer needs and to differentiate themselves in the marketplace. For example, insurers now are creating managed care programs that cover the cost of patients' care while they travel—even if they visit health care providers outside the health plan's network. For instance, the Blue Cross and Blue Shield System's national Medicare HMO network allows members to obtain a full range of health services at any participating HMO—no matter how far from home they travel. Medicare Blue USA also allows members of one participating HMO to become "guest members" in another participating HMO for up to 6 months at a time.

Enhancing portability is just one example of insurers' commitment to constantly adapting to meet consumer needs. Through their Medicare programs, today's insurers are collecting, analyzing and disseminating data about their patients' health care needs and building partnerships with other industry leaders to continuously improve the quality of care they deliver. For example, the Blue Cross and Blue Shield Association (BCBSA) is a major cosponsor of the HMO Workgroup on Care Management, an industry-wide coalition designed to share best practices in caring for elderly and chronically ill people in managed care settings. The Workgroup, spearheaded by the Robert Wood Johnson Foundation health care philanthropy, is creating a training guide to help health professionals address the unique challenges involved in coordinating and integrating the broad range of health care services that older people need. This manual will assist health care providers in determining the medical and social needs of frail elderly patients and in identifying the appropriate providers and community resources to meet those needs.

Additionally, the Blues have joined forces with the American Geriatrics Society (AGS) to offer primary care physicians specific education about older Americans' unique health care challenges. BCBSA and the AGS joined forces in 1997, when the two groups realized that the U.S. health care system desperately needs more health professionals with specialized education in caring for older people. Most practicing physicians who see older patients have had limited training in geriatric health care. As a result, the illnesses of older people are often misdiagnosed, overlooked or dismissed as normal functions of aging. Additionally, many physicians are not trained to recognize how diseases and drugs that are commonly used in the under-65 population can affect older people differently. This lack of education sometimes translates into needless suffering and loss of function for older people, as well as unnecessary costs to Medicare from inappropriate hospitalizations, unnecessary nursing home admissions and multiple visits to specialists who may order conflicting treatment regimes.

To alleviate these problems, BCBSA and the AGS have developed an unprecedented educational program for health professionals who participate in their local Blues Plans' networks. The program, known as The National Blue Initiative for Quality Senior Care, consists of six training modules to help health professionals identify and manage geriatric health problems before they become serious; promote wellness for older adults; and take appropriate actions to help older people live comfortably and independently. The program also provides physicians with reference guides to reinforce the education during actual patient visits. Additionally, the program provides chart forms that can be inserted into patients' medical records to remind physicians about critical tests and screenings.

CARE MANAGEMENT: REVOLUTIONIZING ELDER CARE

Insurers are using their expertise in data collection, coordination of care and health risk analysis to create customized health maintenance programs for older adults. This proactive approach enhances older patients' relationships with their physicians and allows them to access the right health care services, at the right time, in the right setting. The approach also encourages physicians to address each Medicare member's individual needs— whether they are simple or complex. Throughout the care process, the insurer serves as a "broker" or "quarterback," communicating with the patient and the various health care providers to coordinate all necessary services. In addition, specially trained nurses called "care managers" monitor the health plan members' health status and link sicker members with the community resources they need to live comfortably at home. For example, care managers can arrange for home-delivered meals and transportation services for frail older patients who choose to live independently but need assistance with daily household tasks.

These care managers also communicate frequently with the members' primary care physicians to help them develop treatment programs uniquely suited to each patient's needs. For example, when a care manager identifies a patient with congestive heart failure (CHF), the care manager visits the patient at home to explain the symptoms and causes of CHF and to explain the physician's treatment plan. The care manager also helps the patient monitor his or her weight—an important indicator of CHF complications—by recording it in a daily log. After this initial home visit, the care manager calls the patient daily to discuss issues raised during doctor visits, monitor the patient's eating habits and record his or her daily weight. If the patient's weight is increasing, the care manager knows that the patient is probably retaining fluids—a CHF complication that could require an emergency department visit and hospital stay if left untreated. Instead, the care manager can schedule a doctor's appointment or a home visit to provide intravenous medicine. This approach heads off a potential emergency while allowing the patient to rest comfortably at home.

Intensive care management programs such as these allow HMOs to integrate a broad range of health care services—from doctor visits and health education to home care and social services. The care managers' daily or weekly telephone calls often reveal lifestyle problems that could make independent living more difficult. The care managers then work with community agencies to address these routine challenges. An example: A care manager at First Choice 65, the Medicare HMO affiliated with Regence Blue Cross and Blue Shield of Oregon, recently helped a frail older patient modify her home to reduce her risk of serious injury from falling. During a home visit, the care manager noticed that this patient needed hand rails in her bathtub and arranged for a community agency to install the hand rails free of charge. If the insurer had not provided a home assessment, this simple intervention would not have been available for the member—and she could have been seriously hurt. The home visit not only prevented an injury, but also helped inform the member's physician, who otherwise might not be aware of this potential danger.

Research demonstrates that care management programs like these can improve health outcomes and quality of life for older people while reducing health care costs. A recent study in the *New England Journal of Medicine* found that comprehensive health needs assessments for older people living in their communities are more clinically effective and less costly than traditional acute interventions (Stuck et al., 1995). The results of HMOs' intensive care management programs are similarly encouraging. In the 3 years since Keystone Health Plan East, the HMO affiliate of Philadelphia-based Independence Blue Cross, implemented its CHF program, emergency department visits and admissions for CHF complications have dropped by 50%, and patients' ratings of their own health have improved significantly.

Medicare HMOs' care managers also play key roles in preventing complications while patients are hospitalized and in ensuring that patients have adequate support when they return home. Before an older patient is admitted, the care manager speaks with the patient and his or her physician to develop a "game plan" for follow-up treatment and home care. This process can prevent potentially disastrous complications. For example, a care manager at Keystone Health Plan East recently noticed that an older patient being admitted for rotator cuff surgery on his left shoulder was partially paralyzed on his right side, as a result of a stroke 4 years earlier. Clearly, this patient would not have been able to function at home alone until his left shoulder healed. So the care manager arranged for "Meals on Wheels" to provide meals and for another community agency to provide housekeeping services while the patient recuperated.

COLLABORATIONS AND PARTNERSHIPS

Medicare HMOs do not rely solely on their own participating physicians and care managers to address patient needs. Many health plans are actively building partnerships with community providers, local agencies on aging and public health organizations to improve quality of care and to promote wellness among older people. For instance, Shield 65, a Medicare HMO affiliated with San Francisco-based Blue Shield of California, has joined forces with the California Department of Health Services (DHS) to increase adult immunization rates, promote exercise and fitness, and improve the care of chronic diseases among older adults. Shield 65 and DHS jointly operate a flu shot clinic, and care managers from the two organizations are sharing their expertise in monitoring the quality of care for older diabetic patients. Shield 65 also allows patients to supplement their medical and surgical services with "complementary" medicine techniques such as chiropractic services and acupuncture. Additionally, the insurer is participating in a Stanford University study evaluating older adults' interest in and use of complementary medicine. The study is funded by the National Institutes of Health.

Blue Cross and Blue Shield of Florida is another insurer that has launched innovative partnerships with local agencies to promote wellness for older members. The health plan recently joined forces with the Central Florida Adult Day Services Network (ADNet), an umbrella organization that identifies older adults with physical or cognitive impairments and matches their needs with community agencies that provide health and personal care, nutrition services, education, recreation, social activities, transportation and daytime respite for caregivers. ADNet is one of four pilot sites selected to participate in the National Alzheimer's Managed Care Demonstration Project; its member groups include the local Christian Service Center, along with local chapters of the Visiting Nurses Association and Alzheimer's Association. The partnership is designed to help older adults remain more independent and to assist their families in coping with caregiving tasks without seeking unnecessary, expensive medical services or institutional placement.

THE FINANCING CHALLENGE

As these examples illustrate, insurers are developing innovative Medicare health plans that create incentives for providers to personalize and improve quality of health care. Making these partnerships viable financial enterprises, however, remains a formidable task. Though commercial insurers are leaders in setting prospective rates for managed care programs, Medicare still operates primarily on a retrospective, cost-reimbursement model. The federal government is still inexperienced in administering managed care systems, and government officials lack expertise in analyzing prior claims experience and underwriting insurance risks.

The current Medicare HMO payment system also fosters a critical societal problem: Because it does not account for differences in the relative risk of competing health plans' members, it provides incentives for health plans to avoid enrolling those with chronic or expensive-to-treat conditions. Federal program designers must find better ways to adjust HMO payments according to the relative health status of each health plan's members. The Balanced Budget Act of 1997 requires the government to develop such a "risk adjuster" and to submit it to Congress by March 1, 1999. The law also requires the federal government to begin implementing a risk adjustment system by January 1, 2000.

Risk adjusters are important because the cost of providing health care services varies according to the relative age and wellness of a health plan's membership. In general, about 80% of the Medicare population is "low risk." These members are relatively healthy, with few indicators of future complications. Insurers help these members stay well by creating partnerships with providers who can monitor their vital signs, provide them with diet advice, encourage them to exercise and ensure that they receive preventive services. These relatively low-tech interventions are not very expensive. Accordingly, insurers with predominantly low-risk populations should receive lower payments than insurers that enroll predominantly "moderate-risk" or "high-risk" members.

Creating an accurate risk adjustment system is a critical component in the ongoing quest to modernize Medicare and expand health plan choices for beneficiaries. If an effective risk adjustment method is not developed, an opportunity to create a competitive dynamic among health plans to offer the highest quality, most cost-effective care for all Medicare beneficiaries will be missed.

THE INFORMATION CHALLENGE

Along with its risk adjustment provisions, the Balanced Budget Act of 1997 created a new program, Medicare+Choice, that allows beneficiaries to enroll in a broad array of health benefit designs, including HMOs, PPOs and POS plans. This new structure for Medicare—known as Medicare Part C—is modeled in part on the Federal Employees Health Benefits Program (FEHBP), a government insurance program that offers 10 million federal workers, retirees and dependents a choice of more than 300 competing health plans nationwide.

Medicare+Choice is designed to make Medicare operate like a competitive insurance market. Instead of forcing all beneficiaries into one rigid benefit structure, the new program encourages older Americans to choose health plans that best suit their varying lifestyles. Health plans will compete for Medicare beneficiaries' business based on quality and price, but this "marketplace approach" could be confusing for older people if they lack guidance in navigating the expanded pool of options. As more and more older adults opt out of the fee-for-service program, government officials, providers and insurers will need to work together to educate these new customers about the relative advantages and disadvantages of competing health plan structures, as well as the clinical quality of competing provider networks.

Insurers are dedicated to creating appropriate forums for explaining the different models of health care delivery. Many Blue Cross and Blue Shield companies already offer the full spectrum of Medicare coverage, from "Medigap" policies to PPOs to HMOs. The Blues are also leaders in the FEHBP, providing an array of benefit designs for federal workers throughout the nation. Just as they create enrollment guides for the FEHBP, insurers are developing consumer education materials to help older people understand how the new Medicare managed care plans operate so they can select the most appropriate options for their lifestyles. Moreover, insurers are engaged in substantial efforts to develop valid quality indicators that consumers can use to compare the quality of one health plan or provider to another. Capturing valid data comparing clinical outcomes and translating it into consumer-friendly language is a top priority for the nation's insurers.

To ensure vibrant competition in this new Medicare marketplace, government officials will need to develop rules and regulations that explain beneficiary choices and protect consumers without micro-managing health plan operations. During the late 1990s, federal and state legislatures began a troubling trend of passing piecemeal laws mandating that health plans cover specific treatments for specific medical conditions. For example, many state legislatures passed laws requiring two-day hospitalizations for newborns and their mothers, as well as mastectomy patients—even though clinical evidence demonstrates that home recovery for these conditions produces equal or better outcomes. Although these laws are well-meaning, they often produce unintended consequences—freezing medical science in place, protecting the status quo and retarding clinical innovation. As the new Medicare marketplace matures, government officials must create effective, enlightened regulatory structures that ensure access to high-quality care; encourage evidence-based treatment decisions; and stimulate economic competition.

THE CLINICAL CHALLENGE

Now that policy makers are beginning to strengthen Medicare's finances and expand consumers' choices, a national dialogue must be launched on ways to integrate health care services and financing to further improve the quality of care provided to older Americans. Additionally, the health professionals who see older patients must have specific training in identifying and managing their unique health care problems. Many Medicare beneficiaries have no one to serve as their "care manager." Consequently, they are often hospitalized, even when it would be more appropriate for treatment to take place at home or in a nursing home. Policy makers should capitalize on insurers' expertise in creating incentives to provide physicians the education and tools they need to collaborate more effectively with their colleagues in custodial and long-term care settings.

The twenty-first century is poised to become the most exciting era in American health care. Already, we have witnessed remarkable improvements in caring for—and preventing—some of nature's greatest threats. The emergence of hormone replacement therapy has provided a potent new weapon against heart disease and osteoporosis. Other new drugs offer renewed hope for patients with cardiovascular problems, Alzheimer's disease and AIDS. By the turn of the century, scientists are expected to map the entire human genome—opening the door to new treatments for hundreds of inherited illnesses. Insurers—like our counterparts in the provider arena—must continue to invest in this critical research and to find new solutions for acute health care problems.

At the same time, the U.S. health care system must make similar investments in managing the day-to-day manifestations of chronic diseases. Often, these problems do not respond to biomedical interventions, because they are not rooted in bacteria or viruses. Instead, they result from several complex factors, including genetics, lifestyle choices and failures of the body's own immune system. Today, these chronic illnesses—problems like arthritis, diabetes, CHF and dementia—account for 80% of all health care expenditures.

Insurers offer potent new weapons in our efforts to manage these conditions: technology and data. Insurers' computer systems can provide physicians with increasingly sophisticated data showing changes in patients' health status over time so they can decide which treatments are working better than others. Insurers can also capture the data necessary to create clinical practice guidelines that help physicians decide when to intervene with new drugs, surgical procedures, or other treatments.

To promote wellness and independent living, insurers' data must be put to use in creating new, population-based approaches to managing chronic illnesses. The large panels of patients enrolled in managed care plans provide the clinical databases necessary to launch extensive research studies. By analyzing data from thousands of real cases, predictions about which patients at risk will eventually develop complications and which patients will likely respond to different treatments can be made. Coupled with emerging expert systems and artificial intelligence, the possibilities for enhanced health management and quality of life are practically limitless.

The next generation of managed care, if it is permitted to evolve, will be the management *of* care, with empowered physicians fully and actively engaged. Competition among "coordinated care organizations" will encompass not only price, but also value—as defined by return-to-work and return-to-activities-of-daily-living statistics; by quality-of-life measures for those with chronic illness; by employee productivity indices; by outcomes flowing from evidence-based research—in short, as measured by impact on the daily lives of those served. If successful, America will witness the dawn of a truly accountable health care system—a system that promotes, encourages and finances healthy aging for all of its citizens.

REFERENCES

Butler, R.N. (March 21, 1996). On behalf of older women: Another reason to protect Medicare and Medicaid. *N Engl J Med, 334*(12), 794–795.

Committee on Ways and Means. (1997). *U.S. House of Representatives, Medicare and healthcare chartbook.* Washington, DC: 105th Congress. U.S. Government Printing Office.

Frederick/Schneiders Inc. (March 1995). *Analysis of focus groups concerning managed care and Medicare.* Washington, DC: Henry J. Kaiser Family Foundation.

Stuck, A.E., Aronow, H.U., & Steiner A., et al. (November 1995). A trial of annual in-home comprehensive geriatric assessments for elderly people living in the community. *N Engl J Med, 333*(18), 1184–1189.

Vladeck, B.C., & King, K.M. (July 1995). Medicare at 30: Preparing for the future. *JAMA, 274*(3), 259–262.

Zarabozo, C., & LeMasurier, J.D. (1996). Medicare and managed care. *The managed healthcare handbook* (3rd ed.). Gaithersburg, MD: Aspen Publishers, 719.

CHAPTER 18

The Growing Pains of Aging: Disability, Aging and Baby Boomers

Fernando Torres-Gil and Michelle Putnam

WHERE WE STAND

Our nation is growing old. There is no disputing this statistical fact. No matter how many "age-defying" wrinkle creams, miracle vitamins or "abdominizers" we buy for firming up and smoothing out, the reality is that the average number of birthday candles on the cake is rising. Although we envision ourselves as forever young, the day of reckoning is coming—if it is not here already—when a game of one-on-one basketball is lost to your son or daughter because you aggravated your knee again, not because you were trying to boost your child's ego and when the family rafting trip over spring break leaves your college freshman exhilarated, the nagging pain in your lower back reminds you that "extreme adventure" vacations may no longer be in your best interest. Unfortunately, the outcome of these growing pains, which many of us experience as we age, won't be as welcomed as were those we encountered when we passed through puberty into vibrant young adult bodies. Instead, they often represent the beginning of an accumulation of minor aches and pains or chronic health conditions that could develop into functional limitations or disabilities in our later decades.

As the face of our nation begins to add a few wrinkles, we need to confront the sobering picture of what the U.S. population will look like as the baby boom generation moves into old age, and we must examine how we will respond to their health care needs. Throughout this chapter, we will suggest that "disability issues" are no longer the sole concern of individuals born with functional limitations or who acquire a permanent disability sometime between childhood and middle age. In the context of our aging society, where physical functional status is more predictive than chronologic age of independent living, disability becomes a universal concern that touches the lives of all persons with enduring chronic conditions. With the changing demographics, the population of disabled Americans will grow to include persons with lifelong disabilities—those who experience the late onset of disabilities in the second half of life and those who have chronic health conditions. In short, "disability issues" are key in addressing the needs of our aging population and will become a critical component in the public policy debate as baby boomers transition to "aging boomers" and the implications of an older, more diverse society rise to the forefront of the political conscience.

The demographic and social reality is that disability is a common occurrence in old age. Over the past century, we have succeeded in nearly eradicating many of the public health risks that have threatened our citizenry's longevity. In what may be thought of as a remarkable turn of events, through a combination of medical technology and healthier lifestyles, we are succeeding in increasing the life span to such a degree that living to be 100 years of age is no longer headline news. However, despite our ability to add years to life, we are still trying to figure out how to add life to years (Crimmons, Hayward, & Saito, 1994). Today's elders are able to live a quality of life that lends itself to new opportunities in old age more than any previous generation of older adults. However, the potential for everyone to make the most of their increasing years in an aging America will be influenced in part by how the public sector responds to issues of aging and disability. As the baby boomers segue into the senior ranks, the number of persons experiencing chronic conditions and disabilities will increase dramatically. This increase, in turn, will "mainstream" disability issues into the public policy debate, as decision makers come to realize that the new faces of "the disabled community" more closely resemble members of the Rolling Stones than they do the stereotypical images of young adults in wheelchairs presented in mass media.

To make our case, in this chapter we will: address the state of knowledge in the area of aging and disability and overview efforts to bring the disability and aging communities together for purposes of political coalition building; provide a demographic portrait of the current and future disabled population; present the baby boomers as a case study of the changing role of health care in an aging society; and examine the political implications of aging and disability.

THE STATE OF THE KNOWLEDGE:
WHAT WE KNOW TODAY

As our understanding of who comprises the "disabled community" broadens to include young and old, moderately inconvenienced and severely impaired and those with lifelong disabilities, as well as those who acquire impairments in later life, we must begin to develop a knowledge base that reflects the diversity and universality of disability in the United States. At the time of this chapter's writing, it seems fair to say that the ground floor of the knowledge-building in this area is still under construction. Traditionally, disability and aging issues have been investigated independently of each other, with few researchers bridging both fields of study. In the past decade, however, the beginnings of a unified literature have begun to develop, with two main themes emerging. The first theme centers on the long-term care continuum and the need for appropriate care and rehabilitation models for both the disabled and the aging communities. The second theme surrounds the topic of coalition-building between the disabled and aging camps for purposes of pooling scarce resources and increasing overall political clout in the policy-making arena. What follows is a brief overview of each major theme to provide a basic understanding of where we have been in terms of merging aging and disability issues and how far we have to go.

Long-term care seems like a logical topic for aging and disability advocates to share common interests. Both older adults and individuals with disabilities under age 65 have had to steer through webs of red tape to acquire needed home care, personal assistance or skilled nursing care services. Historically, care for individuals aged 65 and older has been provided under what could be termed *aging policy*, which includes the Older Americans Act and Medicare, among others, and disabled individuals have received services under the Rehabilitation Act of 1973. Though many of the services provided for these two populations are fairly similar in terms of actual care delivered, the goals of the two program streams are radically different (Simon-Rusinowitz & Hofland, 1993). The model of disability-related care for the aged has centered on keeping older adults out of institutions and maintaining them in their homes as long as possible. Low goals have been set for rehabilitation, driven perhaps by expectations of diminished levels of functioning in old age. Decisions about service delivery are most commonly made by agency personnel without significant attention to consumer preference. In contrast, younger individuals with functional limitations find themselves in a more consumer-oriented and client-driven program setting with greater control over the services they receive and their choices regarding caregivers or personal assistants (Simon-Rusinowitz & Hofland, 1993).

It is argued that a comprehensive service model is critical for addressing the continuum of need that older persons with physical impairments require to live independently in the community. Therefore, the disability model of service provision may be more appropriate for use, regardless of client's age (Bould, Smith, & Longino, 1997). However, to modify existing program structures, there is a strong need to alert service providers and policy makers to the benefits of geriatric rehabilitation, as well as to the critical public health goal of preventing or postponing future disability, including secondary health conditions, such as heart disease or osteoporosis, that often accompany a primary disability (Campbell, 1997; Wray & Torres-Gil, 1992a). Many policy makers have yet to consider long-term care issues as more than specialized interest group concerns, and their subsequent lack of planning in this area will most likely prove costly (Wray & Torres-Gil, 1992b). Some states are beginning to move toward need-based systems of health care, which have been founded, in part, on a belief that programs should not exclude those who need assistance based on age criteria and which are driven by fiscal necessity to streamline processes and reduce costs (Torres-Gil & Pynoos, 1986). In determining how to reformulate our independent living service models and delivery programs to make them more effective and efficient, it becomes important to create a public and political consensus about who is responsible and to what extent for aging and disability concerns (Torres-Gil & Puccinelli, 1994). To cultivate such a mandate, activists often turn to coalition building.

Building a coalition between the aging and disabled communities is a major challenge (Simon-Rusinowitz & Hofland, 1993). Although older and younger disabled persons share many common problems, each group has traditionally held its own unique set of goals, formed perhaps in part by the different life stages they occupy. Additionally, it cannot be said that either group is a unified coalition on its own, so asking the two to merge is no simple task. Despite the difficulties in assembling a quorum, it is believed that coalition building between the two groups will raise political clout and reduce battles that pit each group against the other (Simon-Rusinowitz & Hofland, 1993). Proponents of bringing the two interests together focus on what can be gained from working as a single unit, citing the ability of older adults to provide lifelong experience and of disability experts to contribute disability-specific and civil rights expertise (Beedon, 1993). In constructing such a political bridge, some advocates warn against becoming identified as one voting block, constituency or social category as if all individuals with disabilities have similar political perspectives or health care needs. They cite the fact that, despite indications that people become more diverse politically and economically as they age, professionals and policy makers alike tend to stereotype individuals with disabilities, basing their images on the population of the severely functionally limited, who tend to most use public and private services (Bass, Torres-Gil, & Kutza, 1991). Research has shown, however, that chronic health conditions have a high prevalence. But a low disability impact should be weighed equally with those conditions that are low in prevalence, yet high in impact when developing appropriate aging policy (Verbrugge, Lepowski, & Imanaka, 1990).

Increasingly, younger and middle-aged adults and their families have come to realize that aging involves more than becoming old chronically. It is about the process of maturing emotionally, spiritually, and physically, which, for many of us, will include facing some sort of physical limitation along the way. For purposes of coalition building, there are more interests at stake than just the aged and the disabled. Taxpayers are demonstrating heightened concern about the extent to which government will respond to its citizenry's longer life span and whether or not the current system of public benefits and services should be modified to address this issue. As the largest birth cohort ever in our nation's history moves into middle and old age, baby boomers and their leaders will face a new set of political realities that will be intimately affected by issues of aging and disability (Torres-Gil, 1988). The challenges will come in correctly reading the demographic tea leaves and adequately preparing for the aging boomers.

A DEMOGRAPHIC OVERVIEW: WHO WE ARE

In 1996, the number of people aged 65 and older was 33.9 million, or about 13% of the total population (Administration on Aging, 1997). For most of us, this figure doesn't seem so unusual. Since 1960, the percentage of adults over 65 has hovered around 9%, increasing to 11% by 1980, and now stands only slightly higher (American Association of Retired Persons

[AARP], 1991). The greatly forecasted old-age population explosion will likely not begin to enter our collective conscience prominently until the year 2010, when the first baby boomers reach age 65. By 2030, the end of the baby boomer maturation period, 69.4 million people, or fully 20% of the general population, will be 65 or older. That is one in every five Americans. Not only will the sheer number of older adults increase, but the average life span will most likely continue to rise as well. In 1996, an individual reaching 65 had an average life expectancy of an additional 17.7 years (19.2 years for women and 15.5 years for men). For those who turn 65 in the year 2000, 26% can expect to survive to age 90. If your sixtieth-fifth birthday isn't until the year 2050, you have a 40% chance of reaching your tenth decade (AARP, 1991).

The current population of the United States is about 268.5 million (Census Bureau, 1997). In 1994, the Census Bureau released data showing that about 21% of the population (54 million) had some level of disability. About half of those individuals—26 million—described themselves as having a severe disability (McNeil, 1997). Disability reaches beyond the individual level, touching nearly one third of all families in the United States. More than 20 million families have at least one member with a disability, the majority of whom are adults (LaPlante, Carlson, Kaye, & Bradsher, 1996). To be counted as *disabled* by the Census Bureau, an individual must have "difficulty in performing functional activities (e.g., seeing, hearing, talking, walking, climbing stairs, lifting and carrying a bag of groceries), activities of daily living (e.g., getting in and out of bed or a chair, bathing, getting around inside the home, dressing, using the toilet, eating), or other activities related to everyday tasks or socially-defined roles." A person with a severe disability is defined as "one who is completely unable to perform one of these activities or tasks or needs personal assistance" (Census Bureau, 1997). To conclude that the Census Bureau figures represent the entire spectrum of individuals facing functional limitations would be misleading. The number of individuals experiencing chronic health conditions in the United States is actually much higher.

In a 1996 study commissioned by the Robert Wood Johnson Foundation, researchers at the Institute for Health and Aging at the University of California, San Francisco (UCSF), reported that nearly 100 million people in the United States had some form of chronic health condition. One in six of these individuals—41 million—had a chronic condition that inhibited life to some degree. The authors of that report defined a *chronic condition* as a general term that includes both chronic illness and impairments. They delineated a chronic illness as "the presence of long-term disease or symptoms" and *impairment* as "a physiological, psychological or anatomical abnormality of bodily structure or function, including all losses or abnormalities, not just those attributable to active pathology" (Robert Wood Johnson Foundation, 1996). UCSF researchers claimed that, by definition, chronic conditions cannot be cured (Robert Wood Johnson Foundation, 1996). Though this definition is less restrictive than that of the Census Bureau, it perhaps is more encompassing of the patterns of gradual function loss that many adults experience with advancing age. Therefore, we feel it is appropriate to consider both groups, acknowledging that most of those termed *disabled* are likely included in the count of individuals with chronic conditions, for policy-making purposes. When the number of individuals with disabilities and chronic conditions is factored in with the projections of our population's increased longevity, the picture of our nation's future needs in the areas of health care and independent living assistance becomes startling.

Although recent medical research has shown that the percentage of older adults who experience severe disability is on the decline, due to both developments in medical science and improved access to services through universal health care programs such as Medicare and Medicaid, it is expected that the total number of middle-aged and older adults with mild or moderate levels of impairment will, nonetheless, dramatically increase (Kunkel & Applebaum, 1992). In fact, current data show that the percentage of people with a disability or chronic condition increases with age. For those individuals aged 22–44, 15% had some form of a disability in 1994. The figure was 36% among middle-aged adults between 55 and 64 and 72% for those 80 and older (LaPlante et al., 1996). For those living in the community with a chronic health condition, the pattern was a bit more even, with 31% of those with chronic conditions falling between the ages of 18 and 44, 29% aged 45–65 and 26% aged 65 and older (Robert Wood Johnson Foundation, 1996). In addition, we now know that co-morbidities, or multiple chronic health conditions, are not unusual. Close to half— 44%—of all persons with chronic conditions had one or more ailments to manage. Of those aged 65 and older experiencing chronic conditions, 7 in 10 had multiple ailments (Robert Wood Johnson Foundation, 1996).

Although not everyone who experiences a chronic health condition or a disability needs personal or home care assistance, a substantial number do. The majority of those in need of assistance with daily living tasks are 65 and older, with those needing the most help at the upper end of the age range (Administration on Aging, 1997). In 1992, only 7% of adults between 65 and 69 needed some sort of assistance with either activities of daily living (ADLs) tasks (e.g., bathing, dressing, eating, getting around the house) or instrumental activities of daily living (IADLs) (e.g., preparing meals, shopping, managing money, using the telephone). However, of those aged 85 and older, 42% needed either ADL or IADL assistance (Administration on Aging, 1997). For many individuals, assistance comes by way of informal care. In 1990, 83% of disabled individuals under 65 and 73% of those 65 and over relied exclusively on informal caregivers be they family or friends (Robert Wood Johnson Foundation, 1996). It is estimated that more than 22 million families are involved in providing some sort of long-term home care (Peterson, 1997). The National Council on Aging reports that nearly seven million Americans provide long-distance care, including locating and paying for provider services, to elders (National Council on Aging, 1997). However, as our society ages, the ratio of the population in the average caregiver age range (50–64 years) to individuals receiving informal care will decrease from 11 to 1 in the year 1990 to 4 to 1 in the year 2050 (Robert Wood Johnson Foundation, 1996). Based on this predictive ratio, the pool of available potential informal caregivers will shrink significantly, and individuals with disabilities or chronic conditions and their families may be forced to rely more heavily on formal care provided by private and public agencies. These demographic and health care trends have long been available for analysis. The questions are, Have we paid attention? and, Are we, as individuals and as a nation, prepared for the arrival of the long-awaited aging boom?

A CASE STUDY OF THE BABY BOOMERS: WHAT WILL BE THEIR FATE?

The test for our society and the social policies it has created will come with the aging of the baby boomers. Our nation's next set of senior citizens were born between the postwar boom period of 1946 and 1964. They are now 79 million strong and have continually redefined the United States socially, politically and economically as they have moved into each new life stage. Who would expect any less? As you walk down the street today, nearly one out of every three people you see will be a baby boomer (AARP, 1991). They are a powerful and plentiful cohort who have already begun to alter our images of aging.

This post–World-War-II cohort is now between 34 and 52 years of age and is a fascinating profile, in some respects similar to their parents, but in many other ways quite different. Much is being written about this generation, so we will provide you with only a brief sketch. Three fourths of baby boomers are white; the remaining quarter is split among the major minority groups, 12% black, 9% Hispanic and 3% of Asian descent. Economically, they are doing about as well as their parents did at the same life stage. Twenty-eight percent of boomer households earn more than $50,000 annually and nearly 6 in 10—57%—own their own homes. Yet, a substantial segment is considered "at risk," which may foretell their future in old age, having one or more of the following characteristics: non–home-owner, single female or having low education. In addition, 1994 figures indicate that about 16% of full-time working adults aged 25–54 years (encompassing the entire boomer age range) had no health insurance coverage. Finally, the typical married baby boom couple has fewer children than their parents, and it is anticipated that 15% of baby boom women will remain childless, which may translate into growing old with few or no children to depend on for support or care (Dennis & Miller, 1996).

Though the baby boomers are reaping the benefits of twentieth-century medical advancements and appear to be in better physical condition than were previous generations, this perception may be deceiving. According to a recent Healthy People 2000 Report, produced by the Department of Health and Human Services (DHHS), the proportion of adults in the United States between the ages of 20 and 74 who are overweight is steadily increasing. Between 1988 and 1991, one third of our national population was overweight. In the same time period, fewer than 25% of Americans were following American Dietary Association guidelines for fat intake or eating the recommended daily amount of fruits and vegetables (Department of Health and Human Services, 1994). Although the rate of adults who perform moderate activity increased to 24% by 1991, the DHHS concluded that substantial progress is needed if goals of a healthier nation are to be met by the year 2000 (Department of Health and Human Services, 1995). Together, these factors point to trouble ahead. Diet and exercise have proven to be moderators for many health conditions. If Americans aren't following them now, can we expect their patterns to change in old age? Current statistics reveal that baby boomers already have a history of some of the most well-known chronic and disabling conditions. (See Table 18–1.) According to the National Center for Health Statistics, high blood pressure, heart disease and diabetes are three of the most prevalent chronic

Table 18–1 Prevalence of Selected Chronic Conditions: U.S. 1990–1992

Ranking	Age 18–44	45–64	65–74	75+
1.	deformities or orthopedic impairments	arthritis	arthritis	arthritis
2.	chronic sinusitis	high blood pressure	high blood pressure	deafness and other hearing impairments
3.	hay fever or allergic rhinitis without asthma	deformities or orthopedic impairments	deafness and other hearing impairments	high blood pressure
4.	headache (excluding tension headache)	chronic sinusitis	heart disease	heart disease
5.	migraine headache	deafness and other hearing impairments	deformities or orthopedic impairments	deformities or orthopedic impairments
6.	high blood pressure	heart disease	chronic sinusitis	cataracts
7.	deafness and other hearing impairments	hay fever or allergic rhinitis without asthma	cataracts	chronic sinusitis
8.	arthritis	hemorrhoids	diabetes	blindness and other visual impairments
9.	chronic bronchitis	chronic bronchitis	tinnitus (hearing)	diabetes
10.	asthma	diabetes	hay fever or allergic rhinitis without asthma	tinnitus (hearing)

Source: National Center for Health Statistics. Vital and Health Statistics, Series 10, No. 194. Reprinted from *Vital and Health Statistics*, Series 10, No. 194, National Center for Health Statistics.

conditions among adults aged 45–64. Arthritis and orthopedic ailments are also high on the list (National Center for Health Statistics, 1997). Though prevalence rates vary, recent figures from the Census Bureau show that disability is already a fact of life for many working-age adults, regardless of profession (U.S. Census Bureau, 1997).

If health and disability projections hold true, the dramatic number of older adults with chronic conditions and disabilities will severely tax the current health care system. As of now, it is debatable whether we are ready for such an increased demand for health care and independent living services. Findings from the Department of Labor show that home health care will have the largest job growth of any industry between 1994 and 2005, accounting for one in every five new jobs. Expectations are that health service occupations will increase more than twice as fast as the economy as a whole (Bureau of Labor Statistics, 1996). Although the demand for increased care is certain, how future health care costs will be paid is still under debate. Amid talk of reform, more than two thirds of Americans are not confident that the Medicare system will continue to provide benefits of equal value to those received by retirees today. Forty-six percent do not believe the Medicare program will still provide health insurance when they retire, and 36% of workers are not confident they will have enough money to take care of their own medical expenses (Employee Benefit Research Institute, 1997). In the face of what may be an uncertain future for publicly financed health care, few baby boomers have taken it upon themselves to plan for meeting their own health care costs in old age.

Despite all the hype that has surrounded the baby boom generation as their first members turned 50, there remains a collective denial among this cohort about the realities of aging that has seemingly left them unprepared for retirement and the medical care they will require as they grow old. In their 1997 Retirement Confidence Survey, the Employee Benefit Research Institute (EBRI) found that, although 69% of current workers save money for retirement, only 27% of Americans have an idea about how much money they will need to save to continue their standard of living after they quit working. Of the 36% who have even tried to compute this, almost one in four workers cannot report that exact figure. Most of us realize that we are underprepared for old age. Only 6% of working and retired Americans believe that, in general, people save enough money to live comfortably throughout their retirement years. However, almost as if everyone decided to stick their heads in the sand at the same time, 68% of those currently working are confident that they personally will have enough money. According to the EBRI, the average 50-year-old who earns $50,000 a year should already have $350,000 put aside for retirement. The reality is that only 27% of individuals aged 45–52 have retirement accumulations of more than $100,000, including employer contributions (Employee Benefit Research Institute, 1997). Given these figures, it appears that baby boomers, much like their parents, will be heavily dependent on federal entitlement programs such as Medicare and Social Security in their later decades.

Although we have provided only a brief sketch of the health and retirement situation awaiting baby boomers, it seems sufficient to warrant a great deal of concern regarding the status of public programs such as Medicare and Medicaid. The directions that these programs take and the extent to which they are prepared to support the aging of baby boomers is heavily dependent on the politics of health and social policy. The fabric of today's health care safety net for older adults is fraught with snags and holes created by a fragmented and incomplete system of care. It is in jeopardy of being distressed further by entitlement reforms aimed at reducing the much-hyped "skyrocketing" costs of Medicare and Medicaid. However, any fundamental changes made to these programs in terms of health care coverage and payment plans should take into consideration the need to prepare not only for an aging society but for one where a significant percentage of the population has a disability or chronic condition. Alterations in these founding programs will directly affect the way we, as a society, including baby boomers and future generations, prepare financially and socially for old age.

POLICY AND POLITICS: PROVIDING A HISTORICAL CONTEXT FOR THE DEBATE

Given this set of circumstances, it becomes important to note at the policy level how disability issues are being addressed in our aging society. Is our nation preparing for the dramatic increase of older adults with disabilities and chronic conditions? The answer is, in short, not exactly. Disability policies and aging policies have developed as two distinct program streams. What exists in the policy and political realms is a fragmented and parallel system of laws and programs that segment older persons and those with disabilities. Few disabled or aging advocates have responded to the crossover occurring between the two populations. However, recent policy debates and political decisions may create an intersection of age, functional limitations, and political alliances that may, in time, bring the issues of disability and age closer together, particularly around the long-term care needs of baby boomers. To understand the current system of laws and programs, we must examine the historical context of social policy in health, aging, and disability.

Aging has a storied history of advocacy, policy and public receptivity (Torres-Gil, 1992). The well-known entitlement programs of Social Security, Medicare, and Medicaid, other important social services provided through the Older Americans Act, volunteer programs such as Senior Companion and Green Thumb, and assorted housing, transportation and social services have their genesis in the Great Depression of the 1930s. The trauma of that period and the resultant insecurities it created highlighted the vulnerability of older persons to the consequences of economic dislocation. What stemmed from that period was a "politics of aging" and a recognition by the federal government that it should provide a safety net for its citizens, largely predicated on age.

The establishment of the Social Security Act of 1935 was the cornerstone for later laws, programs and services that have created a comprehensive system of benefits, entitlements and supports for older persons and their families. The coalescing of older persons during the 1930s to advocate for pensions and income supplements to alleviate the dramatic poverty among their own ranks led to the establishment of organizations such as the American Association for Retired Persons (AARP), the National Council of Senior Citizens, the National Council on Aging, and the Gray Panthers. Together, these policies and advocacy groups, coupled with the high registration and voting rates of older persons, have created a formidable constituency. Elected officials, government agencies, the media and the general public generally listen when the elderly voice their demands to the body politic. Senior lobby groups may not always win their political battles, but they are always taken seriously.

The disabled, on the other hand, have a more recent history (Torres-Gil & Wray, 1993). Though they also have successfully campaigned for an assortment of laws and policies, they do not now enjoy the relative political influence of older persons, although that is changing. Early attempts to organize the disabled as an interest group occurred in the 1960s and early 1970s, with the rise of the independent living movement in the San Francisco Bay area (Young, 1998). Other groups in Massachusetts, Colorado and Texas promoted the civil rights of the disabled and attempted to recast the public image of the disabled from a paternalistic view (e.g., the Jerry Lewis telethons) to one of independence and empowerment. The creation of groups such as the American Coalition of Citizens with Disabilities in 1975 (and its earlier counterpart, the President's Committee on Employment of the Handicapped, created by President Truman in 1947), public activism by groups such as the American Disabled for

Attendant Programs Today and the ongoing work of the National Council on Disability created a public consciousness that the disabled community could promote its own social and public agenda (Young, 1998).

Political success came with the passage of Section 504 of the Rehabilitation Act of 1973 and the Americans with Disabilities Act (ADA) in 1990. The former prohibited discrimination on the basis of disability in all federally funded programs, and the latter provided sweeping civil rights safeguards and equal opportunity provisions in employment, public accommodations, transportation, state and local government services, and telecommunications. Together, those policies created a political climate where the disabled, as an organized interest group, could pressure government and elected officials to view them as a constituency group with its own sense of entitlement and identity.

This quick historical overview signifies the maturation of older persons and persons with disabilities as political forces in American society. It also means that the elderly and the disabled have developed separate and sometimes competing agendas. During the 1960s, 1970s, and 1980s, each group had the luxury of pushing for expanded funding, separate laws, and new programs, largely independent of each other. Thus, we saw the creation of a parallel system of services and programs. For the elderly, an "aging network" of state and local Area Agencies on Aging developed to provide in-home assistance, nutrition, and transportation, among other services. Health care and nursing home coverage came through Medicare and Medicaid. The majority of these services are predicated on age. For the disabled, somewhat similar services became available through state Departments of Vocational Rehabilitation and independent living centers providing a system of supports for young (under 65 years of age) and functionally impaired individuals. Each group, in turn, constructed its own set of terms and conditions for how it viewed its circumstances and proposed unique criteria for how its demands could be met. The elderly, for example, focused on "maintenance of current condition" or prevention of further decline and were most concerned about quality of life in retirement (e.g., pensions, volunteer programs) and availability of long-term care. The disabled, however, pushed for "mainstreaming" functionally impaired individuals (e.g., providing full access to housing, transportation, and work opportunities) and enabling personal independence through the use of rehabilitation services to increase physical abilities and personal attendants assisting in daily activities.

This separate and parallel approach, taken to its logical conclusion, means that those who become disabled can look to one set of policies and programs, and those who reach old age (and meet the eligibility criteria of federal and state entitlement programs) can rely on a separate set of programs and services. What about younger disabled persons who become elderly? What about older persons who become disabled? This intersection of age and disability has become more pronounced in recent years, due in part to the increased life expectancy of younger persons with disabilities such as polio and spinal cord injuries and the increased numbers of middle-aged and older persons living with chronic conditions or functional limitations, such as rheumatoid arthritis or reduced mobility.

In the 1990s, then, we have an interesting and significant confluence of events which, at the moment, is not in synergy with the existing state of policy and politics for both groups. Individuals commonly thought of as disabled can now expect to live into old age and be eligible for old-age programs, especially in the areas of health and long-term care. At the same time, a significant percentage of older adults, particularly aging baby boomers, will face issues of functional limitation and disability in old age and will most likely find that they, too, want independence and empowerment, the very principles embodied in the disability rights movement. Despite the pending merger of the disabled and aging populations, public policy makers have not acted on these trends. Today's system of benefits and programs is still based largely on separate models of care for the disabled and the elderly.

CREATING A POLICY FRAMEWORK FOR AGING AND DISABILITY: LONG-TERM CARE AS A BRIDGE

As Table 18–2 demonstrates, a host of programs and services exists that are targeted for the disabled and the elderly.

The ADA and Section 504 of the Rehabilitation Act are the premiere civil rights vehicles for the disabled. The Social Security Disability Insurance (SSDI) program protects workers from loss of income due to disability. Workers' Compensation provides cash payments and medical and rehabilitation services to workers (or their survivors) who have disabilities because of accidents on the job or occupational diseases. Black lung benefits are paid to coal miners who are totally disabled. The Veterans

Table 18–2 Policy Framework for Aging and Disability

Aging Programs for Individuals 65 and over	Aging-Disability Overlap: Programs Providing Benefits to Both Groups	Disability Programs for Disabled Individuals under age 65
Employee Retirement and Spousal Benefits	Social Security	Supplemental Security Income, Social Security Disability Insurance
Health benefits for qualified individuals aged 65 and older	Medicare	Health benefits for qualified disabled individuals
Health benefits for qualified low income individuals aged 65 and older	Medicaid	Health benefits for qualified low-income disabled individuals
Older Americans Act		Americans with Disabilities Act
Volunteer Programs		Section 504 of the 1973 Rehabilitation Act
		Worker's Compensation
		Black Lung
		Veteran's Administration Disability Compensation Program, Disability Pension Program and Veteran's Health Services

Administration (VA) programs assist veterans with service-related disabilities. Social Security (income supplements), Medicare (hospital and medical coverage for those 65 years of age and older), Medicaid (health care for low-income and medically indigent individuals) and the Older Americans Act (social services for those 60 years of age and older) are heavily predicated on reaching old age or, in the case of Medicaid, are the major public source of funding for nursing-home and long-term care for the elderly.

There is considerable overlap in these programs. Social Security, for example, provides benefit services for disabled individuals who are unable to engage in any substantial gainful activity because of a severe disability.

Medicare, although meant for older persons, does cover disabled persons insured under Social Security. For a time, this overlap appeared to move toward greater integration with proposals to expand long-term care. However, that trend is now uncertain.

The health care reform efforts of the first Clinton-Gore administration resulted in major progress in bridging the long-term care needs of older persons and the younger disabled. Although the ambitious effort to restructure the health care system comprehensively and to provide universal coverage failed, it did result in progress on several fronts, including heightened attention to the uninsured, bipartisan support for expanding coverage to low-income children, creating portability of insurance and making the use of private long-term care insurance more available. A conceptual and political outcome of health care reform was a consensus among advocates for the disabled and the elderly that, henceforth, any expansion of long-term care, especially home- and community-based services, should be based not on age but on need for services. The use of ADLs and IADLs would be the criteria for determining eligibility.

Since the failed attempts at health care reform, there has been some expansion of long-term care. The Health Insurance Portability and Accountability Act of 1996, for example, enhances portability of health insurance, restricts the use of preexisting conditions and provides tax incentives for the purchase of private long-term care insurance. This minimalist approach is not a sign of resistance to such services. In fact, bipartisan support exists for expanding home- and community-based care. It is, however, a resulting effect of budgetary politics and the overarching fear that expanding such services would add major costs to the already overburdened Medicare and Medicaid programs. For example, until the passage of the Balanced Budget Act of 1997, strong bipartisan support existed for expanding respite care to help people caring for persons with Alzheimer's disease. That provision was eventually left out because of deep concerns that it could open up another costly entitlement.

Long-term care and the provision of home and community care to the disabled lie at the intersection of health, aging and disability. The majority of individuals who have difficulty caring for themselves require similar services, regardless of age. With few exceptions, persons with severe disabilities or chronic conditions prefer to stay in their homes, maintain a measure of control and independence, and be helped by family and friends. Yet, public funding of long-term care has largely focused on institutional care for older persons, such as nursing homes, and little emphasis has been placed on restructuring the aging service model to match more closely the disability movement's vision of long-term care, which centers on the use of in-home supportive services and contracted personal assistants. This model may be better suited to the needs of the aging baby boomers, who will have less severe functional limitations, requiring lower levels of care and for which long-term institutionalization may not be appropriate. Clearly, much work is needed to bring current service programs into alignment before they can adequately be united to serve the aging and disabled populations as a universal system of care. However, we must act quickly if we are to be prepared adequately for the largest elderly cohort in American history.

CONTEMPORARY POLITICS: WHERE WE STAND TODAY

As a bridge for meeting the needs of aging baby boomers, the future of disability and aging policies will hinge largely on the political decisions currently being made about the Medicare, Medicaid and Social Security programs. How we handle the politics of those programs will indicate whether we move forward or backward in meeting the needs of older persons who may face chronic conditions and of younger persons with disabilities who will grow old. The "macro politics" of entitlement reform will directly affect the individual and family response to aging and disability.

In the 1990s, addressing the huge federal deficits of the last two decades became a central concern of government, politicians and the public. The growing recognition that the nation could not continue to live beyond its means met with the realization that continued deficits, a huge federal debt and the large proportion of the federal budget used to pay the interest on the national debt were prompting just such a scenario. This "wake-up call" forced corrective action with the Balanced Budget Act of 1997. That law requires a balanced budget by 2002, in large part by reducing overall growth of the Medicare and Medicaid programs. By 1995, Medicare and Medicaid were consuming about 17% of federal spending, compared with 22% for Social Security, 16% for the military and 16% for interest on the national debt. An additional 6% went to means-tested programs (e.g., welfare). Only about 22% of the federal budget was available for all other discretionary spending. Thus, it was clear to many elected officials that if entitlement programs were allowed to continue to grow at their current pace, Social Security and, particularly, Medicare and Medicaid, might not be able to sustain coverage for a projected doubling of the older population early in the next century.

Happily, and somewhat surprisingly, the federal budget is close to being balanced well before the year 2002. But the pressures to revamp Medicare, Medicaid and Social Security continue. The proposed changes to those programs bear close scrutiny by older persons, the disabled and their families. The resultant outcome of any program changes will have significant implications on how disability and aging will be addressed in the coming years.

Medicare, projected to become insolvent within 10 years, is faced with fundamental reform. The Balanced Budget Act of 1997 created the National Bipartisan Commission on the Future of Medicare. This commission will recommend long-term changes to resolve the problems that threaten Medicare's financial integrity. Its report is due in 1999. Options being considered include raising the eligibility age, means-testing parts of Medicare, reducing coverage and raising taxes. These types of considerations may crowd out support for expanding coverage, especially home- and community-based care. The Balanced Budget Act of 1997 did result in some provisions that may benefit persons with disabilities and chronic conditions. Those provisions include making Program for All-Inclusive Care (a comprehensive home- and community-based care program) a permanent Medicaid option, including more preventive services (e.g., pelvic exams, colorectal screening tests, enhanced coverage for mammogram and Pap smears) and introducing new demonstration programs for improving the care of chronically ill individuals enrolled in managed care.

Social Security will face similar pressures and fundamental changes. Its long-term solvency is stronger than that of Medicare, with trust funds projected to last until 2029—well through the retirement of most baby boomers. However, serious consideration is being given to moving up the increase in the eligibility age (currently scheduled to rise from 65 to 67 by 2029) and to partially privatizing Social Security. Such proposals would allow trust fund reserves to be invested in the private market, the creation of a mandatory individual savings plan and a personal security account managed at the individual level. Such changes may also erode the expectations that persons with disabilities can continue to rely on the SSDI program.

However these proposals evolve, it seems certain that some types of changes will occur within Social Security and Medicare that will put a greater onus on individuals to save for their own retirement and health care needs and not to rely solely on federal programs to serve them in old age. To the extent that Social Security and Medicare face fiscal pressures and coverage in either program is reduced, the burden of making up the difference in lost benefits will probably fall heaviest on persons with lower incomes.

Taken together, the politics of entitlement reform will shape the safety net for the next century. The growing political alliances between the disabled and aging organizations, the apparent consensus to support long-term care, based on disability and functional limitations, and the progress made in destigmatizing age and disability could be helped or hindered by the political decisions pending with entitlement programs. The future remains to be seen.

THE NEXT CHALLENGE: ADVANCING THE AGING-DISABILITY AGENDA

The future of aging and disability poses several challenges for health care providers, policy makers, baby boomers and society. The health care industry is undergoing revolutionary changes and faces continued uncertainties. The advent of managed care, the resurgence of high health cost increases, the continued increase in the number of persons without health insurance and the federal and state pressures to reform Medicare and Medicaid ensure an unstable environment for health and long-term care policy. For older persons with chronic conditions and younger persons with disabilities, this ambiguous state creates anxiety and insecurity: What happens if Medicaid reduces coverage and Medicare raises the eligibility age? If current trends continue, whereby the proportion of caretakers to a dependent population drops from 11:1 to 4:1, who will provide caregiving if public funding is constrained? Managed care has been touted as a "magic bullet" for reducing costs, promoting preventive measures and enhancing access. Yet, managed care firms, especially for-profits, are beginning to scale back benefits to Medicare and Medicaid beneficiaries (e.g., by reducing prescription and eyeglass coverage) and have not shown enthusiasm for recruiting members with disabilities. If managed care is not the answer, who will step in to provide health and long-term care coverage?

Those issues will be one of the greatest personal and financial challenges baby boomers will face as they get older. This cohort is used to getting what it wants. Although its members are not yet focused on retirement and their pending old age as a group, they are witnessing what their parents and grandparents encounter as they become older and require health and long-term care. Soon, perhaps within 15 years, the leading edge of the baby boomers will expect adequate health care coverage from the federal government. With increasing numbers of adults facing some type of disability, we may find fertile political soil for renewed advocacy by baby boomers—except that, this time, it will not concern cultural freedom, civil rights, or antiwar protests, but retirement and health care rights. This may also be a milestone for building solid alliances between elderly boomers and the disabled. Taken together, if political consensus can be achieved, we may have a formidable political force during the elections of the next century.

For society, aging and disability go to the heart of how we view our responsibility to take care of ourselves and others. As a youth-obsessed society that values physical beauty and abilities, we continue to shy away from the reality that many of us will face some type of emotional or physiological disability or chronic condition. As we get older, we may understand why, as kids, our parents and grandparents seemed preoccupied with their "maladies." Elderly baby boomers will find that cocktail conversations will center around the latest prescription medication and technological innovations that help us cope with our frailties.

To that extent, there is much positive news. New industries will grow around the technological advances that help us remain active, even if severely disabled. Telecommunications, computers, modified architecture and electronics promise to make up for some of our physical losses. The ADA and the recognition by business and government that persons with disabilities make excellent employees will provide more employment opportunities for persons of all ages who are not physically fit. The media, including advertising, has served the disabled community well by portraying disabled persons in commercials and television shows. Accessibility is quite good in this country, compared with many other nations. One need only travel to Latin America, the Pacific Rim and other regions to know how much progress we have made in this country.

The raising of our consciousness comes with problems, as well. For example, the use of handicap placards to access choice parking has become a serious program in many areas, where relatively healthy people are taking advantage of minor sprains and back problems or, worse, are illegally using handicap placards. The ADA, intended for the severely disabled, is facing a surge of cases where emotional distress and on-the-job stress are being considered as disabilities. However onerous these examples sound, it does signify that society is accepting disability as a natural part of life and of growing older.

We must go back to our original thesis, then, that disability should be central to aging concerns. In an aging society, how we cope with chronic conditions and disabilities will define our quality of life as older persons. Even if we are fortunate enough to age and die without any physical or emotional complications (the proverbial goal of keeling over on the golf course at age 98), we will invariably have loved ones—spouses, siblings, parents, friends—who will face these facts of life. For these reasons, it is important that we interject issues of disability into the political debate and continue to encourage coalition-building between the aging and disabled communities.

REFERENCES

Administration on Aging. (1997). *A profile of older Americans: 1997.* Washington, DC: American Association of Retired Persons. http://pr.aoa.dhhs.gov/aoa/stats/profile.

American Association of Retired Persons. (1991). *Aging America: Trends and projections.* U.S. Senate Special Committee on Aging, American Association of Retired Persons, Federal Council on the Aging and the U.S. Administration on Aging. (DHHS Pub No. [FCOA] 91-28001.) Printed by the U.S. Department of Health and Human Services.

Bass, S., Torres-Gil, F., & Kutza, E. (1991). On the relationship between the diversity of the aging population and public policy. *J Aging Soc Policy, 2*(3/4), 101–115.

Beedon, L. (1993). Moving disability policy into the 21st century. *Top Geriat Rehabil, 9*(2), 18–28.

Bould, S., Smith, M., & Longino, C. (1997). Ability, disability and the oldest old. *J Aging Soc Policy, 9*(1), 13–31.

Bureau of Labor Statistics. Tomorrrow's jobs. www.fedstats.gov/index20.html, 1996.

Campbell, M.L. (1997). Two worlds of disability: Bridging the gaps between the aging network and the disabled community. *Southwest J Aging, 13*(2), 3–11.

Census Bureau web site. http://www.census.gov.

Census Bureau. (1997). *Americans with disabilities: 1994–95.* (Current Population Reports P70-61). U.S. Department of Commerce, Economics and Statistics Administration.

Crimmons, E.M., Hayword, M.D., & Saito, Y. (1994). A long better life: Changing mortality and morbidity rates and the health status and life expectancy of the older population. *Demography, 31*, 159–175.

Dennis, H., & Miller, C. (1996). Some facts about boomers. Andrus Institute. Andrus Gerontology Center, University of Southern California.

Department of Health and Human Services. *Healthy People 2000 progress report for: nutrition,* http://www.odphp.osophs.dhhs.gov/pubs/hp2000, 1994.

Department of Health and Human Services. *Healthy People 2000 progress report for: physical activity and fitness,* http://www.odphp.osophs.dhhs.gov/pubs/hp2000, 1995.

Employee Benefit Research Institute. The 1997 retirement confidence survey: Summary of findings. http://ebri.org/rcs/1997/97rcses.html, 1997.

Kunkel, S.R., & Applebaum, R.A. (1992). Estimating the prevalence of long-term disability for an aging society. *J Gerontol, 47*(5), S253–S260.

LaPlante, M., Carlson, D., Kaye, S., & Bradsher, J. (1996). *Families with disabilities in the United States.* Disability Statistics Rehabilitation Research and Training Center. Institute for Health and Aging. University of California, San Francisco.

McNeil, J. (1997). *Americans with disabilities: 1994–95.* Current Population Reports. Household Economic Studies. (Census Bureau Series P70-61.) U.S. Department of Commerce, Economics and Statistics Administration.

National Center for Health Statistics. (1997). Prevalence of selected chronic conditions: U.S. 1990–92. *Vital Health Stat,* (10), 194.

National Council on Aging. http://www.ncoa.org/pubs/releases/7milLTCB1297.htm (March 12, 1997).

Peterson, K. (1997, 4 September). More spend time caring for elders. *USA Today.*

Robert Wood Johnson Foundation. (1996). *Chronic care in America: A 21st century challenge.* Princeton, NJ: Robert Wood Johnson Foundation.

Simon-Rusinowitz, L., & Hofland, B. (1993). Adopting a disability approach to home care services for older adults. *Gerontologist, 33*(2), 159–167.

Torres-Gill, F. (1988). Process, politics and policy. *Generations, 12*(2), 5–9.

Torres-Gil, F. (1992). The new aging: Politics and change in America. Westport, CT: Auburn House.

Torres-Gil, F., & Puccinelli, M. (1994). Mainstreaming gerontology in the policy arena. *Gerontologist, 34*(6), 749–752.

Torres-Gil, F., & Pynoos, J. (1986). Long-term care policy and interest group struggles. *Gerontologist, 26*(5), 488–495.

Torres-Gil, F., & Wray, L. (1993). Funding and policies affecting geriatric rehabilitation. *Links in Geriat Rehabil, 19*(4), 831–840.

U.S. Census Bureau. Americans with disabilities: 1991–92. Table 7: Occupations of workers with disabilities, 1991–92. http://www.icdi.wru.edu/disability/ustabl7.html, 1997.

Verbrugge, L., Lepowski, J., & Imanaka, Y. (1990). Comorbidity and its impact on disability. *Milbank Mem Fund Q, 67*(3/4), 450–484.

Wray, L., & Torres-Gil, F. (1992a). Availability of rehabilitation services for elders: A study of critical policy and financing issues. *Generations, 16*(2), 31–35.

Wray, L., & Torres-Gil, F. (1992b). Long-term care policy: A California dilemma. In G. Larue and R. Bayley (Eds.) *Long-term care in an aging society: Choices and challenges* (pp. 39–66). Buffalo, NY: Prometheus Books.

Young, J. (1998). Historic research conducted by Jonathan Young, doctoral candidate, Department of history, University of North Carolina, Chapel Hill.

CHAPTER 19

Long-Term Care Choice: A Simple, Cost-Free Solution to the Financing Puzzle

Stephen A. Moses

Healthy aging is the goal and hope of all of the contributors to this book—and of its readers, both from a personal and a theoretical perspective. Certainly, we all strive to encourage attitudes and behaviors that will foster a happy and independent life well into old age.

For many older people, however, the time will come when assistance with the daily tasks of living is needed, perhaps for the long term. With the huge baby boom generation looming on the demographic horizon, how best to provide that assistance and to pay for it is critically important.

Long-term care in the United States is more than a challenging public policy issue. It is a fascinating puzzle as well. In fact, the question of how we will pay for the needs of a rapidly aging population raises a continuum of conundrums. For example, why does a prosperous nation like ours warehouse its World War II generation in welfare-financed nursing homes? Why are most Americans in denial about the risks of long-term care when the media warn us constantly about an impending demographic Armageddon? Why do we agree on so many of the problems and solutions of long-term care service delivery and yet fail, year after year, to initiate decisive corrective action?

A FOUNDATION OF AGREEMENT

Conventional wisdom and scholarly consensus agree: The United States faces a potentially cataclysmic long-term care financing crisis in the foreseeable future. The evidence of impending danger is everywhere we look—undeniable trends in demographics; reduced availability of informal caregivers; doubts about the quality of formal long-term care; inadequate supply of low-cost home- and community-based services; rapidly escalating nursing-home expenses; poorly structured delivery systems; dwindling public finances; increasingly resistant taxpayers; declining ability or willingness of families to pay for long-term care; cracks in our public and private pension systems; and the approaching retirement of the baby boom generation. These are the elements of consensus about the nature of the problem.

Just as the public and the experts have come to agree on the problems, they also concur on the architecture of an ideal long-term care system. Certain optimal features show up consistently in task-force reports, think-tank studies, policy papers and published articles. These include: generous eligibility for assistance; integrated acute and long-term care; easy access at a single point of entry; quality control; case or care management; uniform client needs assessment; asset protection; home- and community-based care; such nonmedical social services as housekeeping and personal care; adult day care; respite care; such supportive housing as assisted living and adult foster homes; preadmission screening; custodial, skilled, and subacute nursing-home care; services to meet the special needs of geriatric, developmentally disabled, mentally ill and other patients; and coordination of public financing sources, primarily Medicaid and Medicare. These are the elements of consensus about the nature of the solution.

Here is the puzzle: We know what is wrong with long-term care in the United States. We know how to design an optimal service delivery system. We live in the world's wealthiest society. Why can't we come together politically and professionally to get the job done?

HISTORICAL PERSPECTIVE

When nothing we do seems to work but our predicament is so desperate that we cannot give up, the best strategy is to reexamine our premises. Most scholarship on long-term care focuses on the status quo, laments the familiar problems, advocates the usual solutions, and blames inaction on a lack of money caused by stingy taxpayers and cold-hearted politicians. If there is a fundamental underlying fallacy in our approach to long-term care, this commonplace analysis will not identify or correct it. The sad fact is that, if we keep doing what we have always done, it is likely that we will keep getting what we have always gotten. Instead, we must ask ourselves,

How did our long-term care system come to be the way it is? What do we need to do differently to achieve more desirable results?

In 1965, America was just starting to have a serious problem with long-term care. People were living longer but dying more slowly of chronic illnesses that caused frailty and cognitive impairment. Older Americans needed more and more long-term care at the very time when women, the traditional caregivers, were entering the formal work force in much greater numbers. This was when a prosperous private market in low-cost home- and community-based services, geriatric care management, and long-term care insurance might have developed in the United States. It did not.

Instead, with every good intention, the new federal Medicaid program offered publicly financed long-term nursing-home care. This benefit, initially unencumbered by restrictions on transfer of assets and estate recovery requirements, confronted families with a very difficult choice. They could pay "out-of-pocket" for the home care and community-based services that elders prefer or they could accept nursing-home care paid for by the government. Most people chose the safety and financial benefits of the government's Medicaid option. Therefore, the market for home care withered, private long-term care insurance failed to develop, and Medicaid-financed nursing-home care flourished.

The nursing-home industry took full advantage of this new source of public financing by building many new facilities. To have failed to do so would simply have been bad business. As fast as the industry could build them, the new nursing-home beds filled with Medicaid residents. Stunned by the cost, Medicaid attempted to control the construction of new beds with certificate-of-need programs based on the principle that "we cannot pay for a bed that does not exist." By the mid-1970s, health planning for nursing homes was in full swing. It worked. Fewer new beds were built.

Capping bed supply, however, predictably drove up price and demand. The nursing-home industry raised charges to compensate for the limitation on new beds. What the government saved by restricting bed supply it lost to nursing-home rate increases. Consequently, Medicaid nursing home costs grew faster than ever. In response, Medicaid capped reimbursement rates. This move impelled the nursing-home industry to increase private-pay reimbursement rates to compensate. The more the government pushed Medicaid rates down, the more the industry pushed private-pay rates up. So began the highly problematic differential between Medicaid rates and private-pay rates. Today, on average, Medicaid pays only 80% of private-pay rates.

Higher private-pay rates made Medicaid more attractive than ever to private payers. The public's desire to obtain public assistance for long-term care expenses led to pressure on legislators to loosen standards for Medicaid eligibility. A long process of eligibility bracket creep gradually made Medicaid nursing-home benefits available even to upper-middle-class people. Anyone who had or could obtain the expertise to manipulate Medicaid's highly elastic eligibility rules became eligible. An entire subpractice of law—Medicaid estate planning—developed to take advantage of this new opportunity. Artificial self-impoverishment, touted, for example, in *SmartMoney* and *Family Circle* magazines in the fall of 1997, became a clever solution to the consumer's long-term care financing problem.

With the supply and price of nursing-home beds capped by government fiat and with Medicaid eligibility increasingly generous, nursing-home occupancy skyrocketed to an average of 95% nationally. Given high demand and severely limited supply, nursing-home operators could fill their beds easily with low-paying Medicaid patients. To achieve adequate operating margins, however, nursing homes had to attract a sufficient supply of full-paying private patients or cut costs drastically.

Yet, if they tried to attract more lucrative private payers with preferred treatment or accommodations, the nursing homes were deemed guilty of discrimination against Medicaid patients. If they tried to cut costs instead, they came under fire for technical violations or quality problems. In response, Congress and state governments pressured the industry to provide a higher quality of care without discriminating against low-paying Medicaid recipients. Given the program's fiscal duress, however, Medicaid could not offer higher reimbursement rates to achieve these goals.

Caught between the rock of low reimbursement and the hard place of quality mandates, the nursing-home industry put up a strong fight. Armed with the Boren Amendment, a federal law that required Medicaid to provide reimbursement adequate to operate an efficient nursing facility, many state nursing-home associations took the battle to court. By this time, however, state and federal Medicaid expenditures were increasing so quickly and taxpayers had become so reluctant to pay for growing public spending that large increases in Medicaid nursing-home reimbursements were out of the question, regardless of which side won the lawsuits. The issue is moot now, of course, because the Boren Amendment was repealed by the Balanced Budget Act of 1997.

In the meantime, a wave of academic speculation in the late 1970s indicated that paying for home- and community-based services instead of nursing home care could save a lot of money. For years, therefore, Medicaid has experimented with home- and community-based service waivers as a cost-saving measure. In time, however, research showed that (desirable as they are) home- and community-based services do not save money overall. Medicaid and, more recently, Medicare expenditures for long-term personal and home care have soared in tandem with nursing home expenditures. It remains true, ironically, that because of the public's aversion for nursing-home care, institutional bias is Medicaid's strongest cost-containment tool, one of its gravest deficiencies, and the biggest single obstacle to the expansion of privately financed home- and community-based long-term care services.

CROSSROADS

In a nutshell, just as heavy demand was building for a privately financed eldercare market in the 1960s, Medicaid co-opted the trend by providing easy access to subsidized nursing-home care. Confronted with a choice between paying out-of-pocket for a lower level of care or receiving a higher level of care at much less expense, elders and their families made the predictable economic choice. Naturally, the potential market for long-term care insurance and privately financed home- and community-based services languished. Medicaid nursing-home case loads and expenditures increased rapidly and drastically. In response, Medicaid capped bed supply and reimbursement rates, which led inevitably to excessively high occupancy, private-pay rate inflation, discrimination against low-paying Medicaid patients, and serious quality-of-care issues.

Over time, Medicaid nursing-home care acquired a national reputation for impeded access, dubious quality, inadequate reimbursement, widespread discrimination, pervasive institutional bias, and excessive cost. Medicaid remains, nonetheless, the only way middle-class people can pay for long-term care without selling their homes or, if they are clever, without exhausting their savings. That is why so many otherwise independent and responsible Americans fail to buy private insurance while they are young and healthy enough to qualify for and afford it. Instead, they end up looking to Medicaid planning as the only way to save their estates or their inheritances. It is the reason why a huge proportion of America's World War II generation is dying on welfare in nursing homes.

Today, these historic trends have almost run their course. We are on the verge of a promising but perilous new world of long-term care. We are floundering forward, compelled by necessity to change the system "somehow." Both the private marketplace and public policy are pushing long-term care in a more consumer-friendly direction. Nursing-home occupancy is declining. The trend toward privately financed assisted living is exploding. Medicare has entered the arena with rapid growth in its home care and skilled nursing components. New buzzwords dominate our professional patois. We look with new hope to concepts like capitation, managed care, dual eligibility, and integration of acute and long-term care.

Is our dream of a seamless long-term care delivery and financing system just around the next bend in public policy? Or are we at risk of making the same mistakes we have made as in the past, but on a wider scale and with more drastic consequences? To answer these questions, we need to find a fresh perspective on the past, present, and future of long-term care financing.

A CONFLICT OF PARADIGMS

Whether we read a newspaper article, a scholarly journal or a book about long-term care financing, we invariably find an argument that goes something like this: "Long-term care, especially nursing home care, is extremely expensive. Very few Americans can afford $3,000–$5,000 per month in extra out-of-pocket expenses. Therefore, when stricken by the tragedy of Alzheimer's disease, Parkinson's disease or stroke, most people spend down their life's savings quickly and collapse into poverty. Once impoverished, they qualify for Medicaid, which steps in to pay their bills. Consequently, Medicaid nursing-home costs are skyrocketing, and the government's ability to meet growing long-term care needs is severely strained."

This scenario—let us call it the *welfare paradigm*—comports with some of the facts. Nursing homes are very expensive; Medicaid is a means-tested public assistance program; approximately two thirds of all residents in nursing homes do receive Medicaid and Medicaid does suffer from severe financial problems. However, let us set these matters aside for a moment, step back from the actual long-term care financing system, and ask, If the welfare paradigm is valid and the biggest problem facing us is widespread catastrophic spend-down, what would we logically expect the long-term care marketplace to look like?

If long-term care impoverishes large numbers of Americans and forces them onto welfare, we would certainly expect certain actions from elders and their families:

1. To worry and plan years in advance about the potentially catastrophic costs of long-term care;
2. To avoid nursing-home care as long as possible because of its expense and because of most people's preference to stay at home;
3. To demand high-quality, low-cost, home- and community-based care alternatives that delay institutionalization and impoverishment;
4. To utilize home equity conversion products (such as reverse annuity mortgages) that can finance home care and postpone liquidation of the family home;
5. To purchase private long-term care insurance that can protect against catastrophic financial loss caused by home or institutional care.

In practice, the opposite of these reasonable expectations holds true. First, most families do not plan in advance for the risk of long-term care. That is why so many of them end up in crisis with nowhere to turn but public assistance. Second, nursing-home care is often the first choice for care, not the last resort. That is why so many people end up in nursing homes when they could be cared for at home more comfortably and for less cost. Third, the home- and community-based care sector of the long-term care marketplace has been very slow to develop. That is why many people have no viable choice aside from nursing-home institutionalization when a health crisis strikes. Fourth, home-equity conversion has failed, to date, as a private-sector financial product, despite strong encouragement from the government. That is why the single biggest financial asset of elders (their home equity) goes virtually untapped as a source of financing for quality long-term care. Finally, only about 6% of older people have purchased private long-term care insurance. That is why nursing-home costs are devastating to most people when they do occur.

Clearly, much of what we would expect rational economic decision-makers to do if the welfare paradigm were valid simply does not happen.

Instead of torturing the old paradigm to account for these anomalies, we might consider a different view—let us call it the *entitlement paradigm*. "In America today, people can ignore the risk of long-term care, avoid the premiums for private insurance, wait to see whether they ever require formal care and, if necessary, shelter all their income and assets to qualify (virtually overnight) for nursing-home benefits paid for by Medicaid."

Viewed from the standpoint of the entitlement paradigm, the puzzling behavior described above becomes far more comprehensible. For example, people do not plan ahead for long-term care because they can wait until the last minute and receive publicly financed care. They often go to nursing homes instead of using home care, despite their preferences, because Medicaid pays generously for nursing-home care but covers very little home care. Few people want to take advantage of home-equity conversion to finance long-term care or purchase private insurance because Medicaid exempts the home and all contiguous property, regardless of value. Finally, long-term care insurance is unpopular because most people will not pay full dollar for something they can get from the government at a deep discount.

Thus, if the entitlement paradigm is valid and the United States has a publicly financed long-term care entitlement program that impedes market-based solutions, it is easy to understand why most people are eligible for Medicaid, even before they enter a nursing home (Sloan & Shayne, 1993). It explains why Medicaid nursing-home census and costs have increased rapidly for many years, why induced demand makes Medicaid financing of home care prohibitively expensive and why private financing of nursing-home care is declining instead of increasing as a proportion of total costs. In 1987, private out-of-pocket expenditures accounted for 49.3% of total nursing-home costs nationally; Medicaid paid for 43.9%, and Medicare paid for 1.4%. In 1996, private out-of-pocket expenditures accounted for 31.4% (down 17.9% since 1987); Medicaid paid for 47.8% (up 3.9%) and Medicare paid for 11.4% (up 10.0%) (Health Care Financing Administration, 1998; Lazenby, 1989).

Furthermore, if the entitlement paradigm is valid, many exciting new public policy options open up for us. For example, it could be possible to save taxpayers a lot of money and to empower many more Americans to pay privately for top-quality long-term care simply by making Medicaid a little less desirable and by providing a stronger incentive for people to plan ahead to avoid public assistance. In other words, the solution to the long-term care financing puzzle may reside in merging the two paradigms to gain the benefits of the welfare system without incorporating its negatives and to eliminate the problems of the entitlement paradigm without sacrificing its benefits.

There is no point, however, in exploring these possibilities further unless the entitlement paradigm is valid. Unfortunately, to most people familiar with the long-term care financing system, the entitlement paradigm will seem highly dubious. Critics of the entitlement paradigm will cite federal and state laws that appear to require impoverishment to qualify for Medicaid. Furthermore, most experts accept the welfare paradigm without challenge. Certainly, until now, no one has made the case in the mainstream gerontologic literature that the welfare paradigm is not valid and that the entitlement paradigm is a much better model of reality.

THE WELFARE PARADIGM: A PHALANX OF FALLACIES

A key fallacy of the welfare paradigm is that most people who need long-term care spend down their life's savings and fall sooner or later into the social safety net of Medicaid. The truth is very different. Seventy-eight percent of all people who enter nursing homes are already eligible for Medicaid before they are admitted to this expensive level of care (Sloan & Shayne, 1993). The vast majority of all patient stays in America's nursing homes are paid for by someone other than the patient. Medicaid alone pays, at least in part, for 71.7% of all nursing home patient days *(McKnight's Long-Term Care News*, 1996). In 1996, more than three fourths of all dollars paid for nursing-home services came from a combination of publicly financed programs, including Medicaid (47.8%), Medicare (11.4%), veterans' benefits and other government sources (2.3%), private health insurance (5.2%) or patient out-of-pocket income (not assets), and Social Security "spend-through"—income in the form of Social Security benefits that must be contributed toward the cost of nursing home services (12.8%) (Health Care Financing Administration, 1998; Lazenby & Letsch, 1990). According to the Health Care Financing Administration, "an estimated 41% of out-of-pocket spending for nursing-home care was received as income by patients or their representatives from monthly social security benefits" (Lazenby & Letsch, 1990). Empirical evidence of widespread catastrophic asset spend-down in nursing homes is nonexistent. In fact, numerous studies have recently shown that only 15–25% of Medicaid nursing-home patients spent down to qualify (including those who did so artificially through asset divestiture), instead of the 50–75% previously thought.

Another important fallacy of the welfare paradigm is that Medicaid eligibility requires impoverishment. The truth is very different. Virtually anyone, regardless of income or assets, can qualify quickly and easily for nursing-home care paid for by the government. Most states place no limit on how much income someone can have and still qualify for Medicaid nursing-home benefits. If a person's total medical costs—including nursing-home care—approximate or exceed that person's income, that person is eligible. Even in the toughest "income cap" states, the median elderly person—in terms of income and assets—qualifies easily for Medicaid nursing-home benefits without complicated estate planning. The income cap increases every year with inflation. For 1997, it was $1,452 per month or $17,424 per year, compared with an average annual income of $16,484 for elderly males and $9,335 for elderly females (Administration on Aging, 1996). The "Miller income trusts" authorized by the Omnibus Budget Reconciliation Act of 1993 (OBRA 93) lifted the lid on income caps altogether for most people.

The widely reported $2,000 Medicaid eligibility limit on assets is highly misleading. Medicaid recipients can also keep exempt assets such as a home, a business, and a car—of unlimited value. Many other assets are exempt as well. Converting such nonexempt assets as cash into exempt assets, such as home equity, is the easiest and most commonplace method of Medicaid planning. For married people, qualifying for Medicaid is even easier than for single people. Couples can shelter up to an additional $80,760 in assets and $2,019 per month in income as of 1998. Furthermore, these levels increase annually with inflation.

For the well-to-do who can afford professional legal advice, even these eligibility limits are easily overcome. Any competent Medicaid estate planner can deliver Medicaid nursing home eligibility almost overnight to practically anyone for less than the cost of 1 month in a private nursing home. Hundreds of law journal articles over the past 15 years attest to the fact that Medicaid is available to anyone with enough money to hire the right attorney. Two mass media legal self-help books do the same (Budish, 1989; Budish & Budish, 1993). The same advisers can evade estate recovery liability for their clients with equal facility. As explained below, these facts remain true, despite strong initiatives taken by Congress and the President in 1993, 1996 and 1997 to close Medicaid loopholes, mandate estate recoveries, and criminalize asset transfer advice.

DISCUSSION

Shall we assume, therefore, that because government pays for or subsidizes most nursing-home care in the United States, older Americans intentionally plan to go on welfare and into nursing homes if they ever need formal long-term care? Is that why so many of them fail to buy insurance or pay privately for lower levels of care? The answer is no. Most people simply do not worry or care about who pays for long-term care. They do not know whether the source is Medicaid, Medicare or Santa Claus. They are aware, however, that somebody else pays and that the horror stories about losing lifetime savings reported by magazine articles and insurance agents can be ignored with impunity. Ironically, they are right.

The easy, almost universal availability of publicly financed nursing-home benefits enables widespread public denial concerning long-term care risk. People insure only against real risks, and they naturally hesitate to pay full price for something that is available by government subsidy. If the social safety net suddenly disappeared—if people really had to become impoverished before the government helped them out—they would quickly realize that they could no longer enjoy the luxury of their denial. They would plan ahead for long-term care risks, buy insurance, tap home equity, employ geriatric care managers to find and coordinate the best available free or fee services and pay privately for the lowest, least expensive and best levels of care they could afford.

The social safety net is not going to disappear, however. The third rail of politics—senior benefits—retains sufficient voltage to stifle any politician who might attempt to eliminate long-term care benefits completely. Fortunately, there is a better way to solve the problem, and we already have many of the legislative and bureaucratic tools in place to implement it.OBRA 93, President Clinton's first budget, provided much of what is needed. OBRA 93 closed many of the loopholes that made Medicaid eligibility so attractive and required every Medicaid program in the country to recover benefits paid from the estates of deceased recipients. In essence, OBRA 93 told the middle class: "Medicaid is a loan, not a grant. If you do not want to die on welfare and pay for the privilege, buy long-term care insurance, pay privately for the long-term care services you prefer and leave public assistance for the poor." The Health Insurance Portability and Accountability Act of 1996 (HIPAA) went even further. It criminalized certain Medicaid asset transfers executed for the purpose of qualifying for public assistance, and it made private long-term care insurance more attractive by making the premiums tax-deductible.

Why have these changes in public policy not already unleashed the full potential of market-based solutions like supportive housing, home equity conversion, private geriatric care management, and long-term care insurance? Unfortunately, America has an entrenched welfare industry that thrives on impoverishing people artificially and profiteering from their dependency. Thousands of Medicaid estate planners throughout the United States work assiduously to reopen the eligibility loopholes closed by OBRA 93 and to weaken estate recovery. Numerous well-intentioned organizations that provide legal assistance to elders aid and abet the private bar by referring affluent elders to for-profit Medicaid planners. The Health Care Financing Administration, which administers Medicaid and Medicare, does not enforce OBRA 93 aggressively, provides little technical assistance to the states and openly advises Medicaid estate planners on how to circumvent the law. State Medicaid programs—experts at providing benefits and spending money—have little aptitude for or interest in controlling eligibility or collecting from estates. Many Medicaid eligibility workers actually help people spend down artificially to qualify for nursing-home benefits. The Balanced Budget Act of 1997 diluted the provisions in HIPAA 96 by aiming criminal penalties at asset transfers by Medicaid planners and other financial advisers but exonerating their clients. Finally, the National Academy of Elder Law Attorneys, the Medicaid planners' professional association, has mounted a nationwide public relations campaign to repeal criminalization altogether or to have the law declared unconstitutional. As so often happens, our public policy makers and the interest groups that lobby them have one foot on the accelerator and one foot on the brake of privatizing long-term care financing.

Clearly, the conventional wisdom that public assistance is available to people only after they have impoverished themselves in paying for long-term care (the welfare paradigm) is wrong. The reality is that most people qualify easily for Medicaid nursing-home benefits, and virtually anyone can qualify quickly with the right advice (the entitlement paradigm). Consequently, it should come as no surprise that most people in America do not worry in advance about long-term care, that they end up in nursing homes on Medicaid instead of in the less institutional settings they prefer and that they fail to tap the equity in their homes for long-term care expenses or to purchase private insurance.

Fortunately, this state of affairs is not irreversible. Today, the political imperatives to reduce government spending and curb entitlements have opened a pathway to major reform. It is no longer necessary to effect incremental change to an obsolete welfare program that is morally, intellectually and financially bankrupt. By virtue of its excessive cost and its reputation for serious access and quality problems, Medicaid is finished as a long-term care financing system for the middle class. America stands poised on the brink of an entirely new approach to long-term care financing.

SUMMARY OF THE PROBLEM

The 1970s should have been the golden age of long-term care in America. The gerontologic wedge pushed into American demographics during that decade could have opened an era of unprecedented entrepreneurial problem-solving. By now, we would have a market-driven continuum of care seamlessly covering everything from chore services to assisted living to subacute care. We would also have an infrastructure of long-term care insurance and home equity conversion to finance it. Public welfare might still have a role to play in long-term care, but that role would not be the tragedy of perverse incentives and unsatisfactory outcomes that it is today.

Instead, with every benevolent intent, Medicaid co-opted long-term care by the late 1960s. It impeded the private market for low-cost eldercare services and housing and discouraged the development of private long-term care insurance by providing free or subsidized nursing-home care. It created a Frankenstein's monster of institutional care by targeting public money only to nursing homes. It stifled competition, thereby impairing access and quality, by constricting bed supply and reimbursement rates artificially. It drove the middle-income consumer out of the private long-term care marketplace by creating a ponderous, publicly financed monopsony. In time, Medicaid choked the nursing home industry almost to death with regulations intended to correct the very problems that the program itself engendered. Nevertheless, in the absence of affordable alternatives and the means to pay for them, middle-class Americans in the hundreds of thousands are still being directed into Medicaid-financed nursing homes by well-intentioned public administrators and Medicaid estate planning attorneys.

PUBLIC POLICY RECOMMENDATIONS

What is the solution? Obviously, we cannot dismantle Medicaid overnight and leave the old, the sick, and the frail to fend for themselves. Rather, the first step is to preserve and improve a publicly financed long-term care program for the truly poor. To command good access and high quality, however, such a program must be able to pay market rates for every appropriate level of care. That will be expensive.

The only way to pay for such a program is to divert the middle class and affluent away from it and into private financing alternatives. This can be achieved only by imposing a strong means test, eliminating all eligibility loopholes and strictly enforcing estate recovery rules. There is no other option. We have to give Medicaid back to the poor and show everyone else how to pay their own way.

We cannot, however, compel middle-class Americans to impoverish themselves before they receive any assistance from their government. That policy already failed. It invites resentment, fraud and legal circumvention of the rules. Instead, we must provide a kinder alternative to families who need long-term care but cannot afford to pay for it without devastating themselves financially.

Given the precarious state of government entitlements, however, public funding for a new middle-class long-term care program is nonexistent. Any new program will have to pay its own way. Fortunately, adequate privately held resources are readily available in this country to pay for market-driven supportive housing and long-term care. In fact, $1.5 trillion lies illiquid and untapped today in older Americans' home equity alone, and another $10 trillion is about to fall into the laps of the baby boomers in the form of inheritance. The secret is to unlock these resources and put them to work paying for long-term care. Forcing elders to sell their homes before they can get help is not an acceptable strategy, however. The need to preserve and protect the family homestead is too deeply ingrained in American culture.

LONG-TERM CARE CHOICE

A better approach is to let older adults keep their income and assets (including their homes) as long as these resources are needed to support themselves or their immediate dependents. When someone requires care for which the family has insufficient cash to pay, let the government guarantee payment of the bill for whatever private service the family chooses. Simultaneously with the initiation of this public assistance, tally the family's income and assets, secure the entire estate with a binding legal encumbrance and subtract the government-sponsored contributions from the ledger every month. Whatever the family is able to and chooses to contribute toward the cost of care is not subtracted from the ledger. Everything the government or its agent contributes, as well as interest, depletes the estate and is recovered upon the death of the last surviving, exempt, dependent relative. If the ledger is depleted entirely, the family is completely destitute and eligible for a newly reformed and financially reinvigorated Medicaid program, that is, welfare.

This approach—let us call it *LTC Choice*—has many advantages over the current situation. Middle-class elders regain their dignity; financial assistance is not welfare if it is repaid. Vulnerable elderly people get red-carpet access to top-quality care; there is never a shortage of preferred long-term care beds or services for full-paying customers. Consumers return to the marketplace; someone else may pay the monthly bill, but it all comes out of the family's estate in the long run, so buyers will be wary of price and quality. Providers receive the full market price for their services; home care companies, assisted living facilities, nursing homes and even previously unforeseen purveyors of housing and eldercare will compete avidly to offer the best possible services for the lowest possible fee. Government and the taxpayers save money; the only up-front cost, which is more than compensated for by savings in the old Medicaid colossus, is a loan guarantee program to attract private lenders to fund the fully collateralized system.

The biggest advantage to LTC Choice, however, is the change in consumer behavior that it will engender. Families will know with strict certainty that they cannot ignore the substantial risk of long-term care. The choices will become stark for 40- and 50-year-olds. They will plan now and buy insurance while they are young and healthy, and good coverage is inexpensive. Otherwise, they will take their chances, hope for the best, accept a dollar-for-dollar loss to their estates if they ever have to rely on the public program and explicitly assume the risk that they may ultimately lose everything—including their home equity—and become dependent on welfare.

Confronted with genuine risk like this, more people will choose to insure privately than have in the past. Fortunately, insurance policies that cover home care, assisted living, and nursing-home care are already easily available and affordable to most people. Those who cannot afford coverage may seek private home equity conversion to generate a sufficient cash flow to enable them to pay their premiums. Heirs, especially adult children who will stand to lose their inheritances entirely otherwise, are likely to encourage their elders to purchase insurance coverage and may also help to pay the premiums. Instead of rewarding people for ignoring the risk, avoiding the premiums and taking advantage of the public dole as the current system does, this approach rewards responsibility and exacts a gradual and predictable penalty for irresponsibility.

One sure way to derail the privatization of long-term care financing and to destroy its promise is to make publicly financed long-term care even more attractive to consumers than it is now. The damage done by easily accessible Medicaid nursing-home benefits has been mitigated by the fact that most people do not want to go into nursing homes. If grand plans now under discussion to pool Medicaid and Medicare monies and provide home- and community-based services for dual eligibles are implemented without a strongly enforced means test and mandatory estate recovery, dire consequences will follow.

Expanded public financing for more desirable kinds of care will not merely exacerbate the "woodwork factor" of induced demand, as other writers have warned. It will make Medicaid estate planning more attractive to consumers and more lucrative to elder-law practitioners. It will inhibit the market for privately financed chore services, home care, assisted living and geriatric care management. It will also decimate demand for private long-term care insurance. Public benefits have always been and will always remain starved for financing. Our only hope to achieve a fully financed, universally available, comprehensive long-term care service delivery system is to draw as heavily as possible on private financing and to depend on public resources only to fill the interstices of need left unfilled by the private market.

Obviously, for LTC Choice to succeed, it cannot be abused and manipulated as Medicaid has been. We will have to ensure that the public understands the high probability of needing long-term care and that individuals and families—not the government—are principally responsible for this huge potential expense. Therefore, before they are too old, frail or sick to save or insure for their own protection, the federal government should deliver comprehensive information on long-term care to aging Americans and require them to make a tough choice about how they intend to protect themselves from this risk. The tough choice is whether or not they will insure privately or rely on the LTC Choice program. If they insure privately, their problem is solved. If they rely on the government-backed LTC Choice program, they must report annually on their income and assets in order to secure their estates as collateral and to eliminate the problem of artificial self-impoverishment that has plagued the Medicaid program. Of course, every American will always be free to dispose of personal wealth as he or she sees fit. The LTC Choice program merely requires that no one who expects to receive public assistance in the future may divest, divert or shelter wealth that could have been used to pay for long-term care.

The best time to present these hard realities of long-term care to the public is as early as possible, but no later than when they become eligible for Social Security and Medicare. At this time of life, elders and their families are most sensitive to the financial and health security challenges of aging. Most of them remain relatively secure financially and are insurable. When it sends information on Medicare and Social Security to aging Americans, the federal government should also provide advice and guidance on the risks and costs of long-term care, on low-cost home- and community-based services options, on home equity conversion, on private long-term care insurance and on the LTC Choice alternative, once it is enacted.

CONCLUSION

Long-term care for a rapidly aging population presents an enormous challenge to the United States. Our country must meet this challenge while confronting similar strains on Social Security and Medicare. To preserve our prosperity and to protect the elderly population, we will need to reassert the traditional values of freedom, independence, and individual responsibility that brought economic greatness to America in the first place. A simple public policy, with which most of our countrymen will agree, would suffice to achieve this goal, if unstintingly observed: "We have very limited dollars available for public assistance. We must take care of the truly poor and disadvantaged first. The middle class and well-to-do should pay privately for long-term care. to the extent they are able without suffering financial devastation. Prosperous people who rely on public assistance for long-term care should reimburse the taxpayers before giving away their wealth to heirs. Older Americans and their heirs who wish to avoid such recovery from the estate should plan ahead, purchase private long-term care insurance and pay privately for the care of their choice when the time comes."

LTC Choice is a viable, simple, and cost-free means to implement this policy and to solve the long-term care financing puzzle once and for all. We need only the vision to see the way, the courage to embrace the change, and the will to follow the course.

REFERENCES

Administration on Aging. (1996). United States Department of Health and Human Services. *A profile of older Americans: 1996.* Washington, DC: http://www.aoa.dhhs.gov/aoa/pages/profil96.html.

Budish, A., & Budish, A.D. (1993). *Golden opportunities: Hundreds of money-making money-saving gems for anyone over fifty.* New York: Henry Holt.

Budish, A.D. (1989). *Avoiding the Medicaid trap: How to beat the catastrophic costs of nursing home care.* New York: Henry Holt.

Health Care Financing Administration. (1998). *Highlights: National health expenditures, 1996, Table 15: Nursing home care expenditures aggregate and per capita amounts and percent distribution, by source of funds: Selected calendar years 1960–96,* http://www.hcfa.gov/stats.

Lazenby, H.C. (1989). Health expenditure analyst. Health Care Financing Administration, Personal communication.

Lazenby, H.C., & Letsch, S.W. (1990). National health expenditures, 1989. *Health Care Fin Rev, 12*(2).

McKnight's long-term care news. (1996). Citing HCFA's guide to the nursing home industry.

Sloan, F.A., & Shayne, M.W. (1993). Long-term care, Medicaid, and impoverishment of the elderly. *Milbank Mem Fund Q, 71*(4).

CHAPTER 20

The Media's Role: Beyond the Medical Model of Journalism on Aging

Paul Kleyman

When the information explosion meets the longevity revolution, whose job will it be to separate health fact from quack fiction? Another baby boomer breaks the age-50 barrier every 7 seconds now to create the age boom. This new cohort of aging Americans—larger, more active and better educated than any demographic group in history—is finding increasingly that quality information can be a needle in the haystack of print, broadcast and Internet information. If healthy aging is to become a core goal of the age boom, older boomers, more than ever, will require reliable sources for health information that are well analyzed and contextualized. They will want to understand their range of choices and to make well-considered decisions.

The current burst of health information on the Internet, both good and bad, should give health professionals pause. A 1997 survey by the marketing research company Find/SVP (http//www.findsvp.com) estimated that there are between 12,000 and 15,000 consumer health-information sites—up from about 10,000 the previous year—and that 43% of all Internet users sought health or medical information, up from 38% only a year before (Brown, 1997).

Michael Brown, author of the report, "HealthMed Retrievers: Consumers Who Use Online Health and Medical Information" (Brown, 1997), noted both positive and negative sides of this eruption of health information. On the one hand, health consumers are increasingly "proactive, often bringing reams of printouts to their doctor's offices." On the other hand, more than half of health-related sites (53%, representing a growing proportion) are from questionable sources, either sales efforts or individually owned Internet pages. The remainder are from legitimate sources, such as universities or health-related associations. Brown found the individually created sites especially troubling. They are the fastest-growing category of Web addresses, accounting for 26% of all consumer health sites in 1997 (up from 8% in 1996). He explained, "Many are great for emotional support for cancer patients and so on, but they often contain nontraditional health information that can be very unreliable." He added that people often begin searching the Internet for health information when they are most vulnerable to quackery or wishful thinking—immediately after diagnosis of a serious illness.

The potential problem is so worrisome that the editors of the *Journal of the American Medical Association* recently published an editorial that included a checklist to be used by medical professionals for evaluating the currency, usefulness and veracity of a health-information Web site (Silberg et al., 1997).

Whether on the Internet or in more customary media, information that can promote healthy aging should be gathered, assessed and interpreted by qualified health and media professionals. Yet, until recently, news organizations have not assigned reporters to focus on the many critical issues in aging. For older more than younger populations, social, behavioral, economic and other factors interact with medical developments to determine an older person's level of wellness and ability to function independently.

Because the news media have historically regarded most stories specific to old age as emerging in the medical context, related concerns such as appropriate housing, economic security, healthy aging, mental and spiritual well being, employment opportunities and discrimination often emerge in coverage as secondary elements of stories anchored in health care. There is, though, a new attitude in journalism about old age. Doubtless, editors and producers at many news organizations in print and broadcast still regard aging as something to be covered in terms of the latest medical breakthroughs or nursing-home scandals. However, increasing numbers of journalists are discovering as they—and their parents—age that growing older encompasses complex interrelationships of social, behavioral, economic, environmental and other factors. They are learning that the dynamic but little-discussed emergence of mass longevity not only extends far beyond the medical model of reporting on aging, but also offers one of the most exciting untold stories of our era—the emergence of a new generation of empowered, vital older adults.

"I think the disease of the week approach happily is disappearing," states Wendy Schmelzer, who covers aging full time for National Public Radio's

(NPR's) Science Unit. She calls aging "a dynamic issue," because "it's not one period; it's anywhere from the age of 65 to 122. Health issues that were relevant in our 70s may completely change when we are 83. A journalist cannot get lazy about it; you cannot assume one size fits all."

A subject such as pain management, for example, requires a reporter to follow the medical literature to discern differences not only in age but in the diversity of the older populations. According to Schmelzer, though health and medical issues are very important, we're giving more credence also to stories that have to do with wellness—things we can do for ourselves and preventive kinds of medicine. Her challenge in covering aging "holistically," she says, is to seek relevant angles and to report on such new developments as diet and exercise. For example, she observes, "When you have a person who is fit in their 70s, exercise means something different than it does for a person who is wheelchair bound."

Although coverage of aging issues is changing, relatively few news organizations have yet to assign reporters to cover aging on a regular basis so that they can adequately develop their knowledge and understanding of the many dimensions of this topic. The misinformation and prejudice that still infect much of the media's approach to how it treats aging was recently addressed by Lawrence K. Grossman, retired head of the Public Broadcasting Service and of NBC News. In a chapter on the media for a book entitled *Life in Older America*, Grossman explains that television has long given short shrift to the information and entertainment needs and interests of older viewers because of the long-held desire to reach the 18- to 49-year-old market and the even narrower 18–34 group, regarded as the most lucrative (Grossman, in press).

Grossman recalls a conversation he had with a print journalist who appeared on a syndicated radio talk show. After the program, he expressed surprise to the show's producer at how young the program's callers seemed to be, based on their voices and kinds of questions they asked. The producer explained, "Our telephone operators filter out older people just in case any advertisers happen to be listening. We don't want them coming away with the impression that our show appeals to old folks. It's bad for sales."

However, asserts Grossman, "the core of [television's] audience—the 76 million baby boomers who were weaned on television, who remain hale and hearty and who have the disposable income that advertisers would love to tap—are putting the medium through its own mid-life crisis. Media ad buyers, who have consistently devalued the over-50 crowd, will have to awaken to the fact of an implacable core audience shift, which they can no longer afford to overlook."

Grossman, a seasoned news professional, comments, "Journalistically, the most interesting aspect of the "grown-ups" movement is that it represents not a special interest beat or what in current media jargon is called a *niche* beat, but one of the most important *general interest* beats of the coming century." Issues and concerns to be covered in aging range from concerns such as the need for our educational system to prepare young people for a lifetime of good habits in health and financial responsibility; the growing call for universal design in products and architecture that will be safe, beautiful and helpful to every user; and how to alter America's long history of denial, in both personal thinking and institutional responses to our era's prolonged experience of death and dying."

A recent example of the new journalism on aging is Michael Vitez's Pulitzer-Prize-winning series written for the *Philadelphia Inquirer*. In "Final Choices: Seeking the Good Death," Vitez described centenarian Ruth Hilsee as "a success story of modern medicine and social progress . . . She has lived nearly a century in excellent health, living independently, staying mentally active, finding joy and fulfillment in each day."

Vitez, whose 1996 series was later released as a book (Vitez, 1997), tells us that Hilsee "is content to die," although she "still has choices to make and intends to make them. What she and her generation want is as much independence as her health will allow." He begins her story as she considers moving from her apartment into a personal care unit within her innovative retirement community.

In the context of modern health care and housing choices, Vitez described the active daily life of Mrs. Hilsee, a trained horticulturist who unhesitatingly stated the botanical Latinate for baby's breath (*gypsophila*); a conscientious reader of her Bible and of issues of the *Biblical Archaeological Review*; a devoted grandmother who hosted a 40th birthday party for one of her three grandchildren and loves to visit with her young great-granddaughters; a patient who asks prudent questions about her medications; an independent resident who prepares her own breakfast and lunch, sometimes struggling to open badly designed food packages; and a smart television viewer who entertains herself by watching "Jeopardy" and "The NewsHour with Jim Lehrer."

In first planning the presentation of the series's five articles, Vitez said that he and his editors first considered beginning with Hilsee's story. Instead, they decided to first publish the four articles about the more challenging and often controversial aspects of death and dying: "Learning

How and When to Let Go," "Going Home to Die with Hospice Care to Help," "Taking Care of Relatives at Home: The Burden" and "Deciding to Die with a Doctor's Help." They determined that it would be best to culminate the articles with Hilsee's story in "Finding More Ways To Stay Independent Longer." Vitez said simply of this article, so much at the heart of his series: "That's what it's about."

"The best stories," Vitez emphasizes, are real yarns. My series was not only about health but about business, growing old, love, national policy, many things. Whether a story is about older drivers or a new development in health, my goal is complex: To give readers an idea of the choices and decisions involved—always told through a good story."

Vitez, a long-time feature writer who won his Pulitzer in the category of explanatory journalism, notes that a strength of the age beat is "the diversity of reporters" who are assigned to it. Among them are feature writers, health and science writers, financial reporters, Washington correspondents and investigative reporters who take traditional—indeed, constitutionally protected—charge of their craft, well beyond American journalism's cursory hit-and-run exposure of health care abuse and fraud scandals.

The thoughtful and thorough approach of these reporters and other reporters like them will provide a critical link between the public and the knowledge that can help foster a healthy aging society. Unfortunately, important elements of the media mainstream work against providing a complete and balanced picture of aging in America. Frequently, television—the news and information source most widely accessed by the public—lends itself to the most dismaying brand of scandal mongering. Professionals in health and aging who are accustomed to systematic analysis and an honest search for solutions can only wince, for example, at television news "investigations" that may employ dramatic, ratings-boosting on-camera confrontations with allegedly larcenous nursing home aides while offering no solutions and paying only passing lip service to the vast majority of truly dedicated long-term care workers across the nation (Grossman, in press).

The press, too, continues to provide coverage in the traditional medical mode. For example, "Fatal Neglect" by Mark Thompson, a *Time* investigation in the traditional "gottcha!" mold of media exposés (October 17, 1997), focused on the findings of two private investigators in California who uncovered records suggesting thousands of possibly questionable deaths ignored by regulators. Such revelations are important, but *Time's* article left readers with the sole impression that nursing homes are horrible places and that neglectful federal and state regulators offer more cause for fear among elders "than either the maggots or the nursing home operators." With this limited and inflammatory approach, *Time* missed an opportunity to set long-term care problems in a meaningful context—national nursing home reform efforts begun in the 1980s, for example, or the need for safe and available home- and community-based care.

Of course, sensationalism will always yellow the pages—and screens—of journalism, but the hope for more comprehensive coverage of issues in aging is more than mere wishful thinking. The aging of the boomers—many of whom occupy the nation's newsrooms—is already yielding a healthier approach, even to investigative reporting in this area. One example of the new journalism on aging that stands in sharp contrast to the *Time* article is the series "Buyer Beware: The Hidden Risks of Home Health Care" (November 11–12, 1996) by Peter Eisler of *USA Today*. Though it carried many of the same admonitions about poor regulatory oversight as did the *Time* article, Eisler's analysis provided a thoughtful examination of "elusive" solutions due to the system's regulatory discontinuity from state to state and the need for coordination between state and federal authorities. In addition, the series did not merely dote on hidden horrors. An entire half-page was devoted to an article headlined "In Troubled Field, Caring Still the Norm." A summary stated, "Theft, abuse and fraud are rising sharply in home healthcare, the United States' fastest-growing industry. But legions of care givers do good work for low wages, and it's easier to find aides who have saved lives, not ruined them" (Eisler, 1996).

In our aging society, says Robert A. Rosenblatt, veteran Washington correspondent for the *Los Angeles Times*, it is the media's responsibility "to try to educate people without just alarming them." He explains that widespread aging is creating "a society that's never existed before, and a huge amount of resources are going to be devoted to it." Whether delving into regional problems or national public policy debates, he says, the role of journalism is to inform Americans in ways that will enable the nation to work out the complications of our changing society "without getting at each other's throats."

WHO IS ON THE AGE BEAT?

Rosenblatt was among 129 respondents to the Second National Survey of the Journalists Exchange on Aging (JEoA), released as a special issue of the group's publication, *Age Beat* (Kleyman et al., 1997). One key finding was that 95.3% of respondents said they had experienced aspects of issues in aging themselves or through their families. Of these journalists, 89.6% said that their personal exposure to concerns of aging had "affected their journalistic perspective." To an overwhelming extent, this group did not feel that its reportorial objectivity—a guiding concern for journalists—was in any way compromised. Instead, they perceived that their personal experience gave depth to their understanding of concerns relating to an aging society.

A typical experience is that of Warren Wolfe, a veteran writer and editor at the *Minneapolis Star-Tribune.* In the early 1990s, this first-wave boomer found himself in search of long-term care for a family elder. His amazement at the extensive research required of people to know where to turn and what to do led to his writing a 25-part weekly series, published during the first 6 months of 1992. The series, eventually published as a book, was the first of at least 10 similar series run during the next 4 years in metropolitan newspapers across the nation, each focusing on family caregiving and related issues through the words of national experts in gerontology, local providers and, most important, the stories of the area's residents (Wolfe, 1992).

The JEoA includes 550 journalism professionals representing all types of media. Although few cover aging full time, the daily newspaper reporters alone who responded to the JEoA's 1997 survey concentrated 47% of their work loads on issues of aging. Significantly, almost two in three respondents indicated that, on average, 30% of their age-beat coverage involved the concerns of aging boomers. One example is NPR, whose audience research shows that the average age of its listeners to programs like "Morning Edition" and "All Things Considered" is 47, which may help to explain why NPR has emerged as a national leader in its coverage of issues concerning an aging society.

To a large extent, the creation of a news organization's age beat was found in the survey results to be "journalist-driven"—started by writers who become fascinated by the issue. For instance, among responding newspaper reporters, more than two in three had initiated regular coverage on this topic at their news organizations. All survey participants constitute a group of journalism veterans averaging 21.1 years in the field and 8.6 years on the age beat.

The study's results belied the impression held by many in the news media that the coverage of aging is largely related to health and medical issues. The good news is that a substantial number of daily news organizations, having looked at the multifaceted world of aging, have stepped ahead of the strictly medical approach to reporting on aging. More than half of the respondents to the JEoA survey were social-issues reporters assigned to the features or lifestyle section, and the rest were spread among newsroom desks focused on health and medical stories, daily news, social issues, editorials and economic and financial coverage. Three said they had no particular desk assignment because their articles run throughout the paper, depending on a story's appropriate placement.

The passion that age-beat journalists have for this subject comes from the realization that there are compelling dimensions to our age of mass longevity at every turn—in changing possibilities for people across their life spans and in the need to adapt our ways of thinking and social institutions to a new and longer view of a typical lifetime. The age beat covers not only the vicissitudes of old age, with its aches and ailments, its burdens on the family, and its costs to society, but it is also about more to do and more to learn; more to contribute and more to understand; more to experience and, perhaps most enticing, more opportunity to carry the best we can be to fruition.

OUTREACH: THE WIRE AND THE WEB

A finding of the JEoA survey that is literally far-reaching is that a high percentage of today's journalists reporting on aging see their work more widely distributed than ever before. Among newspaper journalists in the JEoA study, 88% reported that many of their articles—pieces that not long ago would have appeared locally and quickly yellowed in recycling bins— are increasingly distributed around the nation, thanks to newspaper Web pages and print syndication via increasingly competitive news services. These information suppliers used to carry mainly the output of their own writers but now circulate material from other sources under contract (Kleyman, 1997).

Internet pages are especially exciting additions because they enable journalists to add sections of resource information, frequently with electronic links that enable readers to click directly into the home pages of helpful service agencies. Furthermore, these "cyber pages"—unlimited by the cost and weight of newsprint—allow for more background information on the topic than newspaper space may permit, as well as opportunities for citizens to share their information and ideas. For his Pulitzer-Prize-winning series "Final Choices," Michael Vitez worked closely with the *Philadelphia Inquirer's* Web-page manager to provide relevant details about community hospice, grief counseling and other services.

The public's Internet response to coverage of compelling interest was also demonstrated in November 1997, when NPR launched its year-long project, "The End of Life: Exploring Death in America." The Sunday night before the project was kicked off with a week-long series on "All Things Considered," according to correspondent Howard Berkes, "there were already 50 people on the Web page telling their stories, and we hadn't even done a story yet to trigger that." Both for himself as a journalist and for NPR listeners, he remarked while discussing the unusual project on NPR's "Talk of the Nation" (November 6, 1997) that reporters and the public felt that such major coverage seemed to give them "permission to talk about this issue," a vital concern long considered a taboo topic of conversation in American culture.

Those who visit the Web site http//www.npr.org could click on the words "The End of Life" to screen a page for the project that offers a menu of choices, including transcripts of the radio programs, resources in alphabetical order, a bibliography, additional readings, listener stories and an opportunity for people to add feedback about the programs. Using this and other Web pages, the public, including knowledgeable professionals in relevant fields, has never had such an easy method of interacting with the media.

MEET THE PRESS (HALFWAY)

Leaders in geriatrics and gerontology commonly chuckle among themselves over the calls they occasionally receive from reporters with no knowledge about aging who ask, What are the most important issues about the elderly today? It is easy to sneer, but if professionals in aging and health care could eavesdrop on age-beat journalists who seriously cover these issues, they would hear exasperated comments about the unfounded paranoia of uncooperative agency administrators evidently apprehensive about a journalistic effort to expose them; about articulate academic advocates on aging who simply fail to return calls, faxes or e-mail requests; about health or human service providers who complain that the extensive time they gave a reporter was wasted because the resulting article did not tell readers about their wonderful work; about cagey and arrogant researchers who treated them like undergraduates incapable of representing their meticulous efforts with accuracy.

"Gerontology needs to make some hard decisions," says gerontologist and broadcaster Bernard Starr, "and one is, Do you want to have a private club or to get your message out to the public?" Dr. Starr is in an unusual position to comment. Not only is he the award-winning writer, producer and host of "The Longevity Report" on WEVD-AM radio and other stations, but he holds a doctorate in psychology, directs the gerontology program at Marymount Manhattan College in New York and has long been a series editor of academic gerontologic books. He challenges gerontologists for having been "one obstacle" to the public's understanding of aging because of their "subtle or not-so-subtle disdain . . .for the media or, more broadly, anything that is popular rather than professional or academic." He calls on them to "start tuning in the media, learning about the media."

It is likely that the foremost proponent of active outreach by health care professionals to the media is Robert N. Butler, chief executive officer of the International Longevity Center at Mount Sinai School of Medicine. "If we are dead serious about having an influence on policy and efforts to prepare ourselves for an older society," Butler asserts, "there's no way we can do that without reaching the public through the media." Butler is the winner of a Pulitzer Prize for his 1975 ground-breaking book, *Why Survive: Being Old in America.*

Butler, appointed by President Carter to be the founding director of the National Institute on Aging, is well known among journalists for his accessibility to them. "I'm not there for an ego trip," he states, explaining that three fourths of his interview time is devoted to providing unquoted background information. He urges health and medical professionals to be effective communicators by being "good about the Rolodex, about suggesting other people reporters might talk to."

Over the years, Dr. Butler has invited vigorous local elders to join Mount Sinai medical students for lunch and has assigned many to speak to elders at New York's 92nd Street YMHA, famous for its community programs. The students would have to give a lecture to the members of the seniors program, who average about age 72. "My students would talk about what is type 2 diabetes or Alzheimer's disease or how you handle medications or what you should eat in later years. It was all in an effort to get them to be able to communicate with the larger public, with their patients, and not assume the information was archaic and mysterious that only we physicians should possess. I think this is part of the empowerment of information, the empowerment of the public to know what science is all about."

No professional group is taking Butler's message of empowerment and human perspective more to heart than are the journalists on the age beat. On topics from illness prevention and wellness to family caregiving issues, it is this emerging corps of reporters that can help the public understand the complexities of the longevity revolution and see the importance of valuing the personal and societal steps needed to make progress toward a healthy aging society. No one has stated this more eloquently than Beth Witrogen McLeod, who won the prestigious Pew Journalism Award in 1996 for her writing on caregiving for the *San Francisco Examiner*. Speaking at a spring 1998 symposium on "Covering the Age Boom" at the Freedom Forum Pacific Coast Center, she stressed, "The message that I believe comes out of the age beat is the tremendous humanity and the tremendous heart. We focus so much in the news business on crime, and we should because there's so much to be done about it. But we don't understand that the real heart of humanity is very, very much alive and well in this country. That's what the age beat can bring out, and that's where my passion is (Witrogen-McLeod, 1998).

Bernard Starr has noted that, despite America's devoting a greater percentage of its gross domestic product to health care than any other nation, "a scant 3% of that spending goes for prevention" (Starr, 1996). If the nation will ever accept the old-fashioned wisdom of phrases like "penny-wise and pound-foolish," if we are to foster an environment in which healthy aging becomes our first priority, the public will have to become well-informed partners with health care professionals and policy makers. The information, analysis and enthusiasm of journalists on the age beat can provide much of the mortar needed in building these new partnerships.

REFERENCES

Brown, M. (1997). HealthMed retrievers: Consumers who use online health and medical information. *Find/SVP,* http://www.findsvp.com.

Butler, R.N. (1975). *Why survive? Being old in America.* New York: Little, Brown and Company.

Eisler, P. (1996, November 12). Buyer beware: The hidden risks of home health care. *USA Today*.

Grossman, L.K. (in press, Fall 1998). The media's role. In R.N. Butler, L.K. Grossman, & M. Oberlink (Eds.), *Life in older America*. New York: The Twentieth Century Fund.

Kleyman, P., et al. (1997). *Age Beat.* [Journalists Exchange on Aging newsletter] San Francisco.

Silberg, W.M., et al. (1997, April 16). Assessing, controlling and assuring the quality of medical information on the internet: Caveat lector et viewer—let the readers beware. *JAMA,* 277, 1244–1245.

Starr, B. (1996, January 15). This longevity is killing us: Healthy choices for sick health care. *Barron's.*

Vitez, M. (1997). *Final choices: Seeking the good death.* Philadelphia: Camino Books (Introduction by medical ethicist Arthur Caplan), pp. 53–62.

Witrogen-McLeod, B. (1998, March 26). *Covering the age boom: Health care scandals to the meaning of life.* Speaking at the Pacific Coast Center of the Freedom panel discussion.

Wolfe, W. (1992). Checklist for aging: A workbook for caregiving. *Star-Tribune,* Minneapolis, MN.

PART FOUR

Wellness and Self-Care: The Next Generation

CHAPTER 21

The Past, Present and Future of Self-Care

Molly K. Mettler

Each patient carries his own doctor inside him. He comes to us not knowing that truth. We are at our best when we give the doctor who resides within each patient the chance to go to work.—Albert Schweitzer

The famed Dr. Schweitzer was asking us to expand our thinking as to who might be considered the primary provider of medical care. He was suggesting that by helping patients learn more about their bodies and their conditions, to do more for themselves and their loved ones and to participate more in medical decision making, it is possible to activate the "doctor within."

These internal physicians, the ones who "can go to work" on behalf of individual patients, are perhaps the greatest untapped resource of the health care system. Although it often seems as if the future of health care is in the hands of the government or insurance companies, individuals and groups of consumers have enormous power to affect the health care system. This power centers on what people can do for themselves.

By tapping the wisdom, experience and expertise of countless willing and able medical care consumers, we can reinvent the patient's role in health care, and, by doing so, we can improve quality and reduce cost. This vision reframes the traditional divide between patient and provider. Rather than being a passive recipient of medical services, the new health care consumer is recognized as a capable, essential member of the health care team. In partnership with physicians, these new medical consumers provide appropriate home care, share in medical decisions and assume partial responsibility for outcomes.

The first step in reinventing the patient is to recognize and support Schweitzer's notion of the "doctor within" who practices medical self-care. Medical self-care is what people do to recognize, prevent, treat and manage their own health problems. A woman who diagnoses her own case of flu and takes steps to relieve symptoms is practicing self-care. A man with diabetes who carefully monitors his glucose levels and his diet, and who works closely with a physician to manage the illness, is also practicing self-care. Most of the health care in this country consists of what people do for themselves. Studies report that 80–95% of all health problems are managed at home through medical self-care (Figures 21–1, 21–2) (Dean et al., 1983; Demers et al., 1980; Elliott-Binns, 1986; Willamson & Danaher, 1978).

The actions people take with respect to their own health care make each and every person a bona fide health care provider. However, for the past 50 years, self-care has been the most overlooked part of the health care system. Lay consumers should be considered the "hidden providers" of health care. This is especially true for most older adults. Like everyone

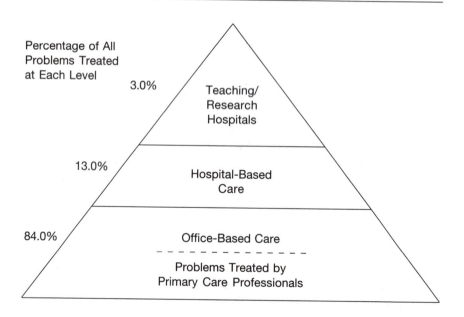

Figure 21–1 Health Care System without Self-Care

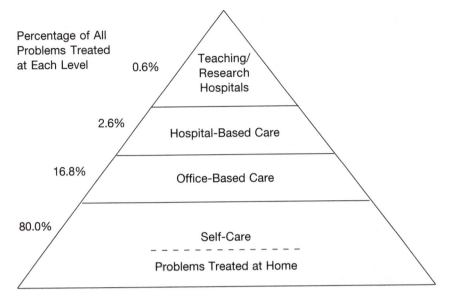

Percentage of All
Problems Treated
at Each Level   0.6%   Teaching/
Research
Hospitals

2.6%   Hospital-Based Care

16.8%   Office-Based Care

80.0%   Self-Care

Problems Treated at Home

Figure 21–2 Health Care System with Self-Care

else, they have to deal with colds, flu and headaches. In addition, many elders also have to cope with and manage multiple chronic conditions such as arthritis and high blood pressure.

There is a widening gap, made even more apparent with the aging of the baby boom generation, between the health care needs of aging adults and the medical remedies of the health care system. Despite the system's best efforts, good health outcomes and good quality of care are not assured. The lives of older adults are often not improved simply by applying technical and professional interventions. Robert Butler has commented that "we have created a health care system in this country that is brilliant but irrelevant to the health needs of most older people" (Taylor, 1992). Typically, our health care system makes heroic and powerful efforts to sustain people through late-life health crises with highly technical, high-cost care, but it does relatively little for them during the years when they are coping with and managing chronic illness. Helping the "hidden providers" of the health care system become more confident and competent in their own medical self-care can bridge the gap and help make the health care system more effective for older adults.

THE HISTORY OF SELF-CARE

A merry heart does good, like medicine, but a broken spirit dries the bones.—Proverbs 17:22

Self-care is a fundamental human activity. Since the dawn of recorded history, health care has been provided primarily by the individual and the family. Ancient Greek and Babylonian texts, as well as the Bible, outlined the importance of daily living patterns in maintaining health and indicated where families could turn when outside advice was needed (Sigerist, 1951).

Although there has been a proliferation of medical self-care texts in the marketplace, books on self-care are not a twentieth-century invention (Kemper et al., 1993). In 1747 the Reverend John Wesley, the founder of the Methodist Church, published a popular self-care book entitled *Primitive Remedies*. Thomas Jefferson was so influenced by the self-care movement that during his tenure as president of the University of Virginia he insisted that incoming freshmen take a course in medical self-care.

Contemporary writers trace the current interest in medical self-care to the feminist movement of the 1970s. Organizations such as the Boston Women's Health Book Collective and their seminal book, *Our Bodies, Ourselves,* called attention to and provided guidelines for lay participation in the health care system. The following decade also saw the publication of several mainstream texts devoted to medical self-care for the consumer, notably *The Healthwise Handbook, Taking Care of Your Child, How To Be Your Own Doctor Sometimes*, and *Take Care of Yourself,* (The Boston Women's Health Book Collective, 1971; Kemper, 1997; Pantell et al., 1994; Sehnert, 1975; Vickery and Fries, 1993).

TODAY'S SELF-CARE DEFINED

If I had known I was going to live this long, I'd have taken better care of myself.—Eubie Blake

The term *medical self-care* has many definitions, and no single one has yet been universally accepted, though there is a growing consensus. Williamson and Danaher conceptualized self-care broadly as "comprising health maintenance, which includes disease prevention and care of self in illness" (Williamson & Danaher, 1978). Levin echoed this definition when he defined self-care as "a process whereby a layperson functions on his/her own behalf in health promotion and prevention" (Levin et al., 1976). Fleming broadens the definition by including several specific self-care activities. These include such diverse behaviors as "consulting with other family members about symptoms, taking nonprescription medications, weight control, self-monitoring of chronic illness, participating in self-help groups such as Alcoholics Anonymous, and consumer political action on health issues" (Fleming et al., 1984).

Barofsky (1978) divides self-care activities into four types: regulatory self-care, such as eating, sleeping and bathing; preventive self-care, such as exercising, dieting, and brushing teeth; reactive self-care, such as responding to symptoms without a physician's intervention; and restorative self-care, such as making healthy behavioral changes and complying with a professionally prescribed treatment regimen. Vickery (1986) defines medical self-care as "actions taken by an individual with respect to a medical problem," which places the emphasis on individual decision making.

When confronted with a symptom or health problem, the practice of self-care encompasses a variety of possible activities by the patient or by caregivers. Preventing, treating and managing health problems can comprise a host of activities, including taking no action; watchful waiting; self-diagnosis; seeking advice from friends and family; self-medication with over-the-counter drugs and home remedies; restricting activity; consulting books, magazines and on-line electronic databases and asking advice of pharmacists and others with professional training (Elliott-Binns, 1986; Levin & Idler, 1983; Verbrugge & Ascione, 1987).

The pervasiveness of what has been humorously described as "people practicing medicine without a license" is well-illustrated by a study that Demers and colleagues conducted (Figure 21–3) (Demers et al., 1980). They analyzed all the health problems recorded by 107 subjects over a 3-week period. They found that less than 6% of the problems received professional medical attention. Of the 348 recorded illness episodes or health problems, 24.7% were not treated, 67.6% were treated with self-initiated self-care measures, and 2.3% were treated with self-care measures after getting telephone advice from a health professional.

Is all this self-care good? The dangers of self-care were addressed by Wilkinson, who studied the self-care actions of 340 subjects over a 2-week period. In only 2% of cases were the actions assessed as "inappropriate and

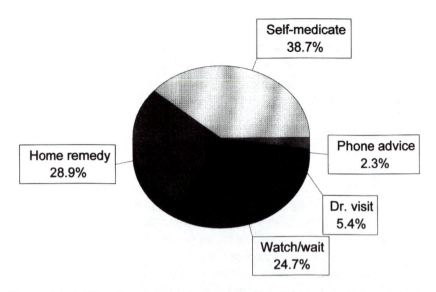

Figure 21–3 What People Do. *Source:* Reprinted with permission from R. Demers et al. An Exploration of the Dimensions of Illness Behavior, *Journal of Family Practice*, Vol. 11, No. 7, © 1980, pp. 1085–1092, Appleton & Lange.

potentially harmful" (Wilkinson et al., 1987). Simply put, most people provide sound and appropriate self-care most of the time.

Several conclusions can be drawn from the studies that have examined self-care behavior and outcomes: It is widely practiced, it is often beneficial and very seldom harmful, and it appears to be a universal behavior.

SELF-CARE IN ACTION FOR OLDER ADULTS

I don't deserve this award, but then I have arthritis and I don't deserve that either.—Jack Benny

Though self-care programs have value for patients of all ages and with afflictions of every kind, self-care is particularly important to older adults. Aging brings with it increasingly higher risks of such chronic problems as arthritis, vision impairment and heart disease. For most chronic illnesses, it is what the patient does for her or his own health on a daily basis that has the greatest impact on quality of life.

Medical information and self-care support for elders are available in several formats: Self-care handbooks and newsletters, self-care workshops, special patient coaching and care counseling services, and on-line databases and information services.

Self-Care Handbooks

Several medical self-care handbooks have been written specifically for older adults (*CareWise*, 1997; Mettler & Kemper, 1996; Mosby Consumer Health, 1997). These books typically answer questions about the common health concerns of elders, present specific home care procedures and make recommendations on when to seek professional medical help.

When older adults are given medical self-care guides by their insurers, employers or retiree programs, they use and appreciate them. Studies report that 73–93% of participants in one self-care program put on by five different organizations reported using their self-care guide at least four times during the first 4–6 months (American Health Consultants, 1996; Colorado State University Cooperative Extension, 1995; National Rural Health Network, 1995; Steelcase Retiree Pilot Program, 1995).

Self-Care Workshops

Though a handbook alone is effective in improving the care given at home, educational and competence-building workshops help increase such other medical self-care and consumer skills as doctor-patient communication. Communication skills are particularly needed to activate the consumer's role in medical decision making. Some self-care workshops that are popular with older adults focus on a particular disease such as arthritis (Lorig et al., 1985) or on a particular skill, such as medication management. Good workshops include written information for home use and an opportunity for participants to discuss and share their personal knowledge on how best to take care of themselves.

Patient Coaching and Care Counseling Services

Older adults are frequently called upon to make major medical decisions, often without complete information or much support. Patient coaching is a relatively new approach to providing that support. Researchers at

Tufts University have developed coaching sessions for patients waiting to see their physician. Trained coaches review the patient's medical records, help them think of questions to ask the physician and urge the patients to take an active role during an office visit. Studies have shown that coached patients received more information during the doctor visit, and, at a 4-month posttest, they reported fewer symptoms and rated their overall health as significantly better than patients who had not asked questions of their doctors (Kaplan et al., 1989).

Nurse Advice Lines

Coaching is also available by phone. Many older consumers have toll-free telephone access to highly trained nurses through care counseling services provided by employers, health plans or community-based health care organizations. Telephone advice-line nurses are often called upon to triage callers and to assist them in determining the severity of their symptoms and whether or not they need to seek professional help. In addition to triage, some advice-line nurses help prepare consumers to participate effectively in care decisions by giving them both the information they need to understand their options and encouragement to be actively involved in the decision-making process.

Using the Internet

Improvements in information technology have contributed to significant advances in medical self-care. In the past, in-depth medical information was restricted to those few patients who had access to medical libraries and were willing to pore over relevant articles in the medical literature. New technology has lifted those restrictions. Now, consumers can get high-quality, in-depth information on almost any health problem easily and inexpensively via the World Wide Web and other electronic information sources installed at public libraries, medical centers and work sites.

Since 1994, personal computers have outsold televisions in the United States. Industry experts now estimate that one in four Americans are Internet users. Older adults are quickly becoming a major force in the use of electronic information services, and people over age 50 are the fastest-growing segment of Internet users.

It is estimated that 25% of all Internet content is health-related (New On-Line Information Network). Older adults have expressed concerns about the quality of medical information on the Internet, and rightly so. Finding good, credible and understandable information on the Web is a little like searching for wild mushrooms. If we know where to look and exactly what to look for, the Web can be amazingly helpful. However, if we do not know, the information might not be good for our health. One solution is to use only highly credentialed Web sources such as **http://www.healthfinder.gov**, for example. This site provides links to many of the federally sponsored Web sites that include useful health care information. Other not-for-profit organizations like the American Diabetes Association (**http://www.diabetes.org**), the American Heart Association (**http://www.amhrt.org**), and the Arthritis Foundation (**http://www.arthritis.org**) have valuable, trustworthy information about specific health conditions.

Because of the Internet's ability to facilitate person-to-person dialogue and support groups, many Web sites are able to electronically model the information exchange and encouragement that is so much a part of self-care. One popular electronic gathering site for older adults with health concerns is SeniorNet, a nonprofit organization founded in 1986 to promote the use of computer technology to elders (**http://www.seniornet.com**). Among other services, SeniorNet hosts "RoundTables" that enable people to share information with their peers and give support and understanding. One particular RoundTable, "Health Matters," allows for consumer-to-consumer discussions on many illnesses and concerns, including arthritis, stroke, depression and caregiver support. By providing high-quality information and the opportunity to compare notes with others in similar health situations, the Internet adds a powerful new resource to the self-care-practicing elder.

THE CONTRIBUTIONS OF SELF-CARE

The time has come for a major conceptual shift. . .from viewing lay people as consumers of healthcare to seeing them as they really are: Its primary providers.—Lowell Levin and Ellen Idler (1983)

The quality, cost and appropriateness of medical care for older adults are often called into question. Medical self-care education, as well as training in self-care skills, can make a significant contribution. Appropriate self-care practiced by older adults could improve the quality of care given at home, which would in turn help prevent complications and improve health outcomes, lower overall health care costs by improving medical consumerism and decision-making skills, and improve satisfaction with medical care by encouraging elders to incorporate their personal values in health care decisions and advance health care directives.

Quality Improvement

Good self-care skills improve the quality of health care, both at home and within the health care system. However, the effectiveness of that care depends on the consumer's knowledge and skills. With reliable information, people can provide appropriate home treatment to manage symptoms and often prevent an illness from getting worse.

With such chronic diseases as high blood pressure and arthritis, self-care is the mainstay of effective treatment. The successful management of these and other chronic conditions is based as much on the quality of home treatment as it is on the quality of professional care. Good self-care includes knowing when to seek professional help. Getting to the right doctor at the right time has a tremendous impact on the quality of care received. With sufficient information, people make more knowledgeable—and appropriate—decisions about the need for and urgency of seeking professional care.

Even after a physician is involved, self-care plays a large role in the quality of care. When a patient presents a complete history of symptoms, the physician's diagnosis is more apt to be accurate. In fact, the American Society of Internal Medicine (1985) has stated that "seventy percent of a correct diagnosis depends solely on what the patient tells the doctor." When a patient prepares properly for diagnostic tests, there are fewer false findings. An informed and involved patient can question the need for service and catch treatment errors before they occur. Active patient involvement results in better medical outcomes and a greater level of patient satisfaction (Greenfield et al., 1985; Kaplan et al., 1989).

Cost Containment

Medical self-care reduces overall health care costs. Evaluations of basic self-care programs have consistently found first-year savings in the range of $2.50 for every dollar spent (Kemper, 1982; Vickery and Levinson, 1993). Cost savings come from fewer clinic visits and a lower cost per visit. Healthtrac's Bank of America Study, which evaluated a self-care and health promotion program for retirees, showed an estimated reduction in direct and indirect costs of 11%, compared with an increase of 6.3% in the control group (Leigh et al., 1992).

Appropriateness and Relevance

Self-care adds appropriateness and relevance to health care for older adults in two important ways. The first is through managing chronic illness. Diagnosis of chronic illness is often a life-changing event. Both patients and their families often feel powerless and angry in the face of such an event. The prospect of years of waning health, increasing demands on caregivers and loss of control can be depressing and fearful. Many patients are placed in nursing homes at staggering expense and with resulting loneliness and despair.

Trends have changed in the management of chronic care, and the burden of chronic illness has become even more immense for patients and their families. In 1995, 99 million people—about 17% of the total population of the United States—were living with chronic illness. The direct cost of their care that year was $470 billion. By the year 2010, it is expected that these numbers will grow to 120 million and $582 billion (Hoffman & Rice, 1995). Chronic illness is a serious concern for our time, not just in terms of quality of life, but also when considering its impact on our national budget.

Home treatments that elders administer themselves can improve the quality of life for many with chronic illness. For example, participants in an arthritis self-management program report less pain and fewer restrictions in daily activities (Lorig et al., 1985; Mullen et al., 1987). In addition, by providing elders with a sense of control over their health problems, self-care programs can strengthen a sense of independence and self-efficacy among older adults. Bandura (1989) defines self-efficacy as "people's judgment of their capabilities to organize and execute courses of action required to attain designated types of performance. It is concerned not with the skills one has, but with judgments or beliefs of what one can do with whatever skills one possesses."

The second way appropriateness and relevance are added to health care is through consumer involvement in medical decision making. Patient-centered medicine helps avoid medical treatments that are not in the consumer's best interest. When major medical decisions need to be made, patients often assume a passive role, thus removing their own values from the decision-making process. By encouraging shared medical decision making, self-care programs promote the careful consideration of the patient's values as a part of the decision process. Studies have shown that educating patients and factoring in patient values result in fewer high-cost, low-benefit treatments (Fowler, 1991).

SELF-CARE AND HEALTH CARE IN THE TWENTY-FIRST CENTURY

If you can see what will be, you can get there before it happens.
—Leland Kaiser

Self-care and shared medical decision making are at the heart of a significant shift in the practice of medicine that we can expect in the twenty-first century. The patient will become recognized as the primary provider of care and a full member of the provider team. The physician's role will focus on partnership with patients in shared decision making. Both physician and patient will share increasingly available, evidence-based information about the outcomes of treatment options.

Consumers are ready for this, and so are physicians. From the consumer's perspective, there are three forces that are shaping the health care system of the future: a recognition of the central role that consumers play in their own health, a greater acceptance among physicians for consumers playing a more involved role in their own health care, and the widespread access and proliferation of medical and health information.

Physician attitudes toward the value of informed, involved patients have changed dramatically over the past 20 years. They will change even more rapidly in the future as the patient becomes a fully recognized and fully supported partner on the provider team.

The future brings with it greater resources for medical self-care and shared medical decision making: Most homes will have a self-care handbook, most families will have access to health advice through nurse call centers and many families will be able to find and use high-quality health information on the Internet. These self-care aids have already been proven effective and are now in the midst of becoming mainstream.

Not only will there be more self-care resources in the future, they will be better. Computers of the twenty-first century will become personalized self-care advocates for the patient. Voice recognition, virtual reality, video-conferencing and interactive multimedia technologies will provide self-care tools never before imagined. Albert Schweitzer's "doctor within" will gain a virtual colleague who will have in-depth knowledge of the diagnosis and treatment of every known medical condition. Computer technology will also allow educational programming to be custom-designed for each patient. Information and behavioral change prescriptions will be based on the psychologic and social profile of the person, as well as on the diagnosis and condition's progression.

For too long, the self-care efforts of lay people have been ignored or undermined. If the health care system is to be relevant, self-care for older adults must be encouraged and supported. Elders need access to sound medical information, training in self-care skills and a welcomed, active role in medical decision making. They need these wherever health care decisions are made—at home, in the doctor's office and in the hospital—for both routine medical care and major medical decisions. Paraphrasing Schweitzer's words, "We will be at our best when we give the doctor who resides within each patient the chance to go to work."

REFERENCES

American Health Consultants. (1996, May). Aetna scores big in satisfaction with nurse counseling service. *Managed Care Quality*, 49–52.

American Society of Internal Medicine. (1985). *Communication: It's good for your health* (Pamphlet).

Bandura, A. (1989). Human agency in social cognitive theory. *Am Psychol, 44*(9), 1175–1184.

Barofsky, I. (1978). Compliance, adherence and the therapeutic alliance: Steps in the development of self-care. *Soc Sci Med, 12A*(15), 369–376.

Boston Women's Health Book Collective. (1971). *Our bodies ourselves*. New York: Simon & Schuster.

CareWise for older adults: Self-care for lifelong health. (1997). Seattle: Acamedica Press.

Colorado State University Cooperative Extension. (1995). Results of a statewide survey sponsored by the Colorado State University Cooperative Extension gerontology team on *Healthwise for Life.*

Dean, K., et al. (1983). Self-care of common illnesses in Denmark. *Med Care, 21*(10), 1012–1032.

Demers, R., et al. (1980). An exploration of the dimensions of illness behavior. *J Fam Prac, 11*(7), 1085–1092.

Elliott-Binns, C. (1986). An analysis of lay medicine: Fifteen years later. *J R Coll Gen Pract, 36*, 542–544.

Fleming, G., et al. (1984). Self-care: Substitute, supplement, or stimulus for formal medical care services. *Med Care, 22*(20), 950–966.

Fowler, F. (1991). Patient reports of symptoms and quality of life following prostate surgery. *Eur Urol, 20*(suppl.1), 255–264.

Greenfield, S., et al. (1985). Expanding patient involvement in care: Effects on patient outcome. *Ann Intern Med, 3*(5), 448–457.

Hoffman, C., & Rice, D. (1995). Estimates based on the *1987 National Medical Expenditure Survey.* University of California, San Francisco: Institute for Health & Aging.

Kaplan, S., et al. (1989). Assessing the effects of physician-patient interactions on the outcomes of chronic disease. *Med Care, 27*(suppl. 3), S110–S127.

Kemper, D. (1982). Self-care education: Impact on HMO costs. *Med Care, 10*(7), 710–718.

Kemper, D. (1997). *Healthwise handbook: A self-care manual for you* (13th ed.). Boise, ID: Healthwise, Incorporated.

Kemper, D., et al. (1993). The effectiveness of medical self-care interventions: A focus on self-initiated responses to symptoms. *Patient Educ Counseling, 21*, 29–39.

Leigh, J., et al. (1992). Randomized controlled study of a retiree health promotion program: The Bank of America Study. *Arch Intern Med, 152*(6), 1201–1206.

Levin, L., et al. (1976). *Self-care: Lay initiatives in health.* New York: Prodist.

Levin, L., & Idler, E. (1983). Self-care in health. *Annu Rev Public Health, 4*, 181–201.

Lorig, K., et al. (1985). Outcomes of self-help education for patients with arthritis. *Arthritis Rheum, 28*(6), 680–685.

Mettler, M., & Kemper, D. (1996). *Healthwise for life* (2nd ed.). Boise, ID: Healthwise, Incorporated.

Mosby Consumer Health. (1997). *Well-advised for people over 50.* Boston: Mosby.

Mullen, P.D., et al. (1987). Efficacy of psychoeducational interventions on pain, depression, and disability in people with arthritis: A meta-analysis. *J Rheumatol, 14*, 33–39.

National Rural Health Network. (1995). Results of a workshop sponsored by the National Rural Health Network on *Healthwise for Life.*

New On-Line Information Network Serves Patients, Providers, Payers. *Healthcare Demand Manage, 2*(9), 133.

Pantell, R., et al. (1994) *Taking care of your child* (4th ed.). Reading, MA: Addison-Wesley Publishing Co.

Sehnert, K. (1975) *How to be your own doctor sometimes.* New York: Grosset & Dunlap.

Sigerist, H. (1951). *History of medicine* (Vol. I). London: Oxford University Press.

Steelcase Retiree Pilot Program (1995). Results of a workshop sponsored by The Steelcase Wellness Center on *Healthwise for Life.*

Taylor, S. (1992, Mar/Apr.). The changing face of aging. *J Health Care Benefits,* 51–54.

Verbrugge, L., & Ascione, F. (1987). Exploring the iceberg: Common symptoms and how people take care of them. *Med Care, 25*(6), 539–569.

Vickery, D. (1986, Summer). Medical self-care: A review of the concept and program models. *Am J Health Promotion,* 23–28.

Vickery, D., & Fries, J. (1993). *Take care of yourself* (5th ed.). Reading, MA: Addison-Wesley Publishing Co.

Vickery, D., & Levinson, A. (1993). The limits of self-care. *Generations, 18*(3), 53–56.

Wilkinson, I., et al. (1987). Self-care and self medication: An evaluation of individuals' health care decisions. *Med Care, 25*(10), 965–978.

Williamson, J., & Danaher, K. (1978). *Self care in health.* London: Croom Helm, 39.

CHAPTER 22

Lifestyle and Longevity: Mind over Matter

Kenneth R. Pelletier

Onset of old age is often seen as a biologic threshold at age 65, but the reality is closer to Bob Dylan's lyrics, "Those not busy being born are busy dying." To work toward optimum health in life's later years, it is necessary for all individuals to see themselves as involved in the process. Managing our lifestyles is clearly one of the most effective means we have to improve health and longevity.

Nearly 2,000 years ago, Virgil lamented that "time bears away all things, even our minds" (*Eclogues* IX). Despite all the vaccination and antibiotic advances of biomedical technology and the limited applications of more holistic approaches to prevention and health promotion, remarkably little has changed since then. Our human condition mirrors Newton's second law of thermodynamics, or the "increasing entropy" law. According to this law, all systems tend to become more disorganized as time passes, unless energy is expended to generate order. Unless molecules are stored at absolute zero and shielded from all forms of radiation, they will deteriorate to less-ordered arrangements of their constituent atoms. Aging can be interpreted as a complex variant of this basic law. Our longevity is a measure of how long order can be maintained within our aging bodies. More individuals attain the average life expectancy now than in the first century BC, but the maximum life expectancy has not increased significantly since Virgil's time.

Isocrates, the Athenian orator of BC 436–338, is said to have lived to be 98; Heraclitus of Ephesus, the Greek philosopher of about BC 556–460, supposedly lived to 96; and the philosopher and mathematician Pythagoras

Source: Copyright © 1981, Kenneth R. Pelletier.

is believed to have lived to 91 during BC 580–489. The maximum life expectancy of yesterday remains about the maximum today. Instances of healthy longevity of 90–120 years have been documented in many societies since at least the sixth century BC. Such instances are an indication of a biologic potential inherent to the human species as a whole.

Psychologic and lifestyle factors have been demonstrated to be among the most significant predictors of both optimum health and longevity. Genetic and biologic influences on longevity are highly dependent on the presence or absence of specific psychologic and lifestyle influences.

AGING AND DISEASE

Every major disease is age-dependent. Although it is not possible to make definitive statements about causation, it is increasingly evident that the progressive degeneration of aging is a precursor to the development of increasingly severe disorders. Once a disorder is manifest, it places increased strain on the organism, thus accelerating the degenerative process.

In attempting to stem this decline, an ironic situation has developed that has been termed the *failures of success* by Ernest M. Gruenberg of the Johns Hopkins University School of Hygiene and Public Health. Gruenberg (1977) and other analysts have noted that a major innovation in medicine occurred in 1936. In that year, a group of investigators with a small grant from the Rockefeller Foundation was searching for a cure for puerperal fever (septic poisoning sometimes occurring during childbirth) and discovered sulfanilamide. Sulfa drugs, with their antibacterial potency, had a remarkable effect in curtailing pneumonia, which had been the most frequent terminal infectious disease. At the same time, the clinical trials methodology was developed in 1937 by Professor A. Bradford Hill and, together, the sulfas and improved clinical trials accelerated the elimination of several terminal disorders. However, as the bacterial diseases were curtailed, the incidence of the "afflictions of civilization," such as heart disease and stroke, were both more evident and actually increasing due to increased stress, inappropriate nutrition, inadequate physical activity, smoking and environmental deterioration. However, faith in biomedical approaches was undaunted. It was popularly believed that, if in its infancy such an approach could cure pneumonia, diphtheria and smallpox, then in its maturity biomedical intervention should certainly be able to "cure" cardiovascular disease and cancer.

Despite the myriad fallacies in this assumption, it has become the rationalization for the predominance of the biomedical model until recent years, as well as the justification for enormous research and technologic investments by individuals and government alike. However, by their very nature, the chronic, degenerative "afflictions of civilization," "the modern plagues" or "diseases of affluence," such as heart disease, cancer, arthritis, Alzheimer's disease, osteoporosis and diabetes, are often too extensive or advanced to be reversed by the time they are detectable. As the number of people over 65 years of age increases, both the percentage and absolute numbers of individuals manifesting these disorders will necessarily increase as well.

All of the major causes of death and disability appear to be secondary to the progressive degeneration of aging. This situation was foreseen by pioneering physician, Sir William Osler, who termed pneumonia "the old man's friend." Currently, many individuals who would have died survive, but with extremely impaired functions. Again, Osler (1978) observed in his classic 1904 textbook, *The Principles and Practice of Medicine*, that "there is truth in the paradoxical statement that persons rarely die of the disease with which they suffer." Secondary terminal infections carry off many patients with incurable disease. Only one pathway seems to lead out of this cruel dilemma of protracted suffering due to the success of certain medical interventions, and that is to turn attention toward the processes underlying both the "afflictions of civilization" and longevity.

One of the single greatest impediments to a health care system devoted to optimum health and longevity is the resistance on the part of individuals and institutions to reorienting their personal habits and economic priorities to recognize that personal behaviors and lifestyle practices can have an enormous impact on one's health. In 1978, physician Steven Jonas (1978) noted in his book, *Medical Mystery: The Training of Doctors in the United States*, that the major shortcoming of contemporary medicine resides in its very structure with its disproportionate emphasis on specialization and pathology management rather than primary care and prevention. Jonas also emphasizes the personal commitment necessary by citing the Hippocratic maxim, "It [is] impossible for a man to remain in perfect health unless he organize[s] his entire life for such a purpose." Though that might be both extreme and unnecessary, it does underscore the effort required by such an orientation.

Increasingly, there is a recognition that morbidity and mortality relate more to psychosocial and environmental factors than to the quality of the medical care system per se. Those same factors appear to have as profound an impact on the quantity of life as upon the quality.

Healthy aging and longevity are phenomena that involve an inextricable interaction between biochemical, psychosocial and socioeconomic influences. Researchers in fields ranging from molecular biology to medical anthropology consistently cite the overwhelming importance of psychosocial influences in the determination of an individual's late life health and his or her potential for longevity. That is not to deny or denigrate current research concerning recombinant DNA or the reversal of cellular processes related to aging, but rather to emphasize the importance of applying available knowledge until the messianic pharmaceutical does emerge from the laboratory. Heroic measures to prolong life after catastrophic illness has already occurred will create only an ever-more-infirm and growing elderly population. Concern for longevity cannot start at an advanced age, and it should not be focused outside the self.

As the percentage of elderly people in the population continues to rise and life expectancy is extended, it becomes increasingly important to avoid lifestyles that lead to an institutionalized, incapacitated old age. It is clearly possible to reorient priorities and the psychosocial milieu to accommodate the lifestyle changes that must occur during the life span between 30 and 100 years of age in order to maintain a high degree of health and fulfillment. In *The Yellow Emperor*, Huang Ti (BC 2697–2597) states: "Hence the sages did not treat those who were already ill; they instructed those who were not yet ill. . . . To administer medicines to diseases which have already developed and to suppress revolts which have already developed is comparable to the behavior of those persons who begin to dig a well after they have become thirsty, and of those who begin to cast weapons after they have already engaged in battle." Though this enumeration could be extended ad infinitum, these points suggest the multiple levels of health that require restructuring if we are to move from pathology management to optimizing health and longevity.

LIFESTYLE AND LONGEVITY

Psychologic and lifestyle factors have been demonstrated to be powerful predictors of both optimum health in maturity and longevity. Modern research also shows that genetic and biologic influences on longevity are highly dependent on the presence or absence of specific lifestyle influences.

Compelling research evidence from a wide range of sources indicates:

1. Lifestyle activities play a large role in shaping one's health status in maturity.
2. Unmanaged psychologic stress is a major influence governing whether or not even the average life expectancy is attained.
3. Women live longer than men, due to lifestyle rather than biologic variables. Not only has this trend been apparent since the turn of the century, but it is accelerating.
4. Studies of isolated and identifiable small communities both in the United States and in cross-cultural research have clarified the nature of the interaction between lifestyle and social and religious support systems in enhancing health and life expectancy.

Taken as a whole, these highly diverse insights point to a common conclusion: that health and longevity observed in later years are largely determined by factors at work both internally and externally throughout the life of the individual. The longevity potential is dependent on the entire developmental process and is not an epiphenomenon that randomly or inexplicably occurs at the end of life.

THE LIFESTYLE FACTOR

Despite the sophistication of genetic, biochemical and neuroendocrine research, *perhaps the single most accurate predictor of longevity is lifestyle*. For example, one particularly important predictor of longevity is work satisfaction. Early research by Erdman Palmore (1969a and b) attempted to clarify the interaction between physical, mental and social factors by developing a longevity quotient, which would give both the relative weight or influence of each of these and explain how they would correlate with longevity. Taking 39 variables, including previous medical history, parents' ages at death, various IQ scores and socioeconomic data, Palmore conducted a 13-year longitudinal study of 268 community volunteers between the ages of 60 and 94 (at the beginning of the study). Employing various statistical analyses, Palmore concluded: "Work satisfaction was the single best predictor among men aged 60 to 69. The evidence suggests that maintaining health, mental abilities and satisfying social roles are the most important factors related to longevity." Following up on his initial research, Palmore studied the same group at a 15-year interval and confirmed his review while refining the results into more specific predictors:

(a) work satisfaction, (b) happiness rating, (c) physical functioning and (d) tobacco use. In the same report, Palmore concluded that "the most important ways to increase longevity are: (1) maintain a useful and satisfying role in society, (2) maintain good physical functioning, and (3) avoid smoking." Thus, family history and long-lived parents are important, but the modifiable lifestyle variables are at least equally important in determining whether genetic potential is realized.

Another influential study was developed from the well-known research of Caroline Bedell Thomas and Karen R. Duszynski (1974) of the Johns Hopkins School of Medicine. Their study of 1,337 medical students for over 30 years yielded great insight into the links between stress, lifestyle and subsequent illness. During 1978, the research team analyzed data from 45 students randomly selected from the Johns Hopkins Medical School class of 1948. At that time, researchers classified the students into three groups based upon psychologic assessments. Subjects were classified as "alphas," who were "cautious, steady, self-reliant, slow to adapt and nonadventurous"; "betas," who were "lively, spontaneous, clever, and flexible"; and "gammas," who were the "most complicated: although often brilliant, gammas were also mercurial and confused. They tended toward extremes."

By 1978, most of the 45 students were practicing physicians in their middle fifties. The researchers screened their records for hypertension, heart attacks, cancer and severe emotional illness. From the results, it was evident that the gammas had the worst medical history, with 77.3% evidencing severe illness, as compared with 25% of the alphas and betas. According to Barbara Betz, the psychiatrist who analyzed the data, the psychologic styles reflect individual neuroendocrine profiles, and these same chronic lifestyles represent a "thread of vulnerability" for the gammas. Most importantly, researchers do not advocate attempts at radical personality change but note that gammas "should try to accept the unevenness in their characters. Such self-acceptance may help the tense gammas to relax and conceivably prolong their lives."

Among other research findings relating lifestyle to longevity are: (1) married couples who are residing together live longer than single, widowed or divorced individuals; (2) positive religious attitudes correlate with happiness, feelings of usefulness, adjustment and longevity; and (3) there is evidence of a "longevity syndrome," exemplified by characteristics such as feelings of well-being, high levels of physical and mental activity, creativity and general enjoyment of life. It is becoming increasingly evident that productivity, psychologic adjustment, and overall life satisfaction are essential factors in increasing life expectancy. Short-sighted public health measures often exclude these variables as extraneous and minimize the preventive potential while maximizing efforts at managing pathology and disease.

STRESS AND LONGEVITY

It has become virtually axiomatic that stress is a major factor governing all states of optimum health, as well as illness. The means that individuals and institutions develop to manage both the positive and negative aspects of stress are, therefore, of greater importance than the stressors themselves.

Pioneering research since the early 1940s by Hans Selye (1956) still remains the primary source of the stress concept:

> Stress is the stereotyped part of the body's response to any demand. It is associated with the wear and tear on the human machinery that accompanies any vital activity and, in a sense, parallels the intensity of life. It is increased during nervous tension, physical injury, infections, muscular work or any other strenuous activity, and it is connected with a nonspecific defense mechanism which increases resistance to stressful or "stressor" agents.

One of the most significant studies demonstrating an interaction between stress, physical health and longevity was undertaken by Harvard University psychiatrist George E. Valliant and his colleagues (1979). From an original sample of 204 men in the Harvard sophomore classes between 1942 and 1944, a research team followed 185 men for over 40 years. During this period of time, the men received periodic psychologic and physical assessments, and responded to interviews and annual questionnaires. Factors considered indicative of the relative degree of illness in the population were psychiatric treatment, little occupational progress, job dissatisfaction, unhappy marriages, little recreation time and general psychologic instability. From the prospective assessments, it was evident that psychologic health not only predicted physical health but that physically healthy men who reacted poorly to stress or evidenced psychologic instability ran a significantly higher risk of developing serious health problems or dying before reaching their fifties. The analysis controlled for such interaction variables as alcohol consumption, tobacco use, obesity, and the life span of the subject's ancestors. Although the study was not oriented toward analyzing for longevity, it did clearly indicate that some of the deterioration of aging is preventable. In discussing the data, Valliant (1979) posits the "tentative conclusions" that:

> Chronic anxiety, depression, and emotional maladjustment, measured in a variety of ways, predicted early aging, defined by irreversible deterioration of health. The data suggest that positive mental health significantly retards irreversible midlife decline in physical health. Stress does not kill us so much as ingenious adaption to stress (call it good mental health or mature coping mechanisms) facilitates our survival.

A great deal of research indicates that responses to life stressors can often be accurate predictors of psychologic stability, physical health and longevity. Many studies confirm that the individual's innate or learned response to stress is more important than the stressors per se. For example, research by Richard S. Lazarus (1966) of the Department of Psychology at the University of California at Berkeley has emphasized the role of "psychologic mediators" governing the actual psychophysiology of the stress response. Findings such as these are sources of optimism because they elevate the individual from the status of passive victim to an active participant in determining how to manage the inevitable and often stimulating stress of life.

This last observation is the key point in the interaction between stress and longevity. Individuals can learn to adapt more positively to stress in order to achieve at least their average life expectancy. Volumes have been and will be written regarding the psychophysiology of stress, its effects, and the clinical treatment of stress disorders. For the most part, these are concerned with health maintenance and are not oriented toward longevity. However, there are related research and observations of centenarian communities indicating that stress and psychologic factors are major determinants of longevity as well.

GENDER ROLES AND LONGEVITY

Closely related to the interaction between lifestyle and longevity is the fact that in all modern societies women tend to live longer than men. Prior to the early 1900s, the ratio of 104–106 male births to 100 female births offset the toll of wars and occupational hazards through the second and third decade of life, but this is no longer the case.

In a series of articles entitled "Why Do Women Live Longer than Men?" Ingrid Waldron of the University of Pennsylvania conducted an extensive inquiry into the possible biologic basis for such a widespread difference (Waldron, 1976a and b, 1978; Waldron & Johnston, 1976). These articles contain an in-depth analysis of the role of influences such as greater male susceptibility to disease due to X-chromosome-linked recessive mutations; the role of female hormones such as estrogen, which does tend to prevent atherosclerosis in premenopausal women; effects of oral contraceptives; as well as cross-cultural studies of this mortality differential. From this extensive review, only the cross-cultural differentiation proved to be of significance. Higher female mortality was observed most frequently in nonindustrial countries, but lower female mortality is the norm in the 10 postindustrial nations studied. Although genetic and hormonal factors are partially responsible for this differential, the conclusion of Waldron's studies unequivocally implicates lifestyle as the major influence:

> Behavioral factors emerge as important determinants for each of the causes of death listed. These causes of death with clear behavioral components are responsible for one-third of the excess male mortality, and arteriosclerotic heart disease is responsible for an additional 40% of the excess deaths among males. . . . Men have higher death rates for arteriosclerotic heart disease in large part because they develop aggressive, competitive, coronary-prone behavior. . . . One third of the sex differential in mortality is due to men's higher rates of suicide, fatal motor vehicle and other accidents, cirrhosis of the liver, respiratory cancers, and emphysema. Each of these causes of death is linked to behaviors which are encouraged or accepted more in males than in females. . . . Thus, the behaviors expected of males in our society make a major contribution to their elevated mortality.

Charles E. Lewis and Mary Lewis of the UCLA School of Medicine have speculated on the potential impact of sexual equality on both male and female health (Lewis & Lewis, 1977). These researchers acknowledge that the major differences "related more to their behaviors and roles in society than to their biologic inheritance."

As sex roles change, will those health-related behaviors that seem highly linked to sex also change—i.e., will women gain equity in death rates for most diseases as they already have for cancer of the lung? Certainly, they will accumulate greater risks as they drive or fly greater distances and acquire different stresses related to occupational responsibilities.

CROSS-CULTURAL PERSPECTIVES ON SOCIAL SUPPORT AND LONGEVITY

Placing the numerous psychosocial influences in an appropriate context that reflects their relative values is a formidable task; there are many variables outside of the immediate social role and lifestyle that exert considerable influence. A study by Richard F. Tomasson of the Department of Sociology at the University of New Mexico attempted to integrate a number of these variables. Statistics indicate that Sweden has been the country with the lowest overall mortality and the highest life expectancy in the world since the early 1960s. From his observations and related research, Tomasson (1976) suggests seven factors that would account for the manifestation of healthy aging:

(1) Sweden's system of compulsory, national health insurance dates only from 1955. . . . The point is that medical care, like education, has been regarded as both a communal responsibility and an individual right in Sweden. . . (2) Sweden has progressed further than the United States in absorbing its lower classes into the conventional living standards of the greater society. (3) Sweden has a highly structured and "tight" social structure in which internal constraints are strong. Constraint has been suggested . . . as a factor in explaining mortality differentials. (4) . . . the extremely low infant mortality that prevails in Sweden is due to the smaller percentage of births to women under age 20 and at ages 35 and over. (5) There is an activist approach toward lessening the dangers of existence in Sweden. (6) Consumption of cigarettes and alcohol are both much lower in Sweden than in the United States. (7) Dietary differences between these two populations are greater than might be expected in the two most affluent societies in the world. Meat and sugar consumption, for

example, is lower in Sweden than in the United States and the consumption of fish is much higher.

Cross-cultural studies are full of evidence that certain lifestyles and attitudes developed early in life do optimize and predict adult health and longevity. There are several studies of groups of individuals and several major longitudinal studies of identifiable groups that indicate the interconnection between psychologic and physical health.

For example, in a study of Mormon men, James E. Enstrom of the UCLA Department of Public Health studied the church records for 15,500 California Mormons during 1968–1975 and for 55,000 Utah Mormons during 1970–1975 to examine cancer incidence. Using age-adjusted statistics, Enstrom noted that for "active Mormon" men (i.e., those who closely followed the dictates of the church), the average life expectancy is over 7 years longer than for comparable U.S. males. When the specific causes of morbidity and mortality are analyzed, they indicated a "mortality ratio of 50% for all cancer," or half the incidence observed in comparable males. Furthermore, when he analyzed the comparisons between active and "inactive Mormons" (who tend to smoke and drink about as much as the general population), Enstrom noted (1978) a higher incidence of cancer in inactive Mormons, concluding:

> Most of the mortality difference between active and inactive Mormons occurs in the smoking-related cancer sites. [But] several additional factors are possibly important: low consumption of alcohol, coffee, tea, soft drinks, and drugs, certain dietary habits, general health practices, including exercise and proper sleep and weight; various social and psychological aspects connected with the nature of their religion; selection factors related to obtaining roles in the Church, and heredity.

From numerous research studies, it has also become clear that religious beliefs and the lifestyles they advocate can have a significant influence on health, usually in a positive direction. Drawing on the research data comparing specific religious groups with control groups from the general population, the results indicate such findings as:

• Mormons in Utah have 30% lower incidence of most cancers.

- Seventh-Day Adventists have 10–40% fewer hospital admissions for epidermoid and nonepidermoid malignancies.
- Regular church attenders in Washington County, Maryland, have 40% less risk from arteriosclerotic heart disease.

There is no intention here to advocate religious beliefs as a prerequisite to health and longevity. However, it seems sensible to conclude that a strong belief and a sense of purpose in life, whether they are identifiably religious or not, can have a profound impact on health.

PROSPECTS FOR THE FUTURE

Improved health and longevity in the future will come from changes in lifestyle and socioeconomic factors, as well as from the medical care system. The psychosocial structure of particularly healthy groups in the United States, the cultural systems evident in centenarian communities, and the lifestyles of long-living women can serve as prototypes for efforts to curb the incidence of premature morbidity and mortality in our society.

The definition of an epidemic is a disease affecting 6% of a given population, and a pandemic is one affecting more than that. Psychosocial influences limiting health and longevity have reached pandemic proportions. Just as major modifications were undertaken in the external environment to stem the infectious plagues, equally significant measures should be undertaken with both the physical and the psychosocial environments to eliminate the modern plagues. Profound changes in human lifestyle could result in increased health and longevity for men and women.

Twentieth-century consciousness has so far been characterized by over-emphasis on the rational, self-assertive, linear and scientific mode of awareness. We have seen an emphasis on dominion over nature and scientific progress outstripping archaic religions. Longevity is a matter of regaining a balance between the masculine, Yang, and feminine, Yin, modes of the human species in the twentieth century. Through a life-preserving balance of activity with contemplation, competition with cooperation, and rational knowledge with intuitive wisdom, the human species can attain its longevity potential.

REFERENCES

Enstrom, J.E. (1978). Cancer and total mortality among active Mormons. *Cancer, 42*(4), 1943–1951.

Gruenberg, E.M. (1977). The failure of success. *Milbank Memorial Fund Quarterly*, *55*(I), 3–24.

Jonas, S. (1978). *Medical mystery: The training of doctors in the United States*. New York: W.W. Norton & Company.

Lazarus, R.S. (1966). *Psychological stress and the coping process*. New York: McGraw-Hill.

Lewis, C.E., & Lewis, M.A. (1977). The potential impact of sexual equality on health. *N Engl J Med*, *297*(16), 863–869.

Osler, W. (1978). *The principles and practice of medicine: Designed for the use of practitioners and students of medicine*. Bermingham: Classics of Medicine Library (first published in 1892).

Palmore, E.B. (1969a). Physical, mental and social factors in predicting longevity. *Gerontologist*, *9*(2), 103–108.

Palmore, E.B. (1969b). Predicting longevity: A follow-up controlling for age. *Gerontologist*, *9*(4), 247–250.

Palmore, E.B. (1971). Longevity predictors—implications for practice. *Postgrad Med J*, *50*(I), 160–164.

Pelletier, K.R. (1981). Longevity: Fulfilling our biological potential. New York: Pelacarte and Pelta.

Selye, H. (1956). *The stress of life*. New York: McGraw-Hill.

Thomas, C.B., & Duszynski, K.R. (1974). Closeness to parents and the family constellation in a prospective study of five disease states: Suicide, mental illness, malignant tumor, hypertension and coronary heart disease. *Johns Hopkins Med J*, *134*(5), 251–270.

Tomasson, R.F. (1976). The mortality of Swedish and U.S. white males: A comparison of experience, 1969–1971. *Am J Public Health*, *66*(10), 968–974.

Valliant, G.E. (1979). Natural history of male psychological health: Effects of mental health on physical health. *N Engl J Med, 301*, 1249–1254.

Waldron, I. (1976a). Why do women live longer than men? *Journal of Human Stress*, *2*(I), 2–13.

Waldron, I. (1976b). Why do women live longer than men? *Social Science & Medicine*, *10*(7–8), 349–362.

Waldron, I. (1978). Why do women live longer than men? *N Engl J Med*, *298*(I), 57–58.

Waldron, I., & Johnston, S. (1976). Why do women live longer than men? *Journal of Human Stress, 2*(2), 19–30.

CHAPTER 23

Exercise, Nutrition and Healthy Aging: Establishing Community-Based Exercise Programs

William J. Evans

Advancing age is associated with a remarkable number of changes in body composition, including reduction in lean body mass, which occurs primarily as a result of losses in skeletal muscle mass (Frontera, Hughes, & Evans, 1991; Tzankoff & Norris, 1978). This age-related loss in muscle mass has been termed *sarcopenia* (Evans, 1995). Loss in muscle mass accounts for age-associated decreases in basal metabolic rate, muscle strength and activity levels, which, in turn, are the causes of the decreased energy requirements that are characteristic of older people.

In sedentary individuals, the main determinant of energy expenditure is fat-free mass, which declines by about 15% between the third and eighth decades of life. It also appears that declining caloric needs are not matched by an appropriate decline in caloric intake, with the ultimate result being increased body fat content with advancing age. Increased body fat, along with increased abdominal obesity, are thought to be directly linked to the greatly increased incidence of Type II diabetes in the elderly population. In this situation, regularly performed exercise is especially important; it can affect the nutritional needs and the functional capacity of elders.

Sarcopenia, the age-associated loss of muscle mass (Evans, 1995), is a direct cause of age-related decreases in muscle strength. Our laboratory (Frontera et al., 1991) examined muscle strength and mass in 200 healthy 45- to 78-year-old men and women and concluded that muscle mass (not function) is also the major determinant of age- and sex-related differences in strength in both men and women. Reduced muscle strength in older people is a major cause of the increased prevalence of the functional disability found in this population. Muscle strength and power form a critical component of mobility (Bassey et al., 1992), and the high prevalence of falls among institutionalized elders may be a consequence of reduced muscle strength.

The question that our laboratory has been attempting to address is, To what extent are these changes inevitable consequences of aging? Our data suggest that changes in body composition and aerobic capacity associated with increasing age may not be age-related at all. By examining endurance-trained men, we saw that the amount of fat the body stores and maximal aerobic capacity were not related to age, but rather to the total number of hours these men were exercising per week (Meredith, Zackin, Frontera, & Evans, 1987). Even among sedentary individuals, energy spent in daily activities explains more than 75% of the variability in body fat among younger and older men (Roberts et al., 1992). These data and the results of other investigators indicate that levels of physical activity are important in determining energy expenditure and, ultimately, the accumulation of body fat. This chapter presents current research findings about the benefits of exercise in older age, as well as guidelines developed in Massachusetts and used in a state-wide exercise program for women and men over 50 years of age.

RESEARCH FINDINGS

Aerobic Exercise

Aerobic exercise has long been an important means of preventing and treating many of the chronic diseases typically associated with old age. These include non–insulin-dependent diabetes mellitus (NIDDM), hypertension, heart disease and osteoporosis. Regularly performed aerobic exercise increases the maximum capacity to take in and use oxygen during exercise. The responses of initially sedentary young people aged 20–30 and older people aged 60–70, both men and women, have been studied (Meredith et al., 1989). Meredith and colleagues found that the absolute gains in aerobic capacity were similar between the two age groups. However, the mechanism for adaptation to regular submaximal exercise appears to be different for old and young people.

Muscle biopsies taken before and after training showed a more than twofold increase in the oxidative capacity of the muscles of older subjects, and that of the young subjects showed smaller improvements. In addition, the storage of glycogen by the skeletal muscles in the older subjects, which was significantly lower than those of young men and women initially, increased significantly.

The degree to which older people demonstrate increased maximal cardiac output in response to endurance training is still largely unanswered. Seals and co-workers (Seals, Hagberg, Hurley, Ehsani, & Holloszy, 1984a) found no increases after 1 year of endurance training. More recently, Spina and colleagues (1993) observed that older men increased maximal cardiac output though healthy older women demonstrated no change in response to endurance exercise. If these gender-related differences in cardiovascular response are real, it may explain the lack of response in maximal cardiac output when older men and women are included in the same study population.

The fact that aerobic exercise has significant effects on skeletal muscle may help explain its importance in the treatment of glucose intolerance and NIDDM. Seals and coworkers (1984b) found that a high-intensity training program provided greater improvements in the insulin response to an oral glucose load than did a lower-intensity program. However, their subjects began the study with normal glucose tolerance. Kirwan and coworkers (1993) found that 9 months of endurance training at 80% of the maximal heart rate resulted in reduced glucose-stimulated insulin levels; however, no comparison was made to a lower-intensity exercise group.

Hughes and coworkers (1993) demonstrated that regularly performed aerobic exercise without weight loss resulted in improved glucose tolerance, improved rate of insulin-stimulated glucose disposal and increased levels of the glucose transporter protein in skeletal muscle (GLUT 4). In this investigation, a moderate-intensity aerobic exercise program was compared to a higher-intensity program (50% versus 75% of maximal heart rate reserve). No differences in glucose tolerance, insulin sensitivity or muscle GLUT-4 levels were seen between the moderate- and higher-intensity aerobic exercise groups. This may indicate that a prescription of moderate aerobic exercise should be recommended for older men or women with NIDDM or at high risk for NIDDM. It might help ensure compliance with the program.

Endurance training and dietary modifications are generally recommended as the primary treatment for NIDDM. Cross-sectional analysis of dietary intake supports the hypothesis that a low-carbohydrate/high-fat diet is associated with the onset of NIDDM (Marshall, Hamman, & Baxter,

1991). This evidence, however, is not supported by prospective studies where dietary habits have not been related to the development of NIDDM (Feskens & Kromhout, 1989; Lundgren,Benstsson, & Blohme, 1989). The effects of a high-carbohydrate diet on glucose tolerance have been equivocal (Borkman, Campbell, Chisholm, & Storlien, 1991; Garg, Grundy, & Unger, 1992).

Hughes and colleagues (1995) compared the effects of a high-carbohydrate diet with and without 3 months of high-intensity endurance exercise in older, glucose-intolerant women and men. Subjects were fed all of their food on a metabolic ward during the 3-month study and were not allowed to lose weight. These investigators observed no improvement in glucose tolerance or insulin-stimulated glucose uptake in either the diet group or the diet-plus-exercise group. However, the group that exercised and followed a carbohydrate diet demonstrated a significant and substantial increase in skeletal muscle glycogen content; at the end of the training, the muscle glycogen stores were considered to be saturated. Because the primary site of glucose disposal is skeletal muscle glycogen stores, it is likely that the extremely high muscle glycogen content limited the rate of glucose disposal. Thus, when combined with exercise and a weight maintenance diet, a high-carbohydrate diet had a counter-regulatory effect. It is likely that the value of a high-carbohydrate/high-fiber diet is in the treatment of excess body fat, which, in turn, may be an important cause of impaired glucose tolerance. Recently, Schaefer and co-workers (1995) demonstrated that older subjects lost weight while consuming a high-carbohydrate diet with no restrictions on the amount they ate.

There appears to be no attenuation of the response of elderly men and women to regularly performed aerobic exercise when compared to young subjects. Increased fitness levels are associated with reduced mortality and increased life expectancy. Aerobic exercise has also been shown (Helmrich, Ragland, Leung, & Paffenbarger, 1991) to prevent the occurrence of NIDDM in those individuals who are at the greatest risk for developing this disease. Thus, regularly performed aerobic exercise is an important way for older people to improve their glucose tolerance.

Aerobic exercise is generally prescribed as an important adjunct to weight-loss programs. Combined with weight loss, it has been demonstrated to increase insulin action to a greater extent than weight loss through diet restriction alone. In the study by Bogardus and colleagues (1984), diet therapy alone improved glucose tolerance, mainly by reducing basal glucose production and improving sensitivity to insulin. Aerobic training, on the other hand, increased carbohydrate storage rates; therefore, "diet therapy plus physical training produced a more significant approach toward normal." However, aerobic exercise (as opposed to resistance training) combined with a hypocaloric diet has been demonstrated to result in a greater reduction in resting metabolic rate than diet alone (Phinney, LaGrange, O'Connell, & Danforth, 1988).

In perhaps the most comprehensive study of its kind, Goran & Poehlman (1992) examined components of energy metabolism in older women and men who engaged in regular endurance training. They found that endurance training did not increase total daily energy expenditure, due to a compensatory decline in physical activity during the remainder of the day. In other words, when elderly subjects participated in a regular walking program, they rested more, so that activities outside of walking decreased and calorie expenditure over a period of 24 hours was unchanged.

Ballor and colleagues (Ballor, Katch, Becque, & Marks, 1988) compared the effects of resistance training to that of diet restriction alone in obese women. They found that resistance exercise results in increased strength and gains in muscle size as well as the preservation of fat-free mass during weight loss. These data are similar to the results of Pavlou and colleagues (Pavlou, Steffee, Lerman, & Burrows, 1985), who used both aerobic and resistance training as an adjunct to a weight-loss program in obese men.

Strength Training

Though endurance exercise has been the more traditional means of increasing cardiovascular fitness, the American College of Sports Medicine currently recommends strength or resistance training as an important component of an overall fitness program. This is particularly important in the elderly population, where weakness and loss of muscle mass are prominent deficits.

Strength conditioning or progressive resistance training is generally defined as training in which the resistance against which a muscle generates force is progressively increased over time. Progressive resistance training involves few contractions against a heavy load. The metabolic and morphologic adaptations resulting from resistance and endurance exercise are quite different. Muscle strength has been shown to increase in response to training between 60% and 100% of the maximum amount of weight that can be lifted with one contraction (the 1RM). Strength conditioning will result in an increase in muscle size, and this increase in size is largely the result of increased contractile proteins.

The mechanisms by which the mechanical events stimulate an increase in RNA synthesis and subsequent protein synthesis are not well understood. Lifting weight requires that a muscle shorten as it produces force. Lowering the weight, on the other hand, forces the muscle to lengthen as it produces force. These lengthening muscle contractions have been shown to produce ultrastructural damage that may stimulate increased muscle protein turnover (Evans & Cannon, 1991).

Our laboratory examined the effects of high-intensity resistance training of the knee extensors and flexors in older men aged 60–72 years. The average increase in knee flexor and extensor strength was 227% and 107%, respectively. Computed tomographic (CT) scans and muscle biopsies were used to determine muscle size. Total muscle area by CT analysis increased by 11.4%, and the muscle biopsies showed an increase of 33.5% in type I fiber area and 27.5% increase in type II fiber area. In addition, lower body aerobic capacity increased significantly while that of the upper body did not, indicating that increased muscle mass can increase maximal aerobic power. It appears that the age-related loss in muscle mass may be an important determinant in the reduced maximal aerobic capacity seen in elderly men and women (Flegg & Lakatta, 1988). Improving muscle strength can enhance the capacity of many older men and women to perform many activities such as climbing stairs, carrying packages and even walking.

We have used this same training program to study a group of frail, institutionalized elderly men and women aged 87–96 (Fiatarone et al., 1990). After 8 weeks of training, the 10 subjects in this study increased muscle strength by almost 180% and muscle size by 11%. More recently (Fiatarone et al., 1994), a similar intervention with frail nursing home residents demonstrated not only increases in muscle strength and size, but also increased walking speed, increased ability to climb stairs and better balance. In addition, spontaneous activity levels increased significantly; the activity of a nonexercised control group was unchanged. This study was designed to determine the effects of augmenting caloric intake by about 20% (without use of a supplement) and providing one third of the recommended daily allowance of vitamins and minerals. Though muscle strength and functional capacity or muscle size were not affected, the men and women who both consumed the supplement and exercised gained weight compared with other participants in the study. The nonexercising subjects who received the supplement reduced their habitual dietary energy intake, so total energy intake was unchanged. It should be pointed out that this was a very old, very frail population with diagnoses of multiple chronic diseases.

The increase in overall levels of physical activity has been a common observation in our studies (Fiatarone et al., 1994; Frontera et al., 1990; Nelson et al., 1994). Because muscle weakness is a primary deficit in many older individuals, increased strength may stimulate more aerobic activities such as walking and cycling.

In addition to its effect on increasing muscle mass and function, resistance training can also have an important effect on the energy balance of elderly women and men (Campbell, Crim, Young, & Evans, 1994). Men and women participating in a resistance training program of the upper and lower body muscles required approximately 15% more calories to maintain body weight after 12 weeks of training when compared with their pretraining energy requirements. This increase in energy needs came about as a result of an increased resting metabolic rate, the small energy cost of the exercise, and what was presumed to be an increase in activity levels.

Though endurance training has been demonstrated to be an important adjunct to weight-loss programs in young men and women by increasing their daily energy expenditure, its utility in treating obesity in elderly people may not be great. This is because, *due to their low fitness levels,* many sedentary older women and men do not spend many calories when they perform endurance exercise. Some 30–40 minutes of exercise may increase energy expenditure only slightly with very little residual effect on calorie expenditure. Aerobic exercise training will not preserve lean body mass to any great extent during weight loss. Because resistance training can preserve or even increase muscle mass during weight loss, this type of exercise for those older men and women who must lose weight may be of genuine benefit.

Bone Health

The increased calorie need resulting from strength training may be a way for older people to improve their overall nutritional intake when the calories are chosen as nutrient-dense foods. In particular, calcium is an important nutrient to increase since calcium intake was found to be one of the only limiting nutrients in the diet of elderly men and women living independently (Sahyoun, 1992). Careful nutritional planning is needed to reach the recommended calcium levels of 1,500 mg for postmenopausal women with osteoporosis or who are not using hormone replacement therapy, and 1,000 mg per day for postmenopausal women taking estrogen.

In one of the very few studies to examine the interaction of dietary calcium and exercise, our laboratory studied 41 postmenopausal women who were placed on a high-calcium diet (1,500 mg) or a moderate-calcium diet (750 mg). Half of these women participated in a year-long walking program, 45 minutes a day, 4 days a week. Independent effects of the exercise and dietary calcium were seen. Compared with the moderate-calcium group, the women on a high-calcium diet displayed reduced bone loss from the femoral neck, independent of whether they exercised. However, walking prevented loss of trabecular bone mineral density, which was seen in the nonexercising women after 1 year. Thus, it appears that calcium intake and aerobic exercise are both beneficial to bone mineral density but act on different sites.

The effects of 52 weeks of high-intensity resistance exercise were examined in a group of 39 postmenopausal women (Nelson et al., 1994). Twenty were randomly assigned to the strength training group and the remaining women were randomly assigned to a sedentary group. At the end of the year, significant differences were seen in lumbar spine and femoral bone density between the strength trained and sedentary women.

Unlike other pharmacologic and nutritional strategies for preventing bone loss and osteoporosis, resistance exercise affects more than just bone density. The women who resistance trained improved their muscle mass, strength, balance and overall levels of physical activity. Thus, resistance training can be an important way to decrease the risk for osteoporotic bone fractures in postmenopausal women.

The Benefits of Resistance Training for Older Men and Women

Virtually anyone can benefit from muscle strength training. Many health care professionals have directed their patients away from strength training in the mistaken belief that it can cause undesirable elevations in blood pressure. With proper technique, the systolic pressure elevation during aerobic exercise is far greater than that seen during resistance training. Muscle-strengthening exercises are rapidly becoming a critical component to cardiac rehabilitation programs as clinicians realize the need for strength as well as endurance for many of the activities of daily living.

As discussed above, the benefits of resistance training for older women and men are increased strength; increased muscle mass; improved balance, walking speed and ability to climb stairs; increased bone density; increased overall levels of physical activity; decreased protein requirements (improved utilization of dietary protein); improved glucose tolerance and decreased risk of type II diabetes; and increased energy requirements, making resistance exercise a safe and important adjunct to a weight-loss program. The following are some practical suggestions for implementation of an exercise program for older people in a community-based setting.

Generally speaking, candidates for the program can include adults of all ages. Older hypertensive patients should be carefully evaluated before beginning a strength-training program. A weight-lifting stress test can be used instead of a treadmill stress test to monitor electrocardiogram and blood pressure responses during the exercise. Patients with rheumatoid or osteoarthritis may also participate. Patients with a limited range of motion should train within the range of motion that is relatively pain free. Most patients will see a dramatic improvement in the pain-free range of motion as a result of resistance training.

Resistance training should be directed at the large muscle groups that are important in everyday activities, including the shoulders, arms, spine, hips and legs. Each repetition should be performed slowly through a full range of motion, allowing 2 or 3 seconds to lift the weight and 4–6 seconds to lower the weight. Performing the exercise more quickly will not enhance strength gains and may increase the risk of an injury.

A high-intensity resistance training program has been shown to have the most dramatic effects at all ages. This is a training intensity that will approach or result in muscular fatigue after it has been lifted and lowered with proper form 8–12 times. A weight that a person can lift 20 or more times will increase his or her muscular endurance, but it will not result in much of a gain in strength or muscle mass.

The amount of weight that is lifted should increase as strength builds. This should take place about every 2–3 weeks. In our research studies, we have seen a 10–15% increase in strength *per week* during the first 8 weeks of training. We have seen significant gains in muscle strength and mass, as well as an improvement in bone density, with only 2 days a week of training over 12 weeks.

People of any age who participate in a resistance-training program should be instructed in correct breathing techniques. This includes inhaling prior to a lift, exhaling during the lift and inhaling as the weight is lowered to the beginning position. Participants should avoid holding their breath during force production. With proper breathing technique, the cardiovascular stress of resistance exercise is minimal. Heart rate and blood pressure should rise only slightly above resting values in older people who follow these guidelines.

Any device that provides sufficient resistance to stress muscles beyond levels usually encountered may be used. Weight-stack or compressed-air resistance machines may be found at many community fitness facilities or purchased for home use. Simple weight-lifting devices might include Velcro-strapped wrist and ankle bags filled with sand or lead shot. Heavy household objects such as plastic milk jugs filled with water or gravel or food cans of various sizes can also be used.

Community-based exercise programs for women and men over the age of 50 are growing in popularity. For individuals participating in such programs, physician screening for every participant may be either impractical or a barrier to participation. The American College of Sports Medicine recommends a physician-supervised stress test for anyone over the age of 50 who wants to begin a vigorous training program. However, if the general recommendation is for an older person to simply walk or participate in a resistance-training program, this test is probably not necessary. A questionnaire can determine whether a physician should examine someone.

The reason for the questionnaire should be obvious. Clearly, the biggest concern is that an individual with cardiovascular disease will have a myocardial infarction during exercise. Questionnaires are designed to determine who may be at greatest risk. One was used in our Massachusetts-wide program ("Keep Moving—Fitness After Fifty"), a community-based walking program for men and women over the age of 50. At its peak, between 7,500 and 8,000 people participated, with an average age of 67. Walking "clubs" were located throughout the state in nursing homes, retirement communities, hospitals and Councils on Aging (buildings that housed many of the activities provided by the Massachusetts Executive Office of Elder Affairs). During the 8 years of the program's existence, there were no reports of myocardial infarction, cardiac arrest or any cardiovascular event during a training session.

Advancing age results in increased muscle stiffness and reduced elasticity of connective tissue. For this reason, proper warm-up and stretching can have a greater effect in reducing the risk of an orthopedic injury in older than in younger men and women. A 5-minute warm-up (exercising at a reduced intensity) followed by 5–10 minutes of slow stretching is highly recommended.

Another important practice for older people is cooling down after exercise. They should never finish a workout by immediately jumping into a hot shower, but rather should end the exercise session with a slow walk and more stretching. Postexercise stretching will be more effective than the stretching done before the exercise. This is because the muscles have warmed up and, along with tendons and ligaments, are much more elastic.

It is always a good idea for people to find a friend to exercise with. The more people exercise together, the more likely they are to stay with the exercise. This is a perfect opportunity for sons and daughters to spend time with their older parents, to the benefit of both generations.

With interest in the establishment of community-based exercise programs for the elderly population increasing, the following are recommendations that may be of help:

- Work with local or state agencies. Often, state offices on aging have some small amounts of resources set aside for health-related activities. The individuals working in these agencies have access to the elderly population in your area.
- Use an already-developed infrastructure. Area agencies on aging may have a facility specifically for programs to serve older people. Also contact the local hospital, YMCA or university.
- Promote and advertise the program as a "social" exercise program. Often, older men and women will join programs because of increased opportunity for socialization, not necessarily for fitness benefits.
- More women than men will join. Use strategies to increase the recruitment of men.
- Plan for a wide variability in functional status. Highly fit and very frail individuals are likely to join. If a walking program is established, plan for at least two groups, slow and fast.
- Form a medical advisory group comprised of local physicians.
- Attempt to incorporate some resistance exercise in any newly established program.

In conclusion, there is no other group in our society that can benefit more from regularly performed exercise than older people. Though both aerobic and strength conditioning are highly recommended, only strength training can stop or reverse sarcopenia. Increased muscle strength and mass in an older person can be the first step toward a lifetime of increased physical activity and a realistic strategy for maintaining functional status and independence.

REFERENCES

Ballor, D.L., Katch, V.L., Becque, M.D., & Marks, C.R. (1988). Resistance weight training during caloric restriction enhances lean body weight maintenance. *Am J Clin Nutr, 47,* 19–25.

Bassey, E.J., Fiatarone, M.A., O'Neill, E.F., Kelly, M., Evans, W.J., & Lipsitz, L.A. (1992). Leg extensor power and functional performance in very old men and women. *Clin Sci, 82,* 321–327.

Bogardus, C., Ravussin, E., Robbins, D.C., Wolfe, R.R., Horton, E.S., & Sims, E.A.H. (1984). Effects of physical training and diet therapy on carbohydrate metabolism in patients with glucose intolerance and non–insulin-dependent diabetes mellitus. *Diabetes, 33,* 311–318.

Borkman, M., Campbell, L.V., Chisholm, D.J., & Storlien, L.H. (1991). Comparison of the effects on insulin sensitivity of high carbohydrate and high fat diets in normal subjects. *J Clin Endocrinol, 72,* 432–437.

Campbell, W.W., Crim, M.C., Young, V.R., & Evans, W.J. (1994). Increased energy requirements and body composition changes with resistance training in older adults. *Am J Clin Nutr, 60,* 167–175.

Evans, W.J., & Cannon, J.G. (1991). The metabolic effects of exercise-induced muscle damage. In J.O. Holloszy (Ed.), *Exercise and sport sciences reviews* (pp. 99–126). Baltimore: Williams & Wilkins.

Evans, W. (1995). What is sarcopenia? *J Gerontol, 50A*(special issue), 5–8.

Feskens, E.J.M., & Kromhout, D. (1989). Cardiovascular risk factors and the 25-year incidence of diabetes mellitus in middle-aged men. *Am J Epidemiol, 130,* 1101–1108.

Fiatarone, M.A., Marks, E.C., Ryan, N.D., Meredith, C.N., Lipsitz, L.A., & Evans, W.J. (1990). High-intensity strength training in nonagenarians. Effects on skeletal muscle. *JAMA, 263,* 3029–3034.

Fiatarone, M.A., O'Neill, E.F., Ryan, N.D., Clements, K.M., Solares, G.R., Nelson, M.E., Roberts, S.B., Kehayias, J.J., Lipsitz, L.A., & Evans, W.J. (1994). Exercise training and nutritional supplementation for physical frailty in very elderly people. *N Engl J Med, 330*(25), 1769–1775.

Flegg, J.L., & Lakatta, R.G. (1988). Role of muscle loss in the age-associated reduction in VO2 max. *J Appl Physiol, 65,* 1147–1151.

Frontera, W.R., Meredith, C.N., O'Reilly, K.P., & Evans, W.J. (1990). Strength training and determinants of VO2 max in older men. *J Appl Physiol, 68,* 329–333.

Frontera, W.R., Hughes, V.A., & Evans, W.J. (1991). A cross-sectional study of upper and lower extremity muscle strength in 45–78-year-old men and women. *J Appl Physiol, 71*, 644–650.

Garg, A., Grundy, S.M., & Unger, R.H. (1992). Comparison of effects of high and low carbohydrate diets on plasma lipoprotein and insulin sensitivity in patients with mild NIDDM. *Diabetes, 41*, 1278–1285.

Goran, M.I., & Poehlman, E.T. (1992). Endurance training does not enhance total energy expenditure in healthy elderly persons. *Am J Physiol, 263*, E950–E957.

Helmrich, S.P., Ragland, D.R., Leung, R.W., & Paffenbarger, R.S. Jr. (1991). Physical activity and reduced occurrence of non–insulin-dependent diabetes mellitus. *N Engl J Med, 325*, 147–152.

Hughes, V.A., Fiatarone, M.A., Fielding, R.A., Kahn, B.B., Ferrara, C.M., Shepherd, P., Fisher, E.C., Wolfe, R.R., Elahi, D., & Evans, W.J. (1993). Exercise increases muscle GLUT 4 levels and insulin action in subjects with impaired glucose tolerance. *Am J Physiol, 264*, E855–E862.

Hughes, V.A., Fiatarone, M.A., Fielding, R.A., Ferrara, C.M., Elahi, D., & Evans, W.J. (1995). Long term effects of a high carbohydrate diet and exercise on insulin action in older subjects with impaired glucose tolerance. *Am J Clin Nutr, 62*, 426–433.

Kirwan, J.P., Kohrt, W.M., Wojta, D.M., Bourey, R.E., & Holloszy, J.O. (1993). Endurance exercise training reduces glucose-stimulated insulin levels in 60- to 70-year-old men and women. *J Gerontol, 48*(3), M84–M90.

Lundgren, J., Benstsson, C., Blohme, G., et al. (1989). Dietary habits and incidence of noninsulin-dependent diabetes mellitus in a population study of women in Gothenburg, Sweden. *Am J Clin Nutr, 52*, 708–712.

Marshall, J.A., Hamman, R.F., & Baxter, J. (1991). High-fat, low-carbohydrate diet and the etiology of non–insulin-dependent diabetes mellitus: The San Luis Valley Diabetes Study. *Am J Epidemiol, 134*, 590–603.

Meredith, C.N., Zackin, M.J., Frontera, W.R., & Evans, W.J. (1987). Body composition and aerobic capacity in young and middle-aged endurance-trained men. *Med Sci Sports Exerc, 19*, 557–563.

Meredith, C.N., Frontera, W.R., Fisher, E.C., Hughes V. A., Herland, J.C., Edwards, J., & Evans, W.J. (1989). Peripheral effects of endurance training in young and old subjects. *J Appl Physiol, 66*, 2844–2849.

Nelson, M.E., Fiatarone, M.A., Morganti, C.M., Trice, I., Greenberg, R.A., & Evans, W.J. (1994). Effects of high-intensity strength training on multiple risk factors for osteoporotic fractures. *JAMA, 272*, 1909–1914.

Pavlou, K.N., Steffee, W.P., Lerman, R.H., & Burrows, B.A. (1985). Effects of dieting and exercise on lean body mass, oxygen uptake, and strength. *Med Sci Sports Exerc, 17*, 466–471.

Phinney, S.D., LaGrange, B.M., O'Connell, M., & Danforth, E. Jr. (1988). Effects of aerobic exercise on energy expenditure and nitrogen balance during very low calorie dieting. *Metabolism, 37*, 758–765.

Roberts, S.B., Young, V.R., Fuss, P., Heyman, M.B., Fiatarone, M.A., Dallal, G.E., Cortiella, J., & Evans, W.J. (1992). What are the dietary energy needs of adults? *Int J Obesity, 16,* 969–976.

Sahyoun, N. (1992). Nutrient intake by the NSS elderly population. In S.C. Hartz, R.M. Russell, & I.H. Rosenberg (Eds.), *Nutrition in the elderly: The Boston nutritional status survey* (pp. 31–44). London: Smith-Gordon and Co.

Saltin, B. (1981). Physical training in patients with intermittent claudication. In *Physical conditioning and cardiovascular rehab* (pp. 191–196). New York: Cohen, Mock and Ringquist.

Schaefer, E.J., Lichtenstein, A.H., Lamon-Fava, S., McNamara, J.R., Schaefer, M.M., Rasmussen, H., & Ordovas, J.O. (1995). Body weight and low-density lipoprotein cholesterol changes after consumption of a low-fat ad libitum diet. *JAMA, 274,* 1450–1455.

Seals, D.R., Hagberg, J.M., Hurley, B.F., Ehsani, A.A., & Holloszy, J.O. (1984a). Endurance training in older men and women: Cardiovascular responses to exercise. *J Appl Physiol: Respir Environ Exerc Physiol, 57*(4), 1024–1029.

Seals, D.R., Hagberg, J.M., Hurley, B.F., Ehsani, A.A., & Holloszy, J.O. (1984b). Effects of endurance training on glucose tolerance and plasma lipid levels in older men and women. *JAMA, 252,* 645–649.

Spina, R.J., Ogawa, T., Kohrt, W.M., Martin W.H. III, Holloszy, J.O., & Ehsani, A.A. (1993). Differences in cardiovascular adaptation to endurance exercise training between older men and women. *J Appl Physiol, 75*(2), 849–855.

Tzankoff, S.P., & Norris, A.H. (1978). Longitudinal changes in basal metabolic rate in man. *J Appl Physiol, 33,* 536–539.

CHAPTER 24

Reversing Disease through Diet and Exercise: The Pritikin Approach

Robert Pritikin

If you want to know how much health care has changed in a relatively short span of time, just consider that Nathan Pritikin, my father, was criticized by cardiologists only a few decades ago for saying that appropriate diet and exercise could prevent and effectively treat coronary heart disease. Back in the 1950s, 1960s and early 1970s, those words were heresy. Not only was heart disease considered incurable, but most doctors believed that diet had nothing to do with the illness. Of course, Nathan Pritikin went even further. He argued that the cause of many serious illnesses, including many common cancers, high blood pressure, adult-onset diabetes and overweight was the high-fat, high-cholesterol diet and sedentary lifestyle of the modern world. Society could all but eliminate the plague of degenerative disease, he said, simply by adopting a diet low in fat and cholesterol and rich in whole grains, fresh vegetables, beans and fruit.

During the past 20 years, more than 70,000 people have come to the Pritikin Longevity Center that Nathan Pritikin founded in 1976. Most have suffered from some form of degenerative disease, such as coronary artery disease, high blood pressure, adult-onset diabetes or overweight. Many had been scheduled for coronary bypass surgery before coming to the center; others had metabolic syndrome—a combination of conditions, including high blood pressure, high insulin, high triglycerides (blood fats) and overweight; still others were at high risk of cancer.

Numerous independent scientific studies of our program have been done to analyze its effects on given populations. Each of these studies has confirmed the remarkable transformations that our participants undergo.

- Research conducted on 4,587 Pritikin participants found that the average drop in blood cholesterol levels was 23% (Barnard, 1991).

361

The National Heart, Lung and Blood Institute (National Cholesterol Education Program, 1994) has calculated that a 1% drop in cholesterol represents a 2% decline in risk for heart attack, which means that the average person who adopts our program sees his or her risk of suffering a heart attack cut in half. These same people experienced an average drop in triglycerides of 33% (Barnard, 1991).

- Eighty-three percent of those studied who come to our center on medication for high blood pressure leave with normal blood pressure and free of medication (Barnard, Zifferblatt, Rosenberg, & Pritikin, 1983).
- One study, which examined a group of people who were scheduled to have coronary bypass surgery when they began our program, found that 80% no longer needed the surgery when they left our Center. Five years later, they were still on our diet, and they still did not need the surgery (Barnard, Guzy, Rosenberg, & O'Brien, 1983).
- Seventy percent of those studied who came to our center with adult-onset diabetes and taking diabetic drugs left with normal blood sugar levels and free of all diabetic medication. Of those adult-onset diabetics who came to our center on insulin, 39% left with normal blood-sugar levels and off of insulin (Barnard, Jung, & Inkeles, 1994).
- When scientists examined the major risk factors for breast and colon cancer among those who attended our program, they found that our participants cut several of these risk factors by as much as 50% (Heber, Ashley, Leaf, & Barnard, 1991; Reddy et al., 1988).

In addition to these results, we have had innumerable medically documented success stories of people who were considered "incurable" by their doctors, only to find themselves restored to health by our program. People have used the program to overcome severe forms of arthritis; immune disorders; chronic pain and joint, eye and ear problems. The Pritikin program is one of the most effective long-term weight-loss programs ever conceived (McCarthy, 1998).

WHERE IT ALL BEGAN

During World War II, Nathan Pritikin, an inventor, engineer and manufacturer, came up with the revolutionary hypothesis that a diet low in fat and cholesterol and rich in plant foods is the basis for good health. Shortly after the war began, the U.S. Army Air Force asked him to improve on the accuracy of its Nordham bombsight, which, because of the technology of the time, was highly inaccurate. Pritikin came up with the idea of photographing an image onto the glass lens, or reticle, then using acid to engrave the image into the glass. The lens that he developed was accurate to within one-thousandth of an inch—an unheard of feat at the time, and many times more accurate than its predecessor.

Not only did the Air Force award him a contract to begin manufacturing the lens, it also gave him top-secret security clearance, which he used to study the subject he was most passionate about—the relationship between diet and health. Armed with his security clearance, he surveyed the military's analysis of health and illness among the European populations during the war. What he found surprised him. Military records showed that deaths from heart attacks were actually falling during World War II. How could that be? The prevailing view among physicians was that heart disease was caused by genetic tendencies combined with the stresses of modern life. Stress, scientists believed, caused the arteries around the heart to harden and gradually narrow, thus blocking blood flow and oxygen to the heart muscle, eventually suffocating it and causing a fatal heart attack. If stress is what caused heart disease, why wasn't there a European epidemic of heart attacks? Surely the German occupation, the constant fall of bombs, and the knowledge that you could be killed any day was the greatest population-based example of stress that modern life had ever produced.

The reason, Pritikin soon discovered, was that European civilians were living primarily on food rations during the war years. German soldiers had confiscated the meat, butter and eggs, leaving the rest of Europe with mostly potatoes, garden-grown vegetables, barley, corn, wheat and small amounts of animal foods (Barker & Osmond, 1986). On this diet, their disease rates plummeted.

Based on the hypothesis that perhaps the diet that the body runs best on was made up mostly of vegetables, with smaller amounts of meat, dairy and eggs, he studied other populations around the world and compared their diets and disease rates. He found that people who ate what westerners would consider more primitive or traditional diets—grains, vegetables, fruits and small amounts of animal foods—were largely free of heart disease, cancer and other illnesses.

This diet was essentially low in fat and cholesterol and rich in nutrition and fiber from unprocessed plant foods. Later, Pritikin would also realize that such plant-based diets were also loaded with immune-boosting and cancer-fighting antioxidants and phytochemicals. All of these factors promoted good health. When, on the other hand, he looked at the populations of people who were plagued by modern chronic degenerative illnesses, he found that these people subsisted on the contemporary western diet—rich in fatty animal foods and processed fare, and low in fiber.

One of the groups of traditional peoples that Nathan Pritikin would point to regularly as an example of this phenomenon were the Tarahumara Indians of Southern Mexico. The Tarahumaras enjoy what most of us would describe as excellent health. They experience virtually no heart disease, high blood pressure, cancer, adult-onset diabetes or other degenerative illnesses. They enjoy optimal weight. Moreover, they are fit. The Tarahumaras play a game that requires the male participants to run more than 100 miles without stopping. The women play the same game and run 60 miles. The diet they consume is composed primarily of plants—grains, vegetables and fruit. The quantity of animal foods they eat is small. Moreover, the animals tend to be low in fat because they are free-ranging and wild (McMurry, Cerqueira, Connor, & Connor, 1991).

By the 1950s the picture seemed clear. Modern western diets and sedentary lifestyles were crippling and killing people prematurely. And the vast majority of this premature death and disability was preventable.

FROM THEORY TO MEDICINE

Nathan Pritikin's insights might have become nothing more than an interesting theory were it not for the fact that in February 1958 he was diagnosed with "incurable" heart disease. An abnormal electrocardiogram and other tests revealed that he had coronary insufficiency, or inadequate blood flow to his heart. At the age of 43, he was told by his doctors to accept his disease and retire—there was nothing they could do for him, except perhaps to use drugs to manipulate his vagus nerve, which controlled his heartbeat.

My parents at the time had just moved from Chicago to Santa Barbara, California. For my father, leaving Chicago for Santa Barbara was something like being released from a tomb into the bright light of a spring day. He had just begun to really enjoy his life in California and he had no intention of surrendering it to retirement. Armed with his precious insight, Nathan Pritikin set out to create a program that would cure himself of heart disease, based on a simple diet and small amounts of exercise. The key, as far as he could tell, was blood cholesterol level. Traditional populations had low cholesterol levels and low rates of disease, including heart disease. On the other hand, most westerners had high cholesterol and high rates of coronary disease. Animal studies had shown that cholesterol could be raised and lowered by either elevating or lowering dietary fat and cholesterol. The primary sources of fat are animal foods, and only animal foods contain cholesterol. Therefore, he surmised that if he drastically reduced animal foods and substituted plant foods for them, his cholesterol level would fall and his coronary artery disease might be reversed.

The diet Pritikin adopted consisted mostly of whole grains—brown rice, barley, wheat, oats and corn, a plethora of fresh vegetables and fruit, beans and small amounts of fish. As he had suspected, his cholesterol level fell like a stone. At one point, just before he was diagnosed with heart disease, his cholesterol level hovered dangerously at around 300 mg/dL. It fell to 150 mg/dL, then to 120 mg/dL.

Nathan Pritikin expected his physicians to celebrate his success. Instead, they were critical of his drastic dietary changes, which they assured him would lead to nutritional deficiencies and other illnesses if he persisted. Unfortunately, he had what seemed like even more radical ideas: He wanted to add exercise to his regime. Now his doctors were appalled. Exercise was out of the question, said one, unless he wanted to wind up face down on the sidewalk one day. However, he had seen research showing that those who exercise regularly have better overall health and greater cardiovascular fitness. He believed that if he began exercising, his heart and general condition would further improve.

Naturally, he started exercising with great trepidation, initially walking short distances and then, after a time, increasing those lengths by small increments. He did that only after he felt sure his heart could tolerate the increase in exertion. After several years of walking, he eventually took up running, a pastime he came to love. Long before the jogging craze took hold, he used to run every day in his specially made sneakers and long pants. Motorists who saw him running through the streets of Santa Barbara thought he looked like a businessman who had just been mugged. He would regularly have to inform passersby who stopped to offer assistance that he was just out for a little exercise.

It took him 8 years to finally overcome his heart disease. In 1966, treadmill tests, electrocardiograms and other tests revealed no sign of illness. By all accounts, his condition was normal and healthy. Throughout his recovery period, he monitored his nutrient levels and never once experienced nutritional deficiencies due to his diet. In fact, in some cases his nutrient intake improved. Many years later, after he had opened the Pritikin Longevity Center, he said that he could have done it all in 9 months. It took him 8 years, he said, because there was no one who could tell him what to do, and his own approach to discovering the answer was through trial and error.

For the next 10 years, Nathan Pritikin continued to study the scientific literature linking diet to disease and in 1974 wrote a book entitled *Live Longer Now: The First One Hundred Years of Your Life*, in which he argued that a long life could be achieved if we adopt a diet and lifestyle for which the human body was designed. If we eat the foods we were designed to eat and get regular physical activity, we can live long lives and enjoy youthful vitality, emotional equilibrium and mental clarity right up to the time of death. Famed cancer researcher Ernst Wynder (Wynder, Weisburger, & Ng, 1992) put the concept nicely: "We should live so that we can die young, as late in life as possible."

In 1975, Nathan Pritikin conducted what came to be known as the Long Beach Study (Pritikin, Kaye, & Pritikin, 1975). The study compared the effects of his diet and exercise program on 19 severely ill veterans from the Long Beach Veteran's Administration Hospital in California. The program was run out of a house to which the men came each day for 6 months for their meals and exercise routine, which consisted of daily walks. I supervised the activities, meal preparation and did much of the recordkeeping.

Though the Long Beach Study showed dramatic improvements in coronary insufficiency, cholesterol levels, adult-onset diabetes, high blood pressure, claudication and walking distance, it was intensely criticized by the National Heart, Lung and Blood Institute for not being double-blind and for having a poorly matched control group. Nevertheless, he was elated with the results. It was obvious, at least to him, that the program was more powerful than any other form of medicine being offered for these illnesses. Even more important, the study gave him an idea: What if a rehabilitation center were created to treat serious illness using a low-fat, low-cholesterol diet and exercise program? The seed had been planted.

THE PRITIKIN LONGEVITY CENTER

On January 5, 1976, Nathan and Ilene Pritikin opened the Pritikin Longevity Center in Santa Barbara. The program, which initially was comprised of 30-day sessions, utilized the gentlest forms of medicine—a plant-based diet and daily walks. From our vantage point at the turn of the millennium, it is difficult for us to understand just how revolutionary my parents' gamble really was. Today we understand that diet plays a key role in causing cardiovascular disease and heart attacks. In the 1970s, no such awareness existed, neither within the general public nor among most doctors and scientists, many of whom were even hostile to the Pritikin claims. The Pritikin Longevity Center was about as bold an adventure in health care as anything that had ever been attempted by a layperson.

Of course, virtually everyone who came to our center in those early years was a medical reject in one way or another. Only those who had run out of medical options dared to show up at our doors. We were regarded as mavericks. Yet we continued to get great results. Despite the severity of their illnesses, participants in our early programs were getting well. Cholesterol levels fell 25%. Eighty-five percent of people who came with high blood pressure and were taking medication were restored to normal blood pressure and stopped needing their drugs. Eighty percent of adult-onset diabetics who were taking diabetic medication left the center with normal blood sugar levels and off all medication. The remarkable analysis went on.

The notable statistics produced by the center cannot possibly convey the story of the Center—not then and not now. Frances Greger of North Miami, Florida, arrived at our earliest sessions in a wheelchair. Her angina pectoris was so bad that she could not walk even a few steps without suffering paralyzing pain. She also had severe claudication in her legs, further limiting her walking. Within 3 weeks at the center, Frances was not only out of her wheelchair, but also walking 10 miles a day.

Charles Tobolsky, a 69-year-old retired construction worker, was told by his doctor in Maple Shade, New Jersey that he was "a walking time bomb." An angiogram performed at Hahnemann Hospital in Philadelphia showed three severely closed coronary arteries. He needed immediate bypass surgery in order to survive, his doctors said. In addition, he had diabetes, for which he took two forms of medication. His physicians told him not to walk up a flight of stairs more than twice a day and never to drive at a speed greater than 40 miles an hour for fear that he would have a heart attack and crash at a potentially lethal speed. Worst of all, at least from Charles's point of view, was that he had to give up golf, a game he loved. By the time he left the center he was off all medication and was walking 10 miles a day. When he returned to Philadelphia he was able to resume golf and, 4 years later, wrote to say that he had recently won a golf champion-ship at his local country club. He never had a bypass operation.

We had people arriving on stretchers and, 3 weeks later, walking out of the center, having returned to "normal function." People not only regained their physical health, but the experience gave them a kind of rebirth. "Nathan and I watched people arrive in fear and, with steady progress, become almost delirious with joy," my mother said in her biography of my father, *The Man Who Healed America's Heart* (Pritikin, 1987). "The group setting required them to spend 30 days together, eating, walking, sharing their fears and their hopes," she wrote. "All of this produced close bonds among people who had previously been strangers. This, of course, is a very rare experience for many adults."

Not everything at the center was a rousing success, however. One of the biggest problems we had, especially in the early years, was the program's most powerful form of medicine: the food. It is important to remember that in the late 1970s and early 1980s there was no established low-fat cuisine. Most of the cookbooks that tell us how to prepare delicious dishes consisting of whole grains, fresh vegetables, beans and fruit had yet to be written. Nor were there healthful, ready-made or easy-to-prepare foods. In addition, there was the problem of learning how to prepare food for large numbers of people. It was one thing for my mother to cook delicious meals at home but quite another to prepare them in quantities for our participants. The people who came to the center called themselves pioneers, and they meant it in more ways than one. Not only were they the first to use this program as medicine, but they were the early guinea pigs on whom we learned to prepare the Pritikin foods.

Pritikin, who, it must be said, had a generally utilitarian approach to food, was occasionally appalled himself at some of our cooks' failures. People respected him too much to express criticism around him, but one day the soup was so bad that a murmur went up around the room, and people looked at each other aghast. Pritikin appeared to those around him to be oblivious to the growing discontent until, finally, he looked up from his soup bowl and said, "My God, what happened to this?" At that, the whole room broke up with laughter.

Nathan Pritikin was so determined that people get the fastest and most dramatic results that he often urged our cooks to avoid putting too much animal foods on anyone's plate, even in soup. Jack Applebaum, one of our earliest participants, caught the spirit of the Pritikin approach when he announced one day that he had found the Pritikin recipe for chicken soup:

"Fill a pot with water," Applebaum said, "put it in the sun, and swing a chicken over it. Serve when ready."

After 20 years of cooking Pritikin foods, it would be a rather extreme understatement to say that we have come a long way. Reviewers of my book, *The Fat Instinct* (1998), were consistently surprised at the creativity and the range of foods incorporated in the Pritikin diet. People who eat our food today or buy one of our books and prepare one of our recipes are invariably surprised by how delicious and satisfying they really are. Of course, if you do something consistently for 20 years, you are bound to become good at it. The fact is, when it comes to making healthful foods delicious, we are.

Ironically, when the flavor of the food stopped being an impediment to adherence, we realized something far more fundamental was driving people's food preferences. That revelation led us eventually to the fat instinct.

WHY SOME PEOPLE REMAIN COMPLIANT WHILE OTHERS CANNOT

For many years, we at the Longevity Center recognized that essentially two types of people adopt our program. Some people have no trouble sticking with the program for life. A larger percentage, however, have trouble maintaining the diet for reasons that, for many years, we did not understand. We have a lot of repeat customers at the Longevity Center. Consequently, I have had the opportunity to talk to people who succeeded on our program but later strayed from the diet. For many years, I thought that the problem was only a lack of discipline, but upon closer examination I realized that there was a greater force at work within people that was far more elemental and far more powerful than simply the temptations of the marketplace or a lack of discipline.

The foods people have the most problem avoiding are those rich in fat and sugar—in other words, those loaded with calories. Why do we crave such foods? I wondered. What makes them so difficult for people to resist?

To find the answer, we did two things: First, we analyzed the lifestyles of people who successfully remain on our program; second, we went back to the scientific literature to see what evidence, if any, might connect those behaviors to successful and healthy living. What we discovered surprised us. In fact, the people who are successful on our program have certain behaviors in common that they have integrated into their daily lives. These behaviors not only promote health, but they also reinforce one another, thus making a health-promoting lifestyle synergistic and easier to manage. Eventually, it becomes second nature to them.

This emphasis on an integrated, health-promoting lifestyle was surprising because, for many years, we tended to emphasize the Pritikin diet above other factors. However, what we learned was that lifestyle habits make it easier to follow the diet. In fact, for most people adherence to the diet depends on integrating these other behaviors into daily life. We also learned that no single behavior is as powerful alone as all of them are together.

At that point, we went back to the scientific literature and tried to understand why this combination of behaviors makes it easier to maintain a health-promoting lifestyle and others make it virtually impossible. We found that the craving to eat fat and calorie-rich foods is part of our instinct to survive. Very early in our evolution, the greatest threat facing human beings, other than the possibility of being eaten by another animal, was starvation. In order to endure food shortages, our ancestors had to have as many calories stored in their tissues as they could to survive the next famine. Fat, of course, is the most calorie-dense substance in the food supply. Thus, whenever our early ancestors had the opportunity to eat a food rich in fat, they gorged on it, consuming as many calories as they could.

What made fat-rich foods even more precious for our ancestors was that they were not as available as were plant foods. For most of our evolution, humans were not particularly good hunters, primarily because we lacked the tools needed to kill enough animals each day to meet our calorie needs. Plant foods, such as roots, leafy vegetables, potatoes and other tubers, were far more abundant and made up the bulk of our ancestral diet. But most plant foods are low in calories, which means that they provided energy for today, perhaps, but offered no long-term protection against the next food shortage. Only fat-rich foods provided that kind of survival benefit. Indeed, foods rich in calories were one of the keys to human survival (Johanson, 1994).

You might say that calories themselves were precious, especially when you consider how our ancestors lived. Each day, they expended enormous amounts of energy as they searched for food and attempted to survive environmental threats. In essence, they were exercising all day long, which meant they were burning calories constantly. In order to survive, they had to learn to conserve calories whenever possible, which meant that, like fat, rest was precious, too (Leonard & Robertson, 1996).

Our biology was shaped by the foods and lifestyle that dominated our ancestors' lives. That, in essence, was a plant-based diet, low in fat and cholesterol, and a high-degree of activity. We also ate frequently throughout the day. Thus, we were accustomed to consuming low-calorie foods frequently—today nutritionists refer to it as "grazing"—and expending enormous amounts of energy every day (Jenkins et al., 1997).

Such a diet and lifestyle made the instinctual desire for fat and the conservation of energy essential to survival. Those who gorged on high-calorie foods and conserved calories whenever possible were the ones who survived famines, were more likely to reach sexual maturity and, therefore, were most likely to pass on their genes to the next generation. Those who lacked the instinct to eat fat very likely starved to death—most of them at an early age—which meant that their genes were eventually extinguished, as well. In time, the fat instinct became woven into our genetic makeup.

Another important instinctual behavior associated with the fat instinct also emerged. Hunger gave rise to an overpowering craving for high-calorie foods. This only stands to reason, of course, since our ancestors were expending enormous amounts of energy searching for food each day. When a food shortage hit, that energy expenditure had to continue until food was found. The only way to replace that lost energy was to gorge on foods loaded with calories. Ideally, that would be a food rich in fat. Thus, hunger aroused, or triggered, our instinct, which encouraged us to gorge on fat and other high-calorie foods. It still does. As a test, go into a restaurant or a supermarket when you are really hungry. Your fat instinct will drive you to purchase as many high-fat, high-calorie foods as you can lay your hands on.

Over many thousands of years, the fat instinct came to be characterized by three behaviors: a preference for high-calorie foods, an instinctual desire to gorge on such foods whenever possible and a natural tendency to conserve calories—in other words, to relax. The instinct is especially aroused whenever we become hungry. These instinctual urges, which were handed down to us from our earliest ancestors, became a fundamental part of our will to survive. Indeed, they dominate us to this day, much to our detriment.

Today, our environment no longer requires a low-calorie diet and high-energy-expenditure lifestyle. The way we live now is just the opposite: High-calorie foods are everywhere and most of us have jobs and ways of living that do not require much physical activity. Nevertheless, our current eating patterns and food choices continually evoke the fat instinct. For one thing, our meals usually include a high-fat food, which triggers the fat instinct and our desire to overeat. Second, because high-calorie meals are so filling, we tend to eat only 2.5 meals per day, giving rise to periods of intense hunger at the lunch and dinner hours. Hunger stimulates the fat instinct, which encourages us to overeat high-calorie foods. That, of course, leads to weight gain and poor health.

Anyone who has dieted and skipped meals to reduce calorie intake knows how ravenous you become by the time you allow yourself to eat. Unfortunately, creating hunger triggers our instinctual desire to consume as many calories as possible at the next meal. Though most dieters do not realize it, eating only one or two meals per day actually encourages weight gain (McNutt et al., 1997), because the hunger associated with dieting actually creates overpowering cravings for high-fat and high-calorie foods.

In an effort to improve their health, many people today are trying to eat more unprocessed carbohydrate-rich foods, such as grains, vegetables and fruits. Unfortunately, they neglect the other essential component that shaped the lives of our ancestors and our own biology: exercise. Without exercise, a high-carbohydrate diet can raise triglycerides, elevate insulin, lower high-density lipoproteins (HDLs, the so-called good cholesterol) and make it difficult to lose weight (Schaefer et al., 1995). This can be very frustrating to people who believe they are doing the right thing but are failing to get the results they want. That frustration only provokes people to eat high-calorie foods, which puts them in the grip of the fat instinct. At that point, their efforts at achieving good health and optimal weight are lost.

OUTSMARTING THE FAT INSTINCT

When we fully understood the fat instinct, we understood why the lifestyle used by people who are successful on the Pritikin program actually works. A health-promoting lifestyle prevents the fat instinct from causing intense cravings for foods rich in fat and calories. People who adopt a health-promoting lifestyle are actually free of the cravings that otherwise control those who live under the influence of the fat instinct (Gambera, Schneeman, & Davis, 1995).

The behaviors that outsmart the fat instinct are now the basis for the Pritikin program. First, we choose natural, unprocessed carbohydrates as the majority of our foods. These include brown rice, barley, corn, millet and oats; a wide variety of leafy vegetables, roots and tubers and fruits. These foods are low in calories, but because they contain water and fiber, they are filling. In the vernacular of food scientists, unprocessed carbohydrates have high-satiety value, meaning that they create feelings of fullness and satisfaction without the high calories. These are the foods on which early humans survived and evolved. They are among the richest sources of nutrition in the food supply. The more of these natural, unprocessed carbohydrates we eat, the lower our risk of getting heart disease and cancer.

Unprocessed carbohydrates also keep insulin levels low (Jenkins et al., 1994), which is important for several reasons. The first is that low insulin maximizes fat burning. The second is that it keeps us from getting hungry. Unprocessed carbohydrate foods also provide long-lasting energy, and they are a rich source of nutrition and immune-boosting and cancer-fighting substances.

Second, we avoid foods rich in fat and calories. High-calorie foods, including fat, trigger the fat instinct and cause us to gorge. Foods that are concentrated in calories have low-satiety value, meaning we have to eat an abundance of them before we feel full and satisfied. Interestingly, high-calorie foods are usually low in nutrition. For our early ancestors, these foods were rare. In order for us to have health today, they must also be rare in our lives, as well.

Third, the Pritikin program advises people to eat frequently. By eating five to six small meals a day, we keep insulin levels low, which, in turn, causes us to burn fat and dampen our appetite and cravings for concentrated calories throughout the day. Studies have shown that frequent eating is associated with low insulin and weight loss (Drummond, Crombie, & Kirk, 1996; Jenkins et al., 1994).

Frequent eating, especially of low-calorie plant foods, keeps us from being hungry, which, in turn, prevents the fat instinct from driving us to eat high-calorie foods. Increased meal frequency gives us the freedom to choose and enjoy health-promoting foods.

Fourth, we urge people to exercise moderately and consistently. There are many health benefits from exercise, but there are three benefits that I would like to highlight. First, exercise lowers triglycerides. Recent studies have found that those who eat high-carbohydrate diets but do not exercise can experience an elevation in triglyceride levels (Schaefer et al., 1995). Triglycerides are a risk factor in the onset of heart disease. Exercise also raises HDL levels, which offer further protection against heart attack and stroke. Finally, exercise promotes weight loss and encourages healthy food choices.

Fifth, it is critically important to maintain consistency. Studies have shown that consistency promotes a desire for the foods you eat regularly, whatever they may be. Those who eat healthful foods consistently end up desiring those foods. This was demonstrated at the Monell Chemical Senses Institute in Philadelphia, where Richard Mattes discovered that when people were asked to refrain from eating fat and fat-substitute foods, they naturally came to enjoy foods that were low in fat (Mattes, 1993). Other studies of free-living populations also demonstrate this same finding (Van Horn, Dolecek, Grandits, & Skweres, 1997). One of the major benefits of consistency is better results.

These five behaviors, which now are integral to the Pritikin approach, replicate some of the patterns of our early ancestors, behaviors that shaped our evolution and biology. The diet our ancestors evolved on is also similar to the Pritikin diet. This is the diet and lifestyle that we were designed to follow. They are a perfect fit, not only with each other, but with our biology. Humans were designed to be active, to eat low-calorie, high-carbohydrate, high-fiber foods. We were designed to eat frequently and to limit the amount of fat we eat. All of these behaviors combine to support our underlying biology and health. In the modern world, they are essential, because without them the fat instinct controls our lives and destroys our health.

The new Pritikin programs represent a continually evolving approach beyond Nathan Pritikin's original thesis. The most recent evolutionary step is the understanding that, given the abundance of fat now available to us, the only way we will survive and thrive is to adopt a lifestyle that defeats the fat instinct painlessly and, at the same time, promotes within us a desire to eat foods that will restore our health.

REFERENCES

Barker, D.J., & Osmond, C. (March 1986). Diet and coronary heart disease in England and Wales during and after the second world war. *J Epidemiol Community Health, 40*, 37–44.

Barnard, R.J. (1991). Effects of life-style modification on serum lipids. *Arch Int Med, 151*, 1389–1394.

Barnard, R.L., Guzy, P.M., Rosenberg, J.M., & O'Brien, L.T. (1983). Effects of an intensive exercise and nutrition program on patients with coronary artery disease: Five-year follow-up. *J Cardiac Rehab, 3*, 83–190.

Barnard, R.J., Jung, T., & Inkeles, S.B. (1994). Diet and exercise in the treatment of NIDDM. *Diabetes Care, 17*, 1469–1472.

Barnard, R.J., Zifferblatt, S.M., Rosenberg, J.M., & Pritikin, N. (1983). Effects of a high-carbohydrate diet and daily walking on blood pressure and medication status of hypertensive patients. *J Cardiac Rehab, 3*, 839–846.

Drummond, S., Crombie, N., & Kirk, T. (1996). A critique of the effects of snacking on body weight status. *Eur J Clin Nutr, 50*, 779–783.

Gambera, P.J., Schneeman, B.O., & Davis, P.A. (1995). Use of the Food Guide Pyramid and US Dietary Guidelines to improve dietary intake and reduce cardiovascular risk in active-duty Air Force members. *J Am Diet Assoc, 95*, 1268–1273.

Heber, D., Ashley, J.M., Leaf, D.A., & Barnard, R.J (1991). Reduction of serum estradiol in postmenopausal women given free access to low-fat high-carbohydrate diet. *Nutrition, 7*, 137–141.

Jenkins, D.J., Jenkins, A.L., Wolever, T.M., Vuksan, V., Rao, A.V., Thompson, L.U., & Josse, R.G. (1994). Low glycemic index: Lente carbohydrates and physiological effects of altered food frequency. *Am J Clin Nutr, 59*, 706S–709S.

Jenkins, D.J., Popovich, D.G., Kendall, C.W., Vidgen, E., Tariq, N., Ransom, T.P., Wolever, T.M., Vuksan, V., Mehling, C.C., & Boctor, D.L., et al. (1997). Effect of a diet high in vegetables, fruit, and nuts on serum lipids. *Metab Clin Exp, 46*, 530–537.

Johanson, D.C. (1994). *Ancestors: In search of human origins*. New York: Villard Books.

Leonard, W.R., & Robertson, M.L. (1996). On diet, energy metabolism, and brain size in human evolution. *Curr Anthropol, 37*(1), 125–128.

Mattes, R.D. (1993). Fat preference and adherence to a reduced-fat diet. *Am J Clin Nutr, 57*, 373–381.

McCarthy, W.J. (1998). Long-term maintenance of weight loss. [Letter]. *Am J Clin Nutr, 67*, 946–950.

McMurry, M.P., Cerqueira, M.T., Connor, S.L., & Connor, W.E. (1991). Changes in lipid and lipoprotein levels and body weight in Tarahumara Indians after consumption of an affluent diet. *N Engl J Med, 325*, 1704–1708.

McNutt, S.W., Hu, Y., Schreiber, G.B., Crawford, P.B., Obarzanek, E., & Mellin, L. (1997). A longitudinal study of the dietary practices of black and white girls 9 and 10 years old at enrollment: The NHLBI Growth and Health Study. *J Adolesc Health, 20*, 27–37.

National Cholesterol Education Program. (March 1994). Second report of the expert panel on detection, evaluation, and treatment of high blood cholesterol in adults (Adult Treatment Panel II) *Circulation, 89*(3), 1333–1445.

Pritikin, N., Kaye, S.M., & Pritikin, R. (1975). *Diet and exercise as a total therapeutic regimen for the rehabilitation of patients with severe peripheral vascular disease.* Presented at the 52nd annual session of the American Congress of Rehabilitation Medicine in Atlanta, Georgia.

Pritikin, I., & Monte, T. (1987). *Pritikin: The man who healed America's heart*. Rodale Press.

Reddy, B.S., Engle, A., Simi, B., O'Brien, L.T., Barnard, R.J., Pritikin, N., & Wynder, E.L. (1988). Effect of low-fat, high-carbohydrate, high-fiber diet on fecal bile acids and neutral sterols. *Prev Med, 17*, 432–439.

Schaefer, E.J., Lichtenstein, A.H., Lamon-Fava, S., McNamara, J.R., Schaefer, M.M., Rasmussen, H., & Ordovas, J.M. (1995). Body weight and low-density lipoprotein cholesterol changes after consumption of a low-fat ad libitum diet. *JAMA, 274*, 1450–1455.

Van Horn, L.V., Dolecek, T.A., Grandits, G.A., & Skweres, L. (1997). Adherence to dietary recommendations in the special intervention group in the Multiple Risk Factor Intervention Trial. *Am J Clin Nutr, 65*(suppl), 289S–304S.

Wynder, E.L., Weisburger, J.H., & Ng, S.K. (March 1992). Nutrition: The need to define "optimal" intake as a basis for public policy decisions. *Am J Public Health, 82*(3), 346–350.

CHAPTER 25

Toward Appropriate Use of Medical Care Among the Aged

Donald M. Vickery

Diabetics attended a self-care course, and their hospital admission rate dropped by 69%. Older men with symptomatic benign prostatic hyperplasia watched a video explaining the risks and benefits of surgery versus "watchful waiting." They chose surgery 50% less often than patients who did not see the video.

These examples from recent research illustrate something of the potential of "demand management"—the use of decision and behavior support systems to enable individuals to use medical care appropriately. They also help to explain, in part, why demand management services have experienced a meteoric rise in popularity and appear to be on the verge of acceptance as a standard part of the health care scene.

THE CURRENT MODEL OF DEMAND MANAGEMENT

Demand management today uses four basic services:

1. Telephone-based decision support. Nurse-staffed telephone services provide information as well as decision and behavior support. Most services focus on triage support—helping people decide whether their symptoms warrant a doctor visit. Some lifestyle programs, especially smoking cessation, are telephone-based. Other services

Portions of this chapter are adapted with permission from D.M. Vickery, Toward Appropriate Use of Medical Care, *Healthcare Forum Journal*, pp. 14–19, © 1996, The Healthcare Forum.

provide comprehensive support for shared decision making, self-management of chronic disease, lifestyle changes and triage.

2. Communications that address self-care. Self-care publications give individuals in-hand resources about self-management of acute minor illness, general information on the use of the medical system and personal lifestyle management. As many studies clearly indicate, these communications do decrease visits among elderly populations.

3. Group and individual education programs. These programs usually are designed to teach patients about the self-management of chronic conditions such as arthritis, asthma, diabetes, hypertension, lung disease and heart disease. Like the Arthritis Self-Help Course mentioned above, the most successful of these programs use a self-help approach.

4. Traditional health promotion programs. These efforts seek to enable individuals to make beneficial lifestyle changes, such as stopping smoking or losing weight. The most successful are based in the workplace.

One market analysis predicts that at least 200 million Americans will be covered by demand management services within the next few years, creating a market well in excess of $2 billion.

Such an estimate is not without support from other sources. For example, a survey of health care marketing first revealed that demand management is the number one marketing theme for the immediate future, and a health care management newsletter's cover story headline recently proclaimed that demand management will soon be a necessity, a "baked-in" utility.

WHY NOW?

How is it that a category of services that was unknown a few short years ago (the demand management model was created in 1992) has achieved such rapid and widespread acceptance, notably among elderly populations? Part of the answer is that many of the tools of demand management—self-care interventions, health promotion and education—have been available for more than two decades. Still, even if a portion of its components have been available for some time, it is fair to ask why demand management has attained such prominence and acceptance now. The answer appears to be that the demand management model offers an important new consolidation of advantages:

- It demonstrates that more appropriate use of health care services by elderly populations can result in lower costs.
- It achieves appropriate utilization among this group by increasing access and satisfaction.
- It is compatible with most forms of supply management traditionally used by managed care organizations and does not require a revolution in the management of care.
- It appears to be a very attractive alternative to rationing as the options within supply management dwindle.

Combining increased quality, access and satisfaction for mature patients with decreased costs is clearly attractive, but is it too good to be true? Perhaps the best way to arrive at this answer is to begin with the demand management model and its scientific underpinnings, then consider current demand management services for older patients and the evidence for their effectiveness.

Demand management relies on information, but it also recognizes that the decisions older consumers make about their care are influenced by other factors, such as their cognitive skills, social support, sense of self-efficacy, and cultural norms. Demand management takes these factors into account as part of its strategy to encourage older individuals to use medical care and self-care appropriately. Note that demand management is not necessarily demand reduction, nor is it necessarily need reduction; these are among its results, but they are not its goals.

Instead, the demand management model postulates that demand for medical services has four sources: morbidity, perceived need, patient preference and non–health-related motives. Though there are no solid boundaries between these components, two of them—perceived need and patient preference—are key to demand management, particularly among elderly populations.

Perceived Need

According to available research, perceived need—a person's view of his or her illness and the health care services needed—is the most important factor influencing a person's use of medical care (even outpacing actual morbidity).

Perceived need is influenced by an individual's knowledge of the risks and benefits of medical care, perceived efficacy of the treatment, ability to access the problem, capability to self-manage the problem and confidence in his or her ability to self-manage the problem (self-efficacy). These factors are, in turn, influenced by cultural norms, education, gender, social support systems and the attitudes of the person's physicians and care providers.

The decision to seek care is strongly influenced by the degree to which a symptom interferes with normal activities, as well as by the presence of stressful life events, combined with inadequate or distant social networks. People who perceive themselves to have poor health seek more medical care than others, even when physicians judge them to be healthy. Conversely, many people with actual health problems sometimes view themselves to be relatively healthy and interact only minimally with the health care system.

Demand management uses self-care interventions such as triage, disease management, and self-help to influence perceived need by directly improving an individual's ability to access and manage medical problems. Many studies support self-care as an effective intervention in decreasing the demand for professional care for all types of illnesses and conditions.

One of the most convincing examples of influencing perceived need comes from researchers at Stanford University. They created the Arthritis Self-Help Course, a series of classes that teach patients how to take charge of their arthritis care. Much of this learning is obtained from other patients with arthritis who have been trained to conduct many of these programs. The course requires a 2-hour meeting each week for 6 weeks. Despite the small amount of time required, arthritis sufferers who attended the self-help course and whose health status was comparable to others who had not taken the course were making 40% fewer doctor visits 4 years after the course concluded. Thus, the impact of the Arthritis Self-Help Course is not only dramatic, but lasting.

Another convincing and thorough account of the efficacy of self-help in reducing perceived need for care among elderly patients is widely known as the "Medicare Study" (Vickery, Golaszewski, Wright, & Kalmer, 1988). As this population is so relevant to readers of this book, I will summarize the study in some detail here.

THE MEDICARE STUDY

To help establish the efficacy of communication-based self-care strategies for older patients, the Cooperative Health Education Program (CHEP) designed a study involving a health maintenance organization's (HMO's) senior population (Vickery et al., 1988). By randomizing senior subjects into four groups (three experimental health education alternatives and one control) and using communications-based strategies, CHEP was able to demonstrate significant decreases in both total and minor illness visits among an average mixed adult population of patients, averaging 17% and 35%, respectively. These decreases yielded cost savings of $2.50–$3.50 for each dollar spent on educational interventions—a substantial savings.

Despite these impressive results, the efficacy of prevention and self-care within Medicare populations was felt to be especially important. The problems of this population group are well known: The elderly have used a disproportionately large amount of medical care, and the proportion of the population in the elderly age group is increasing steadily, along with health care costs.

One might reasonably expect that the elderly would be less interested and less likely to respond in the areas of self-care and prevention than younger people. The elderly may lack the belief that they are capable of changing lifestyle factors or, even if they think they could implement these changes, that, because of their advanced age, there would be any real impact on their health. The purpose of the Medicare Study of Self-Care was to address these concerns and assess the impact on medical care utilization of a low-cost health education program emphasizing decision making. It was hypothesized that improving decision making would decrease ambulatory medical care utilization without deleterious effects on the health of participants and that savings would exceed costs.

The Rhode Island Group Health Association (RIGHA) of Providence was a collaborating agency in the CHEP study and served as the population source for this portion of the research (Vickery et al., 1988). The RIGHA was the first federally funded, qualified HMO and, at the time of the CHEP study in 1988, had about 30,000 members. RIGHA reported 1,009 Medicare-enrolled families containing 1,249 individuals eligible for study. Potential subjects were randomly assigned to an experimental or control group, then given the option of declining participation. Only nine individuals refused to participate.

Interventions consisted of a combination of written materials and a telephone information service. Households in the experimental groups received background information on the purpose of the research and the intervention process through a series of letters from the RIGHA medical director. Households in the control group received no interventions during the 1-year observation period.

Written materials included two self-care books, a monthly newsletter, eight brochures on lifestyle topics and self-help groups in the Providence area, and four newsletters and two self-care education packages designed specifically for the over-60 age group. All materials focused on individual decisions in the areas of self-care, medical care utilization, and lifestyle.

The telephone information service was staffed by the CHEP nurse coordinator and was available at regular hours (8:00 AM to 5:00 PM). It offered information on CHEP, assistance in using the interventions, and a range of information on health and medical topics. This system was operated in addition to the usual telephone information and appointment system at RIGHA.

For the most part, the telephone information system was not used. The probable explanation for this finding was the possibility that participants felt sufficiently comfortable with the information provided through alternative sources. Therefore, it is reasonable to conclude that the powerful results discussed in the following sections relate to the use of written program materials.

Utilization and Costs

The average number of pre-entry visits per year per 65+ individual was 5.10 for the experimental groups and 5.65 for the control group (see Table 25–1). An estimate of cost savings is given in Table 25–2. Summing these cost savings by each provider results in a net change in cost per individual of $30.29 for each experimental subject and $36.65 for each experimental household. These figures are estimates of costs saved for each individual or family because of the impact of intervention.

All costs were determined on a per-household basis; in this case, they were determined on the final household sample size of 300. Therefore, intervention costs were calculated at 16.70 per household (which excluded expenses for the telephone information service). *Comparing the cost of the program versus the above estimates resulted in a benefit-cost ratio of*

Table 25–1 Pre-Entry and Postentry Utilization Total Visits, Minor Illness and Circulatory Diseases[a]

	Pre-Entry Mean (S.E.)	Post-Pre[c] Mean (S.E.)	Analysis of Covariance[b] Mean (S.E.)	Slope
Total Visits				
E	5.105 (0.328)	+0.404 (0.242)	+0.322 (0.237)	-0.351
C	5.665 (0.294)	+1.112 (0.306)	+1.214 (0.266)	-0.285
P value	0.02	0.071	0.013	0.31
Minor Illness				
E	1.078 (0.111)	+0.009 (0.123)	-0.038 (0.094)	-0.791
C	1.222 (0.113)	+0.093 (0.134)	+0.151 (0.105)	-0.628
P value	0.36	0.64	0.18	0.020
Circulatory				
E	1.094 (0.127)	+0.125 (0.121)	+0.094 (0.107)	-0.458
C	1.300 (0.120)	+0.458 (0.120)	+0.497 (0.120)	-0.144
P value	0.24	0.051	0.013	0.0001

[a]N = 363 for group E, 291 for Group C.
[b]Mean post-pre adjusted for pre and linear slope of post-pre on pre.
[c]Reflects 1 year of study.

Source: Reprinted with permission from D.M. Vickery et al., The Effects of Self-Care Interventions on the Use of Medical Service within a Medicare Population, *Medical Care*, Vol. 26, No. 6, pp. 580–588, © 1988, Lippincott-Williams & Wilkins.

Table 25–2 Cost Savings Estimates

Service Provider	Change in Visits vs. Control	Estimated Visit Cost	Changes in Cost
MD	−0.318	$44.63	$−14.19
RN	−0.258	20.64	−5.33
MD & RN	−0.003	32.64	−0.10
Other professional	+0.006	35.99	+0.22
Aide	−0.033	12.88	−0.43
Unspecified	−0.286	36.58[a]	−10.46

Total change in cost per individual:	$−30.29
Total change in cost per household:[b]	−36.65
Intervention cost:	16.70
Ratio of change in visit cost to intervention cost:	2.19

[a]Weighted average based on pretest utilization.
[b]Average Medicare beneficiaries per househould = 1.21.
Source: Reprinted with permission from D.M. Vickery et al., The Effect of Self-Care Interventions on the Use of Medical Service within a Medicare Population, *Medical Care,* Vol. 26, No. 6, pp. 580–588, © 1988, Lippincott-Williams & Wilkins.

$2.19 saved for every dollar spent on intervention. There was no difference in health status between the two groups.

Prior to the implementation of the Medicare Study, there were reasonable grounds for doubting that self-care interventions could have a significant impact on medical care utilization in a Medicare population. Conventional wisdom suggested that this group was dependent on medical care and unwilling or unable to alter its use of the medical care system. Further, it was felt that self-care interventions may be less useful in an older population, in which a greater proportion of ambulatory utilization is for chronic disease and a smaller proportion is for acute minor illnesses than in a younger population. The findings of the Medicare Study indicate that pessimism with respect to the use of self-care interventions in this age group is unfounded. At the same time, these findings make it clear that precisely how the interventions are used by individuals is a complex and little-understood process.

The most striking finding in this study was the significant reduction in total ambulatory visits in the experimental groups, as compared with the control group. After adjustment by covariance for pretest utilization, this reduction is approximately 15.1%.

The decrease in minor illness visits for the experimental groups compared with the control group of 15.9% was not statistically significant. It may well be that older individuals are less likely to identify minor illnesses as a category of problems in which major changes in behavior are possible. Also, visits for minor illnesses constitute a smaller percentage of total visits in the Medicare group than in the non-Medicare population; this decreases the power of the test and makes it more difficult to demonstrate statistical significance for differences found.

Questions remained as to why an overall increase in utilization occurred during the intervention, including the utilization experience of the experimental groups. Increasing utilization over the history of RIGHA was a naturally occurring phenomenon, probably related to the maturation of the HMO population and to a better understanding of how to use and take advantage of the system. Additionally, decreases in the copayment structure were introduced, and branch HMO centers were opened throughout RIGHA during intervention. These administrative factors had the effect of decreasing the cost while increasing the accessibility of service. The percentage of increase experienced by the control group closely matched the overall increase experienced by RIGHA. A comparison of the estimate of savings realized due to reduction in visits and the costs of the educational interventions suggest that the savings associated with the program substantially outweigh its costs.

PATIENT PREFERENCE

The patient's role in shared decision making with physicians is called *patient preference*. Central to this role is the legal standard for informed consent. Within this model, physicians provide patients with treatment options and describe the benefits and risks associated with each one, but patients are responsible for choosing an alternative, based on how they value the benefits and fear the risks. Physicians may be able to define the probability of outcomes, but patients must take an active role in determining the value of those outcomes.

Research on patient education and treatment preference shows that people fully informed about the risks and benefits of all treatment options generally choose options that are less invasive, less risky, and less expensive. In other words, patients are more risk-averse than are their doctors.

Of special interest are the decisions made at the end of life. For some populations, the average cost of medical care during the last year of life can be as much as 80 times higher than the average for all other years. Is such intensive use of medical care actually preferred by patients?

A survey conducted by L.L. Emanuel et al. (Emanuel, Barry, Stoeckle, Ettelson, & Emanuel, 1991) indicated that as many as 93% of patients want advance directives and 71% want life-sustaining treatment discontinued if they become incompetent and have a poor prognosis. Yet, only 9% of Americans have written advance directives (Steiber, 1987), and physicians often are not aware of them when they do exist. Allowing patient preference to be expressed effectively might dramatically impact the use and cost of medical care. In fact, another study's findings (Chambers, Diamond, Perkel, & Lasch, 1994) showed that final hospitalization charges for Medicare patients without advance directives were more than three times higher than for those with directives ($95,305 versus $30,478).

Encouraging informed patient preference does not change the existence of severity of an illness; it does alter the pattern of usual care for illness by involving patients in decision making about that care.

LIMITS OF DEMAND MANAGEMENT PROGRAMS

Demand management has its detractors, of course. Some say that it is nothing more than the nurse advice telephone lines used by established managed care organizations for many years. This confuses the method of delivering a service (i.e., nurses using telephones) with the services being delivered.

Demand management services do not give advice or information that is directive, diagnostic or prescriptive. A quality demand management service provides decision support, not the decision. For example, it does not "tell" a patient to have an operation, but rather provides support in choosing between an operation, medicine, lifestyle changes or some other rational option. Indeed, many of the managed care organizations that have used directive approaches are now switching to a demand management approach.

A legitimate cause of concern with respect to demand management is the confusion of its goal—appropriate use of health care services—with one of its results—reduced costs. Those who have made this transposition have argued that a service that has reduced costs as its goal will inevitably bias its information toward that goal, to the detriment of the individuals using the service. Even if they are reminded of demand management's stated goal (the appropriate use of medical care), skeptics may insist that the real goal is cost reduction, and the effect is the same.

The strongest argument against this is that such a goal simply is unnecessary. Individuals pursuing their own self-interest with the help of demand management use fewer services and less costly services for three simple reasons:

1. They live healthier lifestyles, resulting in fewer preventable illnesses, which decreases the probability that medical care will be considered.
2. Knowing that they have access to effective decision and behavior support, they have confidence in their own ability to deal with medical problems, so perceive less need for professional medical services.
3. Allowed to participate in shared decision making with full knowledge of the risks and benefits of all the alternatives, they tend to choose less risky approaches, which are also less invasive and less costly.

Finally, physicians may be concerned that demand management inserts another party between them and their patients. Again, skeptics may insist that this will happen despite demand management's stated purposes of supporting the doctor-patient relationship.

The best argument against this assertion is that an attempt to intervene in the doctor-patient relationship is simply unnecessary, not to mention that it would create more work and less efficiency for demand management services. Getting between doctor and patient creates a passive patient who is unable to use demand management services effectively. This loss of effectiveness is made worse by the aggravation felt by physicians who will be predisposed to condemn these services rather than support them. In fact, properly executed, demand management will support the patient in interacting with the physician rather than interfere with or replace patient-physician interaction.

Demand management is here to stay. The science upon which it is based suggests that it has the potential to be of substantial benefit in the health care cost-quality crisis, particularly among the nation's elderly. Will it live up to its promise? Perhaps the greatest threat to the success of demand management is that the quality of its services may suffer in the rush to provide them.

REFERENCES

Chambers, C.V., Diamond, J.J., Perkel, R.L., & Lasch, L.A. (1994). Relationship of advance directives to hospital charges in the Medicare population. *Arch Int Med, 154,* 541–547.

Emanuel, L.L., Barry, M.J., Stoeckle, J.D., Ettelson, L.M., & Emanuel, E.J.K. (1991). Advance directives for medical care—A case for greater use. *N Engl J Med, 324,* 889–895.

Steiber, S.R. (1987). Right to die: Public balks at deciding for others. *Hospitals, 61,* 72.

Vickery, D.M. (1996, Jan.). Toward appropriate use of medical care. *Healthcare Forum Journal,* 14–19.

Vickery, D.M., Golaszewski, T.J., Wright, E.C., & Kalmer, H. (1988, June). The effect of self-care interventions on the use of medical service within a Medicare population. *Med Care, 26*(6), 580–588.

CHAPTER 26

Community-Wide Prevention Programs—They Work

John W. Farquhar, Caroline Schooler, and June A. Flora

Health behaviors and health status are influenced not only by biologic and psychologic factors, but also by economic, political and sociocultural factors. For example, the leading causes of death in the United States (cardiovascular disease and cancer) have been shown to be related to such lifestyle elements as diet, exercise and smoking (Department of Health and Human Services, 1991). A primary tenet of community prevention campaigns, therefore, is that efforts to change behavior must go beyond the individual to include family, social and cultural contexts.

The speed and complexity of the world in which we live also provide a rationale for community prevention programs. The rapidly expanding breadth and diversity of communications technology mean that people are exposed to ever more information. This information revolution has altered how people learn and make choices. Much of what we are exposed to does not promote healthful behavior, including infomercials for "quick fix" diets, web sites for junk food or novel marketing strategies for tobacco and alcohol. New technologies, however, also provide opportunities to reach people with health-promoting messages. Research suggests that channels such as computers and video games may reach audiences that traditional health communication materials do not (Boberg, Gustafson, Hawkins, & Chan, 1995; Hawkins et al., 1987). Community-based interventions, there-fore, can disseminate information to diverse segments of society, enhanc-ing their effectiveness through increased opportunity for information

Source: Adapted with permission from Schooler et al., Synthesis of Findings and Issues from Community Prevention Trials, *Annals of Epidemiology*, Vol. 7, No. 7, pp. S54–68, © 1997, Elsevier Science.

exchange and building the social support needed to maintain change (Farquhar, 1978; Farquhar, Fortmann, Flora, & Maccoby, 1991).

These interventions influence both the behaviors of individuals and the social systems in which they live. Education campaigns through mass media and direct interpersonal programs reach the general public as well as health professionals. In addition, community organization strategies create institutional and organizational support for behavioral change. Comprehensive community-based efforts that include multiple types of interventions influence the knowledge, attitudes and behaviors of individuals; they modify the environment so that it supports the initiation and maintenance of individuals' healthy actions or, in some cases, prohibits their unhealthy actions; and they reduce or eliminate factors in the physical or social environment that are detrimental to health. There is a large body of evidence demonstrating the efficacy of community-wide prevention campaigns that attempt to reduce the prevalence of multiple cardiovascular disease risk factors in an intact community.

Two pioneering studies carried out in the early 1970s demonstrated that community prevention campaigns have a significant impact on community members' health-related behavior. The Stanford Three-Community Study (TCS) was conducted in three small agricultural marketing towns in northern California. The total population of these communities was 45,000. In Watsonville, a media campaign was combined with intensive instruction for a randomly selected subset of high-risk residents. In Gilroy, intervention was limited to a media campaign. In the third community, Tracy, only surveys were conducted for comparison purposes (Farquhar et al., 1977; Maccoby et al., 1977; Meyer, Nash, McAlister, Maccoby, & Farquhar, 1980).

The education campaign was conducted in both English and Spanish. It consisted of mass media education for the general public and the identification of a high-risk group for face-to-face intervention. The English-language campaign was conducted predominantly through newspapers and television, and the Spanish-language campaign used primarily radio. Direct mail played a lesser but important role in both languages. The results indicated a significant reduction of about 23% in composite coronary heart disease risk due to decreases in smoking, blood pressure and cholesterol levels (Farquhar et al., 1977). Spanish-speaking residents demonstrated proportionately more reductions in risk for cardiovascular disease than did the Anglo majority (Maccoby et al., 1977).

A second early demonstration campaign, begun in 1972 and still ongoing, is being conducted in predominantly rural Finnish provinces, each of which consists of many villages and a provincial capital. The education campaign consists of radio, newspaper and print messages, as well as direct education and environmental interventions. The project was distinguished from the start by strong partnerships between the public and provincial organizations. Ten-year results demonstrated significant effects on smoking, blood pressure, cholesterol and coronary heart disease risk that were comparable to those seen in the Stanford study (Jousilahti et al., 1994). In addition, favorable net reductions in cardiovascular disease were seen in the first 5 years, followed by continued and parallel declines in mortality in both provinces between 1978 and 1992 (Puska, Tuomilehto, Vartiainen, Korhonen, & Jorma, 1995). Capacity building and extension to the rest of Finland have occurred. However, the presence of an organized health care system in Finland, especially for primary care, probably contributed to the Finnish results and the project's impact on national health policy (Puska et al., 1995). Such an integrated system is absent in the United States.

Considerable informal technology transfer regarding cardiovascular disease community prevention trials began in the mid-1970s and extended to many countries from the U.S. and Finnish centers. The World Health Organization (WHO) established principles for the prevention of cardiovascular disease that included comprehensive population-wide change strategies and mass media programs, as well as policy change. Several studies of campaigns similar to the Finnish and northern California ones were conducted during the 1980s, with equivalent results. Researchers studied campaigns conducted in Australia, South Africa and Italy. All of the studies showed decreases in blood pressure, smoking and composite coronary heart disease risk.

In the United States, the success demonstrated in the 1970s led to funding for three investigator-initiated community-based education and demonstration trials by the National Heart, Lung, and Blood Institute. The Stanford Five-City Project (FCP) was funded in 1978, followed by the Minnesota Heart Health Project (MHHP) and the Pawtucket Heart Health Project (PHHP) in 1980.

In Minnesota, the intervention consisted of mass media, community organization and direct education. A cross-sectional survey of the population indicates decreased smoking prevalence among women and increased physical activity in both men and women (Luepker et al., 1994).

The Pawtucket (Rhode Island) project consisted of a 7-year education campaign launched in 1984. Its components were community organization, print media and environmental programs. Once again, cross-sectional surveys demonstrated significant treatment effects of obesity and reduced coronary heart disease risk (Carleton, Lasater, Assaf, Feldman, & McKinlay, 1995).

The Stanford FCP was conducted in northern California with a total population of 360,000. The education program, which began in 1980, was carried out through television, radio, newspapers, other print materials, direct education and community events. The results showed significant net reductions in smoking, cholesterol, blood pressure, resting pulse and coronary heart disease (Farquhar et al., 1990).

These three large-scale U.S. studies demonstrated that community-wide interventions were feasible and could favorably affect at least some cardiovascular disease risk-factor levels in entire communities. The three projects were based on diverse theoretical and methodologic perspectives, which were reflected in how the education campaigns were implemented.

The Stanford project devoted the most effort to mass media, with 63% of messages delivered via television and 36% in print media. The PHHP did not use broadcast media, and 79% of its messages were delivered via newspaper and such other print sources as booklets and self-help kits. Minnesota mounted many screenings and emphasized face-to-face inter-action, so the bulk of this project was comprised of events (32%) and face-to-face communication (61%) (Flora et al., 1993).

MHHP developed comprehensive face-to-face programs to achieve the feedback, skills building, and efficacy enhancement steps to behavior change. In addition, they used events to prompt for behavior change. The impressive accomplishment of the Minnesota project in screening a large proportion of the population did not seem to enhance the results, reinforc-ing a general impression that although extensive screening has a measur-able impact on those screened, the net effect is diluted when measured on the total population.

In the late 1980s and 1990s, several public education prevention campaigns were conducted outside the United States that considerably enlarged the scope of efforts to date. The German Cardiovascular Pre-vention Study included six different intervention regions representing a total population of 1.2 million inhabitants. The entire population of the former Federal Republic of Germany served as reference. A 7-year education program began in 1985 and consisted of print media, direct education, screenings, events and environmental programs. Cooperation of community leaders, health care professionals, mass media, insurers, supermarket chains, restaurants, and work site cafeterias was an integral aspect of intervention planning and delivery. A study of this project after

3½ years of intervention revealed significant net effects in mean systolic and diastolic blood pressure, uncontrolled hypertension and current smoking among men only (Greiser, 1993). In addition, overall results demonstrate net reductions in cholesterol (Breckenkamp, Laaser, & Meyer, 1995).

In 1985 a 10-year community-based intervention began in Norsjö, Sweden, an inland municipality not far from the Arctic Circle comprising a total of 5,300 inhabitants (Brännström, Weinehall, Pearson, Wester, & Wall, 1993). The intervention was disseminated via newspapers, radio and television. In addition, community organization efforts have enlisted the participation of clubs and local associations, schools, day care centers and primary health care groups. Environmental approaches include modification of school lunches and a food labeling system in local markets. The Norsjö Project emphasized low-fat/high-fiber content in food and eating habits, and results indicate increased sales for low-fat products in local stores. Data from the first 5 years of implementation reveal significant decreases favoring treatment in hypercholesterolemia.

Other recent and ongoing demonstration projects include the Canadian Heart Health Initiative, which began in 1987 to conduct risk-factor surveys and to implement community-level demonstration projects. Principal investigators based in provincial departments of health and university-based evaluation teams are developing a national risk-factor database, establishing provincial coalitions and implementing and evaluating community trials (Health and Welfare Canada, 1992). An important accomplishment of the Initiative is the creation of working partnerships at the federal and provincial levels with involvement of a large number of professional, scientific and voluntary organizations. This infrastructure has led to the development of intervention methods, including policies applicable to other health problems.

In 1987, the WHO established InterHealth to control noncommunicable diseases in developing countries. Currently, InterHealth is involved with 16 demonstration projects in 13 countries. Although animal fat intake is rising in all developing countries and cardiovascular disease rates are approaching those of developed nations, InterHealth projects are demonstrating success for community-based interventions.

In the United States, extension of the technology of community prevention trials has occurred in the area of tobacco control. Two projects have modified earlier intervention models, primarily to enhance community involvement and the emphasis on environmental approaches. The Community Intervention Trial for Smoking Cessation (COMMIT) was the largest National Cancer Institute effort to test methods to help people stop smoking (Department of Health and Human Services, 1995). COMMIT focused on heavy smokers (those smoking more than 25 cigarettes per day). From 1988 to 1992, a standardized intervention was implemented through public education, health care providers, work sites and the promotion of cessation resources in smokers' communities. Results showed significant intervention effects among light-to-moderate smokers but no intervention effects among heavy smokers. The American Stop Smoking Intervention Study for Cancer Prevention is a collaborative effort of the National Cancer Institute, the American Cancer Society, state health departments and other public and private organizations to develop comprehensive tobacco use control programs in 17 states. The two main goals of the project are to reduce adult smoking prevalence to 15% or less and to reduce by 50% the rates of smoking initiation among adolescents by the year 2000. Intervention components are policy advocacy, mass media and program services delivered via work sites, schools, health care settings and community groups.

The major U.S. demonstration projects and the community prevention trials that preceded them provide valuable models, methods and strategies for planning and conducting community-based interventions (Winkleby, 1997). In addition, these programs have advanced community organization and activation principles, social marketing guidelines and evaluation theory and practice (Flora, Jackson, & Maccoby, 1989). These community projects have helped to lay the foundation of numerous cardiovascular disease control programs worldwide.

Research has shown that community-wide prevention projects in different settings, targeting various groups and using diverse methods, can successfully influence health-related behavior or change policy. Overall, studies suggest that to effectively promote behavior change, health education strategies must reach target audiences with sufficient information delivered in a regular, systematic manner. Moreover, intervention strategies must be tailored to the audience and be appropriate to the particular community.

Evaluation of these community prevention trials also reveals synergistic interaction between social groups and settings. For example, in the FCP, family communication, parental behavioral modeling, the education campaign and personal knowledge and self-efficacy interacted to influence adolescents' diets (Rimal & Flora, 1994). Also, interactions between families, schools and children occurred in a school-based nutrition and exercise curriculum, enhancing parental involvement at home in conjunction with classroom activities (Flora & Schooler, 1997). Evidence for the benefit of parental involvement in youth interventions was also shown in the MHHP. For example, a correspondence program requiring parents to work with their children on diet led to significantly lowered fat consumption in participating children (Perry. Klepp, & Sillers, 1989).

Studies of these projects also suggest that dose and consistency of campaign elements strongly shape their effectiveness. Results of health promotion efforts are importantly influenced by the extent to which programs reach or are available to the target audience (Flay, 1986). Experiences from the TCS and FCP suggest a general measure of the minimum "dose" of education needed. Yearly exposure to approximately 5 hours of a combination of mediated and face-to-face education carried out for 2 or more years produced an adequate change in cardiovascular risk factors in the Stanford studies (Farquhar et al., 1991). With as little as 10% of the total exposure devoted to inherently more effective face-to-face communication, behavioral change still occurred at an estimated cost of about $4 per adult per year (Farquhar et al., 1990).

The FCP relied more heavily on mass media for achieving behavior change than did the MHHP or PHHP. The somewhat better population-wide results in the FCP and observation of the strong secular trend regarding cardiovascular disease knowledge and behavior change in the United States suggest that mass media can powerfully shape an individual's health-related knowledge and behavior. Similarly, the earlier Stanford, Australian and South African projects all demonstrated good results in their "media-only" components. Results from the MHHP, on the other hand, suggest that the screening approach may be less effective than such less costly strategies as use of television and a broad distribution of print materials. The apparent effectiveness and lower cost of mediated communication do not imply, however, that face-to-face programs should be eliminated. Results of these studies suggest that some face-to-face interventions are necessary for achieving and maintaining long-term behavior change, and certainly community organizing requires some face-to-face activity. In estimating how much education is necessary in a community prevention campaign, it is important to consider how to achieve a "critical mass" whereby 15–25% of the population adopt a new health innovation to ensure that diffusion occurs rapidly and effectively.

Although many gaps in our knowledge still exist, experience nonetheless leads to many practical methods derived from both common sense and research. Two main characteristics of community interventions proposed as essential for success are that they be comprehensive and integrated. *Comprehensive* means that an intervention is designed to work on multiple dimensions that influence the health-related behavior of individuals as well as a community's environment and policy. Such health-promotion programs target multiple health problems and focus education efforts on multiple audiences. Segmenting the audience into meaningful subgroups enhances the message as well as program design and contributes to successful behavior change (Lefebvre & Flora, 1988; Slater & Flora, 1991).

Efforts to bring about healthful changes in social policies and regulations so that people have access to the facilities and resources necessary for healthful practices are an important facet of community prevention campaigns. In addition, diverse channels of communication (for example, mass media and "mini" media such as direct mail) are needed to reach a wide variety of audience members. Community organizations, workplaces, schools and such local businesses as restaurants and grocery stores can serve as conduits of information, reinforce the change process, enhance resources applied to communication efforts, and ensure the institutionalization of programs (Flora et al., 1993).

Another determinant of success is that such programs be integrated. This means that the multiple intervention modalities, programs and messages of a comprehensive program are designed to complement and supplement each other. Repeating consistent messages in an array of channels increases the number of people who are exposed to them and promotes the memorability and salience of the message. Family, friends, coworkers, and fellow group members provide links to repeat, reinforce, diffuse and ultimately enhance campaign effects. For example, a smoking cessation program using self-help booklets and classes is enhanced through a campaign at local work sites, publicity in the local media, a quit-smoking contest, and legislation to restrict smoking in public areas.

Sequencing the various facets of an intervention is important to ensure that different elements build upon each other in a sensible manner. A theoretical framework for behavior change provides essential guidance for campaign planning. For example, the communication-behavior change model utilized in the FCP helped planners deliver messages to first target awareness, then knowledge, then skills and motivation to prompt actual behavior change. Achieving organizational or policy change also hinges on the planned delivery of intervention components to increase public concern, build consensus for change, and activate constituencies to advocate and vote (Minkler, 1990). A key to effective community organizing in a community prevention program is to begin by building trust between program planners and community members. Moreover, throughout a program, it is essential to incorporate community needs and values in intervention design and delivery.

Perhaps the most important benefit of a comprehensive, integrated community prevention trial that promotes complex interactions is the possibility for synergy. One strategy for achieving synergistic interaction among intervention components is to plan for supplementation. This is a process whereby various intervention formats, such as mass media and face-to-face education, reciprocally reinforce each other. Supplementation can increase the reach of a campaign by prompting individuals who rely on one channel of communication to seek information from another, such as when airing television public service announcements to reduce smoking prevalence results in increased requests for self-help "quit kits" (Pierce et al., 1986). Results from the FCP study indicate that accessible awareness media disseminated early in the education campaign promoted use of information-rich depth media later on (Schooler, Flora, & Farquhar, 1993).

An important aspect of comprehensive and integrated community prevention campaigns is that they are quite cost-effective. First, use of mass media leads to large audience reach and lower costs per community member. Second, supplementation of various program components increases penetration in a community. Finally, synergy between multiple intervention elements targeted to various groups and community institutions enhances program effects and boosts the cost-effectiveness of components.

A crucial challenge for community prevention trials is the extent to which the programs are adopted and maintained by the community when the research phase ends. Research has shown that this involves a dynamic process (Bracht et al., 1994). Community agencies must modify programs to meet changing community needs and agency interests. In addition, the limited "shelf life" of programs may necessitate modifying or terminating specific components. To the extent that agencies have the capacity to tailor existing programs and replace outmoded ones, the potential for long-term maintenance of community health promotion programs is enhanced (Jackson et al., 1994). A primary objective of community organization efforts, therefore, is to foster the capacity and desire of organizations to incorporate health promotion activities into the routines of business, government, and education (Mittlemark, Hunt, Heath, & Schmid, 1993).

Demonstration projects can facilitate institutionalization and plan their eventual departure from communities by promoting empowerment of community organizations and leaders and by relinquishing control over program design and implementation. The FCP, for example, utilized a capacity-building strategy directed at local health educators to maintain its heart disease education program. Long-term maintenance of cardiovascular disease prevention activities was achieved by applying a train-the-trainers model and cooperative learning methods to provide professional development, technical assistance and other resources to a target group of community health educators (Jackson et al., 1994). The MHHP developed "community partnerships" for health, through which community members worked with the research team in decision making and program implementation (Carlaw, Mittlemark, Bracht, & Luepker, 1984). Many of the components developed in the National Heart, Lung and Blood Institute demonstration projects have been adopted for use both in the intervention communities and by other health promotion efforts (Altman et al., 1991; Lefebvre, 1990; Parcel, Perry, & Taylor, 1990). For example, data from the MHHP indicate that 3 years after the withdrawal of federal funding, 61% of MHHP programs were being operated by local providers (Bracht et al., 1994).

To achieve the full potential of community health promotion, researchers and practitioners should incorporate programs to reach the public through health education that uses communication channels natural to community systems, collaborating effectively with community leaders and organizations and leveraging governmental resources. Effectively influencing change in communities involves governmental or "top down" approaches, as well as community activation or "bottom up" strategies. Results from experiences with tobacco control in the state of California underscore the benefits of combining bottom-up educational and community mobilization strategies with policy advocacy and regulatory change efforts (Traynor & Glantz, 1996). Moreover, data from the MHHP indicate that after 5 years of intensive intervention, Bloomington, Minnesota became the largest municipality in the United States to ban the sale of cigarettes through vending machines (Lando, Bluhm, & Forster, 1991).

There is a critical need to disseminate research findings and the technology of community interventions to practitioners through education and advocacy. We must decrease the time lag between the discovery of effective health-promotion strategies and action regarding their implementation. In addition, we should pursue research to investigate how various communities and populations adopt health innovations. Of critical concern is to better understand how to extend the health benefits demonstrated in past community prevention campaigns to different regions and populations, including developing nations, less affluent communities and racial and ethnic minorities. This last point calls for diffusion of research findings and intervention materials to multiple geopolitical settings such as states, provinces, other countries and different parts of the world.

Effective dissemination of the strategies and tactics of community prevention campaigns calls for more training, allocation of more resources, building of networks and coalitions (both public and private), and increased governmental and institutional support. Perhaps the critical first step for dissemination research is to overcome the twin barriers of inertia among policy makers and lack of adequate training of personnel regarding the most effective dissemination strategies. For example, many health professionals and scientists expect that behavior change and new policies and regulations will ensue from publication of research results. Consideration of the field of tobacco control leads to realization that additional tactics are needed to reduce smoking prevalence and to enact tobacco-related laws and ordinances. Recent experiences with passing tobacco excise tax increases in several states in the United States suggest the importance of training more health professionals in advocacy methods and of developing coalitions of health professionals, social scientists, educators and community members to apply political pressure to achieve needed policy change.

One goal of publication and dissemination of research findings should be to provide information that can be used by others to plan their own programs. However a major constraint in providing this information is the publication policies of professional journals, which are typically most interested in "hard" outcome results. More attention, therefore, is generally devoted to examining responses (that is, dependent variables) than to specifying how program outcomes were achieved. Specific interventions, however, are the aspects of a large-scale program that have the most potential for adoption by others because of manageable costs and logistic requirements.

A judicious combination of well-formulated mass media and appropriate community organization can influence behavior on a limited scale in many successful components and on a broad scale in total population samples, organizational changes and resulting community activation. Commercial advertising campaigns, which generally have substantially more resources than do community prevention campaigns, are typically satisfied with quite modest increases in market share. We conclude that the community approach to cardiovascular disease prevention has a high capacity for generalization, cost-effectiveness due to the use of mass communication methods, ability to successfully disseminate information through activation of community networks, and potential for influencing environmental, regulatory and institutional policies that shape health.

REFERENCES

Altman, D., Endres, J., Linzer, J., Lorig, K., Howard-Pitney, B., & Rogers, T. (1991). Obstacles to and future goals of ten comprehensive community health promotion projects. *J Community Health, 16*(6), 299–314.

Boberg, E., Gustafson, D., Hawkins, R., & Chan, C. (1995). Development, acceptance, and use patterns of a computer-based education and social support system for people living with AIDS/HTV infection. *Comput Hum Behav, 11*(2), 289–311.

Bracht, N., Finnegan, J., Rissel, C., Weisbrod, R., Gleason, J., Corbett, J., & Veblen-Mortenson, S. (1994). Community ownership and program continuation following a health demonstration project. *Health Educ Res, 9*(2), 243–255.

Brännström, I., Weinehall, L., Pearson, L., Wester, P., & Wall, S. (1993). Changing social patterns of risk factors for cardiovascular disease in a Swedish community intervention programme. *Int J Epidemiol, 22*(5), 1026–1027.

Breckenkamp, J., Laaser, U., Meyer, S. (1995). The German Cardiovascular Prevention Study: Social gradient for the net effects in prevention of hypercholesterolemia. *Zeitschrift for Kardiologie, 84*(9), 694–699.

Carlaw, R., Mittlemark, M., Bracht, N., & Luepker, R. (1984). Organization for a community cardiovascular health program: Experiences from the Minnesota Heart Health Program. *Health Educ Q, 11*, 243–252.

Carleton, R., Lasater, T., Assaf, A., Feldman, H., & McKinlay, S. (1995). The Pawtucket Heart Health Program: Community changes in cardiovascular risk factors and projected disease risk. *Am J Public Health, 85*(6), 777–785.

Department of Health and Human Services. (1991*). Healthy people 2000: National health promotion and disease prevention objectives*. Publication P115 91-50212. Washington, DC: U.S. Dept. of Health and Human Services.

Department of Health and Human Services. (1995). *Community Based Interventions for Smokers*. NIH Publication No. 954028. Bethesda, MD: U.S. Department of Health and Human Services, Public Health Service, National Institute of Health.

Farquhar, J., Maccoby, N., Wood, P., Alexander, V., Breitrose, H., Brown, B., et al. (1977). Community education for cardiovascular health. *Lancet*.

Farquhar, J. (1978). Community-based model of lifestyle intervention trials. *Am J Epidemiol,* *108*(2), 103–111.

Farquhar, J., Fortmann, S., Flora, J., & Maccoby, N. (1991). Methods of communication to influence behaviour. In W. Holland, R. Detels, & G. Know (Eds.), *Oxford textbook of public health* (Vol. 2). London: Oxford University Press.

Farquhar, J., Fortmann, S., Flora, J., Taylor, C., Haskell, W., & Williams, P., et al. (1990). The Stanford Five-City Project effects of community-wide education on cardiovascular disease risk factors. *JAMA, 264*, 359–365. Available from National Auxiliary Publication Service (NAPS).

Flay, B. (1986). Efficacy and effectiveness trials (and other phases of research) in the development of health promotion programs. *Prev Med, 15*, 451–474.

Flora, J., Jackson, C., & Maccoby, N. (1989). Indicators of societal action to promote physical health. In S.B. Kar (Ed.), *Individual and societal actions for health promotion: Strategies and indicators* (pp. 118–139). New York: Springer-Verlag.

Flora, J., Lefebvre, R., Murray, D., Stone, E., Assaf, A., Mittlemark, M., & Finnegan, J. (1993). A community education monitoring system: Methods from the Stanford Five-City Project, the Minnesota Heart Health program, and the Pawtucket Heart Health program. *Health Educ Res, 8*, 81–95.

Flora, J., & Schooler, C. (1997). Influence of health communication environments on children's diet and exercise knowledge, attitudes and behavior. (In press.)

Green, L., & Kreuter, M. (1991). *Health promotion planning: An educational and environmental approach.* Mountain View, CA: Mayfield Publishing Company.

Greiser, E. (1993). Risk factor trends and cardiovascular mortality risk after 3.5 years of community-based intervention in the German Cardiovascular Prevention Study. *Ann Epidemiol, 3*(suppl), S13–S27.

Hawkins, R., Gustafson, D., Chewning, B., Bosworth, K., et al. (1987). Reaching hard-to-reach populations: Interactive computer programs as public information campaigns for adolescents. *Journal of Communication, 37*(2), 8–28.

Health and Welfare Canada. (1992). *The Canadian Heart Health Initiative (CHHI).* Ottawa: Health Promotion Directorate, Health Services and Promotion Branch.

Jackson, C., Fortmann, S., Flora, J., Melton, R., Snider, J., & Littlefield, D. (1994). The capacity-building approach to intervention maintenance implemented by the Stanford Five-City Project. *Health Educ Res, 9*, 385–396.

Jousilahti, P., Tuomilehto, J., Korhonin, H.J., Vartiainen, E., Puska, P., & Nissinen, A. (1994). Trends in cardiovascular disease risk factor clustering in eastern Finland: Results of 15-year follow-up of the North Karelia Project. *Prev Med, 23*, 6–14.

Lando, H.A., Bluhm, J., & Forster, J. (1991). The ban on cigarette vending machines in Bloomington, Minnesota. *Am J Public Health, 81*, 1339–1340.

Lefebvre, R. (1990). Strategies to maintain and institutionalize successful programs. In N. Bracht (Ed.), *Health promotion at the community level* (pp. 209–228). Beverly Hills, CA: Sage Publications.

Lefebvre, R., & Flora, J. (1988). Social marketing and public health intervention. *Health Educ Q, 15*, 299–315.

Luepker, R., Murray, D., Jacobs, D., Mittlemark, M., Bracht, N., & Carlaw, R., et al. (1994). Community education for cardiovascular disease prevention: Risk factor changes in the Minnesota Heart Health Program. *Am J Public Health, 84*(9), 1383–1393.

Maccoby, N., Farquhar, J., & Wood, P., et al. (1977). Reducing the risk of cardiovascular disease: Effects of community based campaign on knowledge and behavior. *J Community Health, 3*, 100–114.

Meyer, A., Nash, J., McAlister, A., Maccoby, N., & Farquhar, J. (1980). Skills training in a cardiovascular health education campaign. *Journal of Consulting and Clinical Psychology, 48*, 159–163.

Minkler, M. (1990). Improving health through community organization. In K.L.F. Glanz & B. Rimer (Eds.), *Health Behavior and Health Education* (pp. 257–287). San Francisco: Jossey-Bass, Publishers.

Mittlemark, M., Hunt, M., Heath, G., & Schmid, T. (1993). Realistic outcomes: Lessons from community-based research and demonstration programs for the prevention of cardiovascular diseases. *J Health Policy, 14*, 437–462.

Parcel, G., Perry, C., & Taylor, W. (1990). Beyond demonstration: Diffusion of health promotion innovations. In N. Bracht (Ed.), *Health promotion at the community level* (pp. 229–256). Beverly Hills, CA: Sage Publications.

Perry, C., Klepp, K., & Sillers, C. (1989). Community-wide strategies for cardiovascular health: The Minnesota Heart Health Program youth program. *Health Educ Res, 4*(1), 87–101.

Perry, C., Luepker, R., Murray, D., Hearn, M., Halper, A., & Dudovitz, B., et al. (1989). Parent involvement with children's health promotion: A one-year follow-up of the Minnesota Home Team. *Health Educ Q, 16*(2), 171–180.

Pierce, J.P., Dwyer, T., Frape, G., Chapman, S., Chamberlain, A., & Burke, N. (1986). Evaluation of the Sydney "Quit For Life" anti-smoking campaign. Part 1. Achievement of intermediate goals. *Med J Austr, 144*, 341–344.

Puska, P., Tuomilehto, J., Vartiainen, E., Korhonen, H., & Jorma, T. (1995). Mortality changes. In I. Puska, J. Tuomilehto, A. Nissinen, & E. Vartianinen (Eds.), *The North Karelia project* (pp. 159–167). Helsinki: Helsinki University Printing House.

Rimal, R., & Flora, J. (1994). *Psychological and familial influences on children's dietary behavior: Perspectives from a health information campaign.* Presented at the annual meeting of the International Communication Association, Sydney, Australia.

Schooler, C., Flora, J., & Farquhar, J. (1993). Moving toward synergy: Media supplementation in the Stanford Five-City Project. *Commun Res, 20*, 587–610.

Slater, M., & Flora, J. (1991). Health lifestyles: Audience segmentation for public health interventions. *Health Educ Q, 18*, 221–234.

Stokols, D., Allen, J., & Bellingham, R. (1996). The social ecology of health promotion: Implementation for research and practice. *Am J Health Promotion, 10*(4), 257–251.

Traynor, M.P., & Glantz, S.A. (1996). California's tobacco tax initiative: The development and passage of Proposition 99. *J Health Politics, Policy Law, 21*, 543–585.

Winkleby, M. (1997). Accelerating cardiovascular risk factor change in ethnic minority and low socioeconomic groups. *Ann Epidemiol*, S7, S96–S103.

INDEX

A